L'HOMME ET LA NATURE

*Actes de la Société canadienne
d'étude du dix-huitième siècle*

Tome I

publié sous la direction de

Roger L. Emerson, Gilles Girard et Roseann Runte

* * * * * *

pour la Société
par
The Faculty of Education
The University of Western Ontario
London, Ontario
1982

Canadian Cataloguing in Publication Data   909.7

    Main entry under title: M 266

    Man and nature

    (Proceedings of the Canadian Society for Eighteenth-Century Studies; v. 1)

    Title on added t.p.: L'Homme et la nature.
    "Papers selected from those delivered at the general meeting held at the University of Western Ontario 8-10 May 1980."
    Text in English or French.
    Includes bibliographical references and index.
    ISBN 0-920354-14-9

    1. Eighteenth century — Congresses. 2. Civilization, Modern — 18th century — Congresses. 3. Literature, Modern — 18th century — Congresses. I. Emerson, Roger L., 1934- II. Girard, Gilles, 1942- III. Runte, Roseann. IV. Canadian Society for Eighteenth-Century Studies. V. University of Western Ontario. Faculty of Education. IV. Title: L'Homme et la nature. VII. Series.

CB411.M27   909.7   C82-094600-1F

Données de catalogage avant publication (Canada)

    Vedette principale au titre:

    L'Homme et la nature

    (Actes de la Société canadienne d'étude du dix-huitième siècle; t. 1)

    Titre de la p. de t. additionnelle: Man and nature.
    "Les articles . . . ont été choisis parmi les communications présentées au congrès à l'Université de Western Ontario du 8 au 10 mai 1980."
    Textes en anglais ou en français.
    Comprend des références bibliographiques et un index.
    ISBN 0-920354-14-9

    1. Dix-huitième siècle — Congrès. 2. Civilisation moderne — 18e siècle — Congrès. 3. Littérature moderne — 18e siècle — Congrès. I. Emerson, Roger L., 1934- II. Girard, Gilles, 1942- III. Runte, Roseann. IV. Société canadienne d'étude du dix-huitième siècle. V. University of Western Ontario. Faculty of Education. VI. Titre: Man and nature. VII. Collection.

CB411.M27   909.7   C82-094600-1F

83-3478

Printed and bound in Canada by Twin-Offset, 10 Gower Street, Toronto, Ontario, Canada M4B 1E2

MAN AND NATURE

Proceedings of the Canadian Society
for
Eighteenth-Century Studies

Volume I

Edited by
Roger L. Emerson, Gilles Girard and Roseann Runte

* * * * * *

Published for the Society
by
The Faculty of Education
The University of Western Ontario
London, Ontario
1982

The Canadian Society for Eighteenth-Century Studies/La Société canadienne d'étude du dix-huitième siècle
MAN AND NATURE/L'HOMME ET LA NATURE/*Emerson, Girard, Runte*

Faculty of Education, The University of Western Ontario, London, Ontario, Canada archers (pp. 13, 15, 174), à ces bêtes de cirque, les prostituées (p. 178), à l'imbécile portier de Saint-Lazare qui voulait empêcher l'évasion de des Grieux, et qui n'a pas à se surprendre si on lui brûle la cervelle (p. 97), et aux domestiques. Ceux-ci se divisent en deux catégories, selon qu'ils appartiennent au père des Grieux (auquel cas ils sont bons, dévoués et incorruptibles [pp. 21, 35-36]) ou à d'autres maîtres; ce sont alors des espèces d'enfants, susceptibles de réactions affectives primaires, qu'on achète facilement mais qui trahissent pour des raisons aussi futiles que le risque d'être pendus, et toujours suspects de vouloir voler leurs maîtres (pp. 13, 66-67, 104, 120, 154). Enfin, l'histoire de la vocation de des Grieux (pp. 40-42) et ses rapports avec les membres du clergé, dont Tiberge, montrent avec la plus grande clarté que le rôle de l'institution ecclésiastique est essentiellement de servir les intérêts de la noblesse, notamment en ouvrant aux cadets de famille une possibilité d'ascension sociale.

En bref, il n'y a d'hommes dignes de ce nom que ceux qui appartiennent à l'aristocratie. Ce point de vue, confirmé par tout le roman, s'exprime dès les premières pages. J'en citerai comme exemple le beau jugement du marquis de Renoncour, qui commente en ces termes les témoignages de gratitude du héros, à qui il vient de procurer, au prix de quelques louis d'or, le droit de rester aux côtés de Manon jusqu'à l'embarquement pour le Nouvel Orléans: ''La bonne grâce et la vive reconnaissance avec laquelle ce jeune inconnu me remercia, achevèrent de me persuader qu'il était né quelque chose, et qu'il méritait ma libéralité'' (p. 15; voir aussi p. 81). Les bonnes manières et les qualités du coeur s'expliquent par la naissance, et la naissance donne droit aux bienfaits — lesquels, sommes-nous autorisés à conclure, seraient mal employés s'ils tombaient sur des êtres qui n'ont ni naissance, ni, par conséquent, qualités du coeur et de l'esprit.

Le malheur, c'est que l'Histoire de des Grieux n'est pas un roman de Chrétien de Troyes, de La Calprenède ou de Mme de la Fayette. L'idéologie féodale est une bien médiocre boussole pour s'orienter dans la société de la Régence, surtout quant on ne fait pas partie, quoi qu'on veuille se faire accroire, de la classe dominante. Des Grieux oscille entre deux mondes, celui où l'on vaut ce qu'on a et celui où l'on vaut ce qu'on est/naît, sans avoir accès ni à l'un ni à l'autre.

On a souvent commenté la stupeur fascinée du héros devant ces abîmes incompréhensibles que sont l'amour, les femmes, Manon. Je ne sais pas si le mystère est vraiment si impénétrable que cela; ce qui est sûr, c'est que l'univers de des Grieux comporte une autre donnée tout aussi irrationnelle, une autre force devant laquelle il reste absolument désarmé, et qui est l'argent. Il essaie désespérément et maladroitement de calculer, de compter; il en est obsédé au point de faire des équations pour vérifier qu'une moitié de son sang plus une autre partie font bien son sang tout entier (pp. 111-112); le monde qui l'entoure a l'air de fonctionner sur le principe que tout s'échange, que tout s'achète. Mais ce qui lui échappe complètement, c'est l'origine de la richesse. Défavorisé, pour ce qui est des héritages, par sa condition de cadet, ignorant qu'il existe une réalité appelée *travail* (dans tout le roman, d'ailleurs, on ne trouve pas un seul représentant des classes productrices), des Grieux observe le va-et-vient de l'argent, ses apparitions miraculeuses et ses

1. Les Fantasmes de l'argent dans l'Histoire du chevalier des Grieux et de Manon Lescaut

''Il n'y a proprement de Français en France que le petit nombre de ceux qui sont à la tête des autres, et qui sont distingués de ce qu'on appelle peuple.''[1]

Ainsi s'exprime Cleveland, le Philosophe anglais, au livre II de ses mémoires. C'est la même conclusion qu'impose l'*Histoire du chevalier des Grieux et de Manon Lescaut.*

Le marquis de Renoncour, l'Homme de qualité à qui nous sommes redevables de ce récit (écrit, pour ainsi dire, sous la dictée du héros[2]), nous renseigne dès l'entrée en matière sur les circonstances de sa première rencontre avec des Grieux:

Je revenais un jour de Rouen, où [ma fille] m'avait prié d'aller solliciter une affaire au Parlement de Normandie pour la succession de quelques terres auxquelles je lui avais laissé des prétentions du côté de mon grand-père maternel [donc, notons-le en passant, de sa mère à lui] (p. 10).

Il appartient à la classe dominante, dominante par le privilège de la noblesse, mais aussi par la possession héréditaire de ce qui est encore, dans la France de cette époque, la principale source de la richesse, à savoir le sol cultivable. Tout indique que la famille des Grieux, l'''une des meilleures maisons de P.'' (p. 17), est de même rang.

Le reste du monde, aux yeux des représentants de cette classe, consiste en animaux plus ou moins grossiers. Les financiers sont de dégoûtants personnages, qui ne sauraient faire partie du cercle des connaissances de des Grieux père, et à qui il prend bien soin de refuser la particule (pp. 33-34). Son fils, quant à lui, trouve normal de les duper et s'indigne qu'ils osent le lui reprocher; surpris en flagrant délit de proxénétisme et d'escroquerie, son sang noble, juge-t-il, l'autorise encore à réclamer le châtiment de ses victimes (pp. 153-156). La naissance de des Grieux, comparée à celle de ses ennemis, l'innocente pratiquement aux yeux du supérieur de Saint-Lazare et du lieutenant de police aussi (pp. 85sqq., 113, 160-161). La bourgeoisie n'est représentée que par l'estimable famille Lescaut et, sans doute, par Tiberge, le personnage le plus systématiquement bafoué du livre. Quant au peuple, il se ramène en somme à la populace stupide qui gêne des Grieux et l'Homme de qualité dans leurs mouvements (pp. 10-11), aux lâches coquins que sont les principaux moyens mis en oeuvre par la Société ont été les congrès, les bulletins d'information et l'appui accordé à la Société Internationale d'étude du dix-huitième siècle, à laquelle elle est affiliée depuis 1975. Mais depuis ses origines la Société désire aussi produire des publications, qu'il s'agisse d'une revue ou de recueils sans périodicité fixe où se retrouveraient des articles écrits par ses membres ou les actes des congrès. Cet espoir si longtemps caressé trouve enfin un début de réalisation.

Les articles qui composent ce recueil ont été choisis parmi les communications présentées au congrès à l'Université de Western Ontario du 8 au 10 mai 1980. On les a regroupés tout simplement sous les rubriques suivantes: articles relatifs à la littérature française, aux Lumières en Écosse, à la pensée politique, à l'histoire coloniale dans les domaines espagnol et britannique, au Canada français au XVIIIe siècle, à l'histoire de l'art et à l'histoire des sciences. Les éditeurs de ce volume expriment le regret de n'avoir pu publier toutes les excellentes communications présentées au congrès de London.

sinon annuellement, et assurerait une tribune de discussion aux travaux relatifs à la culture et à l'histoire du dix-huitième siècle canadien aussi bien qu'aux sujets qui intéressent habituellement les spécialistes du siècle des Lumières. En ce faisant, la Société veillerait à accorder un statut égal aux langues française et anglaise.

Pendant que des universitaires canadiens examinaient les problèmes reliés à la fondation d'une société nationale, leurs collègues américains discutaient d'une entreprise analogue. Ces discussions conduisirent à la formation de l'American Society for Eighteenth-Century Studies en décembre 1969. Elle fut incorporée, après l'adoption de ses statuts, à son premier congrès annuel (Cleveland, 17-19 avril 1970). Comme plusieurs canadiens se joignirent immédiatement à cette association, il fallut s'interroger sur la viabilité d'une société canadienne. Il était évident que des regroupements régionaux comme la McMaster Association for Eighteenth-Centuries Studies, constituée à cette époque, étaient viables; mais il n'était pas aussi manifeste qu'une association nationale pût survivre dans un pays si vaste, de population clairsemée et linguistiquement hétérogène.

Le 6 mai 1970, une rencontre présidée par David Smith eut lieu à Victoria Collège (Université de Toronto); on y étudia la possibilité de former une Société canadienne et les objectifs qu'elle pourrait se proposer. On décida de solliciter l'avis des spécialistes du dix-huitième siècle au Canada. Si un consensus suffisamment large se dégageait, on mettrait sur pied un comité d'organisation et on ébaucherait des statuts provisoires à soumettre à ceux qui assisteraient au congrès canadien des dix-huitièmistes en mars 1971. Dès le milieu de l'été, il apparut évident que le vif intérêt suscité par le projet justifiait qu'on en poursuive la réalisation. Le Conseil des Arts du Canada répondit favorablement à une demande d'assistance, et il continue à subventionner les congrès depuis lors.

Le comité d'organisation se réunit le 26 septembre 1970 à Toronto pour ébaucher les propositions qui seraient présentées le 17 octobre au congrès de la McMaster Association à Hamilton. Lors de cette rencontre, présidée par David Smith, les débats portèrent sur les statuts provisoires, sur des publications possibles et sur l'affiliation aux Sociétés américaine et internationale. L'ordre du jour incluait également le lancement d'un bulletin d'information sur la Société, à qui ne manquait plus que d'être formellement constituée. En même temps on planifia le premier congrès, qui eut lieu aux Collèges Victoria et Scarborough ainsi qu'à l'Université McMaster du 19 au 21 mars 1971, et qui vit l'approbation des statuts. Les congrès suivants se déroulèrent à l'Université de Saskatchewan (Saskatoon, 1972), à l'Université Laval (Québec, 1975), à l'Université Dalhousie (Halifax, 1976), à l'Université McMaster (Hamilton, 1977), à l'Université de Colombie-Britannique (Vancouver, 1979), et à l'Université de Western Ontario (London, 1980).

La Société canadienne d'étude du dix-huitième siècle s'est fixé pour objectifs ''de soutenir au Canada l'intérêt pour l'étude de la civilisation du dix-huitième siècle aussi bien en Europe qu'au Nouveau Monde, d'encourager, sur une vaste base pluridisciplinaire, la recherche sur le dix-huitième siècle, et de faire connaître aux spécialistes du dix-huitième siècle le travail qui se fait au Canada en ce domaine''. Jusqu'à maintenant les

Readers and Advisors to the Editors
Lecteurs et conseillers des éditeurs

Contents/Table des matières

Acknowledgements/Remerciements

Many people have helped to bring to fruition this first volume of *The Proceedings of the Canadian Society for Eighteenth-Century Studies*. Among those to whom the Society and the editors are most indebted are the following members of The University of Western Ontario: Professor B.B. Kymlicka, Dean of the Faculty of Social Science; Professor John G. Rowe, Dean of the Faculty of Arts; Professors Peter F. Neary and A.M.J. Hyatt, Chairmen of the Department of History; Professor Paul Park, Dean of the Faculty of Education; Professor Geoffrey Milburn, Editor, the Publications Office of the Faculty of Education. In addition to The University of Western Ontario, the Society is grateful for grants in aid of publication to the Samuel and Saidye Bronfman Family Foundation and to the Hannah Institute for the History of Medicine, Associated Medical Services, Inc.

* * *

Plusieurs personnes ont collaboré pour mener à terme ce premier volume des Actes de la Société canadienne d'étude du dix-huitième siècle. La Société et les responsables de cette publication remercient plus particulièrement les membres suivants de l'Université de Western Ontario: le professeur B.B. Kymlicka, doyen de la faculté des Sciences sociales; le professeur John G. Rowe, doyen de la faculté des Lettres; les professeurs Peter F. Neary et A.M.J. Hyatt, directeurs du département d'Histoire; le professeur Paul Park, doyen de la faculté d'Éducation et le professeur Geoffrey Milburn, éditeur, service des Publications de la faculté d'Éducation. La Société manifeste aussi sa reconnaissance pour les subventions d'aide à la publication de la Samuel et Saidye Bronfman Family Foundation et de l'Hannah Institute for the History of Medicine, Associated Medical Services, Inc.

Preface/Préface

The Canadian Society for Eighteenth-Century Studies/La Société canadienne d'étude du XVIIIᵉ siècle grew out of discussions initiated by Professor E.J.H. Greene with scholars who attended the Voltaire conference held at Banff, Alberta in the spring of 1968. Professors Greene, Michel Gaulin, José-Michel Moureaux and David Smith formed a committee to inquire whether or not there was sufficient interest in Canada to warrant the formation of a Canadian society for eighteenth-century studies. Such a Canadian society was conceived as an organization which would hold regular if not annual meetings, which would accord equal status to the French and English languages and which would encourage and provide a forum for the discussion of work concerned with Canadian eighteenth-century history and cultures as well as the topics usually of interest to Enlightenment scholars.

While Canadian academics were considering the problems of founding a national society, their American colleagues were discussing a similar undertaking. Discussions in the United States led to the formation of the American Society for Eighteenth-Century Studies in December 1969. This society was incorporated after the adoption of its constitution at its first annual meeting held in Cleveland 17-19 April 1970. Because many Canadians immediately joined this body, there was some question about whether or not a Canadian society would be viable. It was clear that regional bodies, such as the McMaster Association for Eighteenth-Century Studies which was formed during these years, were viable but it was not equally clear that a national body could be kept alive in such a vast and sparsely populated country which was linguistically diverse.

On 6 May 1970 a meeting chaired by David Smith was held at Victoria College, The University of Toronto, to discuss the feasibility and aims of a Canadian society. It was decided that the views of eighteenth-century specialists in Canada should be canvassed. If there were sufficient support for a society, then an organizing committee would be created and a provisional constitution drafted to be presented to those who should attend a Canadian Eighteenth-Century Congress to be held in March 1971. By mid-summer it was clear that enthusiasm for such a society existed across Canada and that plans could go forward. The Canada Council was approched for aid which it provided; it has continued to subsidize the general meetings.

The Canadian Society for Eighteenth-Century Studies organizing committee met on 26 September 1970 at Toronto to draft proposals which on 17 October were presented to those attending the McMaster Association conference in Hamilton. At that meeting, chaired by David Smith, a provisional constitution was presented, publication possibilities were discussed as was affiliation with the American and International Societies. Other matters of business included the initiation of a newsletter for the Society which was now provisionally constituted. At the same time plans were made for the first general meeting to be held at Victoria and Scarborough Colleges and McMaster University on 19-21 March 1971. In due course this meeting was held and a constitution was approved. Subsequent general meetings have been convened at the University of Saskatchewan, Saskatoon (1972), Université Laval, Québec (1975), Dalhousie University, Halifax (1976), McMaster University, Hamilton (1977), The University of British Columbia, Vancouver (1979), and The University of Western Ontario, London (1980).

The stated purposes of the Canadian Society for Eighteenth-Century Studies are "to advance interest within Canada in the study of the culture and history of the eighteenth century in Europe and the New World, to encourage research and investigation in eighteenth-century studies on a broad inter-disciplinary basis, and to acquaint students of the eighteenth century with Canadian scholarship in this field." Until now the Society's principal means of accomplishing these goals have been in its general meetings, newsletters and the support which it has given to the International Society for Eighteenth-Century Studies with which it has been affiliated since 1975. It has, however, been an aim of the Society since its inception to mount a publication, either a journal or occasional volumes of essays written by its members or presented at its meetings. This volume marks the fulfillment at long last of that much delayed hope.

This collection of papers has been selected from those delivered at the general meeting held at The University of Western Ontario 8-10 May 1980. They have been roughly grouped into papers dealing with French literature, the Scottish Enlightenment, political thought, colonial history in the Spanish and British colonies, French Canada in the eighteenth century, art history and the history of science. The editors of the volume regret that they have not been able to print more of the fine papers presented at the London conference.

* * *

La Société canadienne d'étude du XVIIIe siècle/Canadian Society for Eighteenth-Century Studies s'est constituée à la suite de discussions amorcées par E.J.H. Greene au colloque sur Voltaire tenu à Banff (Alberta) au printemps de 1968. Les professeurs Greene, Michel Gaulin, José-Michel Moureaux et David Smith formèrent un comité afin de vérifier si se manifestait un intérêt suffisant au Canada pour autoriser la formation d'une société. Cette Société canadienne tiendrait des congrès à intervalles réguliers, disparitions par enchantement, comme autant de mouvements sans cause. Logiquement, son seul projet suivi en la matière est d'entretenir Manon au moyen du jeu.

Il faut cependant parler un peu plus en détail de l'héritage, que nous venons d'évoquer. Le budget fort irréaliste de l'ex-abbé de Saint-Sulpice s'établit sur une base de dix ans, au cours desquels, dit-il à Manon, il est impossible qu' "il n'arrive point de changement dans ma famille; mon père est âgé, il peut mourir. Je me trouverai du bien, et nous serons alors au-dessus de toutes nos autres craintes" (p. 50). Trois pages plus loin, il est de nouveau question de ces "changements que j'espérais," allusion bien pudique au désir de tuer le père. Cette mort, au surplus, ne réglerait pas le problème, puisque le vieillard, qui était prêt à vouer son fils au célibat en le destinant à l'ordre de Malte ou à l'état ecclésiastique (p. 18), se survit en un fils aîné, autre lui-même qui avait fort bien fait ses preuves dans l'épisode de la première trahison de Manon, quand il s'était agi d'enlever le frère cadet à Paris et de l'emmener réfléchir quelques mois à la maison, sous bonne garde. Pas grand-chose, donc, à espérer de ce côté-là; aussi bien, quand des Grieux reviendra du Nouvel Orléans, moralement régénéré et définitivement débarrassé de sa catin, il s'en faudra que la maison paternelle s'ouvre toute grande au fils repentant: l'aîné, devenu entre-temps chef de la famille, donne rendez-vous à son frère hors de chez lui, dans la maison d'un parent (p. 204). Reste donc l'autre partie de l'héritage, la seule sur laquelle il faille vraiment compter: "étant dans ma vingtième année, j'entrais en droit d'exiger ma part du bien de ma mère" (p. 117).

Avouons qu'il y a une logique derrière ce rejet que les instances paternelles infligent au Chevalier. En admettant qu'il en eût les moyens matériels, des Grieux ne pourrait prétendre sérieusement à l'intégration dans la classe à laquelle il appartient par sa naissance, ni à la succession. Le roman et son héros ont beau se cramponner à l'idéologie aristocratique, ils n'en présentent en fait qu'une image dérisoire: parodie de la noblesse dans les rituels de l'ordre chevaleresque des escrocs qui détroussent les joueurs à l'hôtel de Transylvanie (pp. 62-64), cynisme de des Grieux lorsqu'il ramène la société à deux classes, les riches stupides et les pauvres astucieux, et nous montre que la vocation providentielle des seconds consiste à sucer l'argent des premiers, en se faisant leurs maquereaux ou leurs précepteurs de vertu — indifféremment, car l'un vaut l'autre (pp. 53-54). La déchéance du Chevalier se marque surtout, et non plus épisodiquement, par un détournement radical de l'idée même de noblesse.

Il serait simpliste de dire que la classe dominante, dans une société donnée, ne fait rien d'autre que de consommer le produit du travail de celles qu'elle exploite, si significative et si fondamentale que soit au demeurant cette consommation publiquement revendiquée. La classe dominante joue aussi d'autres rôles; même si l'analyse de son idéologie révèle qu'elle les survalorise, qu'elle cherche systématiquement à dénier que quiconque puisse l'y remplacer, qu'elle en invente pour se rendre indispensable; bref, même si la vocation qu'elle s'attribue découle moins de la nature des choses que de la façon dont elle a intérêt à voir les choses, il n'en reste pas moins qu'elle fonde sa légitimation — sinon sa légitimité — sur une responsabilité sociale. La

4

classe dominante ne peut réclamer le pouvoir sans se montrer prête à l'exercer effectivement.

Dans le cas de la noblesse d'Ancien Régime, nous savons très bien ce que cela veut dire. Malgré les transformations qu'a subies la féodalité du fait de la montée du pouvoir royal, le noble est toujours un guerrier; il est toujours seigneur, rentier et protecteur de ses vassaux; la participation à l'administration de la justice et à la gestion des affaires publiques continue à faire partie de ses prérogatives héréditaires, même si Versailles les menace. Enfin, sa responsabilité idéologique demeure impérieuse: il est le gardien des valeurs de sa classe, donc des valeurs dominantes de toute la société.

Est-il besoin de dire qu'une conception de la noblesse qui consiste à ruer dans les brancards parce qu'on n'a pas assez d'argent pour risquer plus de deux pistoles au jeu et pour emmener sa maîtresse à l'Opéra deux fois par semaine (pp. 49-50) semble un peu étriquée? Des Grieux se place en marge de l'aristocratie en n'en retenant comme signe distinctif que l'une des formes de la consommation, le divertissement, et surtout en refusant de reconnaître que la vie de l'homme de qualité, par définition, n'est pas que privée (erreur où ne tomberait pas un libertin).

Nous connaissons aussi fort bien le mode sur lequel la condition aristocratique pouvait se vivre subjectivement, et je ne sache pas que ce que Montesquieu écrivit sur l'honneur ait rien perdu de son intérêt. Si la noblesse est la classe qui se déclare prête à risquer sa vie pour le roi, et qui revendique en retour la participation au pouvoir, la richesse, les privilèges et le droit de définir les valeurs dominantes, l'homme de qualité est celui qui se déclare prêt à risquer sa vie pour son honneur et qui réclame en retour d'être reconnu par autrui.

On sait enfin — et c'est par là que je terminerai ce rappel de notions familières — quel lien s'établit dans l'idéologie aristocratique entre l'honneur et l'amour. L'accomplissement du héros, c'est-à-dire de l'idéal du noble, s'atteint lorsque coïncident la reconnaissance de soi comme être social et comme être sexué, reconnaissance qui n'est valide que si le partenaire est digne qu'elle soit réciproque. M. des Grieux père illustre admirablement ce point de vue. Révéler à son fils que c'est Manon elle-même qui s'est vendue à M.B. . . et qui s'est arrangée pour se débarrasser de son amant impécunieux, est à ses yeux un moyen infaillible pour détacher immédiatement l'aveugle, à qui il connaît des "principes d'honneur," d'un objet méprisable; il n'en revient pas lorsque cette manoeuvre échoue, et il reste incapable de croire à une passion aussi invraisemblable (pp. 36-37). De même, à l'autre bout du roman, s'il écoute d'une oreille attendrissable des allusions générales aux ardeurs amoureuses qu'il a pu éprouver dans sa jeunesse (p. 162), il se redresse sous l'outrage lorsque son fils ose comparer sa passion pour Manon à l'amour que lui, le père, avait voué à sa femme. C'est là-dessus que se rompt définitivement le contact entre le père et le fils (p. 172).

C'est dans ce problème de la double reconnaissance — sociale et sexuelle — que je situerais le conflit fondamental du roman. La donnée de base en est que des Grieux doit renoncer à l'une ou à l'autre. Certes, son père, qui n'est pas un monstre, envisage un instant de le marier, croyant qu'il ne peut pas se passer de femme (p. 37); mais cette offre, aussitôt repoussée par le héros, reste sans poids, puisque la seule épouse qu'il puisse accepter est Manon (pp. 22, 26, etc.), qui est exclue, à cause de sa condition et de ses moeurs. D'autre part, des Grieux, chevalier de Malte ou ecclésiastique, aurait pu, pour employer ses propres termes, "n'être pas plus scrupuleux qu'un grand nombre d'évêques et d'autres prêtres, qui savent accorder fort bien une maîtresse avec un bénéfice" (p. 65). Mais les conseils sarcastiques qui sont bons pour Tiberge ne le sont pas pour lui; ce qui serait vraisemblable dans les moeurs de l'époque n'est pas vrai pour le des Grieux réel, c'est-à-dire l'être textuel qui habite le roman de Prévost. Ici, il n'a d'autre alternative que de renoncer à la reconnaissance sexuelle en entrant dans les ordres (militaires ou non), ou à la reconnaissance sociale, en tournant le dos aux seules carrières qui s'ouvrent à un cadet.

En fin de compte, nous le savons, il n'obtiendra ni l'une ni l'autre. Le roman détaille toutes les étapes de la déchéance du Chevalier, et il la figure, comme allégoriquement, en rapprochant deux images: celle du pauvre hère, obligé de vendre sa monture pour suivre une déportée et rentrant d'Amérique, "cavalier désarçonné,"[3] ses guenilles sous le bras, et celle du gamin fringant qui caracole à côté de la chaise où la petite Manon vole vers Paris, comme pour une partie d'amour buissonnier (pp. 14, 16, 183; 24).

Le tableau amoureux ne me semble pas moins sombre, car sans cesse Manon renvoie son amant à sa nullité. Elle l'aime, dit-il et dit-elle; nous n'avons aucun droit de les contredire. Mais elle ne peut supporter l'idée de vivre petitement, de renoncer au plaisir et aux passe-temps.

> Quoiqu'elle m'aimât tendrement, et que je fusse le seul, comme elle en convenait volontiers, qui pût lui faire goûter parfaitement les douceurs de l'amour, j'étais presque certain que sa tendresse ne tiendrait point contre de certaines craintes [la "crainte de la misère", c'est-à-dire surtout l'idée de renoncer à sa voiture, comme cela sera expliqué un peu plus loin, p. 70]. Elle m'aurait préféré à toute la terre avec une fortune médiocre; mais je ne doutais nullement qu'elle ne m'abandonnât pour quelque nouveau B. . . lorsqu'il ne me resterait que de la constance et de la fidélité à lui offrir (pp. 61-62).

Même la frêle assurance qui vient d'être citée s'évanouit d'ailleurs dans la suite: les vivres allaient manquer pour vrai lorsque Manon accueillit les avances de M. B. . ., mais c'est bel et bien l'éblouissement du luxe qui la fait se donner à G. . . M. . . fils, transformant en trahison de l'amour pour l'argent ce qui, au départ, ne devait être qu'une plaisante escroquerie.

Dans son rapport avec Manon, des Grieux apprend donc à se définir comme l'homme à qui il manque quelque chose, puisque ce qu'il est, et qu'elle aime, est impuissant à la satisfaire. Et, par une terrible ironie, elle ne cesse de lui infliger le renouvellement de sa castration. L'argent dont la possession pourrait lui assurer le bonheur dont il rêve, c'est à des figures paternelles qu'elle le demande: à M. B. . ., qui aura tôt fait de se lier avec le père des Grieux pour volatiliser son insignifiant rival — et notre héros, en pénitence au château paternel, retournera à ses livres d'écolier (p. 38); au vieux G. . . M. . . ensuite, ce qui donne lieu à un véritable festival de l'infantilisation: pour introduire son greluchon dans la maison du protecteur,

6

Manon le fait passer pour son petit frère, fraîchement arrivé de province pour se préparer à entrer au séminaire; le cher enfant n'a pas d'autre plaisir que de "faire de petites chapelles" (pp. 76-77). C'est des Grieux lui-même, le des Grieux de Saint-Sulpice, qui se caricature ici sous les traits de l'eunuque demeuré, jeu qui durera jusqu'à ce que la figure paternelle terrible se démasque, chasse du lit l'impuissant et l'envoie dans une autre maison religieuse, la prison de Saint-Lazare.

La troisième trahison a ceci de particulier que des Grieux s'en fait lui-même le complice, qu'il aide à la préparer, tout en en prévoyant fort bien les suites. Autre particularité: ce n'est plus un vieillard qu'il s'agit d'exploiter, mais un jeune homme, l'ami fort estimable de cet incomparable ami qu'est M. de T. . . Le texte insiste sur les similitudes et les affinités qui font de celui-ci un double du héros — mais un double idéal, puisqu'à la jeunesse, à la noblesse, à la sensibilité et à la générosité de des Grieux il ajoute la pleine possession de tous les avantages de l'aristocratie: il est riche, et la première chose que nous apprenions de lui, c'est qu'il est "en âge d'être marié" (p. 99). Il doit cette situation enviable au fait d'être le fils de son père, personnage considérable et administrateur de l'Hôpital, mais ce père, pour comble de bonheur, est absent du roman. C'est le jeune M. de T. . ., donc, qui introduit dans le ménage clandestin de nos deux amants un autre lui-même, G. . . M. . . fils, en le présentant comme l'un de ses meilleurs amis, comme un homme d'honneur et un homme très aimable (p. 125). A voir ces trois garçons ensemble, festoyant à Chaillot avec la belle Manon, on dirait trois frères. Mais G. . . M. . ., lui, a un père pour vrai, que nous connaissons, comme nous connaissons celui de des Grieux.

L'opération érotico-financière qui se trame à partir de là n'a pas le même sens que les précédentes. La première fois, Manon avait agi seule; la seconde, elle avait eu recours à ce frère-janus, Lescaut, qui est le sien par le sang, mais qui sait fort bien se faire passer pour celui du Chevalier quand il s'agit d'introduire un pistolet dans sa cellule à Saint-Lazare; ici, des Grieux est de la partie. D'autre part, le plan ne comporte pas, cette fois-ci, de prostitution réelle: Manon est censée s'évader de la Comédie avant que le jeune G. . . M. . . ait commencé à profiter de son acquisition. Enfin, le but poursuivi est double: renflouer les finances du couple, venger les avanies infligées par G. . . M. . . père.

On peut donc interpréter l'épisode comme suit: des Grieux est toujours à la recherche de ce qui pourrait pallier sa castration, et il croit avoir trouvé l'astuce. Non seulement l'opération pourra se réaliser sans attaquer de front l'instance paternelle, mais revanche sera prise sur les humiliations antérieures. Ce qui manquait ne manquera plus, et ce ne sera pas parce que Manon l'aura soutiré au père en sacrifiant des Grieux; c'est bien des Grieux lui-même, sous les traits de son double, qui le lui aura donné; des Grieux aura coïncidé, dans son double, avec la seule image qu'il puisse tolérer de soi-même: le jeune homme de bonne famille, libre, opulent et aimé.

La catastrophe est épouvantable. Voyons-en d'abord le dernier volet. Devant l'outrage infligé au père, les nuances de rang disparaissent. Des Grieux discute sur la noblesse et la pureté de son sang relativement à celui de ses victimes, regarde de haut M. de G. . . M. . ., ce "vieux monstre d'incontinence" (p. 153). Des Grieux père, lui, trouve normal de rendre visite à ce prétendu coquin, de faire alliance avec lui, d'humilier son fils devant cet homme respectable et offensé, qui s'exprime d'ailleurs, dans la circonstance, de la façon la plus mesurée, la plus digne et la plus patriarcale (p. 165). La victoire de l'autorité est complète; des Grieux retrouve un père-geôlier (pp. 165, 170, 172); Manon est expédiée, littéralement, au bout du monde.

Mais ce qui s'était déroulé auparavant est peut-être pire encore. Manon, on s'en souvient, n'eut pas plus tôt compris l'étendue des bienfaits de son nouveau protecteur qu'elle envoya promener son inutile amant. Au lieu d'exécuter la manoeuvre convenue pour le rejoindre, elle dépêcha à des Grieux l'ancienne maîtresse du jeune G. . . M. . ., pour le consoler en lui faisant passer un bon moment. La scène qui suit est étonnante (p. 133 sqq.). La rencontre a lieu dans un fiacre, à la nuit tombée, et la remplaçante est porteuse d'un billet de Manon. Que l'amant inquiet brûle de le lire, qu'il entre, pour ce faire, dans un cabaret, cela paraît normal, si l'on songe à ce qu'était alors l'éclairage nocturne des rues de Paris. On comprend moins bien pourquoi il s'installe avec la messagère dans un cabinet particulier. La pauvre enfant était payée pour une tâche précise, mais son client ne songe qu'à se livrer à des manifestations de douleur et de rage impuissante, décrites dans des termes qu'un esprit moyennement mal tourné rapportera sans peine à une autre sorte d'efforts inutiles.

Dans ce contexte, les mots que le héros adresse à sa consolatrice abasourdie ont un double sens parfaitement clair:

On t'a trompée, lui dis-je; ma pauvre fille, on t'a trompée. Tu es une femme, il te faut un homme; mais il t'en faut un qui soit riche et heureux, et ce n'est pas ici que tu le peux trouver. Retourne, retourne à M. de G. . . M. . . Il a tout ce qu'il faut pour être aimé des belles; il a des hôtels meublés et des équipages à donner. Pour moi, qui n'ai que de l'amour et de la constance à offrir, les femmes méprisent ma misère et font leur jouet de ma simplicité (p. 137).

Il peut retourner à ses petites chapelles; sa "simplicité" et sa pauvreté font qu'il n'est pas un homme. La fin du roman nous le montre d'ailleurs dans les bras du seul qui l'ait aimé fidèlement, de son vrai double, de son vrai *alter ego*: M. l'abbé Tiberge, chaste poire.

Nous avons donc lu le récit autobiographique d'une homme qui se juge castré, c'est-à-dire dépossédé de son propre corps. Un trouble pareil dans la fantasmation serait-il isolé? Faut-il s'attendre que l'image de la femme, elle, soit normale? C'est ce que nous examinerons maintenant.

Chaussons à nouveau nos besicles historico-sociologiques de tout à l'heure et demandons-nous ce qu'il en est de Manon comme corps social, capable d'entrer dans le cycle des échanges matrimoniaux. L'attitude de des Grieux à cet égard peut sembler fluctuante, mais je retiendrai surtout deux de ses déclarations, situées aux deux bouts du livre; elles me paraissent mériter une créance particulière parce que ce qui y paraît jaillit avec la force du lapsus, et se trouve en profond accord avec le mouvement général du récit.

La première exige, pour être bien comprise, d'être replacée dans son contexte. Nous sommes dans la cour de l'hôtellerie d'Amiens, au moment de la première rencontre. Je demandai à Manon, dit des Grieux,

> ce qui l'amenait à Amiens et si elle y avait quelques personnes de connaissance. Elle me répondit ingénument qu'elle y était envoyée par ses parents pour être religieuse. L'amour me rendait déjà si éclairé, depuis un moment qu'il était dans mon coeur, que je regardai ce dessein comme un coup mortel pour mes désirs. Je lui parlai d'une manière qui lui fit comprendre mes sentiments, car elle était bien plus expérimentée que moi. C'était malgré elle qu'on l'envoyait au couvent, pour arrêter sans doute son penchant au plaisir, qui s'était déjà déclaré et qui a causé, dans la suite, tous ses malheurs et les miens (p. 20).

Nous sommes devant un fragment de récit, plus précisément devant le récit d'un dialogue. Comme partout ailleurs dans le récit de des Grieux, le locuteur est clairement reconnaissable et la source de son savoir, évidente. Mais la dernière phrase, tout à coup, fait problème. "C'était malgré elle qu'on l'envoyait au couvent" peut être en style direct (le narrateur relate ce qu'il sait des sentiments de sa partenaire), mais se lit tout aussi bien en style indirect libre: le locuteur dans le texte serait des Grieux, mais l'énoncé appartiendrait à Manon. La fin de la phrase appartient évidemment au narrateur: "son penchant au plaisir, *qui a causé, dans la suite, tous ses malheurs et les miens.*" Reste l'entre-deux: "on l'envoyait au couvent, *pour arrêter sans doute son penchant au plaisir, qui s'était déjà déclaré.*" Voilà des choses que le narrateur n'a certainement pas apprises ce jour-là (Manon était bien trop expérimentée), et dont le roman ne nous dit nulle part dans quelles circonstances elles lui auraient été révélées. Vaine question, d'ailleurs: "on l'envoyait au couvent, pour arrêter *sans doute* son penchant au plaisir"; c'est à une hypothèse du narrateur que nous avons affaire, hypothèse à laquelle se raccroche grammaticalement un autre énoncé ("son penchant au plaisir, *qui s'était déjà déclaré*"), libre, celui-là, de toute restriction dubitative. Le lecteur reste perplexe, car il reconnaît ici l'une des techniques éprouvées de la diffamation: l'hypothèse désobligeante sur les motifs qu'avaient les Lescaut de mettre leur fille au couvent emprunte sa force à un fait, d'authenticité nébuleuse; le fait, à son tour, gagne en plausibilité d'être intégré à une chaîne causale intelligible: le penchant de Manon au plaisir, qui a causé tous ses malheurs, s'était certainement déclaré fort tôt, et on comprendrait ses parents de l'avoir entourée d'un cordon sanitaire.

Si j'ai parlé de lapsus, c'est que ce genre de perversité dans l'énonciation me semble trancher sur la franchise, l'impudeur même du style de des Grieux. Quant à la portée de la phrase, il est difficile de l'exagérer: "Manon n'a jamais été autre chose qu'une dévergondée," nous dit le narrateur; "c'était un danger public reconnu, comme le confirme la suite de mes malheurs." Des Grieux adopte ici le point de vue de la société sur cette fille "d'une naissance commune," qui prend soin de se faire appeler "Mademoiselle" et qui se trouve "flattée d'avoir fait la conquête d'un amant tel que" lui, d'un gentilhomme (pp. 21-22). Nous sommes assez renseignés sur le lien qu'établit Prévost entre la naissance et les vertus morales pour comprendre qu'à ses yeux aussi, Manon est une ordure.

L'autre phrase que je voudrais commenter provient de l'épisode américain. On sait que le Nouvel Orléans représente une espèce de paradis de simplicité vertueuse, où l'amour et les bonnes qualités des deux amants peuvent enfin fleurir en toute liberté. D'où le désir qui naît en eux de régulariser leur union. Voici comment des Grieux fait sa proposition:

> Nous avons l'âme trop belle, et le coeur trop bien fait, l'un et l'autre, pour vivre volontairement dans l'oubli du devoir. Passe d'y avoir vécu en France, où il nous était également impossible de cesser de nous aimer et de nous satisfaire par une voie légitime; mais en Amérique, où nous ne dépendons que de nous-mêmes, où nous n'avons plus à ménager les lois arbitraires du rang et de la bienséance, où l'on nous croit même mariés, qui empêche que nous ne le soyons bientôt effectivement et que nous n'anoblissions notre amour par des serments que le religion autorise? (P. 190.)

Cette demande en mariage, que Manon n'osait espérer, comble de joie son coeur, où ne règnent plus que l'amour, la religion et l'altruisme.

Nous approchons d'une nouvelle catastrophe, qui donnera à des Grieux l'occasion de gémir sur l'injuste rigueur du Ciel. Il l'annonce en ces termes à son auditeur:

> Je suis persuadé qu'il n'y a point d'honnête homme au monde qui n'eût approuvé mes vues dans les circonstances où j'étais, c'est-à-dire asservi fatalement à une passion que je ne pouvais vaincre et combattu par des remords que je ne devais point étouffer (p. 191).

Qui ne voit que ces excuses ruinent de fond en comble toute la construction? Que sert d'avoir fui la France, l'autorité paternelle et les "lois arbitraires du rang et de la bienséance," de ne dépendre que de soi-même; que sert d'avoir trouvé sous des cieux libres une Manon régénérée, qui déteste son passé et qui n'est plus que modération dans la conduite, générosité envers autrui et amour indéfectible pour l'homme de sa vie, s'il faut, pour justifier le mariage avec elle aux yeux d'un honnête homme, plaider les circonstances atténuantes, se dire ligoté par une passion asservissante et torturé par le remords? Ne sommes-nous pas invités à comprendre qu'il y a des choses qu'un honnête homme ne se permet pas, et qu'on n'anoblit pas une Mademoiselle Manon Lescaut?

Lapsus donc, et lapsus de Prévost, indiscutablement, qui consiste à faire avouer au narrateur ce que ni lui, ni nous ne devrions penser, que Prévost lui-même ignorait sans doute, mais qui est le fil conducteur de son récit: jamais, en aucune circonstance il ne pourra s'envisager que Manon soit la femme de des Grieux.

Le Ciel, bien entendu, se déchaîne, mais nous avons compris que ce qu'il pouvait infliger de pire au héros ne serait que la réalisation de son désir. Aussi bien, si nous avions la tentation de prendre la fiction pour la réalité, de voir des faits là où nous lisons en réalité le dévoilement d'un fantasme, il suffirait de considérer un peu attentivement le gouverneur et son neveu Synnelet pour secouer cette illusion: il est trop évident qu'il n'y a point d'autre fatalité à l'oeuvre ici que la chaîne qui lie un homme à son inconscient, puisque cette nouvelle paire de personnages reproduit en en redistribuant les traits les figures complices du père, de l'entremetteur, du frère nanti et du rival, déjà vues sous les noms des des Grieux aînés, de Lescaut et des deux G. . . M. . . Plutôt que dans je ne sais quelle obscure métaphysique de la passion et du destin, c'est ici qu'il conviendrait de chercher le tragique du roman (si l'on tient à tout prix à y en trouver), dans l'inaptitude de l'être humain à identifier correctement l'objet de son désir. La réalité est déjà assez dure, pourquoi faut-il que nous ne soyons même pas capables de rêver juste?

Si donc il est exclu que Manon soit la femme de des Grieux, pourrait-elle être une femme pour lui? Il faudrait pour cela qu'il fût un homme, ce qui fait problème, comme nous l'avons vu; et nous avions pu être tentés de croire que le roman narrait la quête d'un phallus artificiel, l'argent, qui aurait levé l'obstacle pour qui eût réussi à le détenir avec assez de constance. Je pense que cette lecture est trop courte et qu'en nous y bornant, nous tomberions dans le même piège que des Grieux, car nous nous ferions accroire que c'est à la présence ou à l'absence de l'argent que tiennent les sentiments de Manon envers lui, théorie fétichiste à laquelle il se cramponne bien que ses aventures, les explications de Manon et l'analyse qu'il fait lui-même de la psychologie de sa maîtresse (par exemple pp. 61-62) lui aient démontré le contraire. Ce qu'il désire, c'est le don d'un corps lié à celui d'un coeur, et c'est cela qui n'entre pas dans la tête de Manon.

Parler de la frigidité de cette héroïne serait étrange, dit Raymond Picard en soulevant la question, dans la préface de l'édition qu'il a donnée du roman avec Frédéric Deloffre; des Grieux ne lui fait-il pas "goûter parfaitement les douceurs de l'amour"? "Mais," enchaîne-t-il,

> cette expérience ne semble guère la marquer. L'acte d'amour est pour elle un plaisir parmi d'autres, et qui ne saurait s'inscrire dans un être de façon privilégiée [. . .]. Son corps lui reste extérieur [. . .] (p. cxxii).

Picard rappelle ensuite comment elle croyait satisfaire tout le monde en se donnant au jeune G. . . M. . . et en envoyant une autre fille à des Grieux pour lui faire passer le temps, et ce que fut son étonnement en se rendant compte que son amant n'était pas à l'aise dans un pareil régime d'indifférenciation.

"Son corps lui reste extérieur." La formule est profonde, et Jacques Proust la relève dans sa magnifique étude sur "le Corps de Manon,"[4] à qui j'emprunte à mon tour d'importantes observations, que j'essaierai de pousser plus loin à la lumière de ce que j'ai exposé jusqu'ici.

"Que le célèbre roman de Prévost ne contienne aucune référence descriptive à la belle personne qui en est le sujet n'est pas le moindre paradoxe de son oeuvre," dit Proust (p. 107). Cela a été expliqué diversement, et il est probable que le béguin séculaire de milliers de lecteurs pour Manon s'explique en partie par l'espèce de piège que nous tend le texte en dirigeant sur elle un feu nourri de regards admiratifs, de convoitises immédiates et d'épithètes amoureuses, sans permettre au lecteur d'apercevoir autre chose qu'une sorte de brouillard voluptueusement attirant.

Mais le critique ne s'arrête pas là; au lieu de constater simplement le vague, il nous montre de quoi il est fait, et révèle la présence de plusieurs complexes de signifiants, dont certains fort inattendus. Au risque de ramener une suite d'analyses très fines à un catalogue décharné, j'énumérerai: le rapport de ce voile que le style de Prévost interpose entre nous et la possible vue de Manon avec le geste de se voiler ou de se cacher qui la caractérise en plusieurs moments-clés du livre; le fait "que son visage soit exsangue *chaque fois* que le narrateur juge bon de se référer précisément à sa couleur," ce qu'il faut rapprocher de la prédilection pour des mots comme *langueur* et *languissant*; un mode d'apparition du personnage dans le décor qui s'apparente à celui des spectres (Proust, pp. 110-111). Ces traits convergent avec le rappel d'une donnée fondamentale, à savoir que toute l'histoire des deux amants se raconte après la mort de Manon, se lit sur l'horizon de cette mort, pour conduire Proust à déclarer que, "si l'auteur ne nous montre jamais le corps de Manon, c'est parce qu'au moment où Renoncour — ou des Grieux — nous en parle, ce ne pourrait être qu'un objet d'effroi et de répulsion [. . .]. Manon n'est plus qu'un cadavre décomposé," le contraire donc de ce "composé charmant," de "cette figure capable de ramener l'univers à l'idolâtrie" (Prévost, p. 178), qui faisait délirer le héros. Montrant ensuite quelle fonction matricielle la scène de la mort remplit dans le roman, et quelle importance il faut accorder au sable qui semble en résumer tout le décor, Proust conclut: "Dans le contexte, par le contexte, le sable devient un mot poétique, la figure métonymique d'un objet proprement innommable" (pp. 112-113).

"Son corps lui reste extérieur"; peut-être bien parce qu'il n'est pas un corps, mais un agrégat; non pas une unité concrète et vivante, spécifiée comme personne, mais un ramassis de choses, abstraitement réunies par une dénomination ("Manon"), et qui n'attendent qu'un hasard pour se dissocier et ne plus faire qu'un tas de matière innommable.

Désagrégation, décomposition, anonymat, mort, horreur, tabou linguistique: nous avons là des éléments d'une série. J'en trouve le terme suivant au moyen d'un détour par la morale. Si, reprenant le jugement des contemporains et de la postérité, je dis que Manon est une fille, une catin, une perfide, une traînée, une sans coeur, une coureuse, et que je résume en disant qu'elle est une merde, ce n'est pas, qu'on veuille me croire, pour chercher un effet facile. Aucun autre objet de l'expérience humaine ne réunit avec la même netteté les caractéristiques que nous pouvons attribuer à la maîtresse de des Grieux: infiniment précieuse et infiniment abjecte, instrument de jouissance narcissique interdit par les instances parentales, objet perpétuellement reperdu, qui n'est jouissance que dans le risque et le besoin de le perdre, trésor intime et scandale sans nom pour soi-même et pour autrui, matière morte et produit de la vie, image de la mort et de la séparation d'avec soi-même.

Le dernier élément de la série est, évidemment, l'argent, avatar sans odeur, dit-on, du précédent. Des Grieux ne décrit pas les écus qu'il donne à ses domestiques; pourquoi décrirait-il le corps de Manon, qui appartient à tout le monde, qui va et vient de façon aussi imprévisible que les louis d'or qui remplissent aujourd'hui la bourse du joueur et que les valets auront emporté demain, qui sert à acheter des bijoux et à payer des fiacres, qui peut se remplacer par n'importe quel autre corps de valeur équivalente? Manon est publique, anonyme, divisible, mobile, morte et souillée comme l'argent. Courir après l'argent pour s'assurer son coeur, c'est chercher un fétiche pour acheter un fétiche, c'est prendre une valeur d'échange pour une valeur d'usage.[5]

Ceux qui auront cru pouvoir me suivre jusqu'ici sont désormais persuadés qu'il n'y a, dans l'*Histoire du chevalier des Grieux et de Manon Lescaut*, à un certain niveau de la fantasmation, ni homme, ni femme; mais bien un homme castré et un objet fécal qui lui tient lieu de phallus, fonction que nous pouvons déduire de ce qu'à vingt reprises il déclare que la perte de cet objet est pour lui synonyme de mort,[6] et qu'il est effectivement détruit lorsque cette perte est consommée. Je voudrais maintenant, très rapidement, suggérer une voie de passage vers un autre niveau, mais avec une extrême prudence, car seule la superposition de ce roman-ci avec les autres productions de Prévost donnerait quelque garantie de certitude. Je me conforte, pour le moment, de penser que ce que j'avance est sur la même longueur d'ondes qu'un grand nombre d'observations dégagées par Jean Sgard.

Il y a trois femmes dans ce livre: Manon, sa remplaçante dans l'épisode du jeune G. . . M. . . (sur qui il n'y a rien à dire) et une troisième, qui ne paraît que sur le mode de l'absence. La mère de des Grieux nous est donnée, dans la scène du Luxembourg, comme l'inaccessible, comme celle qui a appartenu au père, celle dont le père interdit même au fils de parler, tant son approche est sacrilège. Elle fait l'objet d'une allusion prodigieusement indirecte, aux premières pages du récit principal, lorsque le narrateur décrit son éblouissement à la vue de Manon: moi, dit-il, "moi qui n'avais jamais pensé à la différence des sexes [. . .]" (p. 19). Il n'a donc jamais pensé qu'il était d'un sexe différent de celui de sa mère? il ignorait donc qu'elle en eût un? Enfin, rappelons la phrase déjà citée: "étant dans ma vingtième année, j'entrais en droit d'exiger ma part du bien de ma mère."

Peut-être bien que ce que le roman raconte, c'est qu'il l'a eue. Intégralement. Il a eu un corps qui ressemblait à s'y méprendre à une femme, et qui était aussi tendre et aussi fidèle qu'une liasse de billets de la banque de Law; et il a eu une morte. Quand, dans une scène (p. 199sqq.) où je suis d'accord avec Jacques Proust (pp. 121-122) pour voir la seule représentation véritable que ce livre nous offre de l'acte d'amour, quand, dis-je, couché à demi nu sur le sable où Manon se décompose, il y tombe dans un orgasme de douleur, il recueille peut-être précisément son legs le plus cher.

* * *

Le moment est venu de préciser ce que j'entendais par mon titre. J'ai voulu montrer à l'oeuvre deux genres de fantasmes reliés à l'argent. Les uns sont de l'espèce qu'on est habitué à rencontrer dans les travaux de psychanalyse et de psychocritique; les autres sont également des produits de l'imaginaire, mais nous savons qu'ils furent consciemment entretenus par des groupes humains considérables, et relèvent de ce qu'on appelle l'idéologie. Telle est par exemple l'idée que les privilèges de certaines familles s'expliquent par une supériorité naturelle, que la richesse leur appartient par harmonie préétablie, etc.

Il me semble avoir fait comprendre assez clairement comment les deux ordres de fantasmes se prêtent l'un avec l'autre à des jeux de métaphorisation: la basse condition et l'immoralité congénitale de Manon, obstacles infranchissables à l'union publique des amants, disent parfaitement, en la voilant, la répugnance du moi à désirer un objet qui, pour lui plaire, doit être ignoble et perdu; l'impossible identification virile ne se marque pas mieux dans l'histoire d'"amour" que dans le statut du héros. Si je n'indique pas de correspondance en sens inverse, cela tient à ce qu'il y a de sommaire et de rapide dans l'essai qu'on vient de lire, et, fondamentalement, à ce que je décris les deux ordres de fantasmes à des niveaux différents: je n'ai pas dépassé, pour ce qui est de l'idéologie, le niveau du manifeste, des attitudes conscientes et explicites, ce qui n'est dans cet ordre, comme dans le psychanalytique, qu'une première et superficielle approche de l'organisation du discours. Même si Prévost s'identifie à des Grieux, comme on a toutes les raisons de le croire, sa vision du monde n'est pas nécessairement identique à celle qu'il pense qu'il a.

Raymond Joly
Université Laval

Notes

*Je remercie les membres du Cercle de psychocritique (Québec), en particulier Jacqueline Gourdeau et Ernest Pascal, pour les observations qu'ils m'ont permis d'utiliser en rédigeant ce texte.

[1] Antoine-François Prévost, *le Philosophe anglais ou Histoire de Monsieur Cleveland,* éd. Philip Stewart dans *Oeuvres,* éd. J. Sgard (Grenoble: Presses universitaires de Grenoble, 1977), II, p. 75.

[2] Prévost, *Histoire du chevalier des Grieux et de Manon Lescaut,* éd. Frédéric Deloffre et Raymond Picard, Paris, Garnier, 1965, pp. 16-17. Dans la suite, un chiffre entre parenthèses suffira à renvoyer aux pages de cette édition — c'est-à-dire au texte de Prévost, mais aussi aux précieuses notes des éditeurs.

[3] Jean Sgard, *Prévost romancier* (Paris: Corti, 1968), p. 236.

[4] Jacques Proust, "le Corps de Manon," dans Jacques Proust, *l'Objet et le texte. Pour une poétique de la prose française du XVIIIe siècle* (Genève, Droz, 1980), pp. 107-126.

[5] Des Grieux, d'ailleurs, est loin d'être insensible aux charmes supplémentaires que l'opulence permet à Manon de se procurer, ni à la valeur marchande de ce corps (et du sien propre). C'est ce que relève Lionel Gossman dans un article (dont je remercie M. Toby Gelfand de me l'avoir signalé): "Prévost's *Manon*: Love in the new world," *Yale French Studies,* 40 (1968), 91-102 (94). Ajoutons aux citations de Gossman ce passage: "L'augmentation de nos richesses redoubla notre affection; Vénus et la fortune n'avaient point d'esclaves plus heureux et plus tendres" (66). Voir également la note suivante.

[6] Cet objet sous ses deux formes: Manon ou l'argent pour entretenir Manon (pp. 53, 108, etc.).

2. *Voltaire et* La Mort de César

Dans l'esprit de Voltaire, comme dans celui d'un certain nombre de ses contemporains,[1] *La Mort de César* représentait une hardiesse telle que l'auteur ne s'étonna guère de devoir attendre plus de dix ans avant de voir sa tragédie jouée sur le Théâtre français.[2] La suppression des intérêts amoureux et des rôles féminins — nous connaissons l'influence prépondérante des comédiennes de l'illustre compagnie dans le choix des pièces, ainsi que le goût du public de l'époque —, l'altération de la forme de la tragédie — *La Mort de César* n'avait que trois des cinq actes prescrits par la dramaturgie classique, — l'interprétation nouvelle d'un mythe séculaire faisant de Brutus le fils de César plutôt qu'un simple conjuré et, enfin, l'idéologie de la pièce, suspecte parce qu'inspirée trop ouvertement d'un modèle anglais qui était jugé révolutionnaire en France à ce moment-là, voilà autant de nouveautés dont Voltaire crut pouvoir s'enorgueillir. Quelque osées que fussent ces innovations et bien que chacune eût sans doute son importance dans l'esprit de Voltaire, une seule retiendra notre attention aujourd'hui, soit l'élimination de l'intrigue amoureuse et la prétention de l'auteur d'avoir réussi, par là, à "guérir le théâtre français de cette contagion [l'amour]," autrement dit, à purger le théâtre des galanteries qui l'affadissaient. Dans sa correspondance et dans ses écrits, Voltaire revient sans cesse sur l'idée qu'il faut opérer une révolution qui débarrasse le théâtre des fadaises amoureuses et détrôner, par conséquent, le despote dont parle le comte Algarotti dans sa lettre à l'abbé Franchini: "L'amore è signor despotico delle scene francesi[3]." A notre humble avis, si la pièce relate le renversement d'un despote appelé César, elle ne réussit pas pour autant à détruire *l'amore despotico,* ni même à purger le théâtre français.

Avant d'aborder le sujet proprement dit, rappelons brièvement l'action de *La Mort de César.* Après avoir subjugué Rome, César est sur le point de se proclamer roi, lorsqu'il avoue à Antoine que Brutus, ce républicain féroce, ennemi des tyrans, est son propre fils qui s'ignore. S'opposant aux conseils d'Antoine qui préconisait l'utilisation de la force pour imposer son règne, César entreprend de se faire aimer de Brutus et du Sénat. A l'acte II, Brutus dénonce avec violence les projets politiques de César et, devant ses amis alarmés, il s'engage à tuer quiconque voudrait détruire la République et la liberté romaine. Survient César, qui produit une lettre prouvant incontestablement à Brutus qu'il est le fils de son ennemi implacable. Abasourdi par cette révélation, Brutus s'acharne tout de même à ne pas reconnaître son père dans le tyran de Rome. A l'acte III, Brutus apprend aux conjurés le secret qui le ronge; Cassius, porte-parole des rebelles, déclare que le sang n'est rien, que seul l'amour de Rome doit remplir le coeur d'un citoyen. Brutus, dans un ultime effort pour dissuader son père, lui avoue qu'il l'aime. Mais César brave les menaces; il meurt assassiné par les conjurés. La pièce se termine par la harangue d'Antoine aux Romains les engageant à punir les coupables.

Outre le fait que, visiblement, la distribution ne comporte pas de rôle pour les femmes et, qu'en apparence du moins, l'auteur se préoccupe uniquement du débat politique mettant aux prises un républicain et un monarchiste, nous ne croyons pas que cela suffise à prouver l'expurgation du théâtre et la défaite de l'amour galant telles que claironnées par Voltaire. Bien au contraire, les critiques relevèrent avec justesse que l'amour, loin d'être banni, s'était métamorphosé. A cet effet, dans l'introduction à son édition de *La Mort de César*, André Rousseau propose l'idée de transmutation:

> La parenté de César et Brutus, très vague soupçon chez Plutarque et Shakespeare. . . s'étale ici avec une complaisance significative. Non seulement se trouve réintroduit le sentiment que l'absence des femmes avait éliminé, mais Voltaire donne un nouvel exemple de sa conception "sentimentale" de la tragédie et du tragique. . . .[4]

Quelle idée attrayante que d'établir la continuité entre les premières tragédies (p. ex. *OEdipe, Artémire*) et *La Mort de César* en posant l'hypothèse que l'amour "galante" des premières se transforme en amour paternel dans la deuxième. Idée intéressante, soit, mais qui se heurte à des objections dès que l'on tente de la vérifier, car ce n'est pas tout de rapprocher *La Mort de César* aux premières tragédies, encore faut-il s'assurer que nous comparons des choses de même nature, susceptibles d'être comparées: la relation Philoctète — Jocaste (*OEdipe*), c'est-à-dire l'amour entre un homme et une femme, disparaît-elle dans les oeuvres subséquentes, transformée en amour paternel (p. ex. Brutus — César)? Ou se maintient-elle sous une forme moins évidente, moins visible? La nécessité d'une théorie de la transmutation dépend de la réponse apportée à cette question. Nous aurons l'occasion d'y revenir.

En fait, cette théorie de la transmutation fut reprise et développée par G. Defaux dans une analyse des idées politiques de Voltaire dans *La Mort de César*.[5] Le critique l'explique ainsi:

> l'amour, qu'il [Voltaire] avait chassé avec éclat par la porte, revient en catimini par la fenêtre. Chez Voltaire, Brutus n'est pas seulement le champion de la Liberté romaine, il est aussi le fils de César. L'auteur voulait par ce moyen compenser l'absence d'amour dans sa tragédie; il ne fait en définitive que réintroduire ce sentiment sous une autre forme.[6]

Pour Defaux, ce palliatif qu'est le retour subreptice de l'amour, s'il pouvait compenser "la sécheresse inhérente à tout débat d'idées," n'entraînait pas moins la tragédie sur la pente du mélodrame; le critique conclut: "le conflit Liberté — Tyrannie. . .prend chez Voltaire l'étroitesse d'une moralité pleurarde, il s'efface devant le drame familial."[7]

Un autre chercheur, Robert Cottrell, signale lui aussi la transmutation de l'amour dans *La Mort de César,* tout en attirant notre attention sur un aspect négligé jusqu'à présent: le langage.

> Others have noted . . . that the tender but anguished relationship between César and Brutus replaces the more traditional love intrigue in contemporary tragedies. Indeed the most striking features of *La Mort de César* is the way in which Voltaire introduces situations and language appropriate to a love story into the economy of his tragedy. . . . By eliminating women from *La Mort de César* he did not rid his tragedy of the contagion of love. The manner in which love, shooed out one door, slips back in through another deserves, I believe, a closer examination.[8]

Après y avoir regardé de plus près, Cottrell est d'avis que l'amour est seul responsable du renversement de César: "The conspirators administer the *coup de grâce,* but it is love that topples César from his seat of power."[9] En effet, selon Cottrell, César est aussi amoureux de Brutus que Phèdre pouvait l'être d'Hippolyte. Pour appuyer ses dires, le critique fait appel au langage employé par César pour parler de son fils: "Although Voltaire is here [dans un extrait] describing paternal love, he has couched it in the traditional language of erotic affection . . . ."[10] Ainsi, quelles que soient leurs divergences d'opinions sur d'autres sujets, tous ces critiques s'entendent sur un point précis: l'amour paternel dans *La Mort de César* est une transmutation de l'amour "galant".

Or, cette opinion semble reposer d'abord et avant tout sur le postulat que nous avons affaire ici à une pièce expérimentale, originale, unique et que, pour cette raison, elle ne se donne pas à lire comme toutes les autres pièces voltairiennes de la même époque. Exception faite de Ronald Ridgway,[11] les autres critiques comparent *La Mort de César* aux premières tragédies, mais ils oublient de la replacer dans son contexte historique et chronologique, de telle sorte que leurs interprétations nous donnent l'impression qu'ils crurent Voltaire sur parole lorsqu'il se vante d'avoir expulsé l'amour galant de cette tragédie. Voilà qui explique pourquoi ils durent créer le concept d'une transmutation de l'amour. Que l'amour soit présent dans cette oeuvre, cela ne fait aucun doute, mais la forme que prend cet amour est problématique.

Il est essentiel, quant à nous, de partir du principe que *La Mort de César* n'est pas une pièce expérimentale, qu'elle contient vraisemblablement tous les éléments qui caractérisent les autres pièces de Voltaire écrites à cette époque, notamment *Brutus* (1730) et *Eriphyle* (1731). Par conséquent, notre première démarche qui consiste à superposer ces oeuvres révèle que, dans les deux dernières, un fils tombe en amour avec une femme aimable et séduisante contre le volonté expresse de son père: Titus, dans la pièce *Brutus,* s'éprend de la princesse Tullie, ce qui le mène à trahir Rome et son père; Alcméon, dans la pièce *Eriphyle,* s'éprend de la reine, ce qui le mène à transgresser l'interdiction du grand-prêtre et à trahir les dieux et son père. Chaque fois, le fils choisit d'aimer plutôt que de se plier à la volonté paternelle, il opte pour l'amour plutôt que le devoir et la fidélité. Dans *La Mort de César,* le père veut également récupérer son fils Brutus, le soustraire à l'influence, non d'une femme, mais des conspirateurs; le fils choisit une fois de plus de trahir son père. Malgré cette trahison, peut-on dire que Brutus sacrifie son père à l'amour d'une femme? En apparence, rien de tel puisqu'aucune femme n'entreprend de séduire Brutus. Néanmoins, notre démarche met en évidence des rapports récurrents d'une pièce à l'autre, rapports qu'il faut tâcher d'élucider davantage.

Il ressort, entre autres choses, que l'amour d'un père pour son fils, loin d'être une transmutation nouvelle et originale dans *La Mort de César* — comme les critiques cités plus haut ont bien voulu nous le faire croire — cet amour, disions-nous, existe comme rapport récurrent dans plusieurs pièces de cette période et, ce qui est plus révélateur, il s'oppose toujours à l'amour du fils pour une femme, ennemie du père. Outre les tragédies de *Brutus* et d'*Eriphyle*, nous pourrions citer les comédies des *Originaux ou Monsieur du Cap-Vert* (1732), de *L'Echange ou Quand est-ce qu'on me marie?* (1734) et même un livret l'opéra, *Samson* (1732). Ainsi, dans *La Mort de César,* au lieu de fabriquer une quelconque théorie de la transmutation et de faire entrer l'amour "en catimini par la fenêtre", ne serait-il pas plus simple — et surtout plus logique — d'y chercher, en dépit des difficultés, le même conflit entre l'amour hétérosexuel et l'amour paternel que nous avons relevé dans toutes les autres pièces de Voltaire écrites à ce moment-là?

Poursuivons cette idée en nous demandant quelle sorte de femme pourrait bien se cacher dans cette oeuvre, en apparence dépourvue de personnage féminin? D'après les résultats de notre superposition de pièces, les personnages féminins de Voltaire se présentent généralement comme des êtres faibles, prisonniers d'un pouvoir étranger, victimes de manigances politiques, enfin, ils constituent des appâts destinés à leurrer un héros sur son devoir politique.[12] Y a-t-il un tel personnage dans *La Mort de César?* Si la réponse est toujours négative, nous devons alors escompter la manifestation de ces idées sous une forme autre que le personnage.

En effet, depuis E. Souriau et A.-J. Greimas, nous savons que toutes les "fonctions" — dramaturgiques ou actantielles — n'ont pas à être présentes au microcosme théâtral dans un personnage distinct, que, parfois, un objet (p. ex. une couronne) ou une idée peuvent incarner le bien souhaité, etc. D'autre part, la poésie utilise constamment le procédé qui consiste à personnifier des choses inanimées. Alors, pourquoi ne pas chercher l'élément féminin qui contrebalance l'influence du père au niveau textuel, comme s'il s'agissait en fait d'un effet de style? La réponse s'impose alors à notre esprit: grâce à la personnification, l'élément féminin séducteur de Brutus s'appelle *Rome*.[13]

En réalité, Brutus et les conspirateurs sont les victimes d'un divorce politique puisqu'ils ont à choisir entre César — qui se veut leur père — et Rome qu'ils considèrent déjà comme leur mère. Cassius en dit autant à César: "Avant que d'être à toi nous sommes ses enfants [à Rome]" (I,E). Cassius, lorsqu'il veut convaincre Brutus de persévérer dans le projet d'assassiner César, demande: "Toi, son fils! Rome enfin n'est-elle plus ta mère?" (III,2) Voilà donc le personnage invisible chargé de séduire le fils de César, chargé d'agir comme pôle d'attraction hostile au père: Rome est la femme fatale pour qui Brutus va tout sacrifier.

Comme Tullie et Eriphyle, Rome est un personnage royal, détenu contre son gré:

Dieux! maîtresse de l'Inde, esclave aux bords du Tibre! Qu'importe que son nom commande à l'univers Et qu'on l'appelle reine, alors qu'elle est aux fers? (I,3)

Comme Tullie et Eriphyle, Rome occupe une position politique diamétralement opposée à celle représentée par l'homme fort au pouvoir: Rome est républicaine, alors que César prétend imposer un régime monarchique; comme Tullie et Eriphyle, Rome est un enjeu politique considérable que chacun s'arrache; comme pour Tullie et Eriphyle, la seule issue pour Rome réside dans la séduction du fils de l'homme fort: Rome doit provoquer Brutus et le tourner contre son père: "Entraîné par César, et retenu par Rome" (III,2), avoue le fils affligé. Rome possède donc toutes les caractéristiques du personnage féminin des autres pièces voltairiennes de l'époque: elle est faible, détenue, appât et rivale.

Par contre, parler de la séduction d'un personnage réel par une abstraction personnifiée dans le texte ne va pas sans créer certains problèmes. Voltaire s'en rendit compte et, pour se tirer d'embarras, dut recourir à un subterfuge peu satisfaisant. Phénomène remarquable, la scène de séduction prend la forme d'un monologue: l'acte II, scène 2. Désemparé devant l'initiative de son père qui veut détruire Rome (tout comme Brutus voulait chasser Tullie et les dieux voulaient détruire Eriphyle), Brutus se lamente: "Et je cherche ici Rome, et ne la trouve plus." Au pied de la statue de Pompée, représentant des vertus romaines, Brutus trouve un billet anonyme: "Tu dors, Brutus, et Rome est dans les fers!" Sans hésiter, Brutus répond à la personne responsable: "Rome, mes yeux sur *toi* seront toujours ouverts;/Ne me reproche point des chaînes que j'abhorre" (c'est nous qui soulignons). Et comme si ce premier billet ne devait pas suffire, Brutus en aperçoit un second: "Non, tu n'es pas Brutus!" Voilà donc que Rome dialogue avec son amant par billets interposés! A cette accusation de sa maîtresse, Brutus ne résiste plus; il se déclare prêt à venger Rome. Voici de quelle façon il s'y prend:

On demande un vengeur, on a sur moi les yeux;
On excite cette âme, et cette main trop lente;
On demande du sang. . .Rome sera contente.

Incapable de préciser quelle femme exige de lui cet effort suprême, Brutus emploie le pronom impersonnel "on" et termine en assurant que sa maîtresse sera satisfaite. Ainsi, sans l'intervention d'aucune femme, Brutus se trouve séduit par des billets qu'il attribue à l'être aimé. Cassius le lui dira un peu plus tard: "C'est Rome qui t'inspire en des desseins si grands" (II,4).

Cette entité féminine anthropomorphe nous permet de tirer quelques conclusions au sujet de *La Mort de César*, dont une première, très importante: la présence de Rome consacre l'échec de Voltaire dans sa campagne d'expurgation du théâtre. Malgré ses déclarations et toutes ses intentions révolutionnaires, l'auteur réintroduit, dans une notion abstraite et personnifiée, les éléments féminins qu'il jugeait indésirables, ce qui a pour effet de rendre cette pièce semblable aux autres. Pas de statut expérimental, par conséquent, et nul besoin d'inventer une théorie de la transmutation puisqu'en fait l'oeuvre reprend le grand thème commun à toutes les pièces de l'époque, soit le conflit entre l'amour hétérosexuel et l'amour paternel, entre l'amour et le devoir. Placé dans une situation pénible où il doit choisir entre son père et sa mère, le fils opte pour la femme et l'amour, provoquant ainsi la catastrophe finale. L'analogie avec *Eriphyle* est ici des plus saisissantes: le spectre du père revient sur terre pour empêcher l'union incestueuse du fils et de la mère. La situation est comparable dans *La Mort de César* où le père tente par tous les moyens de rompre l'attachement malsain de Brutus pour Rome, le tout sans succès: "Rome demande un maître:/Un jour à tes dépens tu l'apprendras peut-être" (III,4). Au dénouement, l'analogie se poursuit: par erreur, Alcméon tue sa mère sur le tombeau de son père et perd l'usage de ses sens; Brutus, quant à lui, permet l'assassinat de son père et, par erreur, plonge Rome dans la guerre civile, perdant alors l'usage de ses sens. Après leur crime, Alcméon, Brutus et même Titus ne sont plus que des loques humaines, victimes trop désireuses du supplice qu'ils ont mérité.

Nous pourrions conclure de la façon suivante: l'amour que Voltaire avait chassé revient, non pas sous forme d'un amour paternel — celui-ci étant déjà présent dans les autres pièces de l'époque —, mais bien dans l'image anthropomorphe de Rome, cette reine "esclave aux bords du Tibre".

Georges-L. Bérubé
Université de Victoria

Notes

[1] Parmi ceux-là, citons le conte Algarotti, LePelletier, Cideville, Desfontaines, etc. Cf. par exemple Best. D426 et D909.

[2] Commencée en Angleterre, *La Mort de César* fut complétée en juin 1731 (Best. D417); elle eut quelques représentations privées avant d'être créée à la Comédie française le 29.8.1743.

[3] Algarotti, *Lettera del signor conte Algarotti,* publiée avec la tragédie de *La Mort de César.*

[4] André Rousseau, *Voltaire: La Mort de César* (Paris: S.E.D.E.S., 1964,), p. 19.

[5] G. Defaux, "L'Idéal politique de Voltaire dans *La Mort de César,*" *Revue de l'Université d'Ottawa,* 40, No. 3 (1970), 418-440.

[6] Defaux, p. 428.

[7] Defaux, p. 428.

[8] Robert Cottrell, "Ulcerated Hearts: Love in Voltaire's *La Mort de César,*" dans *Literature and History in the Age of Ideas,* Ch. Williams éd. (Columbus; Ohio State Univ. Press, 1975), p. 171.

[9] Cottrell, p. 175.

[10] Cottrell, p. 174.

[11] Cf. Ronald Ridgway, *La Propagande philosophique dans les tragédies de Voltaire, SVEC* 15 (1961), 84.

[12] Tullie, dans *Brutus,* est prisonnière de Rome, tout en étant un enjeu politique dont se servira Arons pour séduire Titus. Eriphyle est prisonnière dans son propre palais; elle finit par obtenir l'aide d'Alcméon malgré l'interdiction formelle des dieux.

[13] Ainsi, l'idée d'une transmutation dans laquelle l'amour changerait d'objet — l'amour hétérosexuel qui devient amour paternel — est inutile; il s'agit toujours, dans cette pièce, du même amour hétérosexuel, mais certains procédés d'écriture en ont modifié la *manifestation*.

3. *La Rhétorique amoureuse dans* Les Égarements du coeur et de l'esprit

L'art d'aimer, dans *Les Egarements du coeur et de l'esprit,* se présente comme une *rhétorique.*

Que le roman, à l'époque de Crébillon, reste tributaire d'une définition rhétorique de la littérature, est un fait bien établi. Nous savons, grâce à Georges May, que l'évolution du genre s'explique alors en grande partie par la nécessité où se trouvent les romanciers "de justifier leurs ouvrages soit du point de vue esthétique, soit du point de vue moral,"[1] *Les Egarements* paraissent au moment où la querelle du roman, mettant aux prises Lenglet du Fresnoy, le P. Bougeant (qui attaque Crébillon), le P. Porée, atteint son apogée: à partir de 1737, "la publication des romans," selon Servais Etienne, sera "soumise en France à un régime d'exception qui équivaut presque à l'interdiction pure et simple."[2]

Les attaques contre le roman dans la première moitié du XVIIIe siècle fixent l'attention sur les deux fonctions traditionnellement assignées à la littérature: plaire et instruire. Ces objectifs obligent à considérer la littérature comme un discours persuasif et à insister sur le vraisemblable. En réalité, ils imposent à l'écrivain des impératifs contradictoires. Le désir de persuader le fait recourir à des procédés rhétoriques, mais le souci de la vraisemblance le force à en rejeter l'usage abusif, à la limite, à les dénoncer. Todorov a montré qu'une des tendances de la rhétorique a été d'opposer le discours figuré à un discours naturel impossible à décrire; tendance qui se fait jour, entre autres, dans le célèbre traité *Des Tropes* de Du Marsais.[3] A la fois descriptive et normative, la rhétorique repose sur une dialectique du naturel et de l'artificiel. La théorie de l'art-imitation joue sur la distinction entre vérité et vraisemblance. Si la littérature se situe du côté du vraisemblable, c'est pour valoriser, en creux, le champ de la vérité, pour suggérer que rien ne peut, au fond, remplacer la nature: Derrida a parlé, pour caractériser cette littérature, de "métaphysique de la présence."[4]

Plaire et instruire sont les deux buts avoués par Crébillon dans la *Préface* de son roman. "L'homme qui écrit," précise-t-il, "ne peut avoir que deux objets: l'utile et l'amusant." Et l'application de ces deux critères au roman l'amène à écarter les ouvrages qui ne satisfont pas aux normes de la crédibilité:

> Le Roman, si méprisé des personnes sensées, et souvent avec justice, serait peut-être celui de tous les genres qu'on pourrait rendre le plus utile, s'il était bien manié, si, au lieu de le remplir de situations ténébreuses et

21

forcées, de Héros dont les caractères et les aventures sont toujours hors du vraisemblable, on le rendait, comme la comédie, le tableau de la vie humaine, et qu'on y censurât les vices et les ridicules.[5]

On pourrait songer à dresser la liste des figures les plus fréquemment employées dans *Les Egarements du coeur et de l'esprit*; elle montrerait ce que Crébillon doit à l'esthétique de son temps. Comme dans *La Princesse de Clèves,* les caractérisations physiques — d'ailleurs fort rares — se font par le moyen d'hyperboles. Après la soirée passée à l'Opéra, Meilcour se rend chez Mme de Lursay, qui pour l'attendre, a revêtu "le déshabillé le plus noble et le plus galant" (p. 107). Dans un entretien avec sa mère, il résume en ces termes l'impression produite par la beauté de Mlle de Théville; et Crébillon ajoute à l'hyperbole la gradation et la répétition: "Sa figure, son maintien, son esprit, tout plaît en elle, tout y attache. Ce sont les plus beaux yeux! Les plus tendres! Les plus touchants!" (p. 179).

On ne s'étonnera pas de trouver dans *Les Egarements* un grand nombre de maximes. Expliquant, tout au début du roman, pourquoi il a choisi de séduire Mme de Lursay, Meilcour remarque: "On s'attache souvent moins à la femme qui touche le plus, qu'à celle qu'on croit le plus facilement toucher" (p. 49). Plus loin: "Les leçons et les exemples sont peu de chose pour un jeune homme" (pp. 51-52). Souvent, les maximes s'insèrent dans le mouvement naturel de la narration, dont elles soulignent l'exemplarité:

> Je passe sur les sentiments qui m'occupèrent cette nuit-là. Il n'y a pas d'homme sur la terre assez malheureux pour n'avoir jamais aimé, et aucun qui ne soit par conséquent en état de se les peindre. Si la vanité seule avait pu satisfaire mon coeur, il aurait sans doute été moins agité. (p. 177)

Emaillant dialogues et portraits, les maximes forment la vraie trame du roman et contribuent fortement à sa cohérence. Aristote les définit comme des enthymèmes abrégés; il est donc normal qu'elles jouent un rôle important dans l'argumentation. Vu sous un certain angle, le roman de Crébillon *aboutit* même à la production de maximes: le discours de Versac à Meilcour, dans la troisième partie, se compose de préceptes, règles, conseils, à l'usage du néophyte soucieux d'apprendre à se comporter dans le monde.

Prise dans le contexte narratif, qui l'enferme dans les limites de l'espace et du temps, l'argumentation rhétorique donne naissance au portrait. Le portrait est-il autre chose qu'une maxime appliquée au caractère des personnages et aux situations où ils évoluent? Pour reprendre une formule percutante d'André Breton, le romancier n'a "qu'à mettre l'aiguille de "Beau fixe" sur "Action" et le tour sera joué."[6] Si le portrait relativise la pensée de l'écrivain — dans la mesure où le romancier est un philosophe qui n'a pas réussi à "décoller" du quotidien — on peut penser aussi qu'il généralise les particularités du personnage et les expériences des différents moments de sa vie. Voyons le portrait de Mme de Senanges:

> Madame de Senanges avait été jolie, mais ses traits étaient effacés. Ses yeux languissants et abattus n'avaient plus ni feu ni brillant. Le fard qui achevait de flétrir les tristes restes de sa beauté, sa parure outrée, son

maintien immodeste, ne la rendaient que moins supportable. C'était une femme enfin à qui, de toutes ses anciennes grâces, il ne restait plus que cette indécence que la jeunesse et les agréments font pardonner, quoiqu'elle déshonore l'un et l'autre, mais qui, dans un âge avancé, ne présente plus aux yeux qu'un tableau de corruption qu'on ne peut regarder sans horreur (pp. 151-152).

Ce portrait, l'un des plus "concrets" du roman, permet cependant de prévoir l'essentiel des actions de Mme de Senanges. En insistant sur les attitudes, le masque du fard, le port du vêtement, et en éliminant l'imprévu, il fige la personne dans un choix moral définitif, l'empêche à tout jamais de changer de cap et de se laisser prendre au piège de l'instant. Souvent, l'abstraction est poussée plus loin encore; l'auteur se borne aux caractéristiques morales du personnage, et le portrait se change en éthopée, comme dans cette présentation de Mme de Lursay:

> Coquette jadis, même un peu galante, une aventure d'éclat, et qui avait terni sa réputation, l'avait dégoûtée des plaisirs bruyants du grand monde. Aussi sensible mais plus prudente, elle avait compris enfin que les femmes se perdent moins par leurs faiblesses que par le peu de ménagement qu'elles ont pour elles-mêmes; et que, pour être ignorés, les transports d'un amant n'en sont ni moins réels, ni moins doux. Malgré l'air prude qu'elle avait pris, on s'obstinait toujours à la soupçonner; et j'étais peut-être le seul à qui elle en eût imposé. (p. 53)

Le goût de la maxime et du portrait dans *Les Egarements du coeur et de l'esprit* rappelle que l'habitude des dissertations morales et de l'analyse psychologique est née dans les salons précieux et exprime le lien entre la littérature et les pratiques mondaines. Mais le maniement des figures n'offre pas seulement un intérêt sociologique. Il renvoie à une structure argumentative qui conditionne l'existence même du texte. Ch. Perelman a dénoncé à plusieurs reprises la réduction de la rhétorique à un catalogue de figures. Il souligne, dans un de ses plus récents ouvrages, que les anciens la concevaient "comme la *technique* par excellence, celle d'agir sur les autres hommes au moyen du *logos,* terme désignant d'une façon équivoque à la fois, la parole et la raison"; avec Gérard Genette, il juge significative l'absence d'une théorie des figures dans la *Rhétorique* d'Aristote.[7] Raison et parole fusionnent en effet dans le dialogue, qui est un logos, ordre émergeant de la séparation, de l'affrontement de deux interlocuteurs ou de l'orateur et de son public, du même coup les réunissant (dia-légein). Comme l'a constaté Horst Wagner, le dialogue occupe une place plus importante dans *Les Egarements* que dans n'importe quel autre roman ou récit de Crébillon, et il représente plus de la moitié du texte.[8] Pour Meilcour comme pour les autres personnages, aimer et parler sont presque la même chose; le discours de la séduction se substitue à l'amour-sentiment. Dans la première partie du roman, la possibilité, pour Meilcour, d'avouer son amour à Mme de Lursay, équivaut quasiment à la victoire. "Mais enfin que me demandez-vous?" interroge-t-elle. "Que vous croyiez que je vous aime . . ., que vous me permettiez de vous le dire, et d'espérer qu'un jour je vous y verrai plus sensible." Et le mouvement de pudeur de Mme de Lursay se traduit, comme de juste, par le refus de parler: "Mais non, je n'ai plus rien à vous dire: je vous défends même de me deviner" (p. 90). Faisant allusion à ses tentatives auprès de Madame de . . ., et que Mme de Lursay a finalement fait échouer, Versac explique: "j'étais écouté convenablement, enfin: je persuadais" (p. 135). Mais c'est surtout dans la troisième partie que la persuasion coïncide avec la reddition, corps et âme, de l'objet convoité. Convaincu d'avoir affaire à une femme facile et d'être en droit de la mépriser, Meilcour presse Mme de Lursay de lui accorder un tête à tête; son discours devenu équivoque suggère que parler signifie faire des avances: "j'ai peut-être assez de choses à vous dire," prétend le jeune homme, "pour vous faire passer sans ennui le temps que je vous supplie de vouloir bien m'accorder" (p. 273). C'est effectivement ce soir-là que Mme de Lursay acceptera de se donner à lui.[9]

La conversation ne joue ce rôle déterminant dans l'univers du roman que parce que l'amour y est oblitéré par le lien social. Or les rapports sociaux apparaissent d'abord comme des rapports de domination. Aimer compte moins que séduire. Le tout, dans le monde, est de s'imposer, d'oser prendre même ce qui revient à autrui. Qu'importe si l'on ne peut rendre ce que l'on a reçu? L'homme du monde n'est point embarrassé d'acquitter ses dettes: il lui suffit de payer de mots. Les conseils de Versac à Meilcour ont le mérite d'être simples. Il faut, dit-il, se faire valoir. Comment? En affichant son mérite. "Surtout, parlons toujours, et en bien, de nous-mêmes: ne craignons point de dire et de répéter que nous avons un mérite supérieur." Risquons-nous de dégoûter à force de louer nos qualités? L'inconvénient compte peu, au regard des avantages: "Tout homme qui vous blâme de trop parler de vous, ne le fait que parce que vous ne lui laissez pas toujours le temps de parler de lui: plus modeste, vous serez martyr de sa vanité." Au demeurant, "il est plus sûr de subjuguer les autres, que de leur immoler sans cesse les intérêts de notre amour-propre" (p. 247).

Point n'est besoin d'être pénétré de son mérite pour en convaincre les autres. On peut même sans dommage se prendre intérieurement pour un imbécile, du moment que l'on paraît croire le contraire. Tout est dans ce qu'on dit, non dans ce qu'on sent: "en général vous ne pouvez assez vous emparer de la conversation." A-t-on l'esprit vide, cela ne doit pas encore empêcher de discourir, fût-ce sur les sujets qu'on ignore: "L'arrangement, ou plutôt l'abus des mots, tient lieu de pensées" (p. 251).

Prendre la parole revient ainsi à prendre le pouvoir. Parmi les préceptes que formule Varsac, il en est deux que Meilcour commence par juger contradictoires, mais qui dénotent une connaissance profonde des conditions dans lesquelles s'instaure l'"empire rhétorique". Le premier est d'imiter ce qu'on voit, d'adopter, même de flatter les préjugés d'autrui, c'est-à dire d'être rigoureusement conformiste. Le second, de se singulariser par des impertinences (pp. 243-244). Versac dévoile ici la face la plus cachée de son art. Il comprend admirablement que le rhéteur doit partir des lieux communs et en général s'y soumettre, tout en sachant en temps opportun les bafouer, puisqu'il lui convient autant d'attirer l'attention sur sa personne que d'être approuvé de ceux qui l'écoutent.

Recettes valables non seulement pour la conversation, mais aussi pour les affaires de coeur. Car prendre le pouvoir, c'est d'abord s'emparer des femmes. C'est par elles qu'on parvient aux sommets, elles qu'on doit ménager pour avoir la faveur de l'opinion. Tel que Versac le décrit, l'amour peut être ou ne pas être un sentiment authentique. Dans tous les cas, l'homme du monde le transforme en exercice de manipulation:

> Le moyen le plus simple et en même temps le plus agréable (de rendre son nom célèbre), est de paraître n'avoir dans tout ce qu'on fait que les femmes en vue, de croire qu'il n'y a d'agrément que ce qui les séduit, et que le genre d'esprit qui leur plaît, quel qu'il soit, est en effet le seul qui doive plaire. Ce n'est qu'en paraissant soumis à tout ce qu'elles veulent, qu'on parvient à les dominer. (p. 244)

L'amour, comme la conversation, est affrontement, compétition, parade, défi. C'est un discours à travers lequel chacun cherche à se mesurer, à jauger les forces de l'autre pour finalement le subjuguer. Le langage de la séduction usera d'un vocabulaire belliqueux, puisque l'amour tient de la stratégie: attaque, défense, conquête, résistance, faiblesse, combat, victoire, défaite, honneur, gloire, régner, succomber, soumettre, céder, sont des termes qui reviennent presque à chaque page du roman. Les hommes n'en ont d'ailleurs pas le privilège exclusif. Les femmes usent et abusent, tout aussi bien, des mots qui se rapportent à la guerre. Pour elles, les règles à suivre sont différentes. Si elles se gardent de prendre l'initiative, en se contentant de favoriser l'occasion qui donne envie de les attaquer, ce sont elles qui choisissent les vainqueurs. L'homme croit les soumettre, quand il ne fait que se prendre à leur piège. L'empire des femmes semble donc être la contrepartie de la domination des hommes. Elles dissimulent derrière le voile de la pudeur les manoeuvres qui assurent leur puissance. La rhétorique de la séduction est foncièrement trompeuse et elle cultive l'artifice pour faire oublier ses desseins véritables. Il s'agit, pour les femmes, de vaincre, tout en donnant l'impression d'être vaincues. Elles opposeront à l'homme de faux obstacles qui le persuaderont qu'on cède à son mérite alors que l'issue du combat était arrêtée d'avance. La vanité masculine trouve ainsi à se satisfaire, même si, en définitive, les femmes dictent les règles du jeu. "Plus elle m'oppose d'obstacles, plus ma gloire sera grande," avoue Meilcour à propos de Mme de Lursay (p. 74).

La vanité, qui mise tout sur le paraître, est le principal moteur des actions humaines, comme le langage est leur point d'appui. *Les Egarements du coeur et de l'esprit* illustrent à merveille la célèbre maxime de La Rochefoucauld: "il en est de tels qui n'auraient jamais été amoureux, s'ils n'avaient entendu parler d'amour." Dans la seconde partie du roman, Versac avertit Mme de Senanges que Mme de Lursay et Meilcour sont "bien ensemble" (p. 162), et il n'en faut pas davantage pour que la Senanges, toujours alléchée par une "conquête nouvelle" (p. 170), entreprenne de séduire Meilcour. Dans la troisième partie, Mme de Mongennes défend la réputation de Mme de Lursay, craignant que la Senanges, qui s'acharne à dénigrer sa rivale, ne parvienne à supplanter Mme de Lursay dans le coeur de Meilcour (pp. 213-218). Celui-ci, de son côté, a tout fait pour se débarrasser de Mme de

Lursay depuis qu'il a rencontré Hortense; il a même refusé une invitation à la suivre à la campagne. Mais lorsque Mme de Lursay se résigne à ce changement de fortune, qu'elle adopte à son tour pour lui parler le ton de l'indifférence, Meilcour se sent piqué au vif, voire "malheureux" (p. 263), et il se remet à lui faire une cour effrénée.

Les échanges verbaux entre les personnages, conversations galantes, médisances, persiflages, explorent une figure de rhétorique fondamentale: l'allusion. Au début du roman, Meilcour n'osant déclarer son amour à Mme de Lursay, celle-ci cherche à l'encourager et à lui fournir des prétextes de lui parler. Elle met la conversation sur une comédie alors à l'affiche, dont elle loue un passage contenant une déclaration d'amour. Meilcour convient que cette partie a été bien traitée, d'autant que lui-même trouve difficile "de dire qu'on aime." La difficulté, observe Mme de Lursay, existe surtout pour la femme: "Pensez-vous, dans quelque désordre qu'elle sentît son coeur, qu'il lui convînt de parler la première, de s'exposer par cette démarche à se rendre moins chère à vos yeux, et à être l'objet d'un refus?" (p. 59). Il est clair qu'en posant cette question, Mme de Lursay pense à elle-même: la phrase tend à mettre Meilcour dans le coup, par le procédé de l'association ("vos yeux").

Peu à peu, l'allusion se précise, le dialogue prend un tour plus personnel, même si aucun des deux interlocuteurs n'admet franchement qu'il expose sa propre situation:

— Eh! comptez vous pour rien, Madame, repris-je, l'embarras de le dire, surtout pour moi qui sens que je le dirais mal?
— Les déclarations les plus élégantes ne sont pas toujours, répondit-elle, les mieux reçues. On s'amuse de l'esprit d'un amant, mais ce n'est pas lui qui persuade; son trouble, la difficulté qu'il trouve à s'exprimer, le désordre de ses discours, voilà ce qui le rend à craindre. (p. 60)

Comme Meilcour néanmoins persiste dans son point de vue, Mme de Lursay en conclut qu'il trouve les déclarations embarrassantes parce qu'il en a une à faire (p. 61). L'étape suivante du dialogue conduit les personnages à formuler leurs sentiments comme s'il s'agissait de pures suppositions:

— Mais, Madame, si c'était une personne telle que vous que j'aimasse, à quoi me servirait-il de le lui dire?
— A rien peut-être, répondit-elle en rougissant.
— Je n'ai donc pas de tort, repris-je, de m'opiniâtrer au silence.
— Peut-être aussi réussiriez-vous: une personne de mon caractère peut, continua-t-elle, devenir sensible, et même plus qu'une autre. (p. 63)

Tant et si bien que, renonçant aux expressions fictives, Meilcour a finalement le courage de se découvrir: "Oserais-je, Madame, vous dire que je ne suppose rien?" (p. 64)

La plupart des conversations relatées dans le roman s'inspirent de ce modèle. Dans la dispute entre Mme de Senanges et Mme de Mongennes à propos de Mme de Lursay, il apparaît vite que celle-ci n'est qu'un prétexte. Le portrait peu flatteur que la Senanges fait de Mme de Lursay atteint par ricochet Mme de Mongennes, qui à son tour, prétend apprécier Mme de

Lursay parce qu'elle s'identifie à elle et la compare avantageusement à Mme de Senanges: "Je conviens," reconnaît-elle, "qu'elle n'est plus de la première jeunesse; mais combien ne voit-on pas de femmes, beaucoup moins jeunes qu'elle, inspirer encore des sentiments, ou du moins chercher à les faire naître?" (214)

L'allusion (comme l'emploi du "on", mis pour "je" dans la conversation précieuse) est une forme de mise en abyme. Ce procédé joue, à vrai dire, un rôle majeur chez Crébillon; une étude plus poussée montrerait peut-être qu'il génère la totalité de son univers romanesque. Quand Meilcour voit pour la première fois Hortense de Théville à l'Opéra, il la regarde, ainsi que les gens sur lesquels elle jette les yeux: "Les miens se portaient aussitôt sur l'objet qu'elle avait paru vouloir chercher . . . Sans pénétrer le motif que me faisait agir, je conduisais, j'interprétais ses regards . . ." (p. 76). Meilcour ne parle pas à Hortense, car il ne la connaît pas, mais à un ami qui est avec lui, et il cherche à briller dans la conversation dans l'espoir d'être entendu de la jeune fille (p. 77). Enfin, lorsqu'arrive le marquis de Germeuil, il les regarde se regarder.

Meilcour rencontrera une seconde fois Mlle de Théville aux Tuileries, accompagnée d'une dame. Il écoutera leur conversation. Tout en causant avec Hortense, la dame la questionne sur l'inconnu qui l'avait regardée à l'Opéra (p. 97-98).

Plus tard, chez Mme de Théville, Hortense lit un roman où il est question d'un amant malheureux parce qu'il s'imagine -à tort- n'être pas aimé. Elle raconte à Meilcour cette histoire, qui est probablement la leur (p. 190-191).

Après le séjour à Versailles, Meilcour retrouve Mme de Lursay avec Mlle de Théville. Il remarque que Mme de Lursay le regarde avec ironie pendant que lui-même observe Hortense (pp. 226-227).

La mise en abyme renvoie à une réalité qui se dérobe. Dans *Les Egarements,* le sentiment se perd dans les jeux de miroirs dont les personnages se renvoient mutuellement les reflets, captés dans les mots ou dans les regards. On a parfois comparé Crébillon à Proust et effectivement, chez les Meilcour, les Versac, les Senanges, les Mongennes, l'amour est entièrement socialisé comme l'est aussi, jusqu'à un certain point, l'amour de Swann pour Odette.[10] On est épris parce qu'on croit l'être ou qu'on veut l'être, ou parce que l'autre vous néglige. Les gestes et la parure ont, dans ce contexte, la même fonction que les mots; messages que les personnages déchiffrent à l'aide du code social dont ils ont tous une parfaite connaissance. Après que Meilcour lui a avoué son amour, Mme de Lursay soupire, rougit, tourne vers lui des yeux languissants, se cache derrière son éventail et se tait (p. 64); s'il savait mieux les usages, le jeune homme aurait tôt fait d'interpréter ces façons comme une réponse positive. Voulant séduire Hortense, Versac, qui "avait la jambe belle . . . la fit valoir. Il rit le plus souvent qu'il put, pour montrer ses dents . . ." (p. 159). Quand il verra Meilcour à l'Etoile, il lui apprendra qu'il faut avoir, dans le monde, "une négligence dans le maintien, qui, chez les femmes, aille jusques à l'indécence, et passe, chez nous, ce qu'on appelle aisance et liberté; tons et manières affectés, soit dans la vivacité, soit dans la langueur; l'esprit frivole et méchant, un discours entortillé . . ." (p. 254).

Mais l'éducation sentimentale de Meilcour passe par plusieurs étapes. Au moment où il écrit ses mémoires, il est devenu cynique: Serge Gaubert note l'emploi fréquent d'analepses qui éclairent l'évolution du narrateur par rapport au jeune Meilcour.[11] A son entrée dans le monde, Meilcour s'empêtre dans ses sentiments; il a besoin d'aimer, mais il ignore comment satisfaire ses désirs; il est timide, et ne sait quel objet choisir; il décide d'entreprendre la marquise de Lursay, parce qu'elle est la femme qu'il voit le plus souvent. La marquise lui enseigne à distinguer le respect de la timidité, à ménager sa délicatesse, à accorder la passion aux convenances. Les révélations de Versac sur le passé de Mme de Lursay, les conseils qu'il prodigue sur la manière de se conduire dans le monde le convaincront que la marquise a joué les fausses prudes et qu'il peut l'avoir à la hussarde. Mais il importe de remarquer que Versac n'aura pas le dernier mot. Mme de Lursay prouvera à Meilcour qu'il a manqué de finesse et qu'il a agi comme un mufle. Certes, elle n'est pas telle qu'il l'avait imaginée dans son ignorance et sa candeur. Meilcour n'est pas le premier homme qu'elle ait aimé. Mais elle n'est pas non plus telle que Versac l'a dépeinte: sans principes et sans moeurs. La fin du roman montre que Meilcour a eu tort de douter de la sincérité de Mme de Lursay, de la profondeur de ses sentiments. Elle avait dit: "je hais l'artifice" (p. III), et somme toute, avec raison. Lorsque Meilcour, pour se justifier d'avoir manqué un rendez-vous, avait pris les airs et le ton à la mode, elle avait su les lui reprocher: "Voilà de grands termes . . . si je n'exigeais de vous que des mots, j'aurais lieu d'être contente. Mais vous n'êtes pas de bonne foi . . ." (p. 86). Si prompt que soit Meilcour à suivre les traces de Versac, Mme de Lursay ne sera pas la dupe de ses paroles: elle cédera, non aux manoeuvres du "stratège", mais à la force du sentiment.

Crébillon a sévèrement dénoncé la rhétorique de Versac. "Il s'était fait," dit Meilcour, "un jargon extraordinaire qui, tout apprêté qu'il était, avait cependant l'air naturel" (p. 130). Mme de Lursay le condamne avec encore plus de véhémence: "Il parle," selon elle, "un jargon qui éblouit: il ne se connaît à rien, et juge de tout" (p. 142). Quant à Mme de Senanges, son alter ego, son aspect "ne présente plus aux yeux qu'un tableau de corruption qu'on ne peut regarder sans horreur"; comme Versac, elle utilise des "tournures de Cour, bizarres, négligées et nouvelles, ou renouvelées" (p. 152).

C'est à juste titre que Derrida dérive la mise en abyme de la métaphysique de la présence. Crébillon ne se borne pas à constater que l'amour se réduit à l'usage d'un jargon mis au service de la vanité, il le déplore et il réprouve les conduites dénaturées. Au fond, le roman tout entier justifie la distinction entre "plaire" et "toucher" (p. 54). A la mauvaise rhétorique dégagée de toute loi morale et de toute vérité, s'oppose une rhétorique soucieuse de respecter la raison et les sentiments authentiques. Le jeune Meilcour se leurrait sûrement en s'imaginant qu'il suffit d'être sincère pour faire naître l'amour. Mais la conduite de Mme de Lursay inflige un démenti à l'opinion de Versac: "*Les femmes se rendent promptement, à peine attendent-elles qu'on les en prie*" (p. 168).

A mi-chemin entre nature et culture, l'amour est *à la fois* un sentiment et un art. Il relève autant de l'instinct que de la sémiotique sociale. Présence, mais à renouveler par une attention constante, à empêcher de s'égarer dans les errements de l'esprit et les débordements du coeur.

Jean Terrasse
Université McGill

Notes

1 *Le Dilemme du roman au XVIIIᵉ siècle. Etude sur les rapports du roman et de la critique* (1715-1761) (New Haven: Yale Univ. Press, Paris: P.U.F., 1963), p. 15.

2 *Le Genre romanesque en France depuis l'apparition de la "Nouvelle Héloïse" jusqu'aux approches de la Révolution* (Bruxelles: Maurice Lamertin, 1922), p. 78.

3 Tzvetan TODOROV, *Littérature et signification* (Paris: Librairie Larousse, 1967), p. 102.

4 Jacques DERRIDA, *De la Grammatologie* (Paris: Les Editions de Minuit), p. 41.

5 *Les Egarements du coeur et de l'esprit* (Paris: Folio. 1977), p. 41. Toutes nos citations du roman seront tirées de cette édition.

6 *Manifeste du surréalisme*, Paris, coll. "Idées", (1967). p. 44.

7 Chaïm PERELMAN, *L'Empire rhétorique. Rhétorique et argumentation* (Paris; Librairie philosophique J. Vrin, 1977). pp. 10-11. Voir surtout Chaïm PERELMAN et L. OLBRECHTS-TYTECA, *La Nouvelle rhétorique. Traité de l'argumentation* (Paris: P.U.F., 1958).

8 *Crébillon fils. Die Erzählerische Struktur seines Werkes* (Munich: Wilhelm Fink Verlag, 1972), p. 73.

9 "Sans aucun doute, les confidences osées, les médisances cruelles qui s'échangent dans les salons aristocratiques servent à exciter l'imagination érotique des auditeurs émoustillés, de même qu'elles fournissent matière aux tête-à tête des couples à mousser leurs désirs sexuels" (Ernest STURM, *Crébillon fils et le libertinage au dix-huitième siècle* (Paris: Nizet, 1970), p. 73.

10 Cf. Michel GILOT, "Les doux aveux de Crébillon," dans: *Les Paradoxes du romancier: les "Egarements" de Crébillon* (Grenoble, Presses Univ. de Grenoble, 1975), p. 91.

11 "Synchronie et diachronie ou la naissance du narrateur," dans *Les Paradoxes du romancier*, p. 44.

4. Polemical Intent and Rhetorical Style in d'Alembert's Éloges historiques

In his biography of d'Alembert, Ronald Grimsley quotes from Louis-Sébastien Mercier's *Tableau de Paris* the following description of a typical public meeting of the Académie française on August 25, the feast day of Saint Louis:

> M. d'Alembert est heureux le jour de la Saint-Louis; il va, il vient, il ouvre les tribunes, il commande aux Suisses, il a sous ses ordres deux abbés panégyristes; il place les dames à panaches, il préside les quarante immortels. Assis enfin en haut de la longue table que couvre un tapis vert, il ouvre la séance et distribue des prospectus; puis il donne la médaille immortalisante à son protégé, qui deviendra un petit ingrat.
>
> Il lit ensuite un éloge parfois malin, où il a semé de petites vérités modestes, avec une prudence, un sel, un enjouement qui divertissent l'assemblée. Il ne dit presque rien, mais on voit ce qu'il voudrait dire; on l'entend dans ses petites allusions, et l'on bat des mains. Tout cela ne signifiera absolument rien dans vingt ans.[1]

This description, one commentary among the many we possess on the subject of d'Alembert and his reading of the *éloges,* is particularly provocative. It emphasizes that d'Alembert is performing for a public, a receptive and well-informed body of sympathetic admirers. And second, it underlines the important distinction between what is said and what is meant, between literal text and intended message. A perceptible tension arises in the mind of the listener, who appreciates the separation of form and meaning, and who readily compares one with the other.

D'Alembert was elected to the Académie in 1754, and from the beginning his presence in that body was of great political significance. When in 1772 he succeeded Duclos as *secrétaire perpétuel,* another opportunity was presented to the philosophic party for the dissemination of its thought and ideals. Although some *éloges historiques,* as d'Alembert called them, had already been written before that time,[2] most were composed after 1772. D'Alembert, as *secrétaire perpétuel,* set himself the task of continuing the history of the Académie by writing the *éloge* of each academician who had died from 1700 onwards. In so doing he was following the example of others before him.[3]

Of the ninety *éloges historiques* included in the 1820-1821 Belin edition of d'Alembert's *Oeuvres complètes,*[4] four are not about academicians,[5] and are not typical of the *genre*. Of the remaining 86, fifteen were read in the Académie once (one of these was read after d'Alembert's death[6]), and two were read twice.[7] Those pieces that had been read in the Académie excited the greatest interest, of course, and at least two of them[8] were published almost immediately in the *Mercure*. The thirteen *éloges* that had been read up to 1779 were published, together with some incidental pieces that d'Alembert had also presented to the Académie, in a volume of that year entitled *Eloges lus dans les séances publiques de l'Académie française*. This volume in turn was reprinted as the first of six in the posthumous[9] collection entitled *Histoire des membres de l'Académie française,* edited by Condorcet, and published in 1785 and 1787. The last five volumes of this collection include the numerous pieces that were never read, as well as the voluminous notes to all the *éloges*. The conception of these texts that obtains, then, from the tidy Belin edition, is somewhat misleading. In reality the texts were brought to the attention of the public by various means and over a considerable period of time.

A more important result of this publication history is that d'Alembert the narrator, the historian, the polemicist, appeared to the public in a variety of guises, according to the mode in which the polemic content was delivered. The first and most important of these *personae* was that of the author, the well-known *philosophe* and Encyclopaedist, physically present before the wonderfully cultivated and in part hostile audience in the Académie. The *éloges* presented in this theatre are among the best from the point of view of sustained interest, stylistic variety, and polemic impact. Here the most sparkling and brilliant d'Alembert is revealed. However, the narrator as he presents himself to the *reading* public, in the *éloges* that were communicated only in the printed form, is less gracious, less witty than his more visible counterpart. And in the vast notes that d'Alembert supplied, the narrator is even more frank, more brutal. Irony is much rarer here, and less subtle when it does occur. The author is concerned with communicating facts and opinion that would be either distracting or provocative in the body of the text. Thus we may conclude that d'Alembert intended, in the *éloges* that received a reading in the Académie, to conceal more effectively the polemicist behind the mask of the public eulogist. A greater ironic tension is thus created in the public *éloges,* by the opposing forces of form and real meaning, a tension that results in a delighted clapping of the hands among the audience, as we have seen, and a glowing appreciation for the author's finesse.

* * *

In the *Encyclopédie* article "Eloges académiques", d'Alembert places limits on the degree to which truth, in these texts, can be revealed:

> Ces éloges, étant historiques, sont proprement des mémoires pour servir
> à l'histoire des lettres. La vérité doit donc en faire le caractère principal.
> On doit néanmoins l'adoucir, ou même la taire quelquefois, parce que
> c'est un éloge, et non une satire, que l'on doit faire; mais il ne faut jamais
> la déguiser ni l'altérer.[10]

Truth, in this description, is conceived in a simplistic way to be something concrete, recognizable, accessible; there is a fundamental, obvious difference between truth and untruth. But does not d'Alembert's description of the *éloge académique* contain contradictory elements? While he preaches the inherent value of truth, does he not recognize the advisability, and perhaps even the necessity, of softening it, of presenting it in a way other than in its most obvious, limpid forms? In other words is not d'Alembert suggesting that what he claims should be truth, may be in fact, either by commission or by omission, untruth?

In the *éloges historiques* we witness just such a manipulation of fact. But d'Alembert takes these liberties for polemic reasons, rather than merely to protect the subject's good name. To be sure, one aim of the text is to present a description of past events, of historical personnages, of moods and attitudes, by means of a discussion of the particular academician in question. But in fact d'Alembert's preponderant aim in the *éloges* is to further the cause of the philosophic party, to use the Académie, and later on the published *Histoire*, to put forward the basic platform of the group he is representing. In short, the narrator, at the various levels we have seen, sets out a dialogue between past and present, in the form of a description of historical events revealed and interpreted by a not disinterested commentator. The life of virtually every academician supplies to d'Alembert numerous occasions to reiterate articles of the philosophic creed, to portray, from a partisan point of view, a series of events stretching over a particular period of time. Thus, the vision of the past that we form from these texts is locked into a particular vision of the present, a vision so typical and indeed almost characteristic of the *philosophes,* in which a long-term meliorist optimism is paradoxically tied to general metaphysical scepticism. The past is made to exist as a function of a slow but inexorable process by which better days are in a perpetual state of becoming, and by which old gods will be made to die.

But what is the more precise nature of this manipulation of historical fact? First of all, in the *éloges,* facts are chosen selectively. As d'Alembert advises, again in "Eloges académiques",

> . . . si [les ouvrages de l'académicien] ne fournissent absolument rien à dire, que faire alors? Se taire. Et si par un malheur très rare, la conduite a déshonoré les ouvrages, quel parti prendre? Louer les ouvrages.[11]

However, if facts can be hidden, or neglected, they can also be modified. Such is the case with the basically simplistic historical vision of d'Alembert in the *éloges,* in which the Jesuits are seen only as manipulators, in which Louis XIV does nothing but heed corrupt advisers, in which Fénelon appears not as a *quiétiste,* but only as the author of the *Télémaque,* and in which Bossuet is considered as a religious extremist rather than the firm defender of Gallican liberties. Such carefully chosen and weighted historical views are then placed in an attentively planned and executed narrative. Indeed, what determines the nature of the text is its resultant emotional and propagandistic impact, not its historical objectivity or its universal utility. What is purported to be fact is in reality caricature. Just as a cartoonist presents an abstraction of his subject, so individuals, personalities, and reactions are portrayed by d'Alembert as functions of a polemic aim. The past is interpreted in a way complementary to the philosophic vision of a new, eternal, universal system of values, in which truth, tolerance, justice and enlightenment are upheld.

Fact becomes caricature in the *éloges* in a variety of ways. First of all, and this is perhaps the most important single rhetorical device in the whole body of the *éloges,* the historical past is depicted in a simplistic fashion as a series of conflicts between forces that may be described bluntly as good and evil. The past is, to a great extent, revealed as the dwelling place of the villainous. But through the years, evil presences have begun to recede. Although the victory is far from complete, the evil elements of the *status quo* are seen to be dying out, yielding to the forces of progress, in other words to the forces of *philosophie.* On the other hand, d'Alembert draws our attention to the appearance, in the past, of the humble beginnings of the quest for truth and enlightenment, and describes the process by which progressive ideas have been and are being pushed toward a final triumph. This conception is of course very reminiscent of the idea of historical process revealed in the *Discours préliminaire.*

In his description of villainy in the historical past, d'Alembert sets out a number of discernible categories, for each of which there is an opposing category on the side of good. First, and most obvious, is the presence of perfidious individuals, for whom d'Alembert does not hide his complete contempt. Chief among these are well-known Jesuits,[12] such as La Chaise and Le Tellier, who are also portrayed as notorious manipulators. Jussieu is shown as a repugnant fanatic. Molinos is the originator of the absurd *quiétisme,* and Philip II is a perpetrator of "superstition barbare" (OC III, 88). Best known of this group is of course Bossuet, who, despite his Gallican sympathies, passes into the ranks of the *disgraciés* because of his tepid opposition to the persecution of protestants under Louis XIV, and more importantly because of his struggle with Fénelon.

Set against these villains are d'Alembert's heroes: Fénelon, of course, and Descartes, at least insofar as he represented a renewal of philosophic enquiry, Molière, Fontenelle, Helvétius, and Voltaire. Even the fervent Pascal is seen as a philosophic hero because of the *Provinciales.*

Among those customs and tastes castigated by d'Alembert, we find, for example, the penchant for writing Latin poetry. This is very often portrayed as the pastime of musty clerics. Dull, plodding erudition, similarly because of its link with Biblical studies, is frequently associated with the cast of mind that admits religious intolerance and fanaticism. Ecclesiastics and nobles are too often ruled by a villainous pride, as in the case of the grotesque Clermont-Tonnerre. And finally, courtly flattery[13] is responsible for a multitude of evils, in particular as it influenced Louis XIV, who appears in the *éloges* as a very gullible, but otherwise quite acceptable sovereign.

Villainous institutions mentioned by d'Alembert include the court, which deforms and reduces individual merit, and monasticism, which ensnares the young and binds them to a useless, unproductive existence. But chief among the institutions criticized is of course the Society of Jesus. In all domains the Jesuits are revealed as the complete opposites of the *philosophes*; their active malfeasance is responsible for untold suffering through the encouragement of fanaticism and resultant persecution.

Among those institutions that d'Alembert feels are unjustly maligned, and that possess a nature that is fundamentally good, are the theatre,[14] which he claims teaches virtue and good citizenship,[15] and the Académie itself, which must resist the influence of authority and retain its precious independence. Both the theatre and the Académie were of course seen by d'Alembert and by many others, it should be noted, as areas in which *philosophie* could most effectively exert its influence.

Ultramontanism is portrayed as a vicious political idea, the work of the Jesuits, designed to strengthen the power of the papacy at the direct expense of the central French government. Gallicanism, therefore, is consistently shown as a good and just policy. It is to be noted, however, that Bossuet's important rôle in the debate over Gallicanism is to a certain extent ignored by d'Alembert. Although the part Bossuet played is mentioned, other factors, as we have seen, do not allow him to be accorded the credit that is his due. Ultramontanism, because of its link with the Jesuits, is shown to be an aberration in the same class as religious intolerance and the sadism that characterized religious persecutions of the age of Louis XIV. D'Alembert's feelings about ultramontanism are no doubt strongly influenced by his hatred of the Jesuits, but it is clear that in this domain a most unphilosophic proto-nationalism also plays its part.

Theology and scholastic philosophy are of course described by d'Alembert as frivolous, unprofitable exercises. But he spares no pain to praise the study of mathematics and science, particularly in the very early "Eloge de Bernoulli".[16]

Consistently, then, in the *éloges*, d'Alembert creates balanced, opposing pairs of abstractions, or caricatures, whose express purpose is to call to the mind of the reader or listener, those elements of the philosophic creed that have been so often repeated in the past. There is little that is strikingly new, it must be said, in the list of these elements one is led to compile for oneself while reading the *éloges*. But d'Alembert knew as well as Voltaire and Diderot, and all the other propagandists of whatever stripe in that age or in any other, that the secret of persuasion is repetition of recognizable symbols or simple ideas at a level and in a style that will be appreciated by the persons to whom the discourse is directed. The aim of these *éloges,* then, is to convince, to amuse, and not to provide accurate history.

Although I have dwelt upon the use of caricature in the *éloges,* it is not the only form of distortion that appears in these texts. At times, in his praise of nobility, royalty, legal authority and religion, d'Alembert is telling what we know are outright lies.[17] At other times, he allows himself to offer fulsome praise of an academician's social status and political connections, without offering any valid reasons why the individual should have been elected to the Académie in the first place. The best example of this form of sustained irony is the article on François de Clermont-Tonnerre, an article that, incidentally, is entitled "Apologie" rather than "Eloge". Clermont-Tonnerre's outstanding weakness, the one singled out for ridicule by d'Alembert, is his pride, which predictably is always described in such terms as "une fierté estimable et bien placée" (OC II, 175). D'Alembert mentions a number of times in the text the "ironie perpétuelle" (OC II, 174, for example) that marked the *discours de réception* delivered when Clermont-Tonnerre was admitted to the Académie; such is d'Alembert's way of suggesting that his own text is of a similar nature.

But perhaps one of the most devastating forms of criticism, when one bears in mind the exceedingly sophisticated public for whom the *éloges* were intended, is silence. We must constantly remind ourselves, as no doubt d'Alembert's readers and listeners did, of what he is *not* saying. The most evident lack in the 1200 pages of text of the *éloges,* is that of references to Jean-Jacques Rousseau, who, it would seem, is thus pointed out as one who is no longer associated with the cause, whose political value is reduced to nothing.

Another technique used by d'Alembert to strengthen his philosophic message, is to adapt the tone of his *éloge* to the subject he is discussing.[18] Some *éloges* contain sustained passages explaining a particular theoretical or doctrinal point. Such passages are written in a measured, sober style.[19] In almost every *éloge,* similarly solemn passages appear in which lip service is paid to the usual academic commonplaces of independence, equality, and mutual respect. Bitter, sardonic sarcasm is reserved almost entirely for the notes, and is not common. In contrast to such seriousness, however, many *éloges* are marked by a tone of open, rollicking good humour. The "Eloge du président Rose" (OC II, 161-169), for example, is rather familiar and conversational. D'Alembert seems, in such pieces as the *apologie* of Clermont-Tonnerre, and especially in the *éloges* of two remarkable *originaux,* the *abbé* de Saint-Pierre and the *abbé* de Choisy, to release completely the combination of *rire fin* and *rire polisson* for which he was famous. No reader of the *éloge* of the fatuous Gaspard Abeille (OC II, 516-522), can suppress a smile when he encounters the suggestion that this *abbé* "savait donner [à ses plaisanteries] une forme piquante" (p. 516), and when he reads at least nineteen times in six pages the ridiculous appellation, "abbé Abeille"!

Finally, d'Alembert distributes throughout the *éloges* certain linguistic sign-posts that help the reader or listener to perceive effortlessly the author's attitude in a particular matter. The term *philosophe* is used in a variety of ways, for example,[20] but in general the words *philosophe, philosophie* and *philosophique* are all used to denote individuals, qualities, attitudes and ideas that elicit d'Alembert's wholehearted approval.[21] Similarly, the metaphoric use of *lumière* suggests at the same time the source and end product of *philosophie.*

* * *

Rhetoric had of course long been regarded, by d'Alembert's time, as a set of techniques whose admissibility was to some extent morally questionable. Truth, to use a term favoured by d'Alembert, is disguised in the rhetorical text, which reveals as it were only an obfuscated projection of the originally intended meaning, and which ironically masks the real matter of the author's thought.[22] In the *Discours préliminaire,* d'Alembert presents this sort of criticism. First of all, he suggests, eloquence is defined as the ability to communicate emotion:

> Les hommes, en se communiquant leurs idées, cherchent aussi à communiquer leurs passions. C'est par l'éloquence qu'ils y parviennent. Faite pour parler au sentiment, comme la logique et la grammaire parlent à l'esprit, elle impose silence à la raison même . . . .[23]

Eloquence, however, is quite distinct from rhetorical facility:

> A l'égard de ces puérilités pédantesques qu'on a honorées du nom de rhétorique, ou plutôt qui n'ont servi qu'à rendre ce nom ridicule, et qui sont à l'art oratoire ce que la scolastique est à la vraie philosophie, elles ne sont propres qu'à donner de l'éloquence l'idée la plus fausse et la plus barbare.[24]

True eloquence thus proceeds from the heart, so to speak, rather than the head. Any attempt at rational control of the text inevitably fails: "Tant pis pour tout orateur qui fait avec réflexion et avec dessein une métonymie, une catachrèse, et d'autres figures semblables."[25] D'Alembert would thus have us believe that the eloquent orator expresses his intended message with complete natural sincerity and with effortless facility. His message is not obscured by rhetorical diversions.

But in his letters to Frederick the Great, d'Alembert openly admits that in the composition of the *éloges* he exercises just such a rational control over the text. For example, on 14 August 1772 he writes:

> Je vais cependant essayer la continuation de l'histoire de l'Académie française; mais combien de peine il faudra que je me donne pour ne pas dire ma pensée! Heureux même si, en la cachant, je puis au moins la laisser entrevoir. (OC V, 326)

And on 9 April 1773, he confesses that writing these *éloges* requires wearying effort: "quand je pense que j'ai d'un côté de mauvais auteurs à disséquer, et de l'autre de plats censeurs à satisfaire, la plume me tombe des mains presque à chaque instant" (OC V, 336). Such declarations show that the creation of these texts is by no means a natural, easy process. And, as we have seen, throughout the *éloges historiques,* evidence of a rhetorical consciousness, that is to say a tendency to express thoughts through the use of discernible and classifiable rhetorical techniques, can readily be found.

D'Alembert, along with other members of the philosophic party, and especially the contributors to the *Encyclopédie,* in general strongly favoured the theories of universal grammar propounded by the Port Royal grammarians. Universal grammar theory is seen as the key to understanding the true nature of language and thought, by revealing deep structures of which surface forms ought to be the unretouched model. D'Alembert's ideas about eloquence are similar to the notion of universal grammar, in that both theories suggest the ideal of a sort of transparent language, in which the true intentions of the author are openly revealed. The *philosophe,* whose language is thus indirectly claimed to proceed untrammeled from the depths of his consciousness, is proposed as a being of unquestionable sincerity, incapable of machination or duplicity. D'Alembert's theory of eloquence, like universal grammar theory, contains more than a hint of ideological bias.

To be sure, there were pragmatic reasons for d'Alembert to mask his true thoughts. As a matter of convention he must avoid criticism of the Académie, and as well, as he notes himself, he has censors to satisfy.

But there is another, stronger reason, as I have suggested, for thus modifying, supplementing, and disguising historical fact: d'Alembert wishes above all to convince his readers and listeners of the righteousness of his cause, to convert them to his point of view, to pull them into the sphere of influence of his party. If it is necessary to project a rhetorically determined history in order to further his cause, then he is not unwilling to do so. And theoretical pronouncements condemning rhetorical technique as misleading, only lend force to his own position as a historian, as a narrator, and as an oracle.

Thus, in the final analysis, we may perceive a fundamental contradiction in d'Alembert's claims. He presents untruth as truth; he condemns rhetorical devices and yet indulges in their use; he sets up moral and social principles that he claims to be of universl and eternal value, when in truth they are the principles of the pressure group he represents. Politics is thus never far from the mobile centre of d'Alembert's preoccupations. And for that reason it is exceedingly dangerous for us to accept the portraits that he communicates in the *éloges* of himself, of his circle, of the society of his time, and of the subjects of these texts, without taking into account the polemic importance of each element of the whole.

Dennis F. Essar
Brandon University

Notes

[1] L.-S. Mercier, *Tableau de Paris* (Amsterdam, 1782-1788), VIII (1783), 27-28. Quoted in English by R. Grimsley in *Jean d'Alembert (1717-83)* (Oxford: Clarendon, 1963), p. 93. Spelling and punctuation have been modernized in all quotations.

[2] The *éloges* of Montesquieu, Du Marsais and the *abbé* Mallet had been published in the *Encyclopédie.* Those of Terrasson and Jean Bernoulli had also already been composed but had not been given their final form.

[3] D'Olivet and Duclos in the Académie française, and Fontenelle in the Académie des sciences.

[4] 5 vols. Subsequent references to this edition will be noted in parentheses after the text as OC, together with volume and page number.

[5] The *éloges* of Bernoulli, Mallet, Du Marsais and George Keith.

[6] The *éloge* of Marivaux.

[7] The *éloges* of Fénelon and Boileau.

[8] The *éloges* of Fénelon and La Motte.

[9] D'Alembert died in 1783.

[10] *Encyclopédie*, V (1755), 527.

[11] *Encyclopédie*, V, 528.

[12] It must be remembered that most of the *éloges* were written after the suppression in France of the Society of Jesus in 1767. D'Alembert's important rôle in the battle for expulsion was of course well known.

[13] Flattery is usually spoken of in the *éloges* as *encens*; the ecclesiastical resonance of this metaphor was no doubt pleasing to d'Alembert.

[14] D'Alembert had a remarkable capacity to bear grudges. One is reminded not infrequently in the *éloges* of the great quarrel over d'Alembert's views on the theatre as revealed in the *Encyclopédie* article "Genève" in 1757.

[15] See especially the "Eloge de Nivelle de La Chaussée," OC III, 387-403.

[16] OC III, 338-360. This *éloge* was first published in the *Mercure* in 1748 and was later expanded. See M. Wachs, "A Study of d'Alembert's *Histoire des membres de l'Académie française*" (unpublished dissertation, University of Wisconsin, 1958), pp. 38, 320.

[17] An example is when he protests that it is necessary to have high-born members of the Académie, even if they are otherwise undeserving, to give the assembly stature and to acquire for it the respect of the public (see OC II, 480). D'Alembert contradicts this statement throughout the *éloges*, especially in the notes.

[18] See M. Wachs, pp. 58-60, for pertinent further comment on this aspect of d'Alembert's techniques.

[19] See for example the "Eloge de La Motte" (OC III, 121-174). Other examples are the *éloges* of Montesquieu, Bernoulli, and Du Marsais, but these are not typical (see note 2).

[20] See Peter E. Nitchie, "The *Eloges* in the *Encyclopédie*: genre or strategem?", *Kentucky Romance Quarterly*, XXIII (1976), 506.

[21] D'Alembert even goes so far as to insert this word surreptitiously into a passage he claims is quoted from scripture: "[Daniel] rit en philosophe, de la crédulité du prince et de la fourberie des prêtres, et empoisonna le serpent" (OC III, 489). The event referred to is described in one of the apocryphal chapters of Daniel; however the chapter does not contain this precise description, and no word that could be construed as the equivalent of *philosophe* is to be found therein.

[22] Two useful recent studies of these questions are Pierre Kuentz, "Le 'rhétorique' ou la mise à l'écart," *Communications*, XVI (1970), 143-157, and Ulrich Ricken, *Grammaire et philosophie au siècle des lumières* (Villeneuve-d'Ascq: Publications de l'Université de Lille III, 1978).

[23] *Encyclopédie*, I (1751), x. The whole question of d'Alembert's anti-rhetoric as revealed in the *Discours préliminaire* has been examined by Ralph S. Pomeroy in "Locke, Alembert, and the anti-rhetoric of the "Enlightenment," *Studies on Voltaire and the Eighteenth Century*, CLIV (1976), 1657-1675.

[24] Ibid.

[25] *Encyclopédie*, article "Eloquence," V (1755), 526.

5. Gershom Carmichael and the Natural Jurisprudence Tradition in Eighteenth-Century Scotland

No discussion of the origins of the Scottish enlightenment would be complete without an expression of homage to Gershom Carmichael, the first occupant of the Chair of Moral Philosophy at the University of Glasgow and the predecessor of Francis Hutcheson and Adam Smith. He has sometimes been called, following Sir William Hamilton, "the real founder of the Scottish school of philosophy" but it is not entirely clear what Sir William intended to convey by this pronouncement.[1] His teaching and writings have been characterized more cautiously but perhaps more judiciously by James McCosh as "the bond which connects the old philosophy with the new in Scotland."[2] Carmichael was a transitional thinker of some importance; but McCosh's description, like Sir William Hamilton's, continues to beg the question: in what respect may Carmichael be considered an innovator in his teaching and in his writing? He was not a philosopher of common and of moral sense like the 3rd Earl of Shaftesbury and Francis Hutcheson; Carmichael was aware of this development in moral philosophy in the early eighteenth century and he rejected it. He did not claim to be an experimental philosopher or to be the Newton of the moral sciences; this distinction was claimed by and for later thinkers of the Scottish enlightenment, more skeptical in their approaches to moral and political philosophy than Carmichael. Indeed, considering that he wrote and taught entirely in Latin, and that for most of his teaching career he was a regent in the old system of Scottish university education,[3] it might be more appropriate to locate him in what might be called the pre-enlightenment in Scotland than in the luminous company which was soon to follow.[4] But in one crucial respect at least Carmichael's career as a teacher and writer of moral philosophy was the source of much that was distinctive and of enduring significance in the Scottish enlightenment. For it was above all Carmichael who was responsible for establishing the natural jurisprudence tradition in the Scottish universities. It was not just his decision to make Pufendorf's smaller work, *De Officio Hominis et Civis,* the set text in moral philosophy at Glasgow, a practice also followed by John Loudon and later in Edinburgh by Sir John Pringle, and continued at Glasgow by Francis Hutcheson. It was rather the notes and supplements which Carmichael appended to the text, and which Hutcheson considered of more value than

41

the text itself, which supplied many of the moral and political ideas that lie behind the numerous treatises, tracts and lectures on jurisprudence which were to prove such a fecund source of speculation on human nature and society. In order to appreciate the distincitive turn given the study of moral philosophy and natural jurisprudence in Scotland by Carmichael it may be helpful to provide some biographical details about him.

Gershom Carmichael was born in London, in 1672, the son of a Presbyterian clergyman, Alexander Carmichael, who had been deprived of his church in Scotland and exiled to England earlier in the same year. There he became minister of a congregation of expatriate Scots Presbyterians.[5] Alexander Carmichael and his wife appear to have been acutely sensible of the alien condition of their life in England, as may be inferred from their choice of the name Gershom for their son, which derives from the name of Moses' son given in Exodus 8:22: "a stranger born in a strange land." The elder Carmichael died in 1677, leaving behind a tract which was published as *Believers Mortification of Sin by the Spirit or Gospel-holiness advanced by the power of the Holy Ghost* (London, 1677 and Glasgow, 1730), a document as dour as the title would suggest. Gershom's mother remarried another clergyman, Sir James Fraser of Brea,[6] who brought the family back to Edinburgh in 1687, where Gershom enrolled at the University of Edinburgh and graduated with an M.A. in 1691.[7] Carmichael was appointed a regent at St. Andrews in 1693 but resigned later in the same year to obtain an M.A. from Glasgow where he became a regent in 1694, a position he held until 1727 when he became Professor of Moral Philosophy at the same university.[8] He died in 1729.

Carmichael was a vigorous supporter of the Revolution of 1688 and the Hanoverian succession. His convictions were reinforced no doubt by those of his patrons; in particular, he owed his appointment at Glasgow in part to the patronage of a distant kinsman, Lord Carmichael, who had been made Chancellor of the University of Glasgow in 1692 and Secretary of State for Scotland in 1696.[9] In helping to arrange the appointment of his kinsman, Lord Carmichael was not merely obliging a distant relative, he was contributing to the religious and political realignment of the Scottish universities which occurred at the Revolution. By an Act of Parliament (July 4, 1690) all principals and regents were required to subscribe an oath of allegiance and to declare their belief in the articles of faith of the Presbyterian Church of Scotland.[10] Gershom Carmichael liked to contend (particularly in one notable riposte to Sir Richard Steele) that such subscription in no way inhibited members of the university in their inquiries.[11] And his own theological views were sufficiently unorthodox that we must take him at his word, on this point, at least. As a regent he was responsible for teaching his students moral and natural philosophy, logic, and metaphysics. He published two sets of philosophical theses (on which his students were examined, in 1699 and 1707, on metaphysics and moral philosophy, respectively[12]) and three major works: his edition of Samuel Pufendorf's *De Officio Hominis et Civis juxta Legem Naturalem. Libri Duo. Supplementis et Observationibus in Academicae Juventutis usum auxit et illustravit Gershomus Carmichael* (Glasgow 1718, Edinburgh 1724), an introduction to logic, *Breviuscula*

Introductio ad Logicam (Glasgow 1720, Edinburgh 1722), and *Synopsis Theologiae Naturalis, sive Notitiae, De Existentia, Attributis et Operationibus Summi Numinis . . . Studiosae Juventutis usibus accomodata* (Edinburgh 1729), which contained, he said, the most important part of metaphysics and pneumatology. He insisted in the preface to the last of these works that his teaching be confined in his later years to natural theology and moral philosophy, which he took to be nothing but natural jurisprudence.

In the preface to his edition of *De Officio Hominis et Civis* Carmichael remarked on the great advances in human knowledge which had occurred since the beginning of the seventeenth century. No one with the least tincture of learning could be ignorant, he said, of the remarkable progress made in natural philosophy in the previous century, but no less striking was the improvement in moral philosophy. It was the incomparable Grotius who had restored moral philosophy to the splendour it had enjoyed in ancient times. And from that time, the most erudite and celebrated scholars of Europe, as if aroused by the sound of a trumpet, had vied with one another in the pursuit of moral knowledge. He mentions Selden and Hobbes in this connection, not without profound reservations, however, since Selden's work was confined by his preoccupation with Hebrew learning, and Hobbes, he said, set out not to improve the study of the law of nature but to corrupt it. It was Pufendorf who put the materials of Grotius in a more logical order adding what was necessary to produce a systematic treatise in moral philosophy. The publication of Pufendorf's *De Jure Naturae et Gentium* (1672) and the compendium of that work, his *De Officio Hominis et Civis* (1673) persuaded many that the study of moral philosophy or ethics properly understood was nothing but the study of natural jurisprudence or the demonstration of the duties of man and the citizen from knowledge of the nature of things and the circumstances of human life.

Pufendorf's works were widely adopted by professors of moral philosophy for the use of students in European universities. They became best known perhaps in the translations of those works by Jean Barbeyrac, Professor of Civil Law and History of the College of Lausanne (1710-1717) and later Professor of Jurisprudence at the University of Groeningen (1717-1744).[13] But there were many annotated editions and discussions of Pufendorf's work, particularly of *De Officio Hominis et Civis,* and in 1709 a dozen of these commentaries were collected in a single volume. One comment in that volume had a particular impact on readers generally and on Carmichael in particular. It was an extended critique of the philosophical principles on which Pufendorf had chosen to base his study of the law of nature. The commentator, the famous Leibniz, held that Pufendorf's first principles were basically unsound; this did not prevent the work from having substantial value for the reader, he hastened to acknowledge, since much of the argument in the book did not logically follow from the first principles. There were three basic mistakes in the premises of Pufendorf's discussion of natural law. The first was Pufendorf's insistence that the study of the law of nature should be confined to this life, without consideration of the prospect of happiness or misery after death. Secondly, Pufendorf's understanding of natural law was limited to the external manifestations of human conduct with insufficient consideration of the spirit in which men act, their motives and intentions. Thirdly, given these deficiencies in Pufendorf's understanding of the law of nature, it was not surprising that he had an unsatisfactory notion of the efficient cause of natural law or of what obliges us to obey the law of nature. Leibniz concluded his criticism of Pufendorf on this note:

> "This has not a little relevance for the practice of true piety: it is not enough indeed, that we be subject to God just as we would obey a tyrant; nor must He be only feared because of His greatness, but also loved because of His goodness . . . . To this, lead the best principles of universal jurisprudence which collaborate also with wise theology and bring about true virtue."[14]

Leibniz's proposal that any attempt to offer an understanding of the law of nature more satisfying than Pufendorf's would be well advised to search for it in the collaboration of wise theology with natural jurisprudence found a most receptive reader in Carmichael. He had been remodelling Pufendorf's natural jurisprudence on just these lines in his moral philosophy lectures from the turn of the century. In his edition of Pufendorf, Carmichael advised his readers that he had

> "taken particular care that the obligations imposed by the law of nature be deduced from the existence, the perfection and the providence of the deity: so that the manifest bond between moral knowledge and natural theology might be clearly exhibited."[15]

He also tells us that the first and second supplements which he had added to the text, and which contained a demonstration of the law of nature, its derivation from the supreme being, and its principal maxims or prescriptions were offered by way of response to the criticisms of Pufendorf's theory of natural law made by the excellent Leibniz. Unlike Jean Barbeyrac who defended Pufendorf's separation of natural religion and natural jurisprudence, Carmichael, in an initiative which would have significant consequences for the teaching of moral philosophy, insisted that the two were inseparable.

> "I have asserted more than once," he said, in his *Synopsis Theologiae Naturalis,* "that a genuine philosophy of morals must be built upon natural theology as its foundation, as it were, and that every well founded distinction of good and evil in our actions . . . must be deduced from the perceived relation of those actions to God, that is, to our knowledge of the existence, perfections and providence of the supreme being."[16]

It is worth underlining that it was natural theology which was to serve as the foundation for a system of natural jurisprudence. Carmichael was not concerned to link natural jurisprudence to Christian theology or the study of the revealed word. It was an error, he said, to suppose that one could discover the rights and duties of men and citizens from consultation of holy scripture; in fact, the revealed law, or as he prefers to call it, the positive law of God, offered little guidance in these matters. And, for that reason, he had always opposed the teaching of what is popularly called Christian ethics in the universities.[17] Because the scriptures provided little guidance for the citizen and for the ruler, they had to be supplemented by observations unsystematically culled from pagan writers, and the resulting mish-mash (*farraginem*) had engendered entirely fallacious ideas of governments such as the ideas of divine and indefeasible hereditary right, which Carmichael also characterized by the term, *hallucinatio*. It would have been much better to have followed the lead of the natural theologians and natural jurists who did not attempt to find guidance in holy writ on subjects where the scriptures remain silent but who sought direction instead from the nature of things and of man.

What were the sources of Carmichael's natural theology? In his *Synopsis Theologiae Naturalis* (1729) he appears to combine three distinguishable traditions. He made use of what Hume was to call experimental theology, or arguments for the existence of a supreme being from evidence of design in the physical world. He made reference to the plethora of writings on this subject, mentioning works by Cheyne, Pelling, Ray, Derham and Nieuwent, which one encounters everywhere, he said, and which indicate continued progress in our knowledge of natural things and the confirmation this knowledge affords of the existence of a supreme architect or designer.[18] In this connection, he observed that one might as well suppose that Virgil's *Aeneid* was composed by the ink flowing fortuitously down the pages as suppose that matter somehow accommodated itself to laws of nature without the intervention of an intelligent world orderer; an observation which may bring to mind the remark of the skeptic in Hume's *Dialogues*, that our experience of the creation of universes is so slight that faced with the argument from design, we are in much the same position as an illiterate person who is shown a copy of the *Aeneid* and is asked to form a judgment about the existence and the abilities of the poet.[19] But Carmichael does not attach overriding importance to the argument from design in the physical or corporeal world. He finds more weighty the argument from design in the moral and political world, underlining in particular the description by Malebranche of the way the human mind, by the mediation of the feelings and instincts of the body, unites itself with the perceptible world and with the minds of other men by the instinctive tendency to imitate and sympathize with the feelings of others. Since the ability of men to live in society and in peace with others depends so much upon natural instincts and feelings of this kind which human beings could never have invented for themselves, we must conclude that our instinctive propensities for social life are better traced to the providence of the supreme being.[20] In a third line of argument which proves the most important ingredient in Carmichael's natural theology, we find him calling attention to the imperfections of matter which would lack both form and motion, if it were not shaped and moved by a superior immaterial cause. Even human beings cannot be said to generate their nobler and more sublime modes of thought from their corporeal or material natures. We find rather in man a longing or aspiration to think in ways unbounded by his material existence:

"He arrives by long chains of reasoning at knowledge of the most abstract

46

and recondite truths, not only of things past but of infinite vistas of possible things; thought ascends in its meditations beyond the bounds of earth to contemplate the idea of a perfect being, it aspires to beatific enjoyment of this vision of perfect being. . . ."[21]

The third element in Carmichael's natural theology is the theology of the Schoolmen; the ideas and the language are more reminiscent of Aquinas than of writers in the Presbyterian canon, and, however paradoxical it may seem, Carmichael was quite explicit about his indebtedness to this earlier theological tradition:

"I cannot avoid confessing that the doctrines of the Scholastics, at least of the more ancient ones, seem to me to be more correct and more consistent with reason and even with Sacred Scripture in this, by far the gravest part of philosophy; in particular, in the articles concerning the unity of God, the simplicity and the other communicable attributes thence flowing, likewise concerning the knowledge and decrees of God, and concerning his providence as ruler and preserver, than are those opinions which are opposed to them today. . . and are very much worn in the hands of the student body: whence I have not been ashamed to introduce to them other ideas. . .and I have not refrained from use of words and phrases which are Scholastic, although they may grate on more delicate ears, when a more Latin mode of signifying the sense with equal precision did not occur to me."[22]

Carmichael attached great significance to this element. The principle of aspiration, of longing for complete fulfillment (*beatitudo*) in this life and in the hereafter was the principle that would answer Leibniz's question of the end or aim of the study of the law of nature: the end of the study was knowledge of how one must conduct one's life if one would enjoy eternal happiness.[23] The same principle also pointed to the appropriate inspiration of moral conduct: one must act in a spirit of love and reverence for the supreme being. And finally, it supplied the efficient cause or motivation for observance of the law of nature in a way that avoided the impious notion of the supreme being as a tyrant who enjoys authority over men only because of the penalties he will impose for disobedience. The authority which God enjoys over human beings is authority over rational beings and is properly called *majestas* or *imperium* as distinct from His power over other creatures and things which is properly called *dominium*.[24] The significance of this distinction between *imperium* and *dominium* will become evident in considering Carmichael's contribution to the theory of property and the theory of allegiance to government.

Both the theory of property and the theory of allegiance as one discovers them in Carmichael's writings and lectures are noteworthy above all because they bring to bear upon the thought of Pufendorf and the natural juris-prudence tradition the political ideas of John Locke. We do not know what prompted Carmichael to take up Locke's *Two Treatises of Government* and employ them extensively as a gloss upon the argument of Pufendorf. But as early as 1702-03 in his lectures on ethics, which take the form of a commentary on Pufendorf, we find him referring to the *Second Treatise of Civil Government* for a discussion of property which was found to be preferable to the discussions of property in Pufendorf and Grotius.[25] The date is significant, for there would be no problem of accounting for the use of Locke's *Second Treatise* to provide a corrective for Pufendorf's theories of property and allegiance to government after 1706. Barbeyrac's work was published in that year, and Barbeyrac, through his associations with Pierre Coste, Jean Le Clerc and the Huguenot community in Amsterdam was well acquainted with Locke's political ideas and Barbeyrac corresponded with Locke in the last years of his life.[26] There is no evidence of this kind which connects Carmichael directly with Locke or with the friends of Locke in Holland. But there seems nonetheless some reason to suppose that it was the Dutch connection with the Scottish universities and the fact that the *Second Treatise* was widely acclaimed in Holland in the 1690s that would have called it to the attention of Carmichael. This would be consistent with the close connections between the Dutch and Scottish universities in the sevententh and eighteenth centuries, a connection which was responsible, it has been said, for the great emphasis on Roman law in Scottish legal education in this period, and it would also be consistent with the attempt of William Carstares (the leading adviser on Scottish policy to King William) to reform Scottish university education along Dutch lines.[27] But whatever the source of Carmichael's attachment to Locke's *Second Treatise,* it was his use of that text (along with Barbeyrac's use of it to much the same end) which not only made Locke a political thinker of some importance in the Scottish enlightenment, but also recast Locke's ideas in ways that would stimulate new directions of inquiry by later Scottish thinkers. The recasting was due in part to Carmichael's retention of the frame of reference of Pufendorf's jurisprudence and in part to the Scholastic orientation of his natural theology and jurisprudence.

The immediate attractiveness of Locke's theory of property for Carmichael was that it allowed him to explain how men could have acquired a right of ownership in things not yet owned by anyone. It was a problem which had arisen from the description by Pufendorf of the state of nature or original condition of things as a condition of negative community as contrasted with the condition of positive community in which things were shared by men in accordance with the agreement or consent of all members of the community. What appeared paradoxical to Carmichael was Pufendorf's contention that ownership of property in negative community depended on the same kind of agreement or consent. A much better explanation of the origin of property in the state of nature or of negative community had been provided by Locke: men may be considered to own those things they have occupied by their labour, without waiting upon the agreement or consent of others.[28]

Now it has come to be regarded as controversial whether Locke ever supposed that the state of nature was a negative community in Pufendorf's sense. It has been argued that Locke's theory of the state of nature was a theory of positive not of negative community, that his labour theory of property was a theory of the way men mix their personalities with the things of the common, that it was a theory of individuation not of occupation in the classical juridical sense.[29] But whatever Locke's intentions may have been in elaborating his theory of property, the labour theory of property was recognized by moral philosophers like Francis Hutcheson and George Turnbull, who adopted it, and by critics of the labour theory like David Hume, as a theory of occupation, as a theory of the way men may be supposed to rightfully occupy a previously unoccupied world. It was this formulation of the theory which prompted Adam Smith, Henry Home and others to ask what kind of labour or what sort of occupation men might have engaged in when they began to occupy a hitherto unoccupied world.[30] The form in which the question came to them derives immediately from Francis Hutcheson. But Hutcheson's natural jurisprudence (not his moral psychology) was in turn taken over very largely from the work of Carmichael, as Hutcheson generously acknowledged:

> "The learned will at once discern how much of this compend is taken from the writings of others, from Cicero and Aritotle; and to name no other moderns, from Pufendorf's smaller work, De Officio Hominis et Civis, which that worthy and ingenious man, the late Professor Gershom Carmichael of Glasgow, by far the best commentator on that book, has so supplied and corrected that the notes are of much more value than the text."[31]

Remarkably, perhaps, the labour theory of property became so closely identified with the commentators on Pufendorf's natural jurisprudence in the early eighteenth century, specifically with the names of Barbeyrac and Carmichael, that, in some texts, (as in translations of Bishop Cumberland's De Legibus Naturae) Locke's authorship of the labour theory drops entirely from sight and reference is made only to the presentations of Barbeyrac and Carmichael.[32]

One other feature of Carmichael's formulation of the labour theory of property remains to be mentioned. It is one of the notable features of theories of commercial society in Britain in the eighteenth century that such theories are formulated, typically — by Bernard de Mandeville, David Hume, Adam Smith, John Millar, and others — without reference to Locke and his labour theory of property.[33] But if Hume, Adam Smith and the later thinkers of the Scottish enlightenment formed their ideas of Locke's political thought from compends of natural jurisprudence like Carmichael's, then their diffidence concerning Locke's theory of property may be readily explained and appreciated. For Carmichael's construction of the labour theory of property and his use of Locke's political ideas generally remained within the conceptual horizons of the Scholastic tradition with its insistence on the duties of human beings to limit possessions and transcend attachments to material things.

Carmichael's clearest articulation of these duties appears in his third supplement to the first book of De Officio entitled "On the Duties of Man to His Own Mind." Here he reminds the reader that while external things are needed to preserve life and to provide for the needs of others, no man requires more than a finite and small amount of such things for himself and for his family. Any man who misapplies his mind in the accumulation of wealth is engaged in a purposeless or literally endless activity alien to the nature of man. We have a duty to ourselves not to be overly concerned about our possessions for such things may be lost or stolen or destroyed; we have a duty to avoid appropriation in excess of our immediate and foreseeable needs, for the surplus will surely spoil and thereby frustrate the end of property which is simply to sustain life; we have, at all times, the overriding duty to maintain ourselves in a spirit of reverence for the supreme being, a mental inclination which cannot fail to direct the mind to higher concerns when we have provided by our labour for the needs of ourselves and our dependents.[34] In this highly Scholastic account of human duties with respect to external things one finds little support for a reading of the labour theory of property which would be of service to a theorist of commercial society. It was a monastic or ascetic construction of the labour theory which could only apply in a society characterized by relations of production and exchange very different from those typical of commercial societies. In order to recognize the kind of society Carmichael had in mind when he conceived his theories of property and morality we must turn to his description of the manner in which any legitimate society may be supposed to have begun.

Carmichael's account of the origin of civil or legitimate societies took its point of departure from Pufendorf's theory of the original contract amended, or so he claimed, by Locke's theory of consent. Here the problem addressed by Carmichael had been posed by the skeptical and historical critics of the original contract theory (notably Bayle) who had contended that neither human nature nor history afforded grounds for the belief that societies and governments had their beginnings in agreements or contracts: the origins of all societies were to be found in a perception of the utility or convenience of submission to the craft or force of ambitious men.[35] This skeptical critique of the original contract theory had made an impression on at least two of the commentators on Pufendorf's work; Gerhard Gottlieb Titius (of Leipzig) and Jean Barbeyrac both conceded to the skeptics that the idea of a social contract or original agreement to live peaceably in society was indeed a mistake. But both commentators went on to insist that the skeptical arguments applied only against the first of the contracts in Pufendorf's account of the origin of societies and governments; there was a second contract in Pufendorf's scheme, between members of the society and their sovereign or ruler which was to the first contract "what scaffolds are with respect to the structure of . . . buildings."[36] The second or political contract, the contract of allegiance, had a foundation in history as well as in human nature and the entire case for the theory of the original contract might be best supposed to rest upon it.

This concession to the skeptical critique of the original contract theory by such eminent men (*clarissimi viri*) as Titius and Barbeyrac seemed to Carmichael a most unfortunate lapse on the part of those distinguished jurists. There could be no doubt that crafty and ambitious men were involved in the beginnings of societies, but such men could expect to enjoy support for their schemes only if they presented arguments which seemed persuasive to the people they hoped to induct into the society.[37] The presumption that force could be used to establish a society begged the question: for the presence of armed force presupposed established social arrangements; those who employ force must already enjoy power. And in order to discover the source of power (*imperium*) one must find it in human relations which are quite different from the relations characteristic of the exercise of force, the relations of command and obedience. In pursuit of this theoretical goal Carmichael embarked upon an extended gloss upon the Roman law distinction between *imperium* and *dominium*.

There is a natural power which great landowners or landlords may enjoy which can be called *imperium soli* or power derived from the land. The landlord acquires this power by his willingness to acknowledge that anyone who lives on the land has the right to occupy and work the land and establish a household there. The obligation to acknowledge this right of *dominium* in the land plainly followed from God's gift of the earth to men to occupy and use for the preservation of themselves and their families and the corresponding duty of men to limit their occupancy of the earth so that others may enjoy *dominium* in it. The concession of parts of his estate to others was bound to diminish the wealth of the landlord, but such diminution was entirely consistent with the duties of men with respect to external things: it could not fail, however, to engender a sense of obligation in all his beneficiaries. And this was the source of natural power derived from the land or *imperium soli*. There was no need then to look with the skeptics and historians for the origin of *imperium* in force or in the craft and guile of ambitious men; it was already present in those heads of households who enjoyed recognition and support from all those they had obliged.[38] On this basis, the beginnings of civil power (*imperium civile*) could be readily explained: it must be presumed to have originated in an agreement or contract among men already in enjoyment of natural power to live in society, to establish a government and finally, to transfer their power or *imperium* to the ruler or rulers by particular promises of allegiance. The entire transaction might be distinguished into three separate pacts as Pufendorf had done or more conveniently described as one original contract which contained the force of the various pacts described by Pufendorf. In either case there could be no doubt that the origin of all legitimate societies and governments could be traced to an original contract or contracts and the concessions made by earlier jurists to the skeptics and historians should be withdrawn.

Carmichael thought that his presentation of the theory of the original contract was consistent with Locke's theory of consent as presented in the *Second Treatise*, chapter VIII. And his belief that his natural jurisprudence was supported by the authority of Locke was reinforced, no doubt, in the minds of the later generations of natural jurists and moral philosophers, by Francis Hutcheson's repeated linking of Carmichael's work with Locke's.[39] But just as Carmichael's version of the labour theory of property was found to differ in crucial respects from Locke's formulation of the theory, one finds a similar divergence in their theories of the original contract. One of the most distinctive constituents of Locke's model, his theory of trust, is conspicuously lacking: instead, Carmichael supposed, with Pufendorf, that governments derived their authority from an exchange of promises; and this version of the original contract theory was the version criticised by Hume, Adam Smith and others. Secondly, Carmichael believed that the original contract theory was corroborated in history and experience, as did Francis Hutcheson and the Scottish critics of the theory, notwithstanding the allowance made by Locke himself that arguments taken from history to prescribe how governments ought to be conducted, "from what has been to what should of right be" have "no great force." And finally, it would seem to have been Carmichael's elaborate derivation of civil power from the natural or moral power of the obliging landowners, an argument which may have been suggested to him in part by Locke,' as he claimed, but also by Grotius and by Pufendorf himself, which prompted Hutcheson to conclude that the parties to the original contract were independent landowners and that ownership of land was the best foundation for civil government and for the maintenance of high standards of civic virtue.

Now Hutcheson had his own reasons for supposing that land was the material foundation of government inasmuch as his political thinking was strongly influenced (as Carmichael's was not) by the political writings of Harrington and the classical republican tradition. But Hutcheson's subscription to Carmichael's version of the theory of the original contract and his insistence, with Carmichael and Locke, on the natural independence of individuals and societies, identified for later Scottish jurists and political theorists a tradition in which liberty or independence was supposed to be best secured by an original contract entered into by men who enjoyed independence as owners of land. It was a tradition which was soon challenged. And in this light one may perhaps recognize in the critiques of the theory of the original contract by David Hume in his *Political Discourses* and Adam Smith in his *Lectures on Jurisprudence* one element in the more general argument of both thinkers that the societies which offered the most favourable conditions for liberty or independence were not, as their immediate predecessors had claimed, landed societies. A better prospect for the liberty of individuals and societies was afforded by commercial societies notwithstanding the deleterious effects of commerce on other aspects (mental, moral and military) of social life.[40]

In the revised and quite distinctive form in which Carmichael presented the natural jurisprudence tradition one may find then at least some of the problematic formulations which were taken up by later thinkers of the Scottish enlightenment. It would be necessary in any treatment of Carmichael's work which aspired to be more comprehensive to consider still other features of his natural jurisprudence: his formulation of the law of nature and the manner in which he proposed to reconcile the duties of sociability, and self-preservation; his theory of the family and of the duties of parents with respect to the education of their children; a denunciation of slaves and the right of conquest which claimed the authority of Locke, but was in fact more thoroughgoing in its opposition to slavery and in its defence of the land and the liberty of conquered people than anything written by Locke. And we have seen that it was Carmichael's construction of the labour theory of property and the theory of the original contract (indebted both to Pufendorf and to Locke but different from them both) which was carried over into the moral philosophy of Francis Hutcheson and which challenged the more skeptical and more historically minded philosophers of a later generation. In the range of his concerns, Carmichael was indeed representative, as Dugald Stewart observed, of the natural jurisprudence tradition which dominated the study of moral and political philosophy in the Scottish Universities early in the century.[41] But in the particular turn which Carmichael gave that tradition — in his attempt to ground natural jurisprudence in natural theology, in his concern for the independence of individuals and societies, in his (no doubt idiosyncratic) use of the political thought of John Locke — he must be regarded as a modestly original thinker whose ideas formed an indispensable part of the movement of thought that culminated in the Scottish enlightenment.

James Moore
Concordia University
Michael Silverthorne
McGill University

Notes

The authors take this opportunity to express their gratitude for financial assistance given them by the Social Sciences and Humanities Research Council of Canada and the Humanities Council of McGill University.

[1] This cryptic but often cited remark was made by Sir William Hamilton in a note to Dugald Stewart's "Account of the Life and Writings of Thomas Reid, D.D.," in *The Works of Thomas Reid* (Edinburgh 1846), I, 30n.

[2] James McCosh, *The Scottish Philosophy: Biographical, Expository, Critical,* from *Hutcheson to Hamilton* (London 1875), p. 36.

[3] John Veitch, "Philosophy in the Scottish Universities," *Mind,* II (1877) 74-91 and 207-234 locates Carmichael at the beginning of the era of independent philosophical inquiry in Scotland which followed upon the termination of the regenting system:
   "Remarkably enough with the first man appointed to the professoriate in Glasgow, we have the commencement of independent investigation . . . . Both by date and habit of thought, Carmichael may be taken as the link between the regenting and the professoriate, between the old thought and the new." (p. 209).

[4] For a description of Carmichael's teaching and of the reputation he enjoyed in his own time, see Robert Wodrow, *Analecta: or Materials for a History of Remarkable Providences* (Edinburgh 1842-43), IV, 95-96 and David Murray, *Memoirs of the Old College of Glasgow* (Glasgow 1927), pp. 506-8. For more recent discussion of Carmichael, there is a short article by W.L. Taylor, "Gershom Carmichael: A Neglected Figure in British Political Economy," *South African Journal of Economics,* 13 (1955), 252-55 which is devoted mainly to his contribution to the theory of value or of the natural price of commodities. Hans Medick, *Naturzustand und Naturgeschichte der bürgerlichen Gesellschaft* (Göttingen: Vandenloeck und Ruprecht, 1973), pp. 296-305 also contains useful material. The reader may wish to approach the latter through a review article by David Kettler, "History and Theory in the Scottish Enlightenment," *Journal of Modern History,* 48 (1976), 95-100.

[5] Hew Scott, *Fasti Ecclesiae Scoticanae: the Succession of Ministers in the Church of Scotland from the Reformation* (Edinburgh: Oliver and Boyd, 1928), VII, 489, III, 319; Philip O. Williams, "The Founders' Hall Meeting," *Journal of the Presbyterian Historical Society of England,* 2 (1922), 133-38.

[6] Fraser of Brea enjoyed a certain reputation in Presbyterian circles through the eighteenth century for the sanctity of his life and writings, particularly for his memoirs, or *Memories of the Life of Sir James Fraser of Brea, written by himself* (Edinburgh 1738). See also Hew Scott, *Fasti Ecclesia Scoticanae,* V, 15-16.

[7] *A Catalogue of the Graduates of the Faculties of Arts, Divinity, and Law of the University of Edinburgh since its Foundation,* ed. David Laing (Edinburgh 1858), p. 141.

8   *Munimenta Alme Universitatis Glasguensis* (Glasgow 1854), III, 396. Robert Wodrow, *Analecta*, IV, 95-96 and David Murray, pp. 506-8.

9   *Munimenta*, III, 309, 583.

10 James Coutts, *A History of the University of Glasgow* (Glasgow 1909), pp. 165-72. See also R.L. Emerson, "Scottish Universities in the eighteenth century, 1690-1800," *Studies in Voltaire and the Eighteenth Century,* 167 (1977), 453-74.

11 *De Officio Hominis et Civis* (1724), address to the reader (*lectori benevolo*), pp. XIV-XV, n. A review of Carmichael's edition of Pufendorf in *Acta Eruditorum* (Leipzig) 58 (1727), 45-48 takes Carmichael's response to Steele as its point of departure and goes on to examine the implications of Carmichael's theological ideas for his natural jurisprudence, focusing particularly on his theory of the family.

12 *Theses Philosophicae. . . Sub Praesidio Gerschomi Carmichael* (Glasgow, 1699), and *Theses Philosophicae. . . Sub Praesidio Gerschomi Carmichael* (Glasgow, 1707).

13 Samuel Pufendorf, *Le Droit de la nature et des gens . . . traduit du latin par Jean Barbeyrac avec des notes du traducteur et une préface qui sert d'introduction à tout l'ouvrage* (Amsterdam, 1706). Subsequent references to this work will be to the fourth edition, in English, *Of the Law of Nature and Nations . . . to which are added all the large notes of Mr. Barbeyrac, translated from the best edition* (London, 1729). Barbeyrac's translation of Pufendorf's smaller work, *Les Devoirs de l'homme et du citoyen* was published in Amsterdam in 1707. Subsequent references to this work will be to an edition published together with Jacques Burlamaqui's *Elémens du droit naturel* (1747), (Paris, 1820).

14 G.W. Leibniz, "Opinion on the Principles of Pufendorf," in *The Political Writings of Leibniz,* trans. and ed. by Patrick Riley, (Cambridge: Cambridge Univ. Press, 1972), p. 72.

15 *De Officio Hominis et Civis* (1724), address to the reader, p. xvi.

16 *Synopsis Theologiae Naturalis* (1729), p. 9.

17 *De Officio Hominis et Civis,* pp. x-xi

18 *Synopsis Theologiae Naturalis,* p. 18

19 David Hume, *Dialogues Concerning Natural Religion,* ed. Norman Kemp Smith, (London: Thomas Nelson and Sons, 1947), pp. 166-67.

20 *Synopsis Theologiae Naturalis,* p. 22. Nicholas Malebranche, *De la recherche de la vérité* (Paris, 1965), I, p. 120.

21 *Synopsis Theologiae Naturalis,* p. 20.

22 *Ibid.,* Preface, pp. 7-8.

23 *De Officio Hominis et Civis,* Supplement I, pp. i to xi, address to the reader, p. xvii and notes to author's preface VI (1) and (3).

24 *Synopsis Theologiae Naturalis,* pp. 70-71.

25 *Glasgow University Library Ms. Gen. 168:* "Ethicae sive Jurisprudentiae Naturalis Compendiosum Certamen. Magistro autore Gershomo Carmichael, 1702-03," fol. 152ff. and Hans Medick, pp. 301-03.

26 *Bodleian Library Ms. Locke,* C.3, fol. 140-44. On Barbeyrac's friendship with Le Clerc, Coste, etc. see Annie Barnes, *Jean Le Clerc, et la Republique des Lettres* (Paris: E. Droz, 1938).

27 Peter Stein, "The Influence of Roman Law on the Law of Scotland," *The Juridical Review,* 8, N.S. (1963), 205-45 and Roger Emerson, n.10.

28 *De Officio Hominis et Civis,* I, XII, II, (1) pp. 212-216. See also Barbeyrac's discussion in S. Pufendorf, *Of the Law of Nature and Nations,* IV, 365.

29 James Tully, *A Discourse on Property: John Locke and his Adversaries* (Cambridge: Cambridge Univ. Press, 1980).

30 This discussion is developed more fully in "Locke and the Scottish Jurists," in *John Locke and the Political Thought of the 1680's* (forthcoming), ed. Gordon Schochet.

31 Francis Hutcheson, *A Short Introduction to Moral Philosophy* (Glasgow, 1747) p.i.

32 Richard Cumberland, *A Treatise of the Law of Nature,* trans. John Maxwell, (London, 1727), p. 315 and *Traité philosophique des lois naturelles,* trans. Jean Barbeyrac, (Amsterdam, 1744), pp. 346-48.

33 See J.G.A. Pocock, "The Mobility of Property and the Rise of Eighteenth-Century Sociology" in *Theories of Property: Aristotle to the Present,* ed. Anthony Parel and Thomas Flanagan, (Waterloo, Ont.: Wilfrid Laurier Univ. Press, 1979), pp. 146-47; Donald Winch, *Adam Smith's Politics* (Cambridge: Cambridge Univ. Press, 1978), passim; Thomas Horne, *The*

54

Social Thought of Bernard de Mandeville (New York: Columbia Univ. Press, 1977).

[34] *De Officio Hominis et Civis.* Supplement III, pp. 98-99.

[35] P. Bayle, *Nouvelles Lettres à l'occasion de la Critique générale du Calvinisme de Maimbourg,* Lettre XVII, Sect 2, cited by Barbeyrac in his notes to Pufendorf's *Of the Law of Nature and Nations,* Book VII, Chapter 1, Section VII, note 1, p. 629.

[36] Gerhard Gottlieb Titius, *Observationes in Samuelis de Pufendorf De Officio Hominis et Civis Juxta Legem Naturalem* (Lipsiae, 1703), Observations DLV, Sect. VI, p. 560 and Barbeyrac's note in Pufendorf, *Of the Law of Nature and Nations,* VII, Ch. II, Sect. VIII, n. 1, p. 641.

[37] *De Officio Hominis et Civis,* Book II, Chap. V, Section VII, n. 1, pp. 365-66.

[38] *Ibid.,* Book II, Chap. VI, Section IX, Note 1, pp. 373-79.

[39] Francis Hutcheson, *A Short Introduction to Moral Philosophy,* pp. 286 and 310.

[40] Adam Smith, *Lectures on Jurisprudence,* ed. by R.L. Meek, D.D. Raphael and P.G. Stein, (Oxford: Clarendon Press, 1978), pp. 314-318, 402-4. *An Inquiry into the Nature and Causes of the Wealth of Nations,* ed. by R.H. Campbell and Andrew Skinner, (Oxford: Clarendon Press), I, p. 412. Donald Winch, *Adam Smith's Politics,* chs. 3, 4 and 5.

[41] Dugald Stewart, "Dissertation: Exhibiting the Progress of Metaphysical Ethical and Political Philosophy since the Revival of Letters in Europe," *The Collected Works of Dugald Stewart, Esq., F.R.S.S.,* ed. by Sir William Hamilton, (Edinburgh, 1854). XI, 177-78.

6. "Those Scotch Imposters and their Cabal": Ossian and the Scottish Enlightenment

Many a voice and many a harp, in tuneful sounds arose. Of Fingal's noble deeds they sung; of Fingal's noble race: And sometimes, on the lovely sound, was heard the name of Ossian.

James Macpherson's *Fingal* (1761)

Although the name of Ossian was heard a great deal during the late eighteenth and early nineteenth centuries, it has since become little more than a historical curiosity. We are amazed and amused that so many intelligent, well-educated people could have sincerely believed that the works of Ossian were both completely authentic and (what is perhaps more astounding) aesthetically unsurpassed — even by Homer.[1] We have become accustomed to regarding this strange phenomenon as a case of deliberate deception: the public was simply fooled by James Macpherson, a brash young Highlander who cleverly tricked the literary world into accepting compositions that were in part distortions of genuine Gaelic poems and ballads, in part his own creation, as the original poetry of a legendary third-century Highland bard called Ossian. The world of letters fell for the ruse, so the story goes, because Macpherson was shrewd enough to endow his Ossianic poetry with the primitivism and pathos for which a vast audience of pre-romantics yearned. Ossian was Homer cleaned up for eighteenth-century tastes and then sold to an unsuspecting public by an unscrupulous entrepreneur.[2]

This literary "confidence-man" explanation for the genesis and vogue of Ossian is not exactly false, but neither is it entirely true. For one thing, while Macpherson alone produced the Ossianic "translations" themselves, in a very real sense his Ossian was also the product of a "cabal" of Edinburgh literary men who provided the necessary inspiration, incentive, financial support, editorial assistance, publishing connections, and emotional encouragement. At the heart of this Ossianic "cabal" stood a coterie of Presbyterian clergymen affiliated with the Moderate party in the Church of Scotland — John Home, Hugh Blair, Adam Ferguson, William Robertson, and Alexander Carlyle — but these "Moderate literati" were at various times assisted by other Scottish literati and gentlemen, the most important of whom seem to have been Robert Chalmers and Patrick Murray, Lord Elibank.

55

Furthermore, the sentimental, pre-romantic, primitivist component in Ossianic poetry, while very possibly the most important factor in accounting for the success of Ossian abroad, was only one of several features that made Ossianic poetry so attractive to the Edinburgh "cabal." It is to other, peculiarly Scottish factors that we must turn in order to understand how and why Ossian came to be.

Our account begins in the critical year 1757, shortly before Macpherson introduced Ossian to the Scottish literary community. In July of that year, when David Hume made his famous boast about the Scots being "the People most distinguish'd for Literature in Europe."[3] the literati of Edinburgh were experiencing a sense of national pride and expectation difficult for us to grasp fully today. The Select Society was in full bloom.[4] There was much talk of "improvement." Attempts to censure Hume and Kames in the General Assembly of the church had been decisively defeated by the Moderate party. John Home's *Douglas* and William Wilkie's *Epigoniad* had just proven — at least to the satisfaction of Edinburgh literary men like Hume — that Scotsmen could write first-rate tragedies and epic poems, and several other young Scottish authors, such as Adam Smith, William Robertson, and Adam Ferguson, were soon to publish works of history and philosophy that would give Scotland an enduring name in the republic of letters. There was a growing sense among the cultural elite of Edinburgh that Scotland was on the verge of a new era of civilization and enlightenment which would compel Englishmen to forget past differences and to embrace their northern neighbors as equal partners in a truly united kingdom. The outbreak of the Seven Years War in the previous year had encouraged this spirit of British unity by pitting the Scots and English against a common enemy.[5] In a significant speech in Home's *Douglas,* Lady Randolph articulated the view that England and Scotland were like two foolish sisters who habitually waste their energies fighting each other instead of joining forces against "foreign foes":

A river here, there an ideal line,
By fancy drawn, divides the sister kingdoms.
On each side dwells a people similar,
As twins are to each other; valiant both;
Both for their valour famous thro' the world.
Yet will they not unite their kindred arms,
And, if they must have war, wage distant war,
But with each other fight in cruel conflict.[6]

After half a century of animosity and prejudice it appeared that the time had finally come to "compleat the Union."[7]

Two issues that came to a head in the first half of 1757 demonstrated that Scottish dreams of obtaining political and literary equality in English eyes were not soon to be realized. First, Scotland was excluded by Parliament from the provisions of Pitt's militia bill, ostensibly because of English fears that Scotland would be unable to finance a militia but probably more because of English fears about the danger of arming potential Jacobites, as the Scots were widely perceived to be. To loyal Whigs like the Moderate literati of

Edinburgh, who had fought and preached against the Jacobite menace posed by Bonnie Prince Charlie twelve years earlier, this was a devastating blow not only to Scottish pride but also to Scottish defense. The feeling of vulnerability which had so upset these men during the Forty-Five returned, only this time the immediate threat came from France rather than the Highlands. When a French squadron under Admiral Thurot headed for the North Sea late in 1759 and then actually appeared in Scottish waters early in 1760, Presbyterian Whigs like William Robertson joined with Jacobites like Lord Elibank in proclaiming the militia question the most important issue since the Union.[8] Yet efforts to extend the provisions of the English militia act to Scotland were handily defeated in the House of Commons in April 1760.[9]

The second instance of Anglo-Scottish tension was literary rather than political. It was thought to be bad enough that Home's *Douglas* had been rejected as "unfit for ye Stage" by London's leading actor and theatrical manager, David Garrick.[10] What rankled the Scottish literati still more was the fact that even after *Douglas* had triumphed gloriously in Edinburgh in December 1756 and then enjoyed a successful run at London's Covent Gardens three months later, some English literary critics, including Samuel Johnson, refused to recognize Home's tragic genius. The same pattern occurred when Wilkie's *Epigoniad* put the Scottish literary world "in raptures" during the spring of 1757,[11] only to be either panned or ignored by English critics. The following winter Home's second play, *Agis,* was savagely attacked as a mere party piece — the party being that of Pitt, Bute, and Leicester House that was then associated with the cause of martial virtue[12] — and in 1759 a London edition of Wilkie's *Epigoniad* failed miserably despite the efforts of David Hume to make it less offensive to English readers.[13]

Thus, even before the Earl of Bute's rise to political power in the early 1760s touched off the century's biggest outburst of anti-Scottish sentiment in England, Scottish men of letters were feeling bitterly resentful towards John Bull for denying Scotland her due in military and literary affairs. The Bute era seriously intensified that resentment, especially since Bute himself was so closely connected with the Scottish literati as personal and literary patron. Meanwhile the Scots militia agitation continued, and early in 1762 the Moderate literati, Elibank, and other members of the Edinburgh literary community established the Poker Club for the express purpose of stirring up support for a Scots militia. As in 1760, however, the Scots militia scheme had little political support in England, and in March 1762 Bute and the Scottish members of Parliament decided to shelve a Scots militia bill rather than incur another humiliating defeat in the Commons.

It is surely no accident that the same Edinburgh literati who took the lead in the cause of Scottish literary nationalism, spearheaded the Scots militia campaigns of 1759-60 and 1762, and established the closest relations with the Earl of Bute were the very men who encouraged — one might almost say commissioned — the Ossianic endeavors of James Macpherson. In 1759 Macpherson was an obscure young poet working as tutor to the son of a Highland laird. His first contact with the Edinburgh literati may have been with Adam Ferguson, a fellow-Highlander who is said to have supplied him with a letter of introduction to John Home.[14] At the resort town of Moffat, in early autumn 1759, Home met Macpherson, saw several of his Ossianic fragments in English "translation," and showed them to Alexander Carlyle and another Moderate clergyman, Rev. George Laurie of Loudon. Home and Carlyle then carried their "precious discovery" to Blair, Robertson, and Elibank, and in June 1760 these literary men published at Edinburgh a modest collection of fifteen of Macpherson's little Ossianic poems under the title *Fragments of Ancient Poetry, collected in the Highlands of Scotland,* with an anonymous preface by Hugh Blair.[15]

Two crucial factors should be noted in regard to the events leading to publication of Macpherson's *Fragments.* First, we must be aware that when Ferguson, Home, and Carlyle met Macpherson in 1759 they were obsessed with fear about Scotland's vulnerability in the event of a French invasion and resentment towards England for making such a situation possible. Shortly before his critical meeting with Macpherson at Moffat, Home articulated this theme in a characteristically vehement letter to Lord Bute:

> I am sorry to say My Lord that this country is in the most wretched situation that ever any country was in which the people were allowed to talk of Liberty. The ignorance of the English and I don't [know] what name to give to the conduct of the Scotch has reduced us in the midst of alarms, to a state totally defenceless. No Poet that ever foamed with inspiration can express the grief and indignation of those Scots that still love their country, to find themselves disarmed.[16]

The same obsession characterizes much of the extant correspondence from this period of Ferguson, Carlyle, Elibank, and Robertson, Indeed, Ferguson was only half joking when he told Gilbert Elliot in September 1759 that he and Home actually hoped for a French invasion in order to horrify people into realizing the need for a Scots militia![17] The attraction of Macpherson's Ossianic *Fragments* to these Edinburgh literary men seems to have derived largely from its depiction of a race of heroic Scottish warriors that formed an obvious contrast with their disarmed and sometimes indifferent descendants of the eighteenth century.[18] This militaristic aspect was made all the more appealing because it was sheathed in the polite veneer of sentimental neo-classicism. Here were poems that spoke of noble deeds but little bloodshed, rude manners mixed with lofty sentiments, much weeping and dying but no physical pain. Here, too, were poems with a pedigree, and a pedigree far older than anything the English could produce. English critics could sneer and scoff at Home's tragedies and Wilkie's *Epigoniad,* but could they possibly deny the importance of an authentic third-century Highland bard? In short, Macpherson's Ossianic *Fragments* served Home and his friends both in their ongoing propaganda war against John Bull for recognition of Scotland's literary accomplishments and in their program to encourage martial virtue and a Scots militia.

Secondly, we must realize just how passive Macpherson was in the events leading to publication of the *Fragments.* He did not come to Edinburgh with grandiose claims of a major discovery. On the contrary, he was "entreated and dragged" into the project, as Hugh Blair reminded a skeptical David

Hume some years later.[19] John Home had actually been looking for examples of ancient Gaelic poetry long before his visit to Moffat, and it was only "with some difficulty" that he had prevailed upon young Macpherson to provide him with several short specimens in English translation. The idea to publish a collection of Macpherson's Ossianic fragments had originated with Hugh Blair, and "much and repeated importunity" had been required before Macpherson would agree to it.[20] Blair had secured a publisher and written an enthusiastic preface. Even the style of the fragments had probably been suggested to Macpherson by his Edinburgh backers, for it seems more than likely that they were the unnamed persons whom Macpherson later credited with persuading him to render Ossian in "what is called a prose version" instead of verse.[21]

The factors and individuals that were chiefly responsible for the *Fragments of Ancient Poetry* were also the driving forces behind Macpherson's later and better known Ossianic endeavors, *Fingal* (1761) and *Temora* (1763), only the scale of the enterprise was enlarged and the stakes increased. After the success of the *Fragments,* Macpherson displayed his usual reluctance to participate in any further Ossianic exertions and once again had to be "entreated and dragged" into action by the Edinburgh literary "cabal." This time Blair organized a special dinner party in Macpherson's honor, to which Robertson, Elibank, Home, Sir Adam Fergusson and others came for the specific purpose of persuading Macpherson to undertake a Highland jaunt in search of an epic about the heroic exploits of Ossian's father, an ancient Scottish king called Fingal.[22] Since Macpherson's meager income as a tutor could not provide the necessary funds for such a jaunt, Blair also organized a systematic collection (under the supervision of Robert Chalmers) which is said to have raised £100 for the Ossianic cause.[23] We must imagine a poor, proud, previously unknown young Highland lad being feted and funded by some of Edinburgh's leading literary figures and men of affairs. The pressure to comply with their wishes must have been enormous, certainly more than Macpherson could withstand. Considering these circumstances, the notion of a slick confidence man singlehandedly hoodwinking the Edinburgh literati begins to appear untenable. It would be closer to the truth to say that Macpherson was as much the victim as the victimizer of the Edinburgh literary community.

Macpherson was smart enough to know what was expected of him. The initial Ossianic fragments had been a source of great pride to Edinburgh literary men, but only a complete Gaelic epic, dressed, of course, in neo-classical English garb, could possess the scope and grandeur necessary to elevate Scotland to a new place in the national history of poetry. It is significant that long before Macpherson had even begun to search for *Fingal* and *Temora* Blair was privately referring to those works as *"our* epics."[24] After Macpherson returned from his first Highland excursion early in 1761, Blair kept a watchful eye on his "translating" progress; Robert Chalmers escorted him to London to secure a publisher there; John Home accompanied him on a second Highland jaunt in the spring and summer of 1761; and Lord Bute was persuaded to become Ossian's foremost patron. By the time *Fingal* actually appeared, the Edinburgh literary "cabal" had invested far too much time and energy in the project to tolerate much skepticism about Ossian's authenticity, and they angrily attributed such skepticism to the anti-Scottish prejudices and machinations of the English. "Who but John Bull could entertain the belief of an imposture so incredible as this?", Blair asked David Hume with undisguised hostility in 1763.[25] Yet testimony submitted to the Highland Society indicates that Blair, Carlyle, and Ferguson suspected all along that Macpherson had taken "liberties" in piecing together "separate or broken fragments" to create his Ossianic epics. Those epics were apparently considered too important for nationalistic reasons to be discredited simply because they had never really existed![26]

Scottish literary nationalism was not the only cause for which Fingal's sharp sword did strike. By bravely performing his duty as king and warrior in a world of continual adversity, by fighting only for public virtue, and above all by successfully defending Scotland against armies of foreign invaders,[27] Fingal raised to epic proportions the theme of martial virtue in the service of national defense that had been suggested in a fragmentary way by Macpherson's first book of Ossianic poetry. By contemporary standards Fingal's forces were in fact nothing but a "Raw Militia" — as Alexander Carlyle later termed the army of Highlanders that had beaten Cope's regulars at Prestonpans in 1745[28] — and it seems likely that Fingal was read by its Scottish patrons as a pro-militia statement. How else can we explain the fact that the men who formed the nucleus of the Edinburgh "cabal" responsible for Fingal also constituted the nucleus of the Poker Club, which came into existence within weeks of Fingal's publication for the purpose of spreading Scots militia propaganda?[29] Elibank, Carlyle, and Ferguson (who gave the club its name) head the Poker's membership list, and Home, Robertson, and Blair were also early members. The only other man known to have attended the important Ossianic dinner party of June 1760, Sir Adam Fergusson, was a member, as was Robert Chalmers, the Edinburgh merchant who directed the Ossianic collection drive and accompanied Macpherson to London to secure a publisher for Fingal. Attendance figures for the period 1774-1784 show that Home, Ferguson, Robertson, Carlyle, Blair, and Elibank (until his death in 1778) continued to be among the club's most active participants, and Robert Chalmers attended more meetings during those years than any other member.[30]

Hostile contemporary English critics like Samuel Johnson and Horace Walpole employed such phrases as "those Scotch imposters and their cabal" (Walpole) and "Scotch conspiracy in national falsehood" (Johnson) when privately discussing the Ossian affair.[31] This line of thought would seem to suggest that those contemporary English critics were closer to the truth than they themselves could have known. Ossian *was* a group effort on the part of James Macpherson and a "cabal" of Edinburgh literati who were motivated, largely by topical issues which were in turn situated within the broader context of Scottish aspirations and disappointments in relations with England during the era of the Seven Years War and the political "reign" of the third Earl of Bute.

Such considerations do not render Ossian any less fraudulent, but they do suggest a new view of Macpherson's personality and role in the Ossian affair. Beneath his cocksure exterior, Macpherson now appears to have been an insecure young man who found himself pushed along by the leaders of the Edinburgh literary community, whom he greatly admired and did not wish to disappoint.[32] He perceived what they were after and was manipulated by them into producing it. Far from being merely a "confidence man", he was himself conned into playing a game whose rules and stakes he probably never completely understood until play had already begun. By that time his only alternatives were failure or fraudulence. After some hesitation he opted for the latter and never looked back.

Richard B. Sher
New Jersey Institute of Technology

Notes

[1] John Gordon, *Occasional Thoughts on the Study and Character of Classical Authors, on the Course of Literature, and the present Plan of a Learned Education. With some Incidental Comparisons between Homer and Ossian* (London, 1762), pp. 90-130; S.N. Cristea, "Ossian v. Homer: An Eighteenth-Century Controversy," *Italian Studies* 24 (1969), 93-111.

[2] The classic indictment of Macpherson is Malcolm Laing's edition of *The Poems of Ossian, containing the Poetical Works of James Macpherson*, 2 vols. (Edinburgh, 1805). The revival of serious Gaelic scholarship toward the end of the nineteenth century fostered more sophisticated critiques which dropped Laing's emphasis on plagiarism from classical and English sources in favor of detailed demonstrations of the manner in which Macpherson misused Gaelic materials: Alexander Macbain, "Macpherson's Ossian," *The Celtic Magazine* 12 (February, March, and April 1887), 145-54, 193-201, 241-54; Alfred Nutt, *Ossian and the Ossianic Literature* (London, 1899). These works laid the foundation for J.S. Smart's standard account of the entire Ossian affair, *James Macpherson: An Episode in Literature* (London, 1905), which is little more than a sustained polemic against its subject. Bailey Saunders, *The Life and Letters of James Macpherson* (London, 1894) and Derick S. Thomson, *The Gaelic Sources of Macpherson's "Ossian"* (Edinburgh, 1951) are somewhat more sympathetic. That the pre- romantic and primitivist strain in Ossian constitutes the key to its extraordinary success has been maintained in virtually every piece of Ossianic criticism since Hugh Blair's *Critical Dissertation on the Poems of Ossian, the Son of Fingal* (London, 1763). For a particularly perceptive discussion along these lines, see John L. Greenway, "The Gateway to Innocence: Ossian and the Nordic Bard as Myth," in *Studies in Eighteenth-Century Culture*, vol. 4, ed. Harold E. Pagliaro (Madison, Wisc., 1975), pp. 161-70.

[3] Hume to Gilbert Elliot, 2 July 1757, in *The Letters of David Hume*, ed. J.Y.T. Greig, (Oxford, 1932), I, 255.

[4] Roger L. Emerson, "The Social Composition of Enlightened Scotland: The Select Society of Edinburgh, 1754-1764," *Studies on Voltaire and the Eighteenth Century* 114 (1973), 291-329.

[5] On the importance of the Seven Years War for the emergence of a sense of "Britishness" in Scotland, see Alexander Murdoch, *"The People Above": Politics and Administration in Mid-Eighteenth-Century Scotland* (Edinburgh, 1980), chap. 4.

[6] John Home, *Douglas*, ed. Gerald D. Parker (Edinburgh, 1972), act 1, lines 125-33.

[7] The significance of this popular contemporary phrase is discussed by Rosalind Mitchison in "Patriotism and National Identity in Eighteenth-Century Scotland," in *Nationality and the Pursuit of National Independence*, ed. T.W. Moody (Belfast, 1978), pp. 73-95.

[8] Elibank to Charles Townshend, 21 December 1759, and Robertson to Townshend, 23 February 1760, Townshend Papers, William L. Clements Library, Univ. of Michigan, GD 224/295/3. On Thurot see *Scots Magazine* 22 (February 1760), 99-104.

[9] J.R. Western, *The English Militia in the Eighteenth Century: The Story of a Political Issue. 1660-1802* (London, 1965), chap. 7.

[10] Garrick to the earl of Bute, 10 July 1756, in *The Letters of David Garrick*, eds. David M. Little and George M. Kahrl, (Cambridge, Mass., 1963), I, 246.

[11] John Home to Gilbert Elliot, [August 1757], National Library of Scotland, Minto MSS, EFP 9.

[12] *The Dramatic Execution of Agis* (London, 1758). See Alexander Carlyle's defense of the play in the *Critical Review* 5 (January-June 1758), 233-42.

[13] Ernest Cambell Mossner, *The Forgotten Hume: Le Bon David* (New York, 1943), chap. 4.

[14] Allan Sinclair, "The Authenticity of the Poems of Ossian," *The Celtic Magazine* 5 (June 1880), 311-18.

[15] Unless otherwise noted, information about the role of the Edinburgh literati in the Ossian affair is drawn from the testimonies of Blair, Home, Carlyle, and Ferguson published in the Appendix to the *Report of the Committee of the Highland Society of Scotland, Appointed to Inquire into the Nature and Authenticity of the Poems of Ossian,* ed. Henry Mackenzie (Edinburgh, 1805). On George Laurie see Henry Grey Graham, *Scottish Men of Letters in the Eighteenth Century* (London, 1908), pp. 226-28.

[16] Home to Bute, [26] August 1759, Bute MSS, Mount Stuart, Isle of Bute, box 2 (1759), no. 147. After continuing in this vein several sentences longer, Home adds: "I should make an apology for this declamation, but it is the subject nearest to my heart." I am grateful to the Marquess of Bute and his archivist, Miss Catherine Armet, for permission to examine and cite the Bute manuscripts.

[17] Ferguson to Elliot, 14 September 1759, National Library of Scotland, Minto MSS, EFP 14, fols. 9-10.

[18] More generally, it has been argued that Macpherson consciously borrowed from Hector Boece "the precedent for setting an idealized ancient society against a disappointing modern one." Matthew P. MacDiarmid, "Ossian as Scottish Epic," *Scottish Literary News* 3 (November 1973), 7.

[19] Blair to Hume, 29 September 1763, in John Hill Burton, *Life and Correspondence of David Hume,* 2 vols. (New York, 1967), I, 468.

[20] Although Blair's recollections about Macpherson's reluctance to publish a book of Ossianic fragments were recorded thirty-seven years later, their accuracy is indirectly confirmed by Macpherson's letter to George Laurie of 18 March 1760 in Yale University Library, C1870. I am grateful to N.T. Phillipson for bringing this item to my attention and to Yale University and McGraw-Hill Book Company for permission to cite it.

[21] James Macpherson, Preface to the Fourth Edition of *Fingal* (1773), in *Poems of Ossian,* I, p. lxvii.

[22] The name Fingal, rather than the traditional Finn (or Finn mac Cumail), was apparently invented by Macpherson. For our purposes, a more significant alteration was his substitution of western Scotland for Ireland as the site of Finn or Fingal's domain. See Macbain, "Macpherson's Ossian," p. 145, and Nutt, *Ossian,* p. 49.

[23] The figure of £100 comes from a letter from Mrs. Montagu to Lord Lyttelton, 31 October 1760, in *The Letters of Mrs. Elizabeth Montagu,* (London, 1809-13), IV, p. 320. There is much information about the Ossianic collection in Robert Hay Carnie, "Macpherson's *Fragments of Ancient Poetry* and Lord Hailes," *English Studies* 41 (1960), 17-26, which demonstrates extensive involvement by the Edinburgh legal community in response to Blair's call for financial help. I disagree, however, with Professor Carnie's contention that Macpherson's letter to Blair of 16 June 1760 expressing willingness to head for the Highlands if money could be raised for that purpose (ibid., p. 23) seems to invalidate Blair's testimony about Macpherson's reluctant attitude (ibid., p. 24), for in the first place the letter in question may be read as yet another stalling tactic, and in the second place it apparently was written after the dinner party at which Macpherson was finally won over by the Edinburgh literati.

[24] Blair to David Dalrymple, Lord Hailes, 23 June 1760, in Carnie, *"Macpherson's Fragments,"* p. 22. Emphasis added.

[25] Blair to Hume, 29 September 1763, in Burton, *Life and Correspondence of David Hume,* I, 469.

[26] Carlyle and Ferguson both defended the liberties taken by Macpherson on the grounds that similar liberties had probably been taken by Homer.

[27] The theme of national defense against fearsome Norse oversea-raiders, or *Lochlannach,* was an authentic part of the Ossianic tradition since the Middle Ages (Nutt, *Ossian,* pp. 10, 39), but Macpherson added embellishments, such as introducing Roman as well as Norse invaders. Smart, *James Macpherson,* pp. 104-5.

[28] Alexander Carlyle, *Anecdotes and Characters of the Times,* ed. James Kinsley (London, 1973), p. 76.

[29] Although the title page of *Fingal* says 1762, the actual time of publication was December 1761. The Poker Club was presumably being organized at around the same time and came into existence at the beginning of 1762.

[30] "Minutes of the Poker Club, 1774-1784" and "Poker Club Attendance Analysis" (by Jeremy Cater), Edinburgh Univ. Library, Dc. 5.126 and Dc. 5.126*; Carlyle, *Anecdotes and Characters,* p. 215.

[31] James Boswell, *The Life of Samuel Johnson,* 2 vols. (London, 1927), I, 548; Walpole to William Mason, 22 April 1782, in *The Yale Edition of Horace Walpole's Correspondence,* ed. W.S. Lewis (New Haven, 1937-73), II, 239-40.

[32] Macpherson's admiration for the members of the Ossianic "cabal" remained strong until his death in 1796. His will bequeathed £2000 to John Home as a special sign of gratitude and affection. Alice Edna Gipson, *John Home: A Study of His Works* (Caldwell, Idaho, 1917), p. 26.

7. Sancte Socrates: *Scottish Reflections on Obedience and Resistance*

Socrates was a suicide. That at least appears to have been the verdict of Sir John Pringle who, in February, 1741, addressed at length the question, whether "self murder be in any Case lawful."[1] Although the "first Head" of the Ancients, and thereby (in Pringle's words) "a sufficient law to them," Socrates stands accused here on two counts: first, as contradicting in practice his own views against suicide[2]; and secondly, as contravening the widely accepted rule that if one is determined to die by one's own hand one should not, like Socrates, die "from a Vanity to Show [that one] was not afraid to die."[3] Whether this tarnishing of the Socratic image had any lasting effect on Scottish prelectors in the eighteenth century remains to be seen. What is immediately apparent, however, is that in theory as in practice he represented a "Sufficient law to them" in other domains of human activity.

For was not Socrates also the model agriculturalist of the mind? George Turnbull had thought so, and the image was deeply impressed into the educational outlook of the time.[4] Not the least of those for whom the analogy held promise was Turnbull's own pupil, Thomas Reid.[5] But he was not alone, especially in his native Aberdeen. "[Socrates'] method of teaching was remarkable," extolled David Fordyce to his students at Marischal College in 1743, "being admirably adapted to human nature."[6] Moreover, at the meetings of the Aberdeen Philosophical Society, the possibility of that method's superiority to any other (previous) mode of instruction was raised by Dr. Gregorie.[7] The illustrious place already assigned to Socrates by Alexander Gerard in 1765, beside such modern names as "LORD VERULAM" and "Mr. LOCKE," had virtually assured Dr. Gregorie's "preference."[8] As the much-admired Fordyce had put it, first in his lectures and later in his *Dialogues Concerning Education*, "Man [himself] was the subject of [Socrates'] Philosophy."[9] Cultivation could reach no higher ground than this. "Let the Foundation of the *Socratic* Doctrine be what it will," argued Fordyce,

> it is certain the Practice built upon it, is just and unexceptionable. For whether we say that the Seeds of all Knowledge are actually sown in the Mind, or that it has the Power of conceiving them, by its own generative Force; the interrogating Method sets this Faculty working, and supplies it with Materials to fashion, nay, frequently forms and prepares those Materials, so that it has Nothing to do but to put them together. Yet such is the peculiar Excellency of this Method, that the Mind, all the while,

65

seems to be the *sole* or *principal* Artist. It instructs, convinces or confutes itself.[10]

There was obviously much, then, to honour in this man.

But Socrates was also a "Sacrifice," in the words of Thomas Reid, "to the publick weal." In respect of his "individual" character he may well have been, as Pringle suggested, vain in dying; as a "universal" character, however, he was not.[11] Indeed, to this Glasgow prelector on 11 April, 1765, Socrates appears rather as a living embodiment of the principle of *obedience* to civil authority. In spite of "hardships" and "injuries" under even "the best Government," in spite of the "iniquity of witnesses or of Judges" in the administration of law, that law commands respect. "Every man," declares Reid, "ought to pay . . . obedience to the Laws of his Country which is necessary to the good estate of Government. No state can subsist without a veneration for its laws. Also a Respect to those who have the administration of Government."[12] Under such terms, the "Conduct" of Socrates can only be regarded as "Noble and worthy of the Prince of Philosophers." "*Sancte Socrates*," Erasmus had exclaimed, in a burst of Christianizing fervour. "How fortunate are they who await death in such a spirit!"[13] It is this last face of Socrates, the face of obedience and veneration rather than of guilt or vanity, with which we shall be concerned here.

1. The setting for our inquiry is really threefold. At one side, we are witness to the initial struggle of Adam Smith's successor in the Chair of Moral Philosophy at Glasgow, to define for himself those spheres and principles of "Jurisprudence" and "Politicks" (or political oeconomy) which would form the basis for the concluding portions of his lectures on Pneumatology, to be delivered each spring until his retirement in 1780.[14] Narrowing the focus we find, under the title of "the third and last part of Natural Jurisprudence which treats of the Rights and Obligations arising from the Political State,"[15] a passing but pregnant allusion to "the Doctrine of Non Resistance."[16] A year later, in 1766, the discussion acquires still wider dimensions. With expansion, moreover, the argument grows more complex, the issue less amenable to clear resolve.

Coinciding with the American Revolution, the center of our picture furnishes a glimpse of a theory under trial, transmuted as it were into positive concern. Again, it is obedience to lawful authority, more specifically the right to resist the "Imposition of Taxes," which commands the prelector's attention.[17] As it turned out, there was a final test still to come.

Within a few years of his death, therefore, the subject of revolution is once more on the prelector's mind. The forum for his views is now broader. In November, 1794, Reid addresses himself to the Literary Society of Glasgow. A month later, he publishes those same reflections under the title, "On the Danger of Political Innovation," in the *Glasgow Courier* for 18 December, 1794.

"No young person," reminisced Lord Cockburn, "who came to think for himself soon enough to keep what he heard in remembrance, can ever forget the painful impression made upon him by the intolerance of those times."[18] Whether, and to what extent, Reid partook of that spirit of intolerance is a question which obviously cannot be ignored, and which we will have to raise again. Cockburn's image of the youthful auditor, however, can perhaps be employed to good advantage at this preliminary stage. For as the manuscript evidence clearly suggests, there were numerous occasions when Reid reflected openly upon this matter of "Innovation," without the immediate pressure of what he himself called, in 1794, "atrocious conduct" or at least in philosophical abstraction from it. Those young ears, for example, attending to his apparently extemporaneous comments on the "present disturbances" in the American colonies were treated rather to a lecture on the "rights" of "property" than to a plea for "candour and indulgence" in times of violent stress.[19] Hence, the late public stand taken by this elder philosopher-statesman must be examined and evaluated not only on its own terms and against its historical setting of revolution and counter-revolutionary debate, but also in the light of those earlier prelections to which a privileged few were granted audience. It is thus to what some young persons came to hear that we turn initially.

2. As first broached on 11 and 12 April, 1765, the case for obedience to the civil magistrate gives every appearance of a firm assurance of principle. Although hindered somewhat by a rough and, from this vantage-point, often cryptic set of notes, one may readily surmise that the relation between magistrates and subject has been designed to favour the former even at the worst of times and to the detriment, indeed suffering, of the latter. The investigation into the origins, forms, and ends of civil government had already opened with the candid admission (was it perhaps a forewarning?) that there can be "no civil Government whatsoever which does not in some degree abridge the liberty of those who live under it." Consequent upon this first principle, Reid was able to deduce not only that a "government of Laws [is] better than independence," but also that "Every Man ought in his Station to contribute his best endeavours for the preservation and defence of such a Government. And to be ready to sacrifice his Life and all that is dear to him in so important a Cause." The grounds for *obedience* having been securely laid, in both its "Passive" and its "Active" forms, Reid might then feel prepared to weather even the most forceful arguments for *resistance* to the authority of a "Supreme Power."[20] While the details are sketchy at best, he seems to have chosen excellent company.

Saint Socrates, that doctor of ills to the soul as well as to the body politic, stands of course at the head of the line. Furthermore, Reid adds, any "who have power or have any share of the Legislature ought to be very watchfull to discover the diseases of the body politick and to apply *timely remedies*." The plea for "timely remedies" has to be viewed, however, in the context of the "great mischiefs arising from *violent changes* of Government," which show "that they ought not to be attempted *without urgent Necessity*." It requires little imagination to conjure up the sort of picture which the prelector may have tried to paint for his students with that notion of "urgent Necessity." The list of names attached to his treatment of "the Doctrine of Non Resistance" itself suggests a colourful skirmish of ideas within a particular historical moment. Reid's text at this point reads simply: "The Opinion of [Grotius].

Filmer & Leslie and Atterbury. Sidney Locke Milton Hoadly."[21] In itself seemingly innocent of preference this same list, enlarged within a year to give fuller scope to the issues, will begin to divulge more than just a hint of the prelector's early position.

Once more, Reid's starting-point is the "End of Government, to wit the Good of the Body politick." Measured according to that end, the "Rights and obligations" inherent in and binding upon a sovereign power and its subjects are clearly definable. Hence, it is the *right of the sovereign,* to which respect and obedience are due, to order all "things that are lawfull and are not contrary to the Public Good or to the Constitution." Conversely, "in things unlawfull" obedience may be withheld; moreover subjects are entitled "to defend their Rights against a general & violent Oppression."[22] Reid's arguments in support of resistance swing still further in the direction and apparent favour of the *rights of subjects* as he cites, but turns against him, Calvin's own example of Nebuchadnezzar.[23] A "proud Monarch," he contends, who sets up his own "Gods" or "Golden Image" in opposition to divine authority must be resisted not for political ends, but in the name of "true religion" (in Knox's phrase); for as several earlier challengers to Calvin's authority had maintained, an impious sovereign violates, and thereby puts himself outside, the very covenant by which he was ordained to rule.[24] Reid's exposition of the intricacies of the resistance debate was by no means restricted, however, to scriptural or theological sources.

In September, 1766, Reid makes note of the fact, as was his practice, that he had read "The Law of Nations; or Principles of the Law of Nature applied to the Conduct and affairs of Nations and Sovereigns by M. de Vattel."[25] Although there is a curious discrepancy between the date of his first lecture from these notes (April, 1766) and his reading of de Vattel's work, Reid has clearly been sufficiently impressed by its argument to make it a staple feature of what seems to have become his annual reaffirmation of the principle, that "Active Obedience [is] due onely in things lawfull."[26] Those portions of the "Extracts" designated by a marginal note for citation in class and already mentioned, in substance, on the preceding folio, were presumably intended to give graphic illustration to that vital and singular point on which alone resistance to a sovereign might be countenanced; namely, that the "Supreme power *in doing Hurt to the Society* Acts without Authority, from God, Reason, or human Laws."[27] Nevertheless, while there might well be instances of commands deemed unlawful or socially injurious, or possessing moral turpitude, there must surely be other conditions under which resistance of any sort would be unwarranted.

Again, if only briefly, the "Example of Socrates" is resurrected to redress an apparent disproportion in Reid's argument. Even "where Our Rights are violated," obedience is fitting "wherever the publick good requires it." Unfortunately for the doctrine of non-resistance, however, that measure of "the publick good" can be applied both ways. Socrates notwithstanding, therefore, where "Resistance is necessary to save a Nation from tyranny it is not onely Lawfull but laudable & glorious." Not even the "Precepts of Scripture" can save the non-resistor here, for they are but "General Precepts which therefore admit of Exceptions." Has Calvin then been completely undone?

Apparently not, or at least not fully; for an important "Qualification" — one which, it may be recalled, had been employed during Reid's preliminary assessment of the case in 1765, — is now admitted. "The Causes of Resistance ought to be great and Evident . . . All the certain and probable Consequences of it duly weighed." It is the first of several cautionary notes to be sounded in the discussion; admonitions which include an apparently late addendum which reads, "The Evils arising from Resistance greater than those that arise from Suffering"; a conciliatory gesture in the form, "This Doctrine does not encourage Rebelion, nor tend to disturb Government"; and Reid's final words on the subject at this stage: "Changes in a form of Government that hath been established & acquiesced in ought not to be made without very weighty Reasons[.] Every Good Man respects the Laws and Government."[28] But ultimately, it is the moderate and well-tuned voices of Grotius and, to a lesser extent, Pufendorf which triumph in the end. Both, as Reid appears pleased to affirm, "seem to Give with one hand & [take] with the other."[29]

3. The spirit of "give and take" seems likewise to determine Reid's attitude during his closing lectures of the term, on the subject of "Politicks." Throughout the period under review, and certainly prior to 1776, the issue comes regularly to the fore during Reid's rather lengthy exposition of despotism. Nevertheless, having once planted resistance under that head, Reid quickly withdraws it, preferring instead to place it under "Political Jurisprudence."[30] This rearrangement of parts was no doubt made necessary by his conviction that the domain of *Politicks* ought to be distinguished from that of *Political Jurisprudence* as well as from *Morals*, on which in fact the latter is founded. (As Reid is quick to explain: "All Questions belonging to Jurisprudence are Questions concerning Right and wrong."[31]) The question of the right of resistance to magisterial authority is one which may be regarded, as he himself acknowledges elsewhere, "either in a political or in a Moral Light." In respect of the latter, however, it belongs to that type of query which is concerned, for example, with the rightness or wrongness of the "Tolleration [sic] of those who are not of the established Religion."[32] What then, within the context of a despotic regime, is Reid's moral verdict of that "Right"?

Although it may be reckoned an extreme case, despotic rule affords Reid the opportunity of illustrating two essential conditions of government failing which resistance becomes, to his mind, justified. In the first place, the governed may be said to resemble a moneylender who, when entrusting money to any "Debitor," insists that the latter provide "a Security" against the "just Restitution" of the loan. There is no question here of the integrity of the debitor, nor will any "Debitor however honest [take] it ill that men who entrust him with their Money should take such a Security." It is characteristic of despotism, however, that "there can be no such security," for the simple reason that there is "no Law according to which [the despot] is obliged to Judge." Secondly, the "Rights of Mankind" (to which, incidentally, Reid later adds the rights of domestic animals) provide that any laws set over an individual "be framed and directed with a view to the good & happiness of the Subject." Any law "not directed to this End" is thereby to be judged "contrary to the rights of Mankind." Of course, legislators may mistake the "publick good even when they intend it"; but due allowance being made for such error, the resulting "grievance" will in time be "remedied."[33] In the case of the despot, however, no redress to time or "Experience" is possible, for the good of the public was never his intention.[34] Neither of these conditions being met, therefore, the subject finds himself in a position where, assuming certain other factors, he may have recourse to some form of resistance.

The spelling out of these further impediments to resistance now becomes necessary; for as Reid had observed, in his first account of despotic rule, such "cruel Bashes" of which the "Seraglio" might never hear will, in time, so discourage the one who suffers them that, "banishing all thought of the future and reflexion upon the past [he will sing] in his Chains like a bird confined to a Cage and [make] the best of the present Moment."[35] To the right of resistance, then, one must add the enlightenment to understand and the power to seize that right. Gathering these factors together, Reid pronounces his verdict:

> Every Government . . . which is not directed to promote the good of the Governed is a Usurpation without Right nor can any Length of Time give it a just Title. The people may be subject through fear or through ignorance. But if they are sufficiently enlightened to understand the Rights that belong to them as men, And if at the same time they have it in their power to shake it off and to establish a better and more equitable Government, I have no doubt but they have as good Right to do it as a man has to defend himself against a high way man.[36]

Unlike his classical mentor, Cicero, Reid does not rage against the tyrant.[37] Nevertheless, the calmness of his reasoning scarce conceals the firmness of his resolution.

The inferring of such a right from a set of conditions under which, alone, he who governs may assume and perpetuate that title is not, of course, exceptional. It had long been argued[38] that, armed with the *right* of free disposition and constitutionally stationed *supra regem*, an entire people or at the very least a representative council or assembly may be entitled to depose a pernicious or worthless ruler.[39] Reid's "constitutional" references are seemingly of more recent stock,[40] but serve equally his insistence on the "Importance of Stating truly the Submission due to the Sovereign Power[;] to Princes and to the People, to mankind in General."[41] The conditions, that is, must be well laid; for should any people be compelled to decide, at a critical juncture in their history, whether to claim or to forfeit the right to resist, such conditions will be their only hope against vacillation and possibly prolonged suffering.[42]

4. What happens during what we might call the "middle period" of Reid's deliberations is in fact only a prelude to the apparent vacillations which attend his response to the events of the French Revolution. Although the evidence for this stage is quite patchy — an unseemly mixture of indirect and

fragmentary sources, — it rather suggests that when the theoretically impossible does in fact take place, Reid's argument experiences an uneasy shifting of ground, a temporary dislocation of concepts. Since Reid has been accused of "[bowing] to the [later] storm" and so of running straight from principle into safer confines,[43] it is well to remember that by 1794 he had already weathered one such upheaval, by facing up to the implications of its most unsettling questions.

Rather surprisingly, what emerges from the reconstructed picture — gleaned in part from a student's notes, and in part from Reid's expressed position on several subjects,[44] — is a newly-formed regard for the ultimate right of the state to modify or abrogate the individual's right of private ownership. In view of his generally favourable estimate of Locke's position on this score, as well as his professed admiration for certain provisions made in the Charter of Charles II to William Penn in 1681,[45] Reid might almost be said to court inconsistency here. In earlier pronouncements, he had either reasoned out or at least given tacit assent to two principles: first, that the "Right of Property," while not being "natural" but rather "acquired by [a man's] actions or the Actions of other Men," is inviolable[46]; and second, that any imposition of taxation or customs on a subject's "Lands tenements goods [or] Chattels" wihout the consent of the "Proprietary, or chief Governour, or Assembly, or by Act of Parliament in England" would be tantamount to an attempt to remove or confiscate that property.[47] That a magistrate is bound to "preserve" and never to "take away and destroy the property of the people" had, of course, been a central tenet of Locke's argument in the *Two Treatises* and, more specifically, of his definition of tyranny.[48] Yet if Reid's previous strictures against tyranny had implied acceptance of such a definition, and hence agreement with Locke, on Monday 29th April, 1776, he seems to have made an about-face.

Responding to the contingencies of the historical moment, Reid elects to examine a question "much disputed upon now[,] whether people in a free state should be taxed against their consent."[49] It is, he admits, "a strange notion" and Locke has unfortunately been used. Nevertheless, as he had maintained only a week before, on 26th April, the right of the state to impose taxes or to expropriate property "for the common advantage" (the right known as *dominium eminens*) cannot be denied even "by the American Colonies" now, alas, "very hurtfully taken" with this "notion of Mr Locke."[50] What appears to be "hurtful" in Locke's account is his over-emphasis upon the defence of property as the end of government; the absence of "his usual acuteness [in considering] that the Intention of man's entering into society is . . . [equally] to defend his Life his honour, & his esteem . . ." and his failure to recognize that by analogy with the private debtor who refuses to pay, anyone who resists the paying of a tax imposed by the state "may be forced to do it. . . ." Locke's counsel to the Americal colonists, it seems, had been rather careless in the delivery, but even more incautiously received.

If this was indeed Reid's argument during that period — and there is no compelling reason to doubt the reliability of Jack's record of it, — it would seem that Reid was already moving towards an elucidation of that position which, eighteen years later, he would defend even more openly. The voices of resistance in the American colonies had apparently met their own in the classroom of the Scottish prelector. Perhaps the latter's reading of de Lolme's *Constitution of England* in January of that year had helped to stiffen his own resistance; for among the "Advantages of the british [sic] Constitution" which he extracts from the Genevan's work, Reid singles out for particular attention the "placing the Executive power in One & making it hereditary." This, he seems ready to agree, "renders [that power] sacred & inexpugnable. [It] Checks the Ambition of such as in Republicks from engrossing power have become tyrants, & prevents any Citizen from ever rising to a dangerous greatness."[51] Nevertheless, the challenge of that republicanism was to be sounded once more within Reid's lifetime. Before finally alerting his fellows to the real "Danger of Political Innovation," he would find himself beleaguered, if not actually tempted by the clarion call of French resistance. What, then, was his position at the close?

5. From all accounts, the road to Reid's last stand was a difficult and perhaps even humiliating one. In the first flush of revolutionary enthusiasm, he seems like others to have been raised aloft on the eloquent optimism of Sir James Mackintosh's *Vindiciae Gallicae*.[52] Indeed, the very passion of that plea for "a new aera in history," ushered in by "the authors of the greatest attempt that has hitherto been made in the cause of man,"[53] might almost have played the cathartic to Reid's misgivings. For Mackintosh railed against what he called this "dread of innovation — this horror at any remedy," and would by "reason" have exorcised such fears of a "bolder navigation." The enemy alike of "dastardly coasting" and of "philosophers in theory, and barbarians in practice,"[54] Mackintosh stoked the fires of a "virtuous enthusiasm of liberty"; had events not proved otherwise, he might even have convinced Reid that, unlike the religious sort, this "fanaticism" was not at all "transitory." But it was just that and Reid is purported to have denied its spirit, even after supporting the National Assembly with funds.

Reid's involvement in the first wave of British response to events in France has been variously portrayed not always, it must be said, to his credit. The sardonic allusion of Beattie's friend, Robert Arbuthnot, to the "venerable" Dr. Reid's weakness in remitting money in support of the revolutionary cause leaves a bitter, but unsatisfied taste.[55] Perhaps more reliable are the views of the Rev. Archibald Arthur, an early ally and later assistant of Reid,[56] whose "sentiments . . . concerning the British constitution," are said to have "coincided with those of Dr. Reid, who thought it proper *soon after the commencement of the French Revolution,* and in the situation in which he was placed, to declare, and allow his opinion on this important subject to be published."[57] Unfortunately, the substance of those "sentiments" appears to have been elicited from both men in declarations dated from as late as 1794. To be sure, what they convey is compatible with the tone of Reid's discourse before the Literary Society, a tone which, ironically, reflects that very "dread of innovation" of which Mackintosh had warned so eloquently in 1791, and with which even he himself seems later to have been infected.[58] At the time of the revolution, his biographer claims, Arthur's

sentiment was the same with what reigned in every upright and virtuous bosom. He rejoiced in the emancipation of a nation so vast and powerful. But his rejoicing was not of long continuance. So early as the demolition of the Bastile, his penetrating discernment detected the features of rapacious selfishness, beneath the disguise of a liberal indignation. . . . He saw . . . those alarming taints, which afterwards became a noisome pestilence, to infect the atmosphere of other nations. He heard . . . the outcry of licentiousness, and the screams of anarchy; to be succeeded . . . by the dead and stupifying calm of a portentous despotism. He strove, therefore, as far as his influence could properly extend, to resist and oppose the progress of those principles that governed France.[59]

This is obviously "resistance" in retrospect, and it does little to clarify, although it might serve somewhat to balance our picture of the situation. At the very least, it acts as a corrective to the image of an aging and abject Reid "bowing" ignominiously "to the storm."

The fact of the matter is that Reid could later point to a note of misgiving sounded as early as his initial, and otherwise unqualified, enthusiasm for the "Liberty" not only of the French but of any nation. Although the evidence remains fragmentary, it is known that Reid acted as one of four "stewards" to a meeting of "the Friends of Liberty in Glasgow," held on 14 July, 1791. An advertisement announcing what he himself subsequently described as "a meeting of Friends to the French Revolution" had appeared in *The Glasgow Mercury* on 5 July, with Reid's name listed among the stewards at the bottom.[60] An undated draft of a letter to an unknown party further substantiates and elucidates his involvement in this body.[61] In the spirit of Archibald Arthur's "sentiments", Reid "Rejoice[s] in that Revolution" and with "those who taste the Sweets of Liberty"; for the freedom of a nation, he holds, must reflect a basic knowledge of the "Rights of Man." He is anxious, however, that those who have recently discovered freedom "may not turn giddy but make a wise and sober Use of it." He is concerned, moreover, that friendship with the Revolution should not be construed as enmity towards "the Constitution of . . . Britain." Indeed, he is emphatic that he had only allowed his "Name to be used" (in the advertisement) "upon the Condition & promise of my fellow Stewarts that no unfavourable Reflection direct or oblique either on the Constitution or present Administration, of Great Britain was to be heard." Against an "Anomymous letter in a feigned hand," which he has just received, warning both him and his friends ("political Madmen and Black guards") that they will come to "repent the steps [they] have taken," Reid replies (with self-deprecating wit, but no contrition): "Whether do you think it more odd[:] that an old deaf Dotard should be announced as a Stewart of such a Meeting, or that it should give any Man such offence." While Reid might be seen here as smarting a bit under the public's misrepresentation of his good intentions and (more importantly) of his strict conditions of alliance, he holds resolutely to the position that he has neither said nor done anything of which he need repent.

Nevertheless, if Reid did not recant, having nothing worse to take back than his "rejoicing" at an emancipation so short-lived, he did make a rational virtue out of the "dread of innovation." From the outset, in 1794, he makes it

74

clear that his discourse does not concern the abstract question, which "form, or order of political society . . . tends most to the improvement and happiness of man?" Rather, it has to do with the "very dangerous" *practical* question, how a "long established" and actually existing form of government "may be changed, and reduced to a form which we think more eligible?" His answer, moreover, is brutally realistic: such a change can only be accomplished with great difficulty and, in all likelihood, with much loss. Although this estimate regards only "violent and sudden changes," and not those which are "gradual, peaceable and legal," Reid's conclusion (as he says "from the whole") is that

> such changes are so dangerous in the attempt, so uncertain in the issue, and so dismal and destructive in the means by which they are brought about, that *it must be a very bad form of government indeed*, with circumstances very favourable to a change concurring, that it will justify a wise and good man in putting a hand to them.[62]

The reasons for this bleak prospect are likewise severely drawn: no change of this order and magnitude (that is, in a "great nation") could be effected "all at once," by an ignorant multitude in company with a self-interested faction of "the knowing," whether by open consultation, by election, or even by a constitutional assembly. Human nature, Reid concedes, will simply not support "such a supposition."

Clearly, the only principle at work here is that of consequences; not whether the laws of an existing form of government should always be obeyed (Socrates' argument in the *Crito* 50b-51c), but what would happen *if* . . . . And while the utter wretchedness of a particularly bad government might be grounds for a "wise and good man" to put his hand to it to raze it, even that malignity must be weighed against the effects of resistance. It would appear, then, that Reid has not after all been swayed from that position enunciated during the first few years of his lectures at Glasgow. "The Evils arising from Resistance," he had cautioned at that time, are "greater than those that arise from Suffering."

6. Was this the reasoning of a Socrates? Was it indeed, like the conduct of that ancient figure, "worthy of [a] Prince of Philosophers"? Reid apparently thought so. Both his final declaration and his early arguments draw to a close on a similar note: a note not only of dutiful, if necessary of *passive,* obedience, but also of positive goodness.

"Every Good Man," Reid had affirmed, "respects the Laws and Government of his Country."[63] The implications for the resistance fighter could not be more obvious; nor on this condition could the security of any government be better assured. The obligations, of course, are "reciprocal": "[protection] and the benefit of laws on one hand; respect, submission, and defence in time of danger, on the other." Yet the reciprocity is scarcely one of equals for, as Socrates also had assumed, the protector must play the "father" to the child. Hence, in spite of Reid's late attempt to dress up reform in the guise of "that candour and indulgence with which we perceive the defects of our dearest friends," this is in truth a reformation headed by good men who "'lead quiet and peaceable lives in all godliness and honesty'."[64] Now clearly

the victor, the Calvinist principle of obedience puts to lasting rest, at least in
Reid's mind, the agonizing antinomies of an earlier prelection and upholds,
against either theological or more radical dissenters, the duty to non-
resistance.[65] Consequently, if "*Sancte Socrates*" may be heard once more in
the midst of these reflections, it is as a celebration of divine authority as much
as of reason.

J.C. Stewart-Robertson
University of New Brunswick

Notes

This is a considerably shortened version of a paper originally read for the Canadian Society for
Eighteenth-Century Studies in May, 1980.

[1] Pringle's analysis is recorded in dictates "Collected by JBPS" in 1741 from "Lectures from
Cicero by Dr. John Pringle, Professor of Moral Philosophy att Edinr.," Edinburgh University
Library, MS. GEN. 74D (ff. 8-45). In large measure a commentary on Cicero's De Officiis,
Pringle's lecture material seems here to adopt a more independent line, as he criticizes that
ancient writer's defence of "Catos Exit" [sic] on the grounds that the latter's death failed of the
highest sanction for suicide; namely, that the act be (morally) "examplary." (Wherever
possible in what follows, I have retained the spelling of the original MSS., making exception
only for conjectural readings and for the rendering in full of certain conjunctive or
pronominal abbreviations.) The particular passage which triggers Pringle's antinomy on self-
murder appears at De Officiis, 112: "suicide may be for one man a duty, for another [under
the same circumstances] a crime" (W. Miller, tr., Loeb Classical edition).

[2] *Phaedo* 61c-62c. Pringle's argument against Socrates is that "according to the Established
Maxim that Evry Man who rejects the Means of [providing for] Life is his own murderer in
Effect So Socrates," having refused all means of escape, is thereby "guilty" by omission and of
his own choice. (The words "providing for" are a conjectural reading of an indistinct text, of
which the first three letters only are apparent.)

[3] Significantly, Pringle's complaint against Cicero's reading of the "Exit" of Marcus Cato is at
one with that of Desiderius Erasmus who, in "The Godly Feast," demures at Cato's going out as
being rather "expressive of . . . pride" than of the humility and hope which ought to
characterize the suicide. With respect to the last-named qualities, Erasmus is more generous,
less grudging, in his honouring of Socrates. (His reference is also rather to Cato's final speech
in *De Senectute*.) See *The Colloquies of Erasmus*, tr. Craig R. Thompson (Chicago and
London: University of Chicago Press, 1965), pp. 66-68.

[4] In *Observations upon Liberal Education In all its Branches* (London, 1742), Pt. III, ch. 1, 2.

[5] Reid made frequent use of the analogy in his lectures on the "Culture of the Mind," delivered
to his special "12 o'clock" classes at Glasgow College after 1764.

[6] "A brief Account of the Nature, *Progress and Origin* of Philosophy delivered by the late Mr.
David Fordyce," and presumably transcribed by "his Scholars, before they begun [sic] their
Philosophical course. Anno 1743/44," Aberdeen University Library, MS. 184.

[7] Gregorie's topic (#30) reads, "Whether the Socratic method of Instruction or that of Prelection
is preferable?" and is dated "8 Jan. 1760." An earlier topic (#31) on the "ancient Method of
Education in Public Seminaries from earliest Infancy," again in relation to "modern practice,"
had been delivered by Dr. David Skene on 27 November, 1759. The last in this particular
group of topics (#'s 30 to 37), regarding the best means of cultivating the young "for the
different businesses of life," was given by Professor Gerard. See the original list of "Questions
Proposed in the Philosophical Society in Aberdeen," under the authors' respective hands, in
AUL, MS. 539. I have treated of the still wider setting of these queries in "The Well-
Principled Savage, or the Child of the Scottish Enlightenment," *Journal of the History of
Ideas*, 42, 3 (July-Sept. 1981), 503-25.

[8] See Gerard's *Plan of Education in the Marischal College and University of Aberdeen, with the
Reasons of it* (Aberdeen, 1755), p. 22.

⁹ *Dialogues concerning Education* (London, 1745-48). Reid twice pays tribute to Fordyce's stature as a philosopher of education, in MSS. 2131/4/I/18 and 4/I/31.

¹⁰ *Dialogues*, VIII, 197. The Socratic method is perhaps nowhere better depicted.

¹¹ For this distinction, see Cicero, *De Officiis*, 107.

¹² MS. 2131/8/IV/10 (f. 4); "their" is somewhat indistinct, but highly probable; the phrase "respect and" which follows has been lined out. The numbering scheme for the Reid MSS. is that agreed to by the editor of the Birkwood Collection in co-operation with Mr. Colin A. McLaren, the Archivist and Keeper of Manuscripts, Aberdeen University Library, for the forthcoming serial publication of Reid's papers. The folio numbers are based on my editing to date, and may therefore be subject in some instances to a final revision.

¹³ In "The Godly Feast," the dying words of Peter, Cato, Paul, and Socrates tend to blend into a paean of hope in death. In that mood, moreover, the sanctification of Socrates seems virtually inevitable: "I can hardly help exclaiming," says the character Nephalius, "Saint Socrates pray for us!"

¹⁴ In Reid's very first sketches for a "division of Pneumatology" — undated, but because of their form, script, and resemblance to the lecture notes of his first year, presumed to derive from the period 1764-65, — "Jurisprudence" is not specifically mentioned, although "Ethicks" and "Politicks" are slated to occupy those final segments of the course: *vide* MS. 2131/4/II/11. We do know, however, from lecture notes for the spring sessions of 1765 and 1766, that Jurisprudence took up a position immediately following Reid's treatment of "Justice" — which he had designated, *contra* Cicero, to be the last of the Cardinal Virtues, — this analysis itself falling under the general heading of "Practical Ethicks" (MS. 2131/8/IV/2 and 1, in that order). In observing this order, Reid does not so much depart from what I call the "Pneumatological Tradition" as, in this instance, simply refine it.

¹⁵ MS. 2131/8/IV/9. Although the arrangement of his notes under this head is less than clear, one can, by careful editing and with the occasional help of an external set of notes from one of his students, piece together what appears to have been a fairly standard *three-part* study. Reid begins with a general appraisal of the "Rights and obligations of men grounded upon the laws of Nature," and proceeds to the "more difficult" cases arising, for example, out of a "great inequality of the Persons" or involving "Primitive Christians under persecution" (MS. 2131/8/IV/4). Following a brief note on the "Adventitious Rights of Mankind," such as "Property" (MS. 2131/8/IV/6). He spends several weeks analyzing the rights of "Succession" and of "Contracts and Covenants," before bringing the first Part of Jurisprudence to a close (MS. 2131/8/IV/7). In that first spring of 1765 "Book 2," which concerns "the Rights & Duties arising from the Domestick Relat[ions]" (a frayed edge has rendered the final letters indistinct), occupied the period from 2 to 9 April; at which time Reid turned his attention to the "Rights and duties that arise from the political State or that of Civil Goverment" (MS. 2131/8/IV/7 and 10). In the following spring Reid appears to have reworked, in greater detail, his notes for what is now distinctly labeled "Part 3." A short time later, he has added a discussion of the "Rights of States," of the causes of "injustice" between them, and the "Laws of War"; he quotes extensively on these issues from M. de Vattel's *The Law of Nations; or Principles of the Law of Nature applied to the Conduct and affairs of Nations and Sovereigns*, tr. Newbery (London, 1760), which he had read in "Septr 1766"; cf. MSS. 2131/3/II/5, 8/IV/8, and 8/IV/9. With only minor changes or elaborations (for example, MS. 2131/3/II/5, of the "Just Causes of War" d. 1770), the set of lectures is thereby complete. J. Rennie's notes of Beattie's lectures at Marischal College, at about the same time (1767), reveal a similar progression, but move directly under "Politics" after the investigation of "Oeconomics." See Glasgow University Library, MS. Hamilton 55. Beattie's own record of the lectures, in his *Elements of Moral Science* (Edinburgh, 1790-93), is different again, the analysis of property and contracts having been deleted. We shall see that Reid too effected adjustments, in part to meet the changing times, in part as a reflection of his widening interests and readings.

¹⁶ MS. 2131/8/IV/10.

¹⁷ In the absence of any direct supporting evidence from Reid's own papers, we are here dependent upon the indirect transcription of one of Reid's more reliable student-auditors, Robert Jack, who, by a piece of good fortune, was in attendance at Reid's lectures during the months of April and May, 1776. His notes of Reid's discussions of Jurisprudence and Politics are virtually complete, the only exception being Reid's introductory session under the former head. See GUL, MS. Gen. 116-8.

[18] *Memorials of his Time* (Edinburgh and London, 1910), p. 42. In words that are themselves a memorial, Cockburn remarks further: "Everything rung . . . with the Revolution in France . . . . Everything was soaked in this one event" (73).

[19] Jack's Notes, MS. Gen. 118; and "On the Danger of Political Innovation."

[20] MS. 2131/8/IV/10 (ff. 1, 4, 5); dated "Apr 9 1765."

[21] The date is now "Apr 12." The name of Grotius has been lined out here although it reappears, with that of Pufendorf and with a brief exposition of principles, in the text for the following year. Cf. MS. 2131/8/IV/9. The battle lines are also more sharply defined in that subsequent set of notes, and a few names added. Richard Hooker, Algernon Sidney, Locke, and Benjamin Hoadly (Bishop of Bangor, & c.) are there set "Contra" Hobbes, Sir Robert Filmer, Sir William Barclay (the royalist Governor of Virginia), Alexander Leslie (Earl of Leven), and Francis Atterbury (Bishop of Rochester); in short, against those who had given support, in some manner, to the idea of absolute sovereignty or of the divine origin and right of kingship. See Peter Laslett's very thorough analysis of this clash of ideas in the introduction to his edition of Sir Robert Filmer's *Patriarchia and Other Political Works* (Oxford: Basil Blackwell, 1949).

[22] MS. 2131/8/IV/9 (ff. 4-5); dated 24 April, 1766.

[23] See John Calvin, *Institutes of the Christian Religion*, ed. John T. McNeill, tr. F.L. Battles (Philadelphia: The Westminster Press, 1960), II; Bk. IV, ch. xx, pp. 26-27. Reid would seem here to join forces with George Buchanan and John Knox in opposing Calvin's intransigency and in advocating resistance to any ruler violating or defaulting on divine edict. A slight script change, incidentally, at the point of the example (f.5, bottom) may be indicative of a later insertion (a technique not at all uncommon in Reid's notes).

[24] See, for example, Theodore Beza, *Vindiciae contra tyrannos* (1579) and George Buchanan's *De jure regni apud Scotos*, of the same year. Quentin Skinner has recently added his voice to the contention that Knox's *Appellation from the Sentence Pronounced by the Bishops and Clergy*, of 1558, is "not strictly speaking a *political* theory at all, since his appeal to the nobility ['to take vengeance upon evil doers (and) to maintain the well doers'] is couched entirely in terms of their alleged religious obligations." *The Foundations of Modern Political Thought* (Cambridge: Cambridge Univ. Press, 1978), vol. II. p. 211. It was certainly on religious grounds that Calvin gave apparent sanction to resistance through the *populares magistratus* in his *Institutes* (IV, xx. p. 31).

[25] Reid's reference continues: "Translated from the French Lond 1760 Newbery & c. 2 Vol 4° 1 Vol 254 pages 2^d 170"; MS. 2131/3/II/5. This MS. has erroneously been grouped with two miscellaneous folios (one an abstract of "Lord Herberts Book de Veritate," the other a page from his Jurisprudence notes on the "Just Causes of War"), and unfortunately separated from the remainder of Reid's extracts from the de Vattel work. These have been traced by means of the page numbers and the alphabetical letters according to which Reid identified certain extracts for inclusion in his lecture materials, to MS. 2131/4/III/23c.

[26] MS. 2131/8/IV/9 (f. 6).

[27] Ibid.; (italics mine). The marginal note reads: "See Extracts from Vattel p. 25 &c."

[28] MS. 2131/8/IV/9 (f. 6).

[29] "Grotius acknowledges that there are cases of extreme Necessity wherein it may be lawfull to resist the supreme Power" [cf. *De Jure Belli ac Pacis* (1625), tr. W.S.M. Knight (1922); Bk. II, ch. xxv, p. 8].

[30] His instruction, apparently a subsequent insertion into the text, reads: "All that is marked in the Margin in the two preceeding pages [ff. 1-2] by a line drawn from top to bottom belongs to Political Jurisprudence." MS. 2131/4/III/9 (f.3).

[31] MS. 2131/8/IV/9 (f.1).

[32] MS. 2131/4/III/3.

[33] Due allowance for error *on both sides* is also readily granted, and indeed stressed, by Hutcheson whose argument, in this respect at least, Reid might be seen to follow. Cf. *A Short Introduction to Moral Philosophy, in Three Books; Containing the Elements of Ethicks and the Law of Nature*, tr. from the Latin (Glasgow, 1747), III, vii, p. 2; see also III, viii, p. 12.

[34] MS. 2131/4/III/9 (f.2); dated 6 May, 1765: "where the publick good is not intended there is no remedy to be expected."

[35] MS. 2131/4/III/5 (ff. 1-2).

[36] MS. 2131/4/III/9 (f.2).

[37] Cf. *De Officiis*, III, 32.

[38] By Jean Gerson and John Mair, for example, or later by Lutheran and Calvinist reformers; see Quentin Skinner, pp. 116-23, 206-13.

[39] Cf. MS. 2131/8/IV/9 (f.5).

[40] De Vattel appears again to have been his immediate source, but the arguments of Milton, Sidney, and Locke would almost certainly have been well aired during his expositon of "the Controversy . . . raised and carried on in England" a century earlier. It is unfortunately impossible to infer from the documentary evidence of this first period, for example, just how Reid might have treated Milton's *Defensio pro populo Anglicano* (published in 1651). In the light of his final thoughts on the subject, however, one might hazard the conjecture that Reid may have found himself more than a little sympathetic with the cautious views of Milton's opponent, the French "grammarian" Salmasius.

[41] MS. 2131/8/IV/9 (f.6).

[42] Not the least of Reid's sources at this time was Harrington's *Oceana*. "The Author was a Man of great Genius . . .," extolled Reid (MS. 2131/4/III/6), who was nevertheless severely critical of this writer on a number of counts. Although I was able to treat at length of Reid's attack on the Harringtonian "Model" in the original paper, the limitations of space do not permit its inclusion here.

[43] Henry W. Meikle, *Scotland and the French Revolution* (1912; rpt. New York: Augustus M. Kelley, 1969), pp. 155-56.

[44] The notes are those of "Robert Jack" and, by a quite fortunate concidence, were transcribed during the critical winter and spring of 1775-76. Their value for our purposes lies in the fact, not only that they reveal an unusually careful literary hand, but also that they have been meticulously arranged and chronicled. See GUL, Gen 116-18. Among Reid's own papers, those touching on commerce with the colonies; on Charles the Second's Charter to William Penn; on the Right of Property; and on taxation, have been most useful. See MSS. 2131/4/III/15, 4/III/19, 4/III/18, and 4/III/10. For the most part, these originate in an earlier climate of lecturing needs, and thus comprise the structural components on which Reid is known to have based his subsequent presentations, with only minor additions and modifications. That at least seems to be the inference to be drawn from the extant lecture-notes themselves. The fact that Jack's transcription can only be matched in part against even the most fragmentary of the original notes would seem to point, therefore, towards a topical, possibly extemporaneous, and *ad hoc* delivery, apparently dictated by a genuine concern for the sudden and dramatic reversals in colonial administration during the years 1775 and 1776.

[45] MS. 2131/4/III/19. Reid logs his reading of the Charter as having taken place on "Aug 27 1768."

[46] MS. 2131/4/III/18. The balance struck by Reid between "common" and "private" holdings or ownership owes much, probably directly, to Grotius but ultimately, as Reid himself owns, to the "ancient Moralists"; Cicero, for example, in *De Officiis*, I, 21-22; or Aristotle in his *Politics*, II, 5.

[47] The phrases cited are derived from Reid's transcription of "The Charter of Cha 2^d to William Penn Proprietary & Governour of Pensilvania 4th March 1681"; MS. 2131/4/III/19. See further Quentin Skinner's interpretation of the seeming contradiction in Bodin's defence both of private property and of absolute sovereignty; Skinner, II, 296-97.

[48] Cf. *An Essay . . . of Civil Government*, XVIII, 199, XIX, 22, 226, 228, 229.

[49] From the notes of Robert Jack, MS. Gen. 116-18; Lecture CXXI, (f. 673).

[50] L. CXX, pp. 665, 667. Reid rightly stresses the essential compatibility of the state's *dominium universale* — as Gierke calls it, "a sort of over-ownership," — with the ownership of the *res privatorum*, or the *dominium appropriatus et specialius* of individuals. Only in times of crisis (*de necessitate*), when the state is unable to defend the public advantage (and thereby the private property of each individual) except by taking steps to use or otherwise expropriate portions of that same property, does the *dominium eminens* overrule its "special" counterpart. Even then, as Reid is quick to add, the owner of private property must receive proper indemnification for his loss. The imposing of taxes Reid simply believes to be "another exercise of this dominium eminens." MS. Gen. 116-18; L. CXX, 666. For a detailed examination of the concept's history, see Otto von Gierke, *Political Theories of the Middle Age*, tr. F.W. Maitland (Boston: Beacon Press, 1958), pp. 79-80, 178-79n.. To someone like Thomas Paine, of course, there was no 'common sense' whatever in such an argument. See his address to the "Inhabitants of America" published under that title (*Common Sense*) on 10

January, 1776; particularly the section headed, "Thoughts on the Present State of American Affairs."

51 MSS. 2131/4/III/23a, 4/III/12, 4/III/13. Reid enters his reading for "10 Jan 1776" under the caption, "Read The Constitution of England or an Account of the English Government by J L de Lolme Advocate Citizen of Geneva Lond 1775 8°" (MS. 2131/4/III/23a).

52 *Vindiciae Gallicae. A Defence of the French Revolution and its English Admirers* (1791).

53 See *Vindiciae Gallicae,* in *The Miscellaneous Works of the Right Honourable Sir James Mackintosh* (Philadelphia, 1848), pp. 423, 424.

54 "It is absurd," he writes, "to *expect,* but it is not absurd to *pursue* perfection. It is absurd to acquiesce in evils, of which the remedy is obvious, because they are less grievous than those which are endured by others." *Vindiciae Gallicae,* pp. 422-23.

55 The reference to Reid's folly appears in a letter from Arbuthnot to Beattie in August, 1792, and is quoted by Margaret Forbes in *Beattie and his Friends* (Westminister, 1904) p. 272.

56 He was an "Ally" in the internal struggles which seem to have rocked the Literary Society of Glasgow, during the winter of 1778-79 and on the side of a stricter adherence to the Society's regulations. See Davis D. McElroy's "circumstantial" account of these struggles in his *Scotland's Age of Improvement: A Survey of Eighteenth-Century Literary Clubs and Societies* (Seattle: Washington State Univ. Press, 1969), Introduction and pp. 41-43.

57 See "An Account of some Particulars in the Life and Character of the Rev. Mr. Archibald Arthur, late Professor of Moral Philosophy in the University of Glasgow," by William Richardson; in Archibald Arthur, *Discourses on Theological & Literary Subjects* (Glasgow, 1803), Appendix I, p. 514n..

58 "In the course of the years 1791-92," explains William Ferguson, "the bulk of the upper classes sought refuge in Burke's passionate rhetoric, while the diminishing ranks of upper-class and middle-class reformers availed themselves of James Mackintosh's reply to Burke, *Vindiciae Gallicae . . . .* Mackintosh was a young Scot who had tried both medicine and law none too successfully and who was launched on a moderately successful political career by this controversy. He *later repented of his early democratic sympathies (as so many in his situation did)* and became a fulsome adulator of Burke." *Scotland: 1689 to the Present* (Edinburgh: Oliver and Boyd, 1968), pp. 249-50 (italics mine). There is no evidence that Reid "repented" in quite that sense; nor does his pronouncement "On the Danger of Political Innovation" in any way suggest a contrite spirit.

59 Richardson, p. 512.

60 The advertisement, headed "ANNIVERSARY of the REVOLUTION in FRANCE" (it being in fact the "SECOND"), makes it explicit that its "sole object" is "to celebrate, as a subject of exultation, the overthrow of despotism, and the establishment of civil and religious liberty in France" and thereby, through this testimonial, "to promote the general liberty and happiness of the world."

61 The draft letter appears on a single sheet of folio (*recto*), opposite a geometrical figure: MS. 2131/3/III/8.

62 "On the Danger . . ." (italics mine); in the original — lately recovered, — MS. 3061/6 (f. 4).

63 MS. 2131/8/IV/9.

64 MS. 3061/6 (f. 27); the quotation is from 1 Timothy 2: 1-2.

65 Significantly, Reid ends his discourse with that same scriptural passage on which Calvin had rested so much of his case for "obedience"; see the *Institutes,* IV, xx. p. 23.

8. La Philosophie politique de Kant

La philosophie politique de Kant a été pendant longtemps méconnue des commentateurs, surtout de ceux qui se sont occupés de l'aspect systématique de sa pensée. Les raisons de cet état de choses sont multiples. Non la moindre de ces raisons est sans doute que Kant n'est venu que tard dans sa vie à l'élaboration et à l'expression sous forme écrite d'une théorie politique selon les principes de sa philosophie. Il a par conséquent relativement peu écrit sur des sujets relevant directement de la philosophie politique. En effet, selon l'extension que l'on accorde au mot "politique", seulement entre 1-1/2 et 5 pour cent de ses écrits[1] seraient consacrés à la considération de ce genre de question. Et nous avons le témoignage de Kant lui-même pour nous indiquer le caractère peu systématique de certains de ses textes politiques les plus importants, notamment de son *Projet de paix perpétuelle* (1795), qui ne serait, au dire de Kant, que des "rêveries", une collection d'"opinions avancées au hasard".[2] De plus, en ce qui concerne la partie plus systématique de son oeuvre politique, constituée surtout de la *Doctrine du droit* (1797), il a été suggéré, notamment par Friedrich Paulsen, que celle-ci aurait été rédigée pendant la période de sénilité du philosophe de Königsberg.[3] A cet égard, effectivement, force nous est de reconnaître que la *Doctrine du droit,* ainsi que la *Doctrine de la vertu,* première et seconde parties, respectivement, de la *Métaphysique des moeurs,* présentent des difficultés de lecture considérables. La complexité et l'obscurité syntaxiques, allant parfois jusqu'à l'incorrection grammaticale, assorties d'une terminologie copieuse et, du moins en apparence, flottante, marquent très possiblement une détérioration par rapport aux trois grandes *Critiques* qui avaient précédemment fait la renommée de leur auteur et dont le style ne rendait déjà pas facile la tâche du lecteur. Nous ne retiendrons cependant pas l'hypothèse d'une période de sénilité pour rendre compte de l'impénétrabilité relative du texte de la *Doctrine du droit,* ni surtout pour servir de prétexte à notre paresse, car nous croyons que la détérioration du style de Kant, si détérioration il y a eu, a été voulue dans la mesure où elle est réelle et s'explique moins par l'âge avancé de l'auteur que par des changements survenus dans la situation politique à l'intérieur et à l'extérieur de la Prusse, ainsi que par la prudence qui s'imposait à un auteur qui traitait de questions politiques tout en habitant un pays à régime monarchique quatre ans à peine après la décapitation de Louis XVI. Il est d'ailleurs à remarquer que Kant avait déjà eu de sérieux démêlés avec la censure à propos de sa *Religion dans les limites de la simple raison*

(1793) — et avait même fait l'objet d'une remontrance que lui adressait personnellement le roi Frédéric-Guillaume II.[4]

A Fichte, qui lui avait écrit en 1793 pour dire que son âme était "tout enflammée d'une merveilleuse idée"[5] qui lui permettrait de résoudre le problème proposé par Kant aux pages 372-373 de la deuxième édition de la *Kritik der reinen Vernunft*, Kant répond qu'il souhaite que Fichte le dévance dans cette affaire ou, plutôt, que ce dernier rende "dispensable" le rôle que Kant devait y jouer.[6] Il s'agissait en l'occurrence de tracer les grandes lignes d'"une constitution ayant pour but *la plus grande liberté humaine* fondée sur des lois qui permettraient *à la liberté de chacun de subsister en même temps que la liberté de tous les autres*".[7] Philonenko rapporte que quelques mois plus tard Fichte écrit de nouveau à Kant pour lui annoncer "que son plan de travail intéressant le droit naturel, le droit politique (Staatsrecht) et la politique proprement dite est assez vaste pour occuper la moitié de sa vie — sans préciser que l'autre moitié sera consacrée à fonder plus justement la philosophie transcendentale".[8] Or ce n'est pas par pure générosité que Kant manifeste ce désir de s'effacer devant le jeune Fichte si plein d'enthousiasme. La même année dans une lettre à Spener où il est justement question des difficultés qu'il rencontre vis-à-vis la censure depuis la mort de Frédéric le Grand, Kant écrit que "lorsque les grands de ce monde sont dans un état d'intoxication, un pygmée qui chérit bien sa peau fait bien de ne pas s'impliquer dans leurs querelles".[9] En décembre de la même année, Kant écrit à Kiesewetter qu'"en ce moment où la mode veut qu'on donne l'alarme là où il n'y a que tranquillité et paix, on doit donc patienter, tout en accordant une obéissance exacte à la loi".[10] Plus de quatorze mois plus tard, en mars 1795, en réponse à une requête que lui adressait Schiller de collaborer à un périodique (*Die Horen* — *Les Heures*) dont il était le rédacteur, Kant écrit qu'il doit "demander un assez long délai — *um einen etwas langen Aufschub bitten*".[11] Kant poursuit en constatant que tout "matériel se rapportant à des questions d'état ou de religion se trouve pour le moment soumis à un certain blocus [*Handelssperte*], mais il n'y a guère en ce moment que cette sorte de marchandise qui intéresse la grande majorité des lecteurs". Kant ajoute que "l'on doit observer pendant encore quelque temps ce changement de climat, afin de s'accommoder prudemment du temps — *um sich klüglich in die Zeit zu schicken*".[12] Quelques mois plus tôt Kant avait écrit à son éditeur Lagarde les lignes suivantes:

«Puisque mon sujet est à proprement parler la métaphysique dans l'acception la plus large du mot et s'occupe en tant que telle de théologie, de morale (et, avec cette dernière, de religion aussi), ainsi que de droit naturel (et, avec ce dernier, de droit politique et du droit des gens), mais seulement du point de vue de ce que la simple raison a à en dire, et que la main de la censure [ne] s'abat [pas moins] sur elle à présent, aucune garantie n'existe que l'ensemble du travail entrepris en ce domaine ne soit frustré par un trait de plume du censeur. — Lorsque la paix, qui semble être proche, s'établira, on peut espérer que les limites dans lesquelles un auteur doit se tenir seront plus exactement indiquées par des décrets plus précis, afin que celui-ci puisse se sentir en sécurité dans le domaine qui lui est laissé — *so, dass er in dem, was ihm noch freigelassen wird, sich für gesichert halten kann.*»[13]

N'est-il pas significatif à cet égard, comme l'a fait remarquer Hettner,[14] que Kant ait "publié ses écrits sous son propre nom, tandis que les *Contributions à la juste appréciation de la Révolution française* de Fichte paraissaient de façon anonyme"? Je pense que la conclusion qui s'impose ici est que dans notre lecture des écrits politiques de Kant nous ne devons ni ne pouvons faire abstraction de l'oeil du censeur qui, toujours présent à l'esprit de Kant, lisait, pour ainsi dire, par-dessus son épaule.[15] Il ne serait pas surprenant, dès lors, s'il s'avérait que Kant se soit parfois exprimé par des tours de phrase qui n'auraient pas la même signification pour le lecteur averti que pour le fonctionnaire-théologien moyen. L'un des principes de base de notre lecture de la philosophie politique de Kant sera, en effet, qu'il faut examiner à la loupe pour en déterminer le sens précis, toute proposition qui semble, de prime abord, exprimer une position favorable au régime en place. Nous ne devons cependant pas croire que Kant ait fait imprimer quoi que ce soit qui aille à l'encontre de ses véritables convictions.[16] A cela il aurait préféré le silence: "Rétracter et renier sa conviction intime, on peut lire dans les papiers laissés par Kant, est une bassesse — *Widerruf und Verleugnung seiner inneren überzeugung ist niederträchtig* — et nul ne doit en être supposé capable, mais le silence en un cas comme le présent, est le devoir d'un sujet; et si tout ce que l'on dit, doit être vrai, ce n'est cependant pas un devoir de dire publiquement toute vérité".[17]

Mais si Kant, dans ses écrits politiques, ne s'est pas exprimé avec toute la clarté voulue, et s'il s'avérait de plus qu'il n'ait pas tout dit sur sa véritable position, comment, dès lors, déterminer le sens des textes qu'il s'est néanmoins senti dans l'obligation de faire publier? Nous n'avons pas, il me semble, à cet égard, d'autre recours qu'à une lecture fouillée qui s'appuie sur l'aspect systématique de l'oeuvre de Kant. Or, malheureusement, au dire de Hans Saner, l'oeuvre politique de Kant a été délaissée précisément par ceux-là parmi ses commentateurs qui s'attachaient le plus aux aspects systématiques de sa pensée.[18] D'autres commentateurs, aux préoccupations moins systématiques, ceux qui ne se sont pas laissés complètement rebuter par l'incohérence et l'intelligibilité apparentes du texte, ainsi que par certaines idées apparemment réactionnaires de l'auteur, se sont le plus souvent donné pour unique tâche de retrouver les *origines* des idées politiques de Kant. Et l'on y a si bien réussi, comme le dit encore Hans Saner, que les nombreux pères[19] des idées politiques de Kant ont été retrouvés, mais Kant lui-même a été perdu. Car si l'on a tant cherché à situer la position de Kant par rapport à la pensée des autres, c'est souvent qu'on arrivait mal à la situer par rapport au système kantien dans son ensemble, et qu'on évitait ainsi d'avoir à la confronter en tant que *philosophie* politique. Mais déjà, heureusement, un mouvement contraire s'esquisse. Selon Eric Weil, "Kant, ici comme partout, marque un tournant dans l'histoire de la philosophie", et ce justement en raison des préoccupations systématiques du philosophe de Königsberg, Chez Kant, en effet, selon l'interprétation de Weil, "la politique devient problème parce que la morale et, mais seulement à sa suite, la philosophie de la nature

84

ne permettent plus d'éviter cette question: ni l'une ni l'autre ne seraient achevées, ni l'une ni l'autre ne seraient même vraies, si elles ne donnaient pas de réponse à ce problème qu'elles posent et imposent au philosophe. Ce n'est pas la réflexion politique qui détermine la philosophie kantienne, c'est cette philosophie qui conduit, non aux problèmes politiques, mais au problème de la politique".[20] Les limitations d'espace ne permettent toutefois pas dans le cadre du présent essai de faire le lien entre la pensée politique de Kant et tout le système des *Critiques,* bien que ceci ait déjà été tenté, notamment par Hans Saner. Nous entendons cependant, au cours des remarques qui vont suivre, faire état au moins de la cohérence interne de la philosophie politique kantienne et de ses rapports avec la philosophie morale, en plus de nous servir de cette cohérence comme principe d'interprétation de certains points obscurs ou controversés.

S'il y a pour Kant un problème central en philosophie politique, autour duquel tojustification de la *contrainte juridique,* qui constitue d'ailleurs la condition récessaire de l'existence même d'un Etat politique et d'un système de *lois* garantissant la liberté. Mais, en effet, on ne peut éviter de se poser la question: cette contrainte peut-elle se justifier moralement? Et, si oui, comment et dans quelles conditions? La thèse des anarchistes, qui ne tardera pas à voir la lumière du jour, n'est-elle justement pas que, sauf en cas de légitime défense, la contrainte est toujours et partout une agression indue, une violence perpétrée contre des individus et des groupes, peu importe qu'elle procède du caprice sauvage d'un autre individu ou qu'elle procède de l'Etat et qu'elle s'exerce au nom de la collectivité selon des lois. La question du droit et, partant, de la politique est donc celle de la justification de la contrainte. "Ainsi, dit Kant, le droit et l'autorisation [*Befugnis*] de contraindre sont une seule et même chose".[21]

Or, malgré tout ce qu'on a pu dire pour faire de Kant l'ancêtre du positivisme juridique moderne,[22] l'autorisation dont il s'agit dans ce passage est bien une autorisation *morale,* et la morale en l'occurrence est bien la morale kantienne. Dans la *Doctrine de la vertu,* Kant dit très clairement que "le devoir de vertu se distingue essentiellement du devoir de droit en ce qu'une contrainte extérieure est *moralement* possible par rapport à ce dernier, tandis que le premier repose uniquement sur une libre contrainte personnelle".[23] Dans l'Introduction générale à la *Métaphysique des moeurs,* Kant explique que les "lois de la liberté sont appelées *morales* à la différence des lois de la nature. Lorsqu'elles ne portent que sur des actions extérieures et leur légalité, elles sont dites *juridiques*; mais si, de plus, elles exigent d'être en tant que telles (comme lois) les principes de détermination des actions, elles sont alors *éthiques*" (*Doctrine du droit,* p. 88). Il est donc clair que les devoirs de droit constituent dans l'idée de Kant un sous-ensemble par rapport aux devoirs éthiques.

Sournoisement, par ces définitions, Kant vient de refuser d'accorder un statut proprement juridique à toute mesure prévoyant une contrainte qui soit contraire à la morale! (Ainsi, nous pouvons imaginer que Kant ne dirait pas d'une prétendue loi obligeant chaque citoyen à retourner au propriétaire tout esclave évadé qui se réfugierait chez lui qu'elle est injuste; il dirait bien plutôt que ce n'est même pas une *loi,* puisqu'aucune autorisation morale n'existe pour justifier une telle contrainte, qui ne serait autre chose que violence injustifiée; on obéit à de telles "lois" par prudence seulement, lorsque, effectivement, on y obéit, comme on obéirait à une bande de brigands armés, faute de moyens de résistance mais sans accorder la moindre légitimité à leurs demandes.) Kant s'exprime, il est vrai, un peu moins clairement sur ce point au début du premier chapitre de la *Doctrine du droit* où il s'agit d'expliquer en quoi consiste la "doctrine du droit" — mais il ne faut pas oublier que ce passage, par sa situation au début du premier chapitre ainsi que par le sujet qu'il se donne, serait l'un de ceux sur lesquels le censeur exercerait sa plus grande vigilance. Kant y dit que la "doctrine du droit" est "la totalité des lois pour lesquelles une législation extérieure est possible",[24] en omettant, cette fois, de préciser que la possibilité dont il est question ici est bien une possibilité *morale* et non pas, par exemple, une simple possibilité technique, ou même logique. Kant ajoute que lorsqu'une telle législation existe dans les faits, c'est-à-dire lorsqu'une législation qui est moralement possible existe dans les faits, il s'agit alors de la doctrine du droit *positif.* Kant avait précédemment expliqué que les lois positives sont celles "qui sans une législation extérieure réelle n'obligeraient pas et ne seraient pas des lois" (*Doctrine du droit,* p. 99). Un exemple d'une loi positive serait donc la loi des provinces canadiennes qui oblige les automobilistes à conduire du côté droit, ou la loi britannique qui oblige à conduire du côté gauche du chemin. Ces lois, en plus de faire peser sur l'automobiliste une certaine contrainte exercée par la police et les tribunaux, créent une certaine *obligation morale* de s'y conformer, obligation qui n'existerait pas en l'absence d'une telle législation, comme dans les pays où le côté du chemin duquel on doit se tenir ne fait l'objet d'aucune loi.

L'obligation qui s'attache à ce que Kant appelle une loi *naturelle,* par contre, "peut être reconnue *a priori* par la raison, en l'absence même de législation extérieure".[25] Un exemple d'une loi naturelle serait donc celle qui interdit l'homicide volontaire sauf en certains cas de légitime défense, car la raison reconnaît d'emblée que je ne saurais accepter qu'un autre choisisse de me tuer dans le but de se procurer quelque avantage. Il est à remarquer que, selon cette définition de Kant, une loi ne cesse pas pour autant d'être "naturelle" lorsque l'homme sort de l'état de nature et prend des mesures pour la faire respecter par tous et chacun. Il s'ensuit que ce que l'on appelle aujourd'hui des "lois positives", dans l'acception courante du terme, comprendrait, entre autres, des lois *naturelles* au sens de Kant, lorsque celles-ci seraient l'objet d'une législation extérieure effective. Notre terme "loi positive" comprendrait aussi des lois positives au sens de Kant, ainsi que des mesures gouvernementales auxquelles Kant refuserait jusqu'au titre de "lois".

Kant se demande si une législation extérieure composée uniquement de lois positives, est possible — et répond dans l'affirmative, avec la qualification très importante qu'il faudrait "qu'une loi naturelle précédât pour fonder l'autorité du législateur (c'est-à-dire l'autorisation [*Befugnis*] de lier [les] autres par son simple arbitre [*durch seine blosse Willkür*]". On dirait qu'il s'agit ici d'une distinction pointilleuse, sans beaucoup d'importance, et c'est précisément l'impression que Kant aurait voulu créer dans l'esprit du fonctionnaire-théologien moyen qui assure la fonction de censeur dans l'Etat prussien. Celui-ci n'aurait-il pas tendance à prendre les termes de "lois positives" et de "lois naturelles" dans leurs acceptions habituelles? Ainsi il retiendrait surtout que dans un système politique donné il pourrait n'y avoir que des lois positives, au sens habituel du mot. Nous n'avions évidemment pas besoin de Kant pour nous le dire; mais, penserait notre fonctionnaire, ces vieux professeurs se plaisent à dire des vérités évidentes et, au fond, insignifiantes, en donnant l'impression d'avoir fait une grande découverte et en s'exprimant d'une façon délibérément obscure! La seule "loi naturelle" qui compte, dans l'Etat prussien par exemple, serait celle qui fonde l'autorité du législateur — et ici notre fonctionnaire penserait à l'autorité du roi, son "souverain" — qui contraint ses sujets "par son simple arbitre". Mais, à la vérité, dans ce passage, au contraire de la lecture qu'en ferait notre fonctionnaire, Kant rappelle au lecteur attentif et averti le virement de sens qu'il a effectué par rapport au terme "loi positive": dans l'acception où Kant emploie désormais ce terme il n'y a plus de *loi,* et donc plus de loi positive, dès qu'il n'est plus possible de justifier la coercition qu'elle comporte par le recours à une construction (ou à une reconstruction) rationnelle, ce qui signifie, comme nous verrons plus loin, une dérivation de l'impératif catégorique — ou, plus précisément, une dérivation de l'autorisation de contraindre contenue implicitement dans l'impératif catégorique.

Ce qui est essentiellement le même point revient lorsque Kant tente de lever l'ambiguïté qu'il constate dans l'emploi du terme "état de nature" qui, effectivement, sert tantôt à désigner l'état où l'homme se trouverait en l'absence complète d'influences sociales, tantôt à désigner la situation qui existerait en l'absence de liens proprement juridiques entre les hommes. Ainsi Rousseau, dont Kant ne nous parle pas ici mais dont la présence se devine toujours à l'arrière-plan, ne décrit-il pas dans son *Discours sur l'origine et les fondements de l'inégalité entre les hommes* (1755) l'homme "tel qu'il a dû sortir des mains de la nature"?[26] C'est donc l'homme, abstraction faite de tout ce que la société a pu faire de lui, qui préoccupe Rousseau. Ici, la liberté naturelle de l'état de nature est celle qui *précède* toutes les contraintes que la société fait peser sur l'individu et toutes les autres influences qu'elle exerce sur lui. Mais dans le *Contrat social,* Rousseau nous parle d'un état de nature tout autre, qui surgit dans une société déjà très évoluée par rapport à ce que connaissait l'homme vivant solitaire au fond de la forêt du *Discours sur l'inégalité.* Cet état de nature n'apparaît, effectivement, que lorsque les liens juridiques entre les hommes sont dissous par la rupture du pacte social: "A l'instant où le gouvernement usurpe la souveraineté [qui, selon Rousseau, n'appartient en propre qu'au corps politique constitué de tous les citoyens],[27] le pacte social est rompu; et tous les simples citoyens, rentrés de droit dans leur liberté naturelle, sont forcés, mais non pas obligés d'obéir".[28] L'homme qui se trouve dans l'état de nature, pris dans ce deuxième sens du terme, n'est souvent libre qu'au point de vue moral; en réalité, il se trouve, selon le mot de Rousseau, "dans les fers".[29] Et il ne retrouvera sa liberté que lorsque tous auront contracté avec tous de n'obéir qu'aux lois consenties par ce que Rousseau appelle la *volonté générale.* De façon semblable, Kant écrit:

«L'état juridique est ce rapport des hommes entre eux, qui contient les conditions sous lesquelles seules chacun peut *jouir de son droit,* et le principe formel de la possibilité de cet état, considéré d'après l'Idée d'une volonté législatrice universelle, est la justice publique [qui, selon Kant, comprend nécessairement ce qu'il appelle la "justice distributive"] . . .

L'état non juridique, [par contre,] c'est-à-dire celui où il n'y a pas de justice distributive, s'appelle état de nature (*status naturalis*). Le contraire de celui-ci serait non pas (comme le pense Achenwall) l'état *social,* qui pourrait s'appeler un état artificiel (*status artificialis*), mais plutôt l'état *civil* d'une société soumise à une justice distributive, car dans l'état de nature aussi il peut exister des sociétés légitimes [*rechtmässige Gesellschaften*[30]] (par exemple [la société] conjugale, [la société] paternelle, [la société] domestique en général, et *bien d'autres*[31]), pour lesquelles aucune loi *a priori* ne signifie: "Tu dois entrer en cet état", comme on peut dire, en effet, de l'état *juridique (vom rechtlichen Zustande)* [, à savoir qu'une loi *a priori* exige] que tous les hommes qui peuvent s'engager les uns par rapport aux autres (et ce même contre leur gré) dans des rapports juridiques, *doivent* entrer en cet état.»[32]

On peut se demander quelles sociétés précisément Kant avait en tête en parlant des nombreuses "autres" sociétés qui, dans l'état de nature, sont *rechtmässig,* sans pour autant être *rechtlich.* Quel serait, par exemple, à cet égard, le statut de la monarchie prussienne? Quoi qu'il en soit, il ressort clairement ici que contrairement à ce que suggèrent bien des interprétations de la philosophie politique de Kant, il ne suffit pas que je me trouve dans des rapports *sociaux* avec d'autres et soumis à des règlements contraignants pour que l'on puisse dire que je dois un devoir d'obéissance absolue à ces règlements comme s'il s'agissait d'un état proprement *juridique.* Pour Kant, comme pour Rousseau, il y a des cas où l'on choisit d'obéir (comme à son père après avoir atteint l'âge de raison), mais sans qu'il y ait obligation morale d'obéir; il existe selon les deux auteurs d'autres cas encore où l'on est forcé d'obéir, et où l'on obéit par prudence seulement. L'obéissance que nous devons à de vraies lois positives (et naturelles), nous ne la devons qu'à des mesures qui font l'objet d'une législation extérieure sous un régime proprement *juridique* (et donc en conformité avec la morale).

Mais qu'est-ce qu'un régime ou un Etat proprement juridique selon Kant? Et comment peut-il faire valoir qu'il existe un devoir moral d'entrer en cet état? Revenons donc un peu en arrière pour nous rappeler brièvement les grandes lignes de la théorie kantienne des fondements de la morale. La morale, chez Kant comme chez d'autres théoriciens, se rapporte essentiellement aux actions humaines. Une action, au sens propre du terme, comporte une certaine conscience (du moins en puissance) d'avoir recours à certains moyens (comme par exemple à un certain mouvement de mon bras et de ma main) *afin* d'accomplir un but que l'on se donne (comme par exemple celui de saisir une pomme que l'on a envie de manger). Les mouvements proprement involontaires, par contre, ne comportent pas de telle conscience (pas même en puissance). Les actions proprement dites se distinguent de ceux-ci par le fait qu'en ce qui les concerne le rapport moyen/fin est toujours susceptible de prendre la forme de ce que Kant appelle une "maxime" ou "principe subjectif d'action": J'étends ma main, par exemple, *afin* de prendre une pomme; je prends la pomme *pour* la manger; je la mange *afin* d'assouvir ma faim. Et, de plus, selon Kant du moins, c'est par la considération de la *maxime* de l'action que l'on peut déterminer si l'action en question est moralement permise ou moralement défendue. Le contrôle se fait de la manière suivante: celui qui agit doit se demander si, étant donné le but qu'il cherche à atteindre par son action, il pourrait accepter (ou vouloir) que d'autres personnes tâchent d'atteindre pour elles-mêmes un même but par des moyens semblables à celui qu'il envisage d'employer. Si, par exemple, afin de répondre à mon désir de me rendre dans une ville voisine, je force le conducteur d'une automobile à me la céder à bout de fusil pour ensuite m'en servir, j'aurais commis par là une action qui, selon Kant, est moralement défendue. Car je ne saurais vouloir (ou même accepter) que la maxime de mon action ("je prends cette voiture par la force afin de me rendre là où je veux aller") soit adoptée par d'autres que moi, puisque quelqu'un d'autre, en adoptant une telle maxime, pourrait me ravir la voiture même dont je viens de prendre possession, me frustrant ainsi dans l'accomplissement de mon but. Précisons qu'il s'agit ici du point de vue *rationnel* quant à ce que je *peux* ou non vouloir: en adepte du Zen ou de la résignation chrétienne, je peux évidemment accepter tout ce qui m'arrive. Il n'est cependant pas rationnel, par le même mouvement de l'esprit par lequel je me donne un but, d'accepter ni surtout de vouloir qu'une autre personne agisse précisément d'une façon qui aura pour effet d'empêcher que je réalise le but en question. Voilà le sens de ce que Kant appelle l'impératif catégorique: "Agis seulement d'après une maxime [telle] que tu peux vouloir . . . qu'elle devienne une loi universelle [, c'est-à- dire qu'elle serve de principe d'action à n'importe qui ayant des buts semblables aux tiens]".[33]

Dans le contexte de la philosophie politique et juridique, il s'agit donc de se demander si la *maxime* qu'on se donnerait en établissant une législation extérieure contraignante peut être celle d'une action qui soit moralement permise. Kant écrit:

> «La résistance opposée à ce qui fait obstacle à un effet fait avancer celui-ci et s'accorde avec lui. Or, tout ce qui est injuste est un obstacle à la liberté suivant des lois universelles; mais la contrainte est un obstacle ou une résistance exercée sur la liberté. Il s'ensuit que si un certain usage de la liberté même est un obstacle à la liberté suivant des règles universelles (c'est-à-dire est injuste), alors la contrainte qui lui est opposée, en tant *qu'obstacle à ce qui fait obstacle à la liberté*, s'accorde avec cette dernière suivant des lois universelles, c'est-à-dire qu'elle est juste; par conséquent une autorisation (*Befugnis*) de contraindre ce qui lui est préjudiciable est, suivant la loi de contradiction, liée . . . au droit.»[34]

Voilà pour la preuve que dans certaines circonstances du moins il peut être moralement permis, au nom même de la plus grande liberté de tous selon des principes universels, d'imposer par moyen de la contrainte extérieure des limites à l'exercice de la liberté personnelle. Mais ce n'est pas n'importe quelle contrainte qui a pour effet d'augmenter la liberté de tous selon des principes universels. Pour préciser les conditions et les modalités de l'application d'une telle contrainte un plus long développement sera nécessaire. Mais Kant en dégage néanmoins tout de suite le principe de base: le droit, selon lui, "ne peut pas être pensé comme constitué de deux moments: à savoir de l'obligation suivant une loi — et de l'autorisation [Befugnis] de celui qui oblige les autres par son arbitre de les contraindre à accomplir cette obligation".[35] Au contraire, le droit strict exigerait "une contrainte réciproque complète", comme dans la doctrine de la volonté générale de Rousseau.[36] Chez Kant, en effet, comme chez Rousseau, "le pouvoir législatif ne peut appartenir qu'à la volonté unifiée du peuple" (Doctrine du droit, p. 196). Les membres d'une société vivant sous une condition proprement juridique y retrouvent "la liberté légale de n'obéir à aucune autre loi qu'à celle à laquelle ils ont donné leur consentement". Ainsi, le souverain, "considéré selon les lois de la liberté, ne peut être autre que le peuple uni lui-même" (Doctrine du droit, p. 198).

Il reste que le souverain, chez Kant comme chez Rousseau, ne statue que sur les conditions générales des rapports qui existeront entre les citoyens et ne peut pas, par la force des choses, s'occuper de l'application des lois à des cas particuliers. Le souverain ne peut donc ni assumer les fonctions d'un tribunal ni exercer celles du gouvernement proprement dit. Kant écrit:

> «Le régent de l'Etat (rex, princeps) est la personne (morale ou physique) investie du pouvoir exécutif . . .: c'est l' agent de l'Etat, qui installe les magistrats, prescrit au peuple les règles d'après lesquelles conformément à la loi (par subsomption d'un cas sous cette loi), chacun peut . . . acquérir ou conserver ce qui est sien. . . . Les ordres qu'il donne au peuple . . . sont des ordonnances, des décrets (non des lois), car ils ont pour objet une décision en un cas particulier et ils se donnent comme révocables. Un gouvernement, qui serait en même temps législateur, devrait être appelé despotique. . . .» (Doctrine du droit, p. 199)

Inversement, si le régent n'a pas l'autorisation de légiférer, le législateur ou souverain ne peut pas gouverner à la place du régent:

> «Le souverain [Beherrscher] du peuple (le législateur) ne peut ainsi être en même temps le régent; car ce dernier est soumis à la loi et est donc obligé par celle-ci, et donc obligé par un autre (le souverain). Le souverain peut lui ôter son pouvoir, le déposer, transformer son administration, mais il ne peut le punir . . .; car il s'agirait là encore d'un acte du pouvoir exécutif, auquel revient, suivant la loi, la faculté [Vermögen] de contraindre d'une manière suprême, qui néanmoins serait soumis à une contrainte; en quoi il y a contradiction.» (Doctrine du droit, p. 199)

C'est d'ailleurs en raison de cette dernière déclaration et d'autres semblables qu'on a si souvent reproché à Kant d'avoir nié le droit de résistance aux autorités établies, même en cas d'abus grave des pouvoirs du gouvernement. Et, effectivement, il est exact de prétendre que la résistance armée n'est nullement, selon Kant, un moyen d'action juridique. On ne saurait, par exemple, inscrire dans la constitution même d'un Etat juridique quelque droit que ce soit de s'opposer par la force au gouvernement. Cette idée, que l'on retrouve chez Achenwall, Fichte et les auteurs des premières constitutions française et américaine, serait, selon Kant, contradictoire. Toute révolution constitue pour lui, en effet, une destruction du système juridique en place. Mais ce que Kant ne dit pas ici d'un ton trop haut, c'est qu'il se pourrait que le *régent* se soit déjà conduit d'une façon qui détruise le caractère juridique de la contrainte qu'il fait subir au peuple. Cette contrainte ne s'exerçant plus conformément à la loi, le peuple se retrouverait replongé dans un état de nature par rapport à son ancient régent, contre qui le peuple aurait le même droit de légitime défense que contre n'importe quel autre agresseur. Le devoir de contraindre celui qui se maintient par rapport à nous dans un état de nature, à entrer avec nous dans un état juridique s'appliquerait d'ailleurs tout autant dans le cas d'un ancien régent que dans le cas de n'importe quel autre individu. Là où il existe un véritable Etat juridique, certes, le régent est irrésistible; mais si l'on réussit à déposer par la force celui qui se donnait pour régent, on démontre seulement que ce dernier n'était pas le régent d'un Etat juridique, puisque la violence sauvage a eu raison de lui. Il lui manquait le pouvoir unique et suprême de contraindre selon des lois, condition *sine qua non* de l'Etat juridique. Voilà le véritable sens de la formule de Kant selon laquelle dans un Etat juridique le pouvoir exécutif est irrésistible.

James Crombie
Université Ste-Anne

Notes

[1] D'après l'estimé de Hans Saner, *Kant's Political Thought: Its Origins and Development,* trad. de l'allemand par E.P. Ashton (Chicago/Londres, 1973), p. 2.

[2] Lettre à Kiesewetter (1795), citée par Saner, *ibid.*

[3] Cf. Friedrich Paulsen, *Immanuel Kant, sein Leben und sein Lehre,* 5⁰ éd. (Stuttgart, sans date), p. 364; cité par Saner, *op. cit.,* p. 316, note 16: "L'exposition systématique des fondements métaphysiques de la *Doctrine du droit* (1797) appartient à la période de sénilité. . . . Ceci est vrai également du deuxième essai, qui fait partie du *Conflit des facultés* (1798)". Tel n'est cependant pas l'avis de J. Gibelin, qui, dans son "Introduction du traducteur" *au Conflit des facultés* de Kant (Paris, 1973), pp. iv-v, répond à l'affirmation de K. Fischer selon laquelle Kant "savait que dans ses exposés oraux et écrits se manifestaient déjà visiblement les traces d'une intelligence décroissante. . ." par ce qui suit: "En ce qui concerne le *Conflit des facultés,* cette opinion nous paraît exagérée, sinon erronée. La différence entre les trois parties du traité a été, comme on le verra, voulue par Kant et s'explique aisément si l'on tient compte des circonstances, de l'ambiance intellectuelle et des principes mêmes de la philosophie de l'auteur."

[4] Cf. Theodore M. Greene, "The Historical Context and Religious Significance of Kant's *Religion*", dans Kant, *Religion within the Limits of Reason Alone,* trad. de l'allemand par Greene et John R. Silber (New York, 1960), esp. pp. xxxii-xxxvi.

[5] "*Dans glüht meine Seele von einem grossen Gedanken . . .*", cité par A. Philonenko, *Théorie et praxis dans la pensée morale et politique de Kant et de Fichte en 1793* (Paris, 1968), p. 80

[6] Lettre à Fichte (1793), citée par Saner, *op. cit.,* p. 2.

[7] *Critique de la raison pure,* trad. par A. Tramesaygues el B. Pacaud, (Paris, 1965), p. 264.

[8] Philonenko, p. 80.

[9] Lettre à Spener (1793), citée par Saner, p. 2.

[10] Lettre à Kiesewetter (1793) citée par Werner Haensel, *Kants Lehre vom Widerstandsrecht: Ein Beitrag zur Systematik der Kantischen Rechtsphilosophie* (Berlin, 1926), p. 76. Haensel, cependant, cherche à démontrer que ni la position de Kant en ce qui concerne l'autorité de l'Etat ni sa façon de la présenter n'ont été déterminées par l'"Aufluss von Zensurrücksichten".

Nous sommes pleinement d'accord avec Haensel sur le premier point, mais en désaccord sur le deuxième.

[11] Lettre à Schiller (1974), citée par Saner, p. 77.

[12] Cf. *ibid.*: "... ausser diesen [Materialen] kaum noch, wenigstens in diesem Zeitpunkt, andere die grosse Lesewelt interessierende Artikel gibt. ..."

[13] Lettre à Lagarde (1794), citée par Saner, p. 76.

[14] *Literaturgeschichte des 18. Jahrhunderts* (Braunschweig, 1879), p. 46; cité par Haensel, p. 74.

[15] Pour une bibliographie sommaire de cette question du "Conflit de la censure", voir Georges Vlachos, *La Pensée politique de Kant* (Paris, 1962), p. 541, note 76.

[16] Suivant Friedländer, "Kant in seiner Stellung zur Politik", *Deutsche Rundschau*, 9 (1876), 241 et sqq.; cité par Haensel, pp. 74 et 77.

[17] 2e "Pièce annexe" au *Conflit des facultés*, trad. Gibelin, p. 143; citée en raccourci par Haensel, p. 77.

[18] Voir Saner, p. 3; dans la note qui intéresse la remarque en question (n° 18 à la p. 316), Saner poursuit en donnant le nombre de pages consacrées aux théories politiques de Kant dans les ouvrages suivants, respectivement: J.E. Erdmann, *Der Entwicklung der deutschen Spekulation seit Kant*, vol. I (Stuttgart, 1931) [8 sur 232 pages]; Paulsen [20 sur 420 pages]; Bruno Brauch, *Immanuel Kant* (Berlin/Leipzig, 1971) [13 sur 470 pages]; Ernst Cassirer, *Kants Leben und Lehre* (Berlin, 1918) [15 sur 460 pages]. La seule exception à cette règle, selon Saner, serait Karl Jaspers qui, pour la "première fois", accorderait aux idées politiques de Kant le "rang métaphysique" qui leur revient.

[19] Dans la liste de ceux à qui on a déjà attribué une telle paternité, Saner mentionne (note 17, p. 316) les noms de Machiavel, Hobbes, Locke, Hume, Grotius, Pufendorf, Thomasius, Leibniz, Wolff, Baumgarten, Vattel, Achenwall, Fichte, Humboldt, Gentz, Montesquieu, Rousseau, Voltaire, Condorcet, d'Argenson, Turgot, Mirabeau, de Sieyès, et "d'autres encore".

[20] Eric Weil, "Kant et le problème de la politique", dans *La Philosophie politique de Kant* (Paris, 1962), pp. 1,3.

[21] *Métaphysique des moeurs, première partie: Doctrine du droit*, trad. par A. Philonenko (Paris, 1971), p. 106. D'autres références à cette oeuvre seront signalées dans le texte. Nous n'avons pas cependant retenu la traduction du terme "*Befugnis*" par "faculté" adoptée par Philonenko: "Recht und Befugnis zu zwingen bedeuten also einerlei." — *Die Metaphysik der Sitten, Erster Theil: Anfangsgründe der Rechtslehre*, dans *Kants Werke: Akademie Textausgabe*, vol. VI (Berlin, 1968), p. 232.

[22] Voir à cet égard, Michel Villey, "Kant dans l'histoire du droit", dans *la Philosophie politique de Kant*, pp. 53-76.

[23] *Métaphysique des moeurs, deuxième partie: Doctrine de la vertu*, trad. par A. Philonenko (Paris, 1968), p. 52; cf. *Die Metaphysik der Sitten, Zweiter Theil: Metaphysische Anfangsgründe der Tugendlehre*, dans *Kants Werke*, VI, p. 383.

[24] *Rechtslehre*, p. 229; cf. *Doctrine du droit*, p. 103.

[25] *Rechtslehre*, p. 224.

[26] *Oeuvres complètes*, présentation par Michel Launay (Paris, 1971), II, p. 213.

[27] Cf. Livre I, ch. vi; *loc. cit.*, pp. 522-523.

[28] Livre III, ch. x, p. 554.

[29] Livre I, ch. i, p. 518.

[30] Comment traduire "*rechtmässig*"? Le *Dictionnaire de poche des langues française et allemande* de Langenscheidt (Berlin, 1940), 2e partie, p. 305, suggère les trois traductions suivantes: "légal ..." légitime ... ; juste".

[31] C'est moi qui souligne ces quatre petits mots, possiblement lourds de signification. Voir *infra*.

[32] *Rechtslehre*, pp. 305-306; cf. *Doctrine du droit*, pp. 187-188.

[33] *Ibid.*, p. 225; cf. *Doctrine du droit*, p. 99. Il s'agit d'une version améliorée de la formulation de 1785 (cf. *Grundlegung zur Metaphysik der Sitten*, dans *Kants Werke*, vol. IV, p. 421). C'est le principe fondamental de nos devoirs éthiques. Ces derniers sont soit de vertu, soit de droit. Pour le principe fondamental de chacune de ces catégories de devoir, cf. *Doctrine de la vertu*, p. 67 (*Tugendlehre*, p. 395) et *Doctrine du droit*, p. 105 (*Rechtslehre*, p. 225), respectivement.

[34] *Rechtslehre*, p. 231; cf. *Doctrine du droit*, pp. 105-106. H. Cohen, *Kants Begründung der Ethik*, insiste à juste titre que chez Kant la contrainte est "conditionnée" par la liberté. Haensel, notamment, (*op. cit.*) attribue aux "tendances socialistes" de Cohen, ce qu'il qualifie

de certaines erreurs d'interprétation de la pensée politique de Kant.

[35] *Ibid.*, pp. 232/106.

[36] Cf. *Contrat social,* I, i, pp. 522-524.

9. "The Romance of Real Life": Autobiography in Rousseau and William Godwin

To readers in late eighteenth-century England there were two Rousseaus, Rousseau the political and moral philosopher, author of the *Discourses,* the *Social Contract,* and *Emile,* and Rousseau the man and legend, author of *Julie,* the *Rêveries,* the *Dialogues,* and the *Confessions.*[1] Those who were seeking rational solutions to the problems of human nature and society found in the "political" Rousseau new but often "paradoxical" insights into man's individual and social existence; while those in increasing numbers who believed that reason could be at best but a feeble and unreliable guide found in the "autobiographical" Rousseau new and exciting prospects for the sympathetic reconciliation of individual man with nature, his fellow men, and himself. There were few in England after Rousseau's death who were better prepared to recognize the achievement of his political thought than the English Dissenters and their allies, the "eighteenth-century Commonwealthmen."[2] They shared with Rousseau a common inheritance of ideas from English political theorists of the seventeenth century and British epistemologists and moral philosophers of the eighteenth;[3] moreover, they were prepared by a century and a half of evolving political experience and religious thought to welcome the religion of the Savoyard Vicar, the political and moral philosophy of the citizen of Geneva, and the bourgeois utilitarianism of this son of a Swiss artisan.

They were also beginning to appreciate the confessional and autobiographical writings of the "Solitary Walker," for although they too had shared in the century's disposition to observe and analyze, to institutionalize the Spectator, and to provide rational or empirical proofs for everything, they were also coming increasingly to believe that merely intellectual knowledge was sterile and nihilistic without the support of religion and human feeling. English Dissenters and "Commonwealthmen" could easily share Rousseau's view of man as naturally good but socially depraved, and they could share his philanthropic passion to replace this fallen and divided world with a new Eden in which man would be once more in harmony with himself and with the physical and social world around him. Therefore it was appropriate for them in 1789 to celebrate the Revolution which Rousseau had anticipated in his *Considerations on the Government of Poland,* and which invoked

93

Rousseau as one of its tutelary spirits.[4] But if the Revolution seemed at first to confirm the ideas and the predictions of the "political" Rousseau, it soon seemed to take a different course, away from a paradise of social justice and harmony towards the unrestrained passions of the Terror and all the horrors and injustice of war. Events now seemed to vindicate the other Rousseau, the persecuted "Solitary Walker," and those who turned to his autobiographical writings found consolation in the possibility that Eden might still exist, not in the external world of society, politics, and power, but within.[5] When the Revolution destroyed its first, more moderate leaders, and therefore betrayed its English sympathizers, Rousseau, a different Rousseau, was still there to offer solace, and to speak to those who would carry the spiritual and intellectual impetus of English Dissent into a new movement, English Romanticism.

One of the most powerful early influences on the English Romantic poets, essayists, novelists, and historians was William Godwin.[6] Godwin had inherited the intellectual and cultural tradition of English Dissent when it was at its height, and he adapted it completely to the needs of the Revolutionary decade in England. The son of an East Anglian Calvinist minister, he had received a thorough training in eighteenth-century philosophy, science, and rational religion at Hoxton Dissenting Academy,[7] and although he had lost his clerical vocation by the late 1770s and his religious faith by the late 1780s, he retained into the 1790s all the essentials of the Dissenting experience, philosophy, and mythology. Like other Dissenters and "Commonwealthmen" he could appreciate Rousseau's radical analysis of society, government, and civilization because the Dissenting tradition had in a sense prepared him for it;[8] and when, in September 1791, he began to write his own reply to Burke's attack on the French Revolution and its English Dissenting sympathizers, he prepared himself by reading through the most important of Rousseau's political works.[9] Like the Dissenting thinkers of the previous generation, Godwin tried in his *Enquiry Concerning Political Justice* (1793) to provide a rational demonstration of virtue and philanthrophy, to deduce liberty, equality, and fraternity from essential human nature. Both his contemporaries and posterity judged Godwin to be the most thoroughgoing rationalist of his time, and it was a judgment he accepted willingly at first; but once he had completed *Political Justice* he began, like many of the young men he influenced in the middle years of the decade, to see how much his rational philosophy was a creature of his heart's desire, a rationalization of his own emotional and intellectual experience. Over the next three years he wrote a novel which demonstrated the emotional springs of social oppression and rebellion (*Things As They Are,* better known as *Caleb Williams,* 1794), published a condemnation of overly-zealous pursuit of rational reform (*Considerations,* 1795), and tried to revise *Political Justice* itself to give greater place to feeling in his philosophy of man and society (second edition 1796, third 1798). As he began to understand the sociology of his own knowledge and of the "English Jacobin" philosophy, Godwin began to believe that he had seen only the truth he wished to see, and that if he were to see the truth whole, he must know himself as a whole man. By 1796 he was beginning to appreciate and to explore the "sentimental" side of his nature, and soon after he fell in love with Mary Wollstonecraft, herself a student of the autobiographical Rousseau, he began to re-read *La Nouvelle Héloïse*.[10] Wollstonecraft's death in September 1797 left him alone, with an enhanced appreciation for the "Solitary Walker," and soon he was beginning to compose his own autobiographical reflections. By the end of the decade, when the Revolution had failed, when the Dissenting drive for reform had been stifled, when his wife was dead and he was once again alone, Godwin, like the young Romantics, had come to believe it was a terrible error to deny the "domestic affections" and to try to separate individual feeling from general considerations of "political justice". Many forces had helped to shape Godwin's new and Romantic sensibility, but he had discovered, like Rousseau from whom he drew, that "a vision of regenerated humanity could be presented only by a man who had just discovered it in his own heart."[11]

It is, then, highly appropriate that from 1789 to 1804 Godwin should have worked intermittently on a translation of Rousseau's *Confessions*.[12] He had always valued Rousseau's autobiographical writings as documents in the "science of mind," as evidence for the empirical epistemology and necessitarian metaphysics of his English Jacobin philosophy. Rousseau himself had intended that his *Confessions* be "une pièce de comparaison"[13] for future students of human nature. But it was during the period of self-examination and self-discovery which followed Godwin's revision of his philosophy in 1795-96, and which co-incided with his marriage to Mary Wollstonecraft and the aftermath of her death in 1797, that he came to concentrate fully on the autobiographical writings of Rousseau. It was during the same period that he composed the first and most important of his own autobiographical reflections. Only then, it seems, could he fully appreciate this aspect of Rousseau's achievement. However, once experience and the evolution of his "English Jacobin" philosophy had taught Godwin to value the sensibility of Rousseau, once he had made sense of his own sensibility, he turned again to his favourite task of using every form of moral and philosophical writing for the enlightenment of his fellow-man.

Godwin's interest in the "autobiographical" Rousseau falls into three main periods, then: up to 1795, 1795-1802, and after 1802. In the first of these periods, he used Rousseau's autobiographical works as material to substantiate his own philosophy; in the second he used them as a guide in his own struggle for self-awareness; and in the third he used them again, in conjunction with an enhanced sense of his own sensibility, to substantiate the revised version of his philosophy. Clearly, it is the second and central period which is of greatest interest and complexity.[14] Godwin was not just interested in coincidental factual parallels between his life and Rouseau's. Rather, it was the way in which Rousseau regarded his life, explored it, and described his feelings about it, which interested him as he searched for the roots of his own sensibility. For although Godwin's autobiographical MSS vary from mere outlines of dates and events to lyrical effusions in the manner of the *Rêveries,* all are concerned with tracing the origins of their author's mind and personality, and all illustrate the same pattern of experience: a childhood dominated by fancy and feeling, a youth consequently passed in solitude, and a resulting tendency in maturity towards a radical view of society and its institutions; the anti-social outlook enhances the imagined isolation, and the only compensations are a sense of conscious virtue, the pleasures of nature, the influence of women (society's underdogs), and a sublime and transcending idealism. Reading Rousseau helped Godwin to perceive this pattern in his own life.

Firstly, then, helped by Rousseau, Godwin began (in middle-age) to see that his mind too had always been dominated by imagination. This may have been because the early years of both were passed in a Calvinist cultural milieu, and perhaps that dark religious doctrine, against which both later rebelled,[15] fostered in both a counter-vailing vigour of fancy. Godwin was obviously writing of himself and very much under the influence of Rousseau, for example, when he had the hero of his novel *Fleetwood* (1805) describe how the solitude of his childhood led to a tendency to mental abstraction or "reverie" (Vol. I, p. 9). This same withdrawal from reality to an imagined world also led to a passionate interest in history, to a zealous identification with the republican heroes of classical antiquity. Rousseau found his heroes in Plutarch, Godwin his in Rollin, but for both the identification was an impassioned one; as Jean Starobinski puts it, "la distance historique n'est plus que distance intérieure . . . ."[16] Hence reverie joins history just as history joins fiction, in the form of romance; and although Rousseau and Godwin differed somewhat in their favourite youthful fictions (*Confessions, O.C.,* I, 171), in both the appeal was from the form of romance, a form that influenced their conception of the pattern of their own lives. Godwin was probably still guided by Rousseau, for example, when he described reading Rollin at the age of twelve: "No book ever occasioned me such sublime and transporting emotions. I now for the first time [a phrase that recurs again and again in the *Confessions*] perceived the glorious energies of which the species is capable among whom I was an individual."[17] The same emotions were experienced when Godwin read *Tom Jones* at sixteen,[18] and he concluded that "it was an essential part of my early character, that I read for feeling, and not for criticism. . . ."[19] Books, whether history or fiction, contained a world created by and for the imagination,[20] and kept the physical eye away from the imperfect world of everyday reality.

Secondly, Godwin, like Rousseau, saw the connection between imagination and solitude. Perhaps Rousseau, like Godwin, would have traced part of his tendency to mental abstraction and indulgence in imagination to the simple fact that he too had poor eye-sight;[21] but certainly both linked the tendency and the indulgence to a preference for solitude in later life.[22] The solitude of youth, however, is not that of embittered maturity; it is mingled with the pleasure born of fantasy, a fairy-tale element described by Ruffigny in Godwin's Romantic novel, *Fleetwood* (II, 43); and so the imagination creates a sense of the self's uniqueness, and this special sense persists into maturity. Only when there is a realization that one's self-consciousness is not understood by others does the sense of uniqueness become disturbing and dangerous. The punishment of Rousseau for supposedly breaking Gabrielle Lambercier's comb comes as a complete revelation to him, for it reveals that others cannot see him as he sees himself, and therefore creates the possibility of injustice (I, 20). Godwin came to a similar rude awakening when he received his first beating from his tutor at Norwich, and although he drew somewhat different conclusions, the point of departure for his recollection of the incident could easily have come from the *Confessions*: "It had never occurred to me as possible," Godwin writes, "that my person, which hitherto had been treated by most of my acquaintances . . . as something extraordinary and sacred, could suffer such ignominious violation. The idea had something in it as abrupt as a fall from heaven to earth" (Kegan Paul, I, 11; probably written February, 1800). Thenceforth all relations with others were shadowed by insecurity, for the immediate understanding of others could no longer be taken for granted, and had instead to be constantly striven for and frequently missed. Desiring to return to that blissful state of innocence in which one's sense of oneself was instantly communicated to others, both Godwin and Rousseau desperately worked to please, and consequently failed to do so. "Past doubt," Godwin writes, "if I were less solicitous for the kindness of others, I should have oftener obtained it." And later in the same passage of self-analysis he remarks, "Perhaps one of the sources of my love of admiration and fame has been my timidity and embarrassment. I am unfit to be alone in a crowd, in a circle of strangers, in an inn, almost in a shop" (Kegan Paul, I, 359; dated Sept. 1798). Once again Godwin's reflection seems to have been stimulated by a passage from the *Confessions,* although Rousseau was characteristically more explicit about making a virtue out of necessity: "Je me fis cynique et caustique par honte; j'affectai de mépriser la politesse que je ne savois pas pratiquer" (*Confessions, O.C.,* I, 368).

Thirdly, then, the sense of not belonging in polite society easily developed into a sense of not belonging to society in general, indeed, developed into a sense of persecution. And yet it was this otherness which created the basis for their critical view of social conventions and institutions. The feeling of isolation which stemmed from their early self-consciousness thus contributed greatly to the passion with which they conceived their philosophical work,[23] for these philosophies would demonstrate the benevolence and humanity of their authors to all the world. But once again, the fantasy foundered on experience. As a young man Godwin had already been marked out for the singularity of his religious views (Kegan Paul, I, 14, 16, 18-19), although not with the violence which Rousseau experienced at Môtiers; and as with Rousseau, each book he published for the service of truth and his fellow-man only seemed to raise the chorus of abuse and vilification against him. In fact, at the very time when, after the death of Mary Wollstonecraft, Godwin was becoming deeply interested in the "autobiographical" Rousseau, he was also becoming the *bête noire* of the Anti-Jacobin press. And what stung Godwin and Rousseau most was that they were most abused by erst-while friends. In Godwin's eyes it would be an irony only more likely to incline him to sympathy for Rousseau that his one published attempt to explain the conduct of himself and Mary Wollstonecraft (his *Memoir* of her, 1798) should have contributed most to wrecking his reputation. He learned the lesson that Rousseau did not learn, and therefore transformed his confessions into fictions.

Fourthly, then, Rousseau published his autobiography as such, whereas Godwin did not. Indeed, Godwin did little more in his autobiographical MSS than to sketch out the form Rousseau had helped him to perceive in his own life, and, influenced by Rousseau, to trace the main aspects of his personality to their origins in his early experience. Perhaps Godwin left his autobiography in fragments and in manuscript because when he wrote these fragments he was still in the midst of re-forming his philosophy, his sensibility, and his sense of himself. Once this reformation was complete, he was more interested in applying his new knowledge to his old vocation of serving truth and his fellow man through philosophy, history, and fiction, through, that is, conventional, even if seriously renovated, forms of public discourse, rather than through personal discourse immediately made public. Godwin's major autobiographical MSS were written during the period of his crisis of sensibility, from 1797 to 1801. After that his intellectual and emotional energies were poured into new work (*The Life of Chaucer*, 1803, and the novel *Fleetwood*, 1805) and a new family (he had married Mrs. Clairmont in December 1801 and she bore him a son in 1803). On one MS, begun apparently in February 1800, Godwin added in 1805: "I shall probably never complete it. My feelings on the subject are not what they were. I sat down with the intention of being nearly as explicit as Rousseau in the composition of his Confessions" (Kegan Paul, I, 13). But although he almost ceased to write autobiography,[24] Godwin's autobiographical impulse did not slacken, and both *The Life of Chaucer* and *Fleetwood* contain passages from his own life, subjected to a variety of transformations. The autobiographer became absorbed in the philosopher-as-artist. Godwin did complete his exploration of the meaning of his existence, and he did so according to the pattern revealed in Rousseau's autobiographical writings; but he preferred to assimilate his own confessions to a variety of "conventional" literary forms in history and fiction.

No doubt Godwin's utilitarian "English Jacobin" philosophy encouraged him to break out of the confessional syndrome which Rousseau could not escape. Moreover, Rousseau himself had once turned to fiction, as he explained it in the *Confessions,* to embody both personal and universal truths which neither philosophy nor autobiography could compass (I, 427, 431). Philosophical writing could be seen as demonstrating truth without referring to the personal feelings which in reality gave it birth. Autobiography on the other hand could seem to dwell on mere facts or personal feelings and make truth almost an idiosyncratic by-product of individual experience. But in the novel, life and general truth could be reconciled under the public conventions of art. Fiction could also elicit from the imagination acts of compensation, confession of the recompense as well as the expense of living for passion and truth. As he read Rousseau's account in the *Confessions* of how he had felt while writing *La Nouvelle Héloïse,* Godwin saw that he too had become a confessional novelist when he wrote *Caleb Williams* in 1793-4, that he too had turned from philosophy to fiction in order to purify his conscience, indulge unlived passions, idealize personal and social realities, and balance the particularity of experience against what would seem to be the universal truth of an accepted form of public, yet artistic and therefore personal, discourse.

Finally, then, although he did not publish — or even complete — his autobiography as such, all of Godwin's novels do embody a pattern similar to that found in the autobiographical writings of Rousseau. The protagonist struggles against a social and political world so corrupt that it construes benevolence as misanthropy and counts virtue a crime. At the same time that Godwin's heroes struggle, like Rousseau and his St. Preux, against "things as they are" (the original title of *Caleb Williams*), Godwin himself struggled to reconcile the pessimism born of experience with the optimism born of hope and demonstrated by reason. Godwin's philosophy, like Rousseau's, was born of his personal experience; and when the experience and the philosophy conflicted, when experience pointed to a despair that his philosophy could not recognize, Godwin, like Rousseau, was faced with a dilemma that was both personal and philosophical. Only in fiction constructed as romance could this dilemma be faced, for only there could the imagination reconcile philosophy and autobiography according to the demands of form. Godwin's personal problem, like Rousseau's, became an artistic one, that was resolved by recourse to "romantic" compensations — love, self-knowledge, conscious virtue, sympathetic nature, and an all-embracing idealism that transcends imperfect reality. Of course, in the autobiographical writings of Rousseau and in Godwin's novels despair is the only true evil, but like the enchantress it has its fascinations. Godwin's heroes and Rousseau's St. Preux become more or less anti-social and misanthropic because of their experience of society; Godwin's heroes and Rousseau himself come to see the social and political world as a prison, and the simile descends through Gothic fiction and the poetry of Byron, sanctioned by the last book of the *Confessions* in which Rousseau, ejected from his self-exile on the Ile de Saint-Pierre, pathetically requests the government of Berne to imprison him for life in order to free him from life (I, 647-8). But in both Rousseau and Godwin the triumph of hope is made more affecting by the passage through despair. The structure and furniture of romance, assimilated by Rousseau in his attempt to make sense of his own sensibility, and adapted by Godwin in his attempt to make art out of experience, were ready to be used by the Romantics themselves. The final optimism of Rousseau and Godwin is the optimism of Romantic sensibility rather than of Enlightenment or "English Jacobin" philosophy, because it is an optimism won through experience of feeling, of persistent self-reflection, and of self-awareness.

Godwin kept Rousseau before him over the entire period of his philosophical and sentimental development, but through the last three years of the 1790s and the first few years of the nineteenth century it was the autobiographical writings on which he concentrated, so that Rousseau must have seemed an almost living presence and could almost be included among his "principal oral instructors." Always a man apart, one who kept his distance, Godwin proceeded very much by a kind of detached sympathy which enabled him to remain within himself at the same time that he "felt" with or for another. This was the sympathy which, according to Rousseau, joined men together at the same time that it made them independent of one another. It was also the feeling which became the grand theme of the English Jacobin novel after 1794, and one of the dominant themes of nascent English Romanticism. Within Godwin's breast of course, sympathy did not vibrate as extravagantly as it did in Rousseau's, but worked on a more mental, though not an abstract or purely intellectual plane. Godwin allowed the extravagance to manifest itself in his confessional fiction, especially in *St. Leon* (1799), and this partly explains the novel's failure. In his own life sympathy worked in more covert ways. It could, for example, take the form of that excessive "ductility"[25] of which his friend Coleridge complained,[26] an androgynous willingness to receive the influence of others which was, again, a mark of Rousseau's character. Or it could take the more active if still largely covert form of open-mindedness. Godwin himself, in an autobiographical note, described his mind as "dependent on others for its determination to any particular point, working subtlely and actively on the suggestions it receives or collects."[27] His mind was like the aeolian harp of the Romantic poets, it worked not by passive influence, but by active sympathy.

It was this sympathizing power which was always ready to respond to the spirit of Rousseau, a sympathy for the man as much as for his ideas. For at whatever point in his life Godwin picked up the autobiographical writings of Rousseau he, like his friend Thomas Holcroft, would have been struck by similarities between himself and the "Citizen of Geneva." But there was more than just a surface similarity between the two; there was in the last three years of the 1790s a profound and complex "confrontation" between Godwin's sense of himself and his sense of the man Rousseau. In the years immediately after the death of Mary Wollstonecraft, Godwin, apparently for the first time, attempted to record both the origins and the essence of his own existence. It was a peculiarly Rousseauist endeavour, carried on no doubt with the necessitarian rigour of which Holcroft would have approved; but an examination of these scattered MSS shows that Rousseau had found, in the somewhat unlikely person of Charles Lamb's "Professor," the man who would vindicate in his reformed sense of himself the painful candour of Rousseau's own autobiographical method. More important, Rousseau helped Godwin to see life itself as a romance which contained a truth of form superior to the truths of both reason and historical and social reality. Always a philosopher of necessity, Godwin learned from Rousseau that only the imagination could perceive the romance of real life.

Gary Kelly
University of Alberta

Notes

1. The influence of the two Rousseaus has been studied in detail by Henri Roddier, *J.-J. Rousseau en Angleterre au XVIIIe siècle* (Paris, 1950) and Jacques Voisine, *J.-J. Rousseau en Angleterre à l'époque romantique* (Paris, 1956).
2. See Caroline Robbins, *The Eighteenth-Century Commonwealthman* (1959, rpt. New York, 1968), and Carl B. Cone, *The English Jacobins* (New York, 1968).
3. See Rousseau's *Confessions* in *Oeuvres complètes*, ed. Bernard Gagnebin and Marcel Raymond, I, 237, 409 n.1. All further references are to this edition. Rousseau received the influence of the English political theorists through Locke and Montesquieu; see John C. Hall, *Rousseau, An Introduction to his Political Philosophy* (London, 1973), p. 149.
4. For an interesting account of the relationship between Rousseau and the Revolutionary sensibility, see Gita May, *De Jean-Jacques Rousseau à Madame Roland. Essai sur la sensibilité préromantique et révolutionnaire* (Geneva, 1964). Madame Roland had probably been known to Godwin's wife, Mary Wollstonecraft. See also Joan McDonald, *Rousseau and the French Revolution 1762-1791* (London, 1965), ch.xii, "The Revolutionary Cult of Rousseau."

5 See Northrop Frye, "The Drunken Boat: The Revolutionary Element in Romanticism," in *Romanticism Reconsidered*, ed. Northrop Frye (New York and London, 1968). See also Marc Eigeldinger, *Jean-Jacques Rousseau et la réalité de l'imaginaire* (Neuchâtel, 1962).

6 For Godwin's influence on Wordsworth, see Leslie F. Chard, II, *Dissenting Republican: Wordsworth's Early Life and Thought in their Political Context* (The Hague and Paris, 1972), pp. 181-3; for Coleridge's attitude to "Godwinism" see Coleridge's *Lectures 1795 On Politics and Religion*, ed. Lewis Patton and Peter Mann (London and Princeton, 1971), introduction, pp. lxvii-lxxx; and for Godwin's influence on Shelley see Kenneth N. Cameron, *The Young Shelley* (London, 1951), pp. 61-70. For Godwin and Southey, see Geoffrey Carnall, *Robert Southey and His Age* (Oxford, 1960), pp. 25-8.

7 Charles Kegan Paul, *William Godwin: His Friends and Contemporaries*, 2 vols. (London, 1876, rpt. New York, 1970), I, 14-16. Henceforth referred to as Kegan Paul.

8 On the relationship between the writings of the "Commonwealthmen" and the young Romantics, see Zera S. Fink, "Wordsworth and The English Republican Tradition," *JEGP*, 47 (1948), 107-26; Chard, pp. 83-91. On Godwin and the Dissenting tradition see F.E.L. Priestley's edition of *Political Justice* (Toronto, 1946), III, 78-81, and the dissertation being prepared by Peter Marshall of Sussex University.

9 Godwin's MS Journal, in the Bodleian Library, Oxford. I am grateful to Lord Abinger for permission to use this material.

10 MS Journal, 28, 29 October 1796.

11 Ronald Grimsley, *Rousseau and the Religious Quest* (Oxford, 1968), p.x.

12 According to the MS Journal he undertook the translation for Robinson, his publisher, on December 1789, and worked at it 24-28 August 1792, the first half of August 1797, July and August 1801, and February, March, and April 1804.

13 Jean-Jacques Rousseau, *Oeuvres complètes*, I, p. 1149; see also the first pages of the *Confessions*.

14 According to the MS Journal Godwin composed the following autobiographical fragments between 1797 and 1802: (1) "Life," 19 pp. 1-5, 11 August 1797; (2) "My Own Life," approximately 20 pp., February-March 1800; (3) "Memoirs," 21 August 1800; (4) "Creed," 3 pp., 28 July 1801; (5) "Life," 5 pp., 29-30 July 1801; (6) "Life," 2 pp., 13 September 1802. These deal with Godwin's education and early sensibility, and all but (3) and (6) were preceded, accompanied, or followed by readings in either *Emile, La Nouvelle Héloïse*, the *Confessions*, or the *Rêveries*.

15 Godwin's "Creed," written 28 July 1801. Printed in Kegan Paul, I, 27-8. The "creed" is very close to Rousseau's *Lettre à Voltaire*, which Godwin read 16 August 1798 and 5 March 1801.

16 *Jean-Jacques Rousseau. La Transparence et l'obstacle* (1957), rev. Paris, 1971), p. 31.

17 MS, autobiographical fragment, dated 29 July 1831. A similar passage occurs in a fragment probably written July 1801. I am grateful to Lord Abinger for permission to use this material.

18 MS autobiographical fragments, undated, but probably written July 1801.

19 Ibid.

20 See Godwin's unpublished MS essay on "fictitious history," written in 1797, and discussed in my *The English Jacobin Novel, 1780-1805* (Oxford, 1976), ch.v.

21 MS autobiographical fragment dated 29 July 1831. Cf. *Confessions, O.C.* I, 37.

22 *Confessions, O.C.*, I, 41. Godwin would probably have translated this passage from Book II in 1797. The work went slowly and by 1801 he had only got to Book III.

23 The Second of the *Lettres à Malesherbes, O.C.*, I, 1135. MS autobiographical note, dated 10 October 1824.

24 Several autobiographical fragments were written after 1804, and may be found in the Abinger collection, but most of them repeat the major points of the earlier MSS. Godwin did print some autobiographical reflections in the *Essay on Sepulchres* (1809), and the *Thoughts on Man* (1831).

25 "Ductility is a leading feature of my mind," he wrote, in an undated autobiographical note. Kegan Paul, I, 13. On Rousseau's ductility see Ronald Grimsley, *Rousseau*.

26 Letter to Godwin, 23 June 1801, *Collected Letters of Samuel Taylor Coleridge*, (Oxford, 1956), II, 736. Coleridge was complaining of Godwin's "retractions" in the second edition of *Political Justice* (1796) and his reply to Parr (1801).

27 Undated. Abinger MSS.

10. Problèmes du monde hispanique au XVIIIe siècle: les Comuneros de Nouvelle-Grenade et l'oeuvre de Francisco Antonio Moreno y Escandón (1781)

L'Espagne déploie au XVIIIe siècle, sous les Bourbons, un certain effort de redressement à tous les points de vue après sa grande décadence du XVIIe siècle, l'extinction en 1700 de sa dynastie des Habsbourgs, et les traités d'Utrecht qui ont mis fin entre 1713 et 1715 à la guerre provoquée par la succession de Charles II. Malgré l'influence des nouvelles orientations intellectuelles et politiques marquant alors la civilisation occidentale, c'est avec une lenteur relative que le monde hispanique paraît évoluer durant la majeure partie de la période. L'exemple extérieur ne saurait-il avoir prise sur des structures sclérosées? En posant le problème à partir de ses bases économiques, on peut se demander si le succès du redressement bourbonien est vraiment possible à long terme. Il semblerait que non si nous en croyons l'analyse des Stein[1] qui nous démontraient, il y a plus d'une décennie, l'ampleur de la dépendance économique rendant la force de l'Espagne illusoire déjà même lors de la *Conquista* du XVIe siècle. Qu'en est-il donc de l'effort novateur qui nous intéresse ici en relation avec ses retombées américaines? L'Amérique espagnole doit attendre le règne de Charles III (1759-1788) pour qu'interviennent les principales transformations politico-administratives, militaires, commerciales. Le point culminant de la réforme bourbonienne serait à situer entre 1787 et 1792[2]. Mais l'année suivant la mort de Charles III sera lourde de conséquences pour l'Espagne et le Portugal puisqu'elle va signifier, avec l'irruption de la Révolution française, le début de la violente crise internationale devant disloquer pour de bon les vieux empires ibériques dans le premier quart du XIXe siècle. Pour mieux évaluer l'effort espagnol de réforme avant la secousse fatale venue de l'extérieur, nous allons jeter un coup d'oeil sur les déchirements de ce monde hispanique par le biais de l'exemple colombien. Que signifie, en cette époque de timide philosophie des Lumières et de despotisme éclairé bien prudent, la critique des Comuneros face aux activités de Francisco Antonio Moreno y Escandón?

La Nouvelle-Grenade, Colombie de l'époque coloniale, a vu commencer en 1778 l'inspection générale que dirige un envoyé de la Couronne espagnole,

Juan Francisco Gutiérrez de Piñeres. La pratique de l'inspection générale, venant examiner *in vivo* le fonctionnement de l'administration en territoire hispano-américain, remonte au XVIe siècle mais a été abandonnée au XVIIe siècle car l'autorité métropolitaine la jugeait peu efficace et génératrice de litiges interminables. Elle est néanmoins reprise par Charles III. Le monarque réformiste élargit cette *visita general* pour en faire l'instrument principal de sa politique américaine: non plus contrôle de routine, comme autrefois, mais prétexte à un remaniement des structures.[3] L'expérience initiale et exemplaire a été menée par José de Gálvez en Nouvelle-Espagne, le Mexique colonial, de 1765 à 1771. Devenu en 1776 ministre des Indes, c'est-à-dire responsable des colonies d'Amérique, Gálvez a entrepris d'étendre son expérience d'inspecteur à l'ensemble de l'Empire espagnol. En mars 1776, l'inspection générale du Pérou était confiée à José Antonio de Areche. En décembre suivant José García de León y Pizarro et Juan Francisco Gutiérrez de Piñeres se voyaient attribuer l'inspection de l'Audience de Quito, actuel Equateur, et de la Nouvelle-Grenade respectivement. Quels résultats peut-on remarquer? La mission d'Areche est liée dans une certaine mesure à la crise profonde qui va secouer de 1780 à 1783 la société péruvienne avec l'insurrection de Túpac Amaru et ses 80.000 ou 100.000 morts.[4] Plus au nord, la démarche prudente de León y Pizarro prévient les troubles graves que pouvait laisser craindre le passé turbulent de Quito. Gutiérrez de Piñeres, pour sa part, agit avec moins d'habileté. Sans avoir le tragique de la péruvienne ni le calme de l'équatorienne, l'expérience colombienne que nous invoquons à présent illustre bien les déchirements du monde hispanique.

Déterminé quant à l'essentiel par la montée de l'impôt depuis une vingtaine d'années, le soulèvement des Comuneros[5] connaît — schématiquement — ses origines immédiates dans les réformes fiscales de 1778 à 1780, ses grandes manifestations de mars à juin 1781, et sa liquidation jusqu'en 1783-84. La résistance ouverte et soutenue aux décisions de l'inspecteur général débute au centre-nord du Nouveau Royaume de Grenade avec une première manifestation, le 16 mars 1781, dans la dynamique petite ville d'El Socorro, de la province de Tunja. "Vive notre Roi d'Espagne!, hurle la foule en colère, mais nous n'admettons pas le nouvel impôt. . . .!" Ce cri traditionnel est vite repris de proche en proche. Les émeutes se multiplient rapidement. Comme par ailleurs la guerre fait rage entre l'Espagne et la Grande-Bretagne, le vice-roi est parti commander au port de Cartagena les troupes disponibles en prévision d'une éventuelle attaque britannique. Après l'échec humiliant d'une petite expédition punitive, la capitale sans défense qu'est devenue Santa Fe de Bogotá voit converger à ses portes des milices réunissant de 15.000 à 20.000 rebelles venus surtout des départements colombiens actuels de Boyacá, Santander et Santander del Norte. Les plénipotentiaires dépêchés par le gouvernement d'urgence, et parmi lesquels s'affirme l'archevêque Antonio Caballero y Góngora, doivent accepter le rejet de la nouvelle réglementation fiscale. C'est ce que veulent dire, le 8 juin, les Capitulations de Zipaquirá. Triomphe bien bref des insurgés, cependant. L'arrivée à Bogotá d'un premier contingent de 500 militaires au mois d'août, et l'expédition pacificatrice de l'archevêque joignant la campagne politique à la tournée pastorale, modifient le rapport de force pour amener la population à accepter docilement le retour des réformes fiscales. Cette fiscalité n'est d'ailleurs réintroduite qu'avec d'habiles modifications de détail par Caballero y Góngora, bientôt vice-roi de 1782 à 1789.

Ce n'est pas vraiment la lutte contre l'impôt qui représente, à notre avis, l'aspect révélateur du soulèvement colombien de 1781. Les protestations de l'éternel contribuable méritent bien sûr une analyse détaillée pour renseigner l'historien sur l'économie et la société du territoire en révolte. Pourtant l'étude de Phelan[6] en 1978, n'a pas voulu creuser la dimension économique du phénomène, et a refusé pareillement d'y rechercher la manifestation des antagonismes sociaux,[7] pour y voir plutôt une riposte du peuple à la subversion institutionnelle que constituerait la réforme bourbonienne, relativement centralisatrice après le contrôle plus lâche exercé par les Habsbourgs aux XVIe-XVIIe siècles.[8] Nous souscrivons à cette dernière approche qui nous paraît plus juste que celle, répandue naguère dans l'historiographie colombienne, faisant des Comuneros de Nouvelle-Grenade de véritables précurseurs de l'indépendance politique. La présente communication voudrait, dans la même optique, souligner deux points de la réaction face aux réformes de Charles III. L'une et l'autre critiques s'expriment dans le *pasquin* ou placard anonyme trouvé sur un mur de la capitale le 7 avril 1781, communiqué à la ville insurgée de Socorro, utilisé dorénavant comme principal instrument de la propagande rebelle, et que tous désignent comme "nuestra cédula", notre cédule ou billet. Que dit le texte? Cette longue harangue en 332 vers, adressée alternativement à l'inspecteur général et aux insurgés, dépeint en termes d'apocalypse la désolation du Nouveau Royaume qu'elle attribue à la scandaleuse réforme fiscale. A l'ombre de ce scandale majeur sont dénoncées aussi deux oeuvres d'iniquité que perpétrait naguère Francisco Antonio Moreno y Escandón. Il s'agit de l'inspection en 1777-78 des réductions indigènes de la province de Tunja, simple occasion de dépouiller le misérable troupeau indien, et de l'offensive sournoise frappant la sainte religion par le bouleversement des programmes d'étude.[9]

Comment interpréter pareilles attaques? Que le placard désigne à la vindicte populaire la figure de l'inspecteur général n'a rien pour nous surprendre. Le sort fait ici à Moreno y Escandón, par contre, ne laisse pas de nous étonner. Ce fonctionnaire, considéré comme l'un des hommes politiques les plus brillants qu'ait connus l'Amérique espagnole au XVIIIe siècle,[10] semble avoir été tout le contraire d'un prévaricateur. Quand il quitte sa Nouvelle-Grenade natale pour le Pérou, en mai 1781, il n'a même pas les moyens d'emmener immédiatement sa famille avec lui.[11] Sa mutation à l'Audience de Lima ne paraît pas être un exil déguisé, comme le prétend notre satire, mais plutôt une promotion que suivra, de 1789 à son décès en 1792, le poste de régent à l'Audience de Santiago du Chili.[12] Les grandes lignes de sa carrière à Bogotá expliquent quand même facilement les accusations portées contre lui par les Comuneros à la veille de son départ. Les multiples charges qu'il assume depuis une vingtaine d'années, notamment celle de Procureur du Roi, lui ont nécessairement valu quelques solides inimitiés. Pour comble de motif à l'impopularité en cette période de crise, il a l'estime de l'inspecteur général dont il paraît avoir été un conseiller officieux en matière de finances.[13] Pour résumer, à l'origine des accusations figure tout simplement le zèle réformiste qu'il a déployé pendant quelque deux décennies. Quant à la politique amérindienne et à la politique culturelle qu'on lui reproche maintenant, une brève évaluation s'impose.

Le problème des terres enlevées aux autochtones fait partie d'un vaste processus englobant toute la période coloniale, à commencer par la conquête. Dans son effort de compromis entre la sauvegarde du monde indigène et les exigences concrètes du développement territorial, la Couronne avait élaboré en effet, de 1595 à 1642 pour la Colombie coloniale, sa politique du *resguardo*. D'après une telle solution, les communautés amérindiennes recevaient du pouvoir royal l'usufruit de terres inaliénables réservées à leur usage exclusif, les *resguardos*. Une inspection menée en 1755-57 dans les provinces de Tunja et Vélez avait cependant révélé un déclin démographique notable des bénéficiaires autorisés pendant qu'augmentaient les autres groupes ethniques comme usurpateurs ou le plus souvent locataires de ces réserves.[14] De 1774 à 1778, Moreno y Escandón a fait ou dirigé comme Protecteur des Indiens une autre tournée d'inspection qui a constaté l'accentuation du phénomène dans les provinces de Santa Fe, Tunja et Girón. Chargé officiellement d'effectuer les regroupements administratifs nécessaires, il a voulu profiter de l'occasion pour rayer de la carte les villages indigènes dépeuplés où Métis et Blancs avaient pris la place des occupants légitimes. Ceci a impliqué des transferts de populations et la vente pour le Trésor des biens communautaires ainsi récupérés dans 18 villages indiens.[15]

Parallèlemement à la question des *resguardos,* et pour la même raison du déclin démographique des autochtones, avait également surgi le problème des salines laissées à l'exploitation des indigènes. A propos de celles de Zipaquirá, Tausa et Nemocón, les principales du vice-royaume, Moreno y Escandón a décidé de regrouper tous les bénéficiaires légitimes à Nemocón, dont l'exploitation a été placée sous la tutelle d'un administrateur gouvernemental.[16] En politique culturelle, d'autre part, les positions novatrices de Moreno y Escandón se sont affirmées après l'expulsion des Jésuites, en 1767, et devant la lente pénétration d'idées nouvelles dans le petit monde cultivé de la colonie. On sait l'impact que devait représenter au niveau de l'enseignement la mesure prise en février 1767 par Charles III d'expulser de tous ses territoires la Compagnie de Jésus. Celle-ci régissait en Nouvelle-Grenade, parmi plusieurs institutions, les collèges de Tunja et de Honda ainsi que surtout, à Santa Fe de Bogotá, le Colegio Máximo. Les Dominicains auraient voulu combler à leur profit un tel vide culturel en faisant prévaloir leur collège et leur université thomistes dans la capitale. Moreno y Escandón pourtant, chargé en 1774 d'élaborer un nouveau programme d'études, leur a manifesté son opposition en voulant supprimer dans la liste des cours la traditionnelle philosophie scolastique et introduire plutôt celles de Descartes, Newton, etc., projet que la Cour a d'ailleurs rejeté.[17]

Que viennent faire, dans la révolte contre l'impôt qu'est l'insurrection des Comuneros, ces critiques visant les initiatives du haut fonctionnaire que nous avons signalées? En ce qui concerne la politique amérindienne, la question est beaucoup trop vaste pour être disséquée ici. Peu importe, du reste. Que le triste sort des indigènes ait été invoqué par les promoteurs du soulèvement relève tout simplement de la stratégie insurrectionnelle: ne s'agissait-il pas de dresser contre les représentants de la réforme bourbonienne la plus vaste coalition possible de tous les mécontentements? Quant aux griefs religieux invoqués contre un partisan des Lumières, l'explication détaillée devrait bien sûr recourir à toute l'histoire culturelle du territoire. Sans entrer dans de vastes considérations philosophiques, bornons-nous à dire qu'une première donnée fort simple tient à l'identité probable de l'auteur anonyme du texte appelé *Nuestra Cédula*. Il s'agirait, selon toute vraisemblance, de Fray Ciriaco de Archila. Frère d'un chef rebelle de la région insurgée, cet homme est convers chez les Dominicains et exprimerait donc, tout naturellement, le point de vue de l'ordre prêcheur combattu par Moreno y Escandón. Plus profondément, l'hostilité des Comuneros à l'égard d'un porte-parole de la Philosophie des Lumières concorde avec ce que l'on remarque par ailleurs sur le caractère fondamentalement religieux, et même réactionnaire jusqu'à un certain point, des Comuneros durant le soulèvement colombien de 1781.

Nous voyons, en conclusion, que despotisme éclairé de même que Philosophie des Lumières ont pu signifier, dans le monde hispanique du XVIIIe siècle, de nouvelles sources de conflit. Non seulement conflit entre les exigences de la métropole et les répugnances financières de la colonie, mais conflit entre deux âges à l'intérieur d'une même civilisation. La portion américaine du monde hispanique resterait dans une large mesure à l'heure du XVIIe siècle tandis que sa portion européenne, l'Espagne "éclairée" qui a d'ailleurs ses disciples outre-atlantique, essaie lentement d'évoluer pour rejoindre les autres sociétés plus modernes du monde occidental.

Jean-Marie Loncol
Université de Montréal

Notes

1 Stanley J. and Barbara H. Stein, *The Colonial Heritage of Latin America. Essays on Economic Dependence in Perspective* (New York: Oxford University Press, 1970).
2 Jacques A. Barbier, "The Culmination of the Bourbon Reforms, 1787-1792", *The Hispanic American Historical Review*, 57 (1977), 51-68.
3 Cf. Guillermo Céspedes del Castillo, "La Visita como institución indiana", *Anuario de Estudios Americanos* (Sevilla), III (1946), 984-1025.
4 Parmi les monographies, soulignons au moins celle de Boleslao Lewin, *La Rebelión de Túpac Amaru y los orígenes de la emancipación americana* (Buenos Aires, 1957), et celle de Lillian E. Fisher, *The Last Inca Revolt, 1780-1783* (Norman, Okl., 1965).
5 Nous renvoyons pour l'essentiel à notre *Réforme et révolte dans la Colombie coloniale: le soulèvement des Comuneros (1781)* (Montréal: Les Presses de l'Univ. de Montréal, 1976).
6 John L. Phelan, *The People and the King: The Comunero Revolution in Colombia, 1781* (Madison: The Univ. of Wisconsin Press, 1978).
7 Cf. par exemple, à ce dernier point de vue, les dissensions que révèlent à l'Archivo Histórico Nacional (Bogotá) *Comuneros*, VI, ff. 164 et 67.
8 John L. Phelan, *The Kingdom of Quito in the Seventeenth Century: Bureaucratic Politics in the Spanish Empire* (Madison: The Univ. of Wisconsin Press, 1967).
9 "Salud señor Regente", *Testimonio del Segundo Quaderno* . . ., ff. 251v.-259, Archivo General de Indias, Sevilla (à l'avenir: A.G.I.), Santa Fe, leg. 663-A.
10 Mario Hernandez Sanchez-Barba, "La sociedad colonial americana en el siglo XVIII", *Historia social y económica de España y América* (Barcelona, 1958), IV. p. 359.

108

[11] Rapport d'Antonio Caballero y Góngora au Roi, 15 août 1782, A.G.I., Santa Fe, leg. 594.

[12] Roberto María Tisnes J., *Capítulos de Historia zipaquireña* (Bogotá, 1956), p. 80.

[13] Dépêche confidentielle no. 34 de Gutiérrez de Piñeres au ministre Gálvez, 31 mars 1778, A.G.I., Santa Fe, leg. 659.

[14] Les réductions indigènes de la province de Tunja comptaient 42.334 âmes en 1635-36 pour seulement 22.543 en 1755-57 d'après Magnus Morner, "Las comunidades de indigenas y la legislation segregacionista en el Nuero Reino de Granada", *Anuario Colombiano de Historia Social y de la Cultura*, 1 (1963), 74. A.G.I., Santa Fe, leg. 595.

[16] Flórez à Gálvez, 29 octobre 1778, A.G.I. Santa Fe, leg. 701.

[17] J. Manuel Marroquin, "Biografía de Don Francisco Antonio Moreno y Escandón", *Boletín de Historia y Antigüedades* (Bogotá), XXIII, No. 264 − 265 (septiembre y octubre de 1936), 538-539; Gabriel Porras Troconis, *Historia de la cultura en el Nuevo Reino de Granada* (Sevilla: E.E.H.A., 1952), pp. 424-436.

11. The Massachusetts Superior Court and the American Revolution: The Professionalization of a Judicial Elite, 1740-1775

The Massachusetts Superior Court was in a transitional position in 1750. It represented both the traditional western system of enforcing law and state policy by utilizing the power and prestige of the social elite and a more recent tendency to employ trained legal specialists. This tendency would be fully developed in the nineteenth and twentieth centuries. There was thus a latent contradiction between the concept of a judiciary drawn from the governing class that promoted and gave effect to government policy and one whose participation in the governing process was limited to interpreting the law and applying it to disputes that came before the court. This paper is concerned with the resolution of that dilemma.

Courts frequently played an important part in the politics of pre-industrial western societies, acting as intermediaries between the central power and those who exercised effective local authority.[1] For instance, the English tribunals which served as the jurisdictional model for the Superior Court of Massachusetts had functioned as an effective link between the two levels of political power in the late sixteenth and seventeenth centuries.[2] Well-born judges of assize communicated crown policy to local justices who had the primary responsibility for enforcing it, influenced the selection of men to fill those posts, and attempted to mediate county disputes that might hinder the effective administration of justice and government policy. They also provided legal guidance for the numerous lay judiciary, and exercised "the amalgam of coercion and authoritative advice which formed the basis of the judges' control over the rural bench" in the interests of the national government and those who composed it.[3] "The success of domestic policy . . . turned in practice on the existence of reliable media for conveying to provincial agencies the content and implication of relevant legislation and for ensuring that the programmes therein expressed were fully and persistently implemented. . . . This function was most regularly and successfully discharged by the judges of assize."[4]

Recent scholarship views the Massachusetts high court in a similar light. Kinvin Wroth argues that "the circuits of the Superior Court brought the authority and image of the central government directly to the counties," and "that the courts of Massachusetts were an effective agency of social control in all areas of human conduct on the local level." The high court not only impressed citizens but had the power to enforce its decisions through sheriffs, constables and coroners; those decisions were numerous and seizures of persons and property functioned as vivid reminders of the power of the judiciary and the government it represented. In addition, laws announced by the judges were "constraints upon individual conduct at the stage at which private activity is planned."[5] David Flaherty agrees, noting that judges "were prominent and powerful people both in their local communities and at the provincial level of politics," making especially "active and powerful agents of the central government" in an essentially orderly and well-behaved society.[6] Like its English predecessors, the Massachusetts bench took full advantage of the opportunity of delivering a charge to the grand jury to educate courtroom crowds on current political and social issues as well as the fundamentals of criminal law.[7]

In pre-Revolutionary Massachusetts, political leadership was exercised by wealthy, educated men from the leading families of seaboard mercantile communities.[8] Such men were the backbone of government, for they brought to their work as legislators the prestige derived from prominent families, wealth, culture and seats on the county judiciary.[9] The respect in which they were held was a crucial factor in giving effect to the policies of a provincial government which, lacking significant coercive resources, had to rely on the compliance of the local authorities and populace.[10] Such cooperation could best be secured by having the colony's laws and policies framed and implemented by men whose authority was readily accepted in the towns.[11]

The same is true of the Superior Court. While commercial towns did not produce the majority of its judges, the long-settled eastern counties did.[12] In addition, both legislative leaders and high court jurists came from old, socially prominent families whose standing was intimately related to the acquisition of a college education and a seat on the powerful county courts.[13] Nominations to the principal court of law were thus clearly related to the methods by which the colony was governed.

The mid-eighteenth century was an important period in the evolution of Massachusetts' judicial elite, for access to the Superior Court was increasingly restricted to men from families with several generations of judicial service, and nominees themselves were now generally drawn from those with extensive experience on other provincial tribunals. The growing tendency to appoint experienced judges to the highest court combines with the fact that most governors had some legal background to suggest a deliberate policy, or at least awareness of the importance, difficulty, and perhaps distinctiveness of the judicial function and the qualities needed to perform it well.[14]

Both reliance on members of the established political and social elite and the choice of men with legal expertise were evident in other contemporary western societies as well. In both England and France, major courts were no longer filled with randomly selected representatives of the governing class who held no regular judicial office, functioned sporadically as judges, and were not appointed on the basis of legal skill. Instead, the monarchies chose men to perform an identifiable adjudicatory function on a continuous basis, taking into account social origins, professional training, and experience in the application of legal principles.[15] For instance, eighteenth-century English judges were generally members of influential families and had attended university, trained at the Inns of Court, and practiced law.[16]

Colonial judges in Brazil, appointed by the Portuguese monarchy, were the sons of gentlemen, lawyers, officials or international merchants in the mother country. These jurists possessed university law degrees, had taught or practiced law, served in the bureaucracy or held office in the lower courts before joining the high court. Once in Brazil, they occupied an ambiguous position between the crown and the creole planter elite.[17] Like Spain, Portugal feared the weakening of royal control that might result from judges' forming close ties with powerful elements in colonial society.[18] The crown strove to prevent such links but failed to isolate its judges from their environment; they bought property, joined organizations, and befriended and married members of leading Brazilian families. However, the court "never became the creature of any one group in Brazilian society" and generally maintained "institutional autonomy in the face of pressure" from both sides. The home government came to realize the judges' value as a mediating force in conflicts with its often fractious colonists and as an interpreter of crown policies to those whose compliance was essential to their successful implementation.[19]

Because of their general lack of coercive resources, many governments in the early modern period still had to rely on social elites to secure the compliance of the populace in law enforcement. In England, France and Massachusetts, members of the indigenous "better sort" manned the highest courts, while in Brazil the crown employed prominent Portuguese with strong connections to important elements in creole society. Law could best be enforced when the visibly active agents combined the authority of the monarchy with that of the most influential and respected elements in society itself. In addition, governments in England, France and Portugal had long been aware that judges not only had to represent royal authority and the prestige of the ruling class, but to render effective decisions in often complex legal disputes. As a result, their criteria for judicial appointments had come to include the possession of a degree of legal expertise. Massachusetts, the youngest of the four societies, was clearly moving in that direction by the 1760s.

This increasing emphasis on the Superior Court's juridical function is closely related to the increase in complexity and sophistication that occurred in American law during the eighteenth century. The expansion of settlement and commerce brought more numerous and difficult cases before colonial courts, leading to greater reliance on the complex doctrines of the English common law and a search for lawyers and judges capable of interpreting and applying them successfully.

Superior Court judges heard a very wide range of private disputes, criminal charges and local conflicts as they travelled from county to county.[20] Their caseload was as heavy as it was varied, for by the time of the Revolution the Court was hearing more than ten times as many actions as it had sixty years earlier. Table 1 illustrates the dramatic increase.

		TABLE 1			
		CIVIL LITIGATION AND POPULATION, 1710-1773			
Year	No. Lawsuits	Pct. Increase	Population	Pct. Increase	Lawsuits Per Thousand
1710	83		62,390		1.33
1750	1013	1120.5	188,000	201.3	5.39
1773	1128	11.4	235,308ª	25.2	4.79
Overall Increase		1259.0		277.2	

ª1770 population.

Source of population figures: Jack P. Greene, ed., *Settlements to Society, 1584-1763* (New York, 1966), p. 238; figures derived from U.S. Bureau of Census, *Historical Statistics of the United States* (Washington, 1960), p.756.

Litigation was clearly increasing much faster than population. This does not mean that resorting to the judicial system was a new activity for Massachusetts colonists — far from it. They had inherited their English forebears' "national addiction to the adversary process" and developed their own multi-level legal system in the seventeenth century.[21] New England merchants had long been known for actively continuing the tradition of "the instinctive litigiousness of the Puritan Fathers."[22]

Nonetheless, by the middle of the eighteenth century even local contemporaries were complaining of the readiness with which their countrymen went to court. Harvard College President Edward Holyoke spoke in 1741 of their "want of Brotherly Love evident by their quarrelsome, litigious Disposition, and Lawsuits without numbers."[23] Fifteen years later the legislature remonstrated, not for the first time, that "trials of civil actions, upon appeals and reviews, have been unnecessarily multiplied, to the great charge [expense] and grievance of many of his majesty's subjects."[24]

Colonial Americans' growing addiction to the law also attracted the attention of English observers. Attorney General William DeGrey told Parliament, likely in the late 1760s, that American protests would show "how well these Americans are versed in the Crown [criminal] Law. I doubt whether they have been guilty of an overt act of treason; but I am sure they have come within an hair's breadth of it."[25] The more sympathetic Edmund Burke made the famous observation a few years later that in the colonies

all who read — and most do read — endeavor to obtain some smattering in that science [law]. I have been told by an eminent bookseller, that in no branch of his business, after tracts of popular devotion, were so many books as those of the law exported to the Plantations. The Colonists have now fallen into the way of printing them for their own use. . . . General Gage . . . states that all the people in his government [Massachusetts] are lawyers, or smatterers in law.[26]

Judge Peter Oliver also applied the concept to Massachusetts, writing that "the People of the Province seem to be born with litigious Constitutions . . . [a] general Foible."[27] Twenty-four years on the bench had given him ample opportunity to observe the phenomenon. Pauline Maier, no admirer of the British, agrees with DeGrey, Gage, Burke and Oliver, stating that "in Massachusetts . . . every man thought himself a lawyer."[28]

Their disputes sent colonists not only to justices of the peace and county courts of common pleas, but to the province's highest court of law, for payment of debts was often delayed and impatient creditors were not reluctant to use the legal system as a collection agency.[29] Because appeals to the Superior Court were inexpensive and access relatively frequent due to the circuit system, many suitors disappointed at the county level pursued their remedies in the high court.

Massachusetts provincials were contentious but not disorderly under normal circumstances. A disciplined people, they generally kept their conflicts within socially approved bounds, avoiding serious illegal activities in favor of such forums as town meetings and courts of law. (Even riotous group departures from the letter of the law were viewed by participants as measures to give effect to the proper meaning of that law.)[30] Unlike the situation in New York, serious criminal activity was rare throughout the provincial period, though increasing slightly toward its end.[31] People generally looked to the law and the courts for preservation of their rights, even against officialdom.

The Superior Court thus functioned as an important agency of social control, giving people an accessible forum in which to resolve their conflicts. Its judges possessed the experience in social, economic, political and legal affairs to deal effectively with a large and complex workload and direct the jury panels in deciding the small proportion of cases that came before them.

In exercising those functions, the bench received considerable assistance from a legal profession and body of law that were coming to resemble those of England more closely. Similar developments were under way in other colonies, for with the growing availability of British law books and trained lawyers,[32] "colonial common law courts were making a self-conscious effort to replicate the behaviour of their English counterparts." As a result, the eighteenth century was "the era of more sophisticated adoption of the common law."[33] In Massachusetts these developments "continued relentlessly . . . with a cumulative effect that was momentous."[34] Not only the Superior Court was affected, for by mid-century both procedural and substantive law in the courts of Middlesex County were coming "to approximate English models."[35] The transformation was still incomplete in 1775, for Massachusetts retained its traditional easy access to all courts and relatively simple, flexible procedures,[36] and some areas of law showed little evidence of Anglicization as yet; for instance, divorce law, applied by the governor and council rather than the Superior Court, still "diverged significantly from that of England."[37] The over-all trend, however, was not toward divergence but toward greater conformity. Massachusetts and its fellow colonies were moving in parallel fashion toward greater reliance on English law, thus requiring the presence of more technically sophisticated high courts.

It was this juridical aspect of the Superior Court's activities on which contemporaries commented before 1760. Whether they were unaware of the judges' governmental role, latently hostile to it, or took it for granted as a necessary and proper part of traditional society does not appear in the sources. The latter began with the statute of 1698 which prescribed the oath to be sworn by newly appointed jurists requiring them to "serve our sovereign lord the king and his people . . . and . . . do equal law and execution of right to all people, poor and rich."[38] Reverend Samuel Moody expressed much the same idea in 1741 when he wrote glowingly of judges[39]

> Lynd, Dudley, Remington and Saltonstall,
> With Sewall, meeting in the judgment Hall,
> Make up a learned, wise and faithful Set
> Of God-like judges by God's Counsel met.

Chief Justice Benjamin Lynde was embarrassed by the fulsome tribute; likely he would have preferred the comment of William Douglass, who described the Superior Court as "perhaps the most upright of any in our national Plantations and Colonies."[40] Not all mid-century colonists shared the favorable opinions of Moody and Douglass, however. On April 9, 1752 Judge Benjamin Lynde Jr. "found a small pox letter enclosing scabs and a plaster put into the window of kitchen, with design to infect us."[41] The governor offered a reward of £500 O.T. for information leading to the conviction of the "Evil-minded Person" responsible.[42] The incident was neither punished nor repeated.

The death of Chief Justice Stephen Sewall in September 1760 occasioned several observations on the qualities requisite in a successful judge. An anonymous newspaper correspondent praised the deceased for "the nicest sense of honour, and an uncommon delicacy of conscience . . . wisdom . . . singular fidelity . . . [and] great dignity."[43] Prominent clergyman Charles Chauncy complimented Sewall for his "quickness of apprehension and a capacity to look thoroughly into a subject."[44] His fellow cleric Jonathan Mayhew added the late judge's "great decorum in the court" and the "strict impartiality . . . [of] the knowing lawyer, and the upright judge."[45] The members of Massachusetts' highest court were expected to be men of integrity, impartiality, intelligence, learning and dignity.

The Revolutionary years from 1760 to 1774 brought about the erosion of the respect in which the Court was held. The bench was involved in a series of crises that aligned it with Lieutenant Governor Thomas Hutchinson, the royal customs service, the British army, and the ministry and Parliament in London. Its critics argued vociferously that, instead of upholding the constitution and the law, the judges appeared to abet their violators and to be willing to profit from such complicity. Fortunately the high court's acts elicited not only intemperate denunciations but articulate criticism that probed the nature of the proper relationship between judiciary, politics and society. Not surprisingly, radical spokesmen rejected the bench's traditional role as an elite instrument of government because of its potential for conservative political partiality. The judges' persistent adherence to that concept of their function caused the administration's critics to attempt to educate the public on the importance of having a judiciary that could maintain its integrity and impartiality by eschewing political controversy in favor of the adjudication of legal disputes. These arguments had sufficient effect by 1774 to cause the people to repudiate the Superior Court for a position that it had taken almost reflexively, thus demonstrating perhaps a greater awareness of recent changes in the judiciary's social role than the judges themselves possessed.[46]

Seventeenth-century English judges had suffered similar fates in revolutionary situations. Their emphasis on the legal rights of the crown in the 1630s soon proved unacceptable to Parliament. The latter was unwilling to believe that the law could favor its opponents and therefore blamed the men who applied it.[47] Although there was yet no formal doctrine of the separation of powers, there was "a growing feeling that some kind of demarcation could and should be made" between the judicial and political spheres.[48] It is not clear whether the post-Restoration judiciary had learned this lesson. On one hand, its important role as political intermediary between capital and provinces was taken over by other agencies, notably the lords lieutenants of the counties.[49] On the other hand, judges were highly visible partisans again in the 1680s, "securely identified . . . with James II and with the prerogative excesses which had brought on the Revolution." What seems most likely is that revulsion at the conduct of James's judicial henchmen like Chief Justices Jeffreys and Scroggs reinforced the trend toward defining a new and less partial role for the high courts. "Retribution [against such men] did not . . . usher in immediately a new era of independent and politically non-aligned judges,"[50] but it probably ensured that judicial behavior moved closer to that standard in the eighteenth century.[51]

Thus the mid- and late eighteenth century saw Massachusetts share in important legal trends that were also evident in other western societies. The higher judiciary was becoming more of a distinct and specialized profession with an increasingly high level of expertise in the complex techniques of interpreting and applying the law. This development was a necessary precondition to the emergence of a "formative era" in the early nineteenth century when American judges played a major role in creating and adapting institutions appropriate to a dynamic and expanding society.[52]

The appearance of a more technically skilled and less overtly politicized judiciary also suggests a society approaching "modernity." One feature of this widely discussed process was the change from the "convergence of roles" characteristic of the seventeenth century to a social system that "multiplies and separates them."[53] In the legal sphere, modernization has usually been seen in the organization of hierarchical court systems, greater use of rules "ascertainable from written sources by techniques that can be [rationally] learned and transmitted," selection of trained experts to operate the system, and a tendency to greater technical complexity. In short, "the task of finding law and applying it to concrete cases is differentiated in personnel and technique from other governmental functions."[54] Processes of this sort were going on in late colonial Massachusetts and other colonies as well. While the Bay Colony's judicial system was not quite the "strikingly modern" and "remarkably sophisticated" organization described by Hiller Zobel,[55] even less was it the rigid conservator of a static, Puritan-dominated social order characterized by William E. Nelson.[56]

The work and personnel of the Superior Court reflected significant processes of legal, social and political change which Massachusetts shared with other sectors of western society.[57] The Bay Colony, once quite separate and aloof, had become an integral part of a larger and modernizing culture.

Peter E. Russell
The University of Western Ontario

Notes

[1] Stuart B. Schwartz, *Sovereignty and Society in Colonial Brazil: The High Court of Bahia and its Judges, 1609-1751* (Berkeley, 1973). Mark A. Burkholder & D.S. Chandler, *From Impotence to Authority: The Spanish Crown and the American Audiencias, 1687-1808* (Columbia, Mo., 1977). Leon G. Campbell, "A Colonial Establishment: Creole Domination of the Audiencia of Lima During the Late Eighteenth Century," *Hispanic American Historical Review*, 52 (1972), 1-25. Franklin L. Ford, *Robe and Sword: The Regrouping of the French Aristocracy After Louis XIV* (Cambridge, Mass., 1953, rpt. New York, 1965).

[2] J.S. Cockburn, *A History of English Assizes, 1558-1714* (Cambridge, Eng., 1972), especially the Introduction and ch. 8 & 9.

[3] *Ibid.*, ch. 8; quotation from p. 171.

[4] *Ibid.*, 179. W.J. Jones, *Politics and the Bench: The Judges and the Origins of the English Civil War* (London, 1971), pp. 18-19.

[5] L. Kinvin Wroth, "Possible Kingdoms: The New England Town From the Perspective of Legal History," *American Journal of Legal History*, 15 (1971), 320-322. Hereafter cited as *AJLH*.

[6] David H. Flaherty, "Review of William E. Nelson, Americanization of the Common Law," *University of Toronto Law Journal*, 26 (1976), 111-112.

[7] Cockburn, pp. 67-69. John D. Cushing, "The Judiciary and Public Opinion in Revolutionary Massachusetts," in George Athan Billias, ed., *Law and Authority in Colonial America* (Barre, Mass., 1965), pp. 168-186.

[8] Robert M. Zemsky, "Power, Influence and Status: Leadership Patterns in the Massachusetts Assembly, 1740-1755," *William & Mary Quarterly*, 3rd Ser., 26 (1969), 502-520. To the same effect are Edward M. Cook, *Fathers of the Towns: Leadership and Community Structure in Eighteenth-Century New England* (Baltimore, 1976) and Richard D. Brown, *Revolutionary Politics in Massachusetts: The Boston Committee of Correspondence and the Towns, 1772-1774* (Cambridge, Mass., 1970, rpt. New York, 1976).

[9] John J. Waters, *The Otis Family in Provincial and Revolutionary Massachusetts* (New York, 1975), pp. viii-ix. Waters & John A. Schutz, "Patterns of Massachusetts Colonial Politics," *WMQ.* 3d ser., 24 (1967), 567. John M. Murrin, "Anglicizing an American Colony: The Transformation of Provincial Massachusetts" (unpub. Ph.D. diss., Yale Univ., 1966), pp. 265-266.

[10] David H. Flaherty, "Law and the Enforcement of Morals in Early America," *Perspectives in American History*, 5 (1971), 201-253. See also Brown, pp. 1-4 for a briefer discussion.

[11] On a larger scale, the British government recognized the value of acting through locally prominent men in New England, for nearly half of the royally appointed governors there were native to their provinces. (In other mainland royal colonies the figure was one in eight or ten.) Such men were almost always members of leading families, Harvard graduates and possessed of intellectual capacity and interests — Leonard W. Labaree, "The Royal Governors of New England," Colonial Society of Massachusetts, *Publications*, 32 (*Transactions*, 1933-1937), 120-131.

[12] The careers of all Superior Court judges appointed between 1692 and 1774 are analyzed in Peter E. Russell, "His Majesty's Judges: The Superior Court of Massachusetts, 1750-1774" (unpub. Ph.D. diss., Univ. of Michigan, 1980), ch. 2 & Biographical Appendix.

[13] *Ibid.* John M. Murrin, "The Legal Transformation: The Bench and Bar of Eighteenth-Century Massachusetts," in Stanley N. Katz, ed., *Colonial America: Essays in Politics and Social Development* (Boston, 1971), pp. 423-425. Charles Robert McKirdy, "Lawyers in Crisis: The Massachusetts Legal Profession, 1760-1790" (unpub. Ph.D. diss., Northwestern Univ., 1969), pp. 39-40.

[14] Russell, pp. 36, 39.

[15] John P. Dawson, *History of Lay Judges* (Cambridge, Mass., 1960), pp. 1-4, 69-83, 129-136, 274-280, 293-299, and *Oracles of the Law* (Ann Arbor, 1968), pp. 3-12, 29-49, 306-314, 339-341, 358-362.

[16] Peter E. Russell, "A Profile of the English Superior Court Judiciary, 1714-1775" (unpub. paper, Univ. of Michigan, 1974).

[17] Schwartz, pp. 283-313.

[18] On Spanish America, see Burkolder & Chandler, *From Impotence to Authority*, and Campbell, "A Colonial Establishment."

[19] Schwartz, pp. 78, 171-190, 265-267, 280-281, 313-343; quoted portion at 184.

[20] The analysis that follows is based on the Superior Court Record Books for 1710, 1730, 1750 & 1773 in the office of the Clerk of the Supreme Judicial Court, Suffolk County Court House, Boston, and on the Minute Books for 1750, 1757, 1763, 1768 & 1773.

[21] Hiller B. Zobel, "The Pompeii of Paper," *Boston Bar Journal*, 22, 7 (1978), 20. Hereafter cited as *BBJ*.

[22] Bernard Bailyn, *The New England Merchants in the Seventeenth Century* (New York, 1964), p. 165.

[23] Edward Holyoke, *The Duty of Ministers* (Boston, 1741).

[24] Preamble of an Act for Further Regulating the Course of Judicial Proceedings, Province Laws, 1756-1757, ch. 28, in Ellis Ames et al., eds., *Acts and Resolves of the Province of Massachusetts Bay, 1692-1780*, 21 vols. (Boston, 1869-1922).

[25] Quoted by George G. Wolkins in "Daniel Malcom and Writs of Assistance," Mass. Historical Society, *Proceedings*, 58 (1924-1925), 22. Society hereafter cited as MHS.

[26] Quoted in Alan McKinley Smith, "Virginia Lawyers, 1680-1776: The Birth of an American Profession" (unpub. Ph.D. diss., Johns Hopkins Univ., 1967), pp. 59-60.

[27] *Origin and Progress of the American Rebellion*, eds. Douglass Adair & John A. Schutz (Stanford, 1975), p. 27.

[28] *From Resistance to Revolution: Colonial Radicals and the Development of American Opposition to Britain, 1765-1776* (New York, 1974), p. 133.

[29] Robert J. Brink, "Boston's Great Anthropological Documents," *BBJ*, 22, 7 (1978), 12.

[30] Pauline Maier, "Popular Uprisings and Civil Authority in Eighteenth-Century America," *WMQ*, 3d ser., 27 (1970), 3-35. John Phillip Reid, "In a Defensive Rage: The Uses of the Mob, the Justification in Law, and the Coming of the American Revolution," *New York University Law Review*, 49 (1974), 1043-1091.

[31] Douglas Greenberg, *Crime and Law Enforcement in the Colony of New York, 1691-1776* (Ithaca, 1974). David H. Flaherty, "Crime and Social Control in Provincial Massachusetts," paper read at the Annual Meeting of the Organization of American Historians, April 1975.

[32] Richard B. Morris, *Studies in the History of American Law* (2d ed., 1958, rpt. New York, 1974) and "Legalism Versus Revolutionary Doctrine in New England," *New England Quarterly*, 4 (1931), 195-215.

[33] Stanley N. Katz, "The Politics of Law in America: Controversies Over Chancery Courts and Equity Law in the Eighteenth Century," *Perspectives in American History*, 5 (1971), 263, 272.

[34] Murrin, "Anglicizing an American Colony," 151.

[35] Hendrik Hartog, "The Public Law of a County Court: Judicial Government in Eighteenth-Century Massachusetts," *AJLH*, 20 (1976), 297-298, 302.

[36] G.B. Warden, "Inequality and Instability in Eighteenth-Century Boston: A Reappraisal," *Journal of Interdisciplinary History*, 6 (1976), 615.

[37] Nancy F. Cott, "Divorce and the Changing Status of Women in Eighteenth-Century Massachusetts," *WMQ*, 3d ser., 33 (1976), 612.

[38] Province Laws, 1698, ch. 23.

[39] Quoted in The Saltonstall Papers, 1607-1815, ed. Robert E. Moody, MHS, *Collections*, 80 (1972), 79.

[40] Benjamin Lynde Sr., *Diary, 1690-1742*, ed. Fitch E. Oliver (Boston, 1880), pp. 111-112.

William Douglass, *Summary, Historical and Political . . . of the British Settlements* (Boston, 1749, rpt. New York, 1972), I, 517-518.
[41] Benjamin Lynde Jr., *Diary, 1721-1780,* ed. Fitch E. Oliver (Boston, 1880), p. 175.
[42] *Proclamation, May 28, 1752* (Boston, 1752).
[43] *Boston Evening Post,* Sept. 22, 1760.
[44] Quoted in John Eliot, *Biographical Dictionary* (Boston & Salem, 1809), p. 420.
[45] *Discourse Occasioned by the Death of the Honourable Stephen Sewall* (Boston, 1760). See to the same effect Judge Addington Davenport's obituary in *Boston Evening Post,* Apr. 19, 1736.
[46] The extensive sources on which this paragraph is based are analyzed in Russell, "His Majesty's Judges," ch. 4.
[47] Jones, pp. 13, 20-21, 129-129, 137-139, 147-148.
[48] *Ibid.,* pp. 16-17.
[49] Cockburn, pp. 184-187.
[50] *Ibid.,* p. 259.
[51] *Ibid.,* pp. 184-187.
[52] Nineteenth-century developments are ably discussed in Roscoe Pound, *The Formative Era of American Law* (Boston, 1938); James Willard Hurst, *The Growth of American Law: The Law Makers* (Boston, 1950), *Law and the Conditions of Freedom in the Nineteenth-Century United States* (Madison, Wis., 1956), *Law and Social Process in United States History* (Ann Arbor, 1960); Leonard W. Levy, *The Law of the Commonwealth and Chief Justice Shaw: The Evolution of American Law, 1830-1860* (Cambridge, Mass., 1957); Charles M. Haar, ed., *The Golden Age of American Law* (New York, 1965); Stanley I. Kutler, *Privilege and Creative Destruction: The Charles River Bridge Case* (Philadelphia, 1971); Morton J. Horwitz, *The Transformation of American Law, 1780-1860* (Cambridge, Mass., 1977).
[53] Thomas Bender, *Community and Social Change in America* (New Brunswick, N.J., 1978), p. 61.
[54] Marc Galanter, "The Modernization of Law," in Myron Weiner, ed., *Modernization: The Dynamics of Growth* (New York, 1966), pp. 155-156.
[55] Hiller B. Zobel, "Law Under Pressure: Boston, 1769-1771," in Billias, ed., pp. 187-188.
[56] William E. Nelson, *Americanization of the Common Law: The Impact of Legal Change on Massachusetts Society, 1760-1830* (Cambridge, Mass., 1975), pp. 16-63.
[57] Recent literature stressing the importance of transatlantic links in the eighteenth century includes R.R. Palmer, *The Age of the Democratic Revolution: A Political History of Europe and America, 1760-1800* (Princeton, 1959); Bernard Bailyn, *The Ideological Origins of the American Revolution* (Cambridge, Mass., 1967); John Clive & Bernard Bailyn, "England's Cultural Provinces: Scotland and America," *WMQ,* 3rd ser., 11 (1954), 200-213; Michael Kraus, *The Atlantic Civilization: Eighteenth-Century Origins* (Ithaca, 1949); Carl Bridenbaugh, *Mitre and Sceptre: Transatlantic Faiths, Ideas, Personalities and Politics, 1689-1775* (New York, 1962); I.K. Steele, *Guerrillas and Grenadiers: The Struggle for Canada, 1689-1760* (Toronto, 1969); Louis Gottschalk & Donald Lach, *Toward the French Revolution: Europe and America in the Eighteenth-Century World* (New York, 1973). The field is surveyed by Jack P. Greene, I.K. Steele and others in the *Journal of Imperial and Commonwealth History,* 8 (1980).

12. The Competition for American Seamen during the War of 1739-1748

In June of 1739 the British Privy Council authorized the issuing of letters of marque and reprisal against the property of the King of Spain and all of his subjects.[1] This action allowed Britons to fit out privateers and legally capture the commerce of the Spanish Empire. Colonial reaction to this aggressive change in policy was exuberant. Newspapers from Boston to the West Indies reported the colonists' "universal Joy" at being able to prey upon Spanish shipping.[2] When the conflict expanded in 1744 to include France, the American response remained enthusiastic. Press reports testified to the strength of the "privateering Spirit" in colonial seaports.[3] To ensure that the colonies fit out privateers, imperial administrators instructed the American governors to encourage such ventures in their colonies "as effectually as possible."[4] Throughout the War of 1739-1748, the colonial chief executives complied with those instructions. They published proclamations to encourage privateers, aided in lowering customs duties on prize goods, and, of course, issued hundreds of letters of marque and reprisal.

As a result of these policies, scores of British colonial privateers plied the Atlantic in quest of Spanish and French merchantmen. These predators succeeded in capturing hundreds of prizes and greatly distressed Spanish and French shipping.[5] In this way private men-of-war augmented Britain's power at sea. At the same time, however, privateering ventures helped to cause serious problems for colonial governors. The lure of rich prizes attracted thousands of seamen to sail on private men-of-war. This drain on colonial mariners coincided with increased manpower requirements of the Royal Navy. Moreover, most of the British colonies in North America and the Caribbean began fitting out vessels to patrol their coasts. To make matters worse, British and American merchantmen began carrying larger crews in an effort to defend themselves against enemy predators. All of these avenues of maritime endeavour created competition for colonial seamen which greatly hindered the governors' abilities to man colonial coast guard vessels and assist Royal Navy commanders in filling their complements for the king's ships stationed in America. Thus, the maritime prize war created serious administrative difficulties for colonial and naval officials.

The imperial hostilities increased the demand for able seamen and created a shortage of mariners in British colonial ports. The ships of force of the navy, coast guard, and private men-of-war all required large crews to capture enemy merchantmen and escort them to friendly ports. Vessels employed as warships carried many more men than comparable craft engaged in peacetime commerce.[6] The manpower requirements of the navy alone increased by more than 700 percent over the peacetime decade of the 1730s. Only about 7000 or 8000 officers and men comprised the Royal Navy's establishment during the quiet years of the 1730s. By contrast, at the peak of its strength in 1746 and 1747, between 50,000 and 60,000 men sailed on the king's ships.[7] British colonial privateers also attracted large numbers of sailors. During King George's War colonial private men-of-war provided more than 29,000 berths and averaged 4700 berths annually after 1744.[8]

The shortage of seamen affected all areas of maritime enterprise. Numerous letters from a Charles Town rice merchant, Robert Pringle, reveal that the most important port in the southern colonies experienced difficulties manning its merchant vessels.[9] The seabourne commerce of other colonies as well as the mother country also suffered.[10] The sailors' belief that they could earn greater financial rewards on privateers aggravated the shortage of merchant mariners. Advertisements frequently appeared in the colonial press offering rewards for the return of men who had jumped ship to join privateers;[11] other advertisements sought to recruit sailors for private men-of-war.

Contemporaries (and subsequent historians) believed that countless sailors deserted from the merchant marine, Royal Navy, and the coast guard to join privateering cruises, but despite these defections private men-of-war not infrequently experienced problems in manning their vessels. A 1739 press report from Jamaica indicated that island privateers shared this shortage. "There are only two Privateers gone out . . . tho' several others would be fitted out if they could get Hands, who are so extream scarce."[12] In 1741 the Newport privateer *Revenge* left her home port short-handed and spent thirty-six days in New York trying to recruit men. While the *Revenge* was in Manhattan the commander of the New York private man-of-war *Humming Bird* resigned himself to the fact that there was an insufficient number of mariners to fill his requirements at home, and he headed, therefore, to Philadelphia.[13] Other privateers were forced to search for crews beyond their home port. Two London predators, the *Garland* and the *London,* sought hands in Ireland.[14] The owners of the New York privateer *Prince Charles* placed a recruiting advertisement in a Philadelphia newspaper; so did the owners of the Norfolk, Virginia cruiser *Raleigh.* Even with this expanded area from which to enlist mariners, the *Raleigh* had to delay its departure for three months.[15]

Although merchant vessels and privateers often faced a shortage of seamen, the Royal Navy and colonial coast guard vessels suffered more serious manpower problems. The existing evidence clearly reveals that eighteenth-century sailors preferred to serve on merchantmen or privateers rather than in the navy or the coast guard. Throughout the war, naval commanders' advertisements placed in the colonial press to recover deserters often mentioned that the absent mariners had been enticed by the higher wages paid by the merchant marine.[16] Massachusetts Governor William Shirley informed his colony's legislature in 1742 of Admiral Vernon's complaint "that the Masters of Merchant Ships . . . in this Province, make a Practice of enticing away their [ie, the navy's] Seamen."[17] Shirley called upon the legislators to enact a new law to curb merchant vessels and privateers from employing naval deserters, but he was unsuccessful.[18]

Deserters plagued the navy in other colonies as well. Captain Peter Warren informed the Admiralty that the king's ships in New York had great difficulty keeping their men: "It is impossible . . . to keep any of them that have an inclination to leave their ships, to which they are greatly prompted by the success of the privateers."[19] Naval vessels in Philadelphia encountered similar problems. Replying to a request for wharf space from Captain Masterson of HMS *Hector,* Pennsylvania Council President Anthony Palmer expressed his fears that the *Hector's* crew would probably jump ship *en masse:*

> The danger mostly apprehended by the Council is, that you will not be able to keep your Sailors; this Port is on this account one of the worst in the World, as their is an abundance of bad People to conceal & assist Runaways. Captn. Ballet [commander of HM Sloop *Otter*] experienc'd this & found it a hard matter to get Men.[20]

Royal Navy commanders stationed in Charles Town were also often forced to place advertisements in the *South Carolina Gazette* offering rewards for the return of absent mariners.[21] Naval officers in the West Indies seemed to face a never ending struggle to prevent their men from jumping ship to sign on privateers or merchant vessels.[22]

The operations of the colonies' guard vessels were also hampered by manpower shortages. The Massachusetts House of Representatives anticipated a lack of volunteers to serve on the province's new guard vessel in 1740 and, therefore, authorized the governor and council to press a sufficient number of sailors to man the craft.[23] Expecting an exodus of mariners during the preparations for the expedition against the French fortress at Louisbourg, the Bay Colony's legislature enacted a statute "to prevent seamen removing into distant parts to avoid their being impressed into His Majesty's service."[24] A year later the commander of the *Massachusetts Frigate* petitioned Governor Shirley "setting forth the great Difficulty he meets with in manning the said Ship."[25] Other Massachusetts vessels suffered from the same problem. "The Commander of the *Boston-Packet* is inlisting Seamen . . . but it has been represented to me by the Committee of War, that it is not probable that many Men will inlist upon our Pay, when they can have much greater Wages in the Merchant Service." Governor Shirley did not think the colony would obtain a sufficient number of mariners "without some extraordinary Methods."[26]

The Rhode Island coast guard experienced similar difficulties. In order to obtain full complements for the sloop *Tartar,* the legislature was forced to press sailors.[27] An inquiry into the capture of a French vessel off Point Judith, Rhode Island in 1748 highlighted the problem of the *Tartar.* The sloop's commander had committed a serious breach of discipline by sailing without orders. In the subsequent investigation of Captain James Holmes's conduct, the coast guard's lack of popularity was evident:

It was resolved by the committee [of inquiry], that his [Holmes's] going out without orders . . . from the Governor, or the Deputy Governor, was a great misdemeanor; but it appeared to the committee, that it was without any bad design, and principally to keep his men on board from deserting their service.[28]

It is ironic that the Narragansett Colony had such difficulty attracting and keeping sailors in its employ. Moreover, it is surprising that the Rhode Island government issued press warrants. Throughout King George's War — especially after the French entered the conflict — Rhode Island was attacked as a haven for seamen who wished to avoid impressment into the navy. William Shirley, the chief protagonist in this assault on the Newport government, was particularly strident in criticizing Rhode Island's contribution to the Louisbourg expedition. In June of 1745 he wrote Rhode Island Governor Gideon Wanton and excoriated him for inadequate efforts to supply mariners for the incursion. Shirley went on to describe how Massachusetts's attempts to secure seamen were doomed to failure because of Rhode Island's ineffective recruiting policies:

I find my endeavors will be to little purpose, whilst all mariners subject to be impressed here into His Majesty's Service, fly to Rhode Island to avoid it (as indeed has been long the practice) and are there sheltered and encouraged, where (I am credibly informed) there are at this time many hundreds of foreign Seamen daily walking the streets of Newport, whilst scarce one is to be found in Boston.

After leveling this charge, Shirley stated that the King had authorized him to supply Commodore Warren with men and shipping. The Massachusetts governor then instructed Wanton, in effect, to put his colony in order and provide the necessary sailors:

You will exert yourselves in the most effectual manner, for furnishing Mr. Warren with Seamen, which I am satisfied it is in the power of your Government to do, either by offering the same bounty to volunties as this government has done [i.e., £3 (Mass.)], or by impressing; and that you will not permit your Colony to be an Asylum to all mariners coming into New England, for screening themselves from His Majesty's Service.[29]

Shirley continued to level similar criticisms throughout the war. He also cast aspersions on the willingness of New York and Pennyslvania to supply manpower for the navy. In a long letter to the Duke of Newcastle, Shirley revealed that his attempts to secure seamen for the king's service had caused Massachusetts serious economic problems. Forcing men into the navy had driven hundreds of mariners out of the province and into the neighboring colonies. This exodus had caused the Bay Colony's trade to suffer while the commerce of Rhode Island, New York, and Pennsylvania expanded. Moreover, riots had erupted in Boston, murders had been committed during a confrontation between sailors and press gangs, and the colony's council had been intimidated from issuing additional press warrants. Shirley refrained from suggesting a solution to this problem, but he stated emphatically that he would be unable to raise any more men for the navy "unless some method is at the same time found to oblige the other Colonies, especially the neighbouring ones of Rhode Island, New York and Pennsilvania to furnish their proportion of Mariners for the King's Ships."[30]

The attacks on Rhode Island's willingness to send sailors and troops to Cape Breton and for the subsequent assault on Canada prompted numerous letters from Newport to Richard Partridge, the colony's London agent. This correspondence urged Partridge to defend the colony's actions by insisting that Rhode Island was only a small province which had provided all the men it could spare. These letters illustrate clearly how privateering created difficulties: "The Colony was then exhausted of Men to an uncommon degree," Governor Wanton explained to Partridge, "not twenty had return'd from the West India Expedition [the unsuccessful 1741 attempt on Cartagena], We had lost many more in the Privateers and had then ten or twelve sail on a Cruise so that it was morally impossible to raise such a Number of Volunteers here at that Time as was desired."[31]

It is difficult to evaluate this dispute between the New England governments. Rhode Island had offered large bounties to attract recruits, and the colony was not adverse to impressment.[32] It is possible, therefore, that much of what the Rhode Islanders said was true — that the Narragansett Colony did, indeed, face a shortage of sailors. It is, of course, naïve to accept all of their claims at face value; after all, Rhode Island's politicians did not want to incur ill will in England. The colonists had expended monies in the expeditions against the French, and they wanted to be reimbursed. At the same time, however, Shirley's charges are also not above suspicion. It was to his advantage to blame other colonies — especially Rhode Island — for the impressment riots that had erupted in Boston in 1747. Moreover, the less the Narragansett Colony received from the parliamentary grant to cover the expenses of the Cape Breton campaign, the more there would be for Massachusetts.[33] The major point that emerges from these charges and counter charges is that the naval and the colonial coast guard vessels were undermanned. It also appears that as many seamen as possible attempted to find berths on merchantmen or private men-of-war rather than on vessels in the navy or the coast guard.

When Governor Shirley informed the Massachusetts legislature that it was improbable many sailors would enlist in the coast guard "upon our Pay," he mentioned one of the main reasons for this: seamen could earn much higher wages in the merchant marine than they could aboard the men-of-war. Moreover, service on a privateer offered even greater potential for financial gain.

One important consequence of the wartime demand for mariners was an increase in the level of seamen's wages. Throughout most of the peacetime decade of the 1730s wages in the merchant service averaged 23-25 s. (sterling) per month.[34] After the outbreak of hostilities in the fall of 1739, mariners' wages rose dramatically. The *Boston Evening Post* reported on 5 November that seamen in Jamaica "may have 20 Guineas, besides many other Advantages, for the Run Home [i.e., England]."[35] In Britain, sailors demanded 50 s. (sterling) a month from merchant shippers in 1740 but from

1745 to 1748 wages averaged 55 s. (sterling) per month.[36] Wages in North America also reflected the increased demand for sailors. Writing from Charles Town, Robert Pringle informed his business associates of the high cost of maritime labor, "There being now Fifteen and Twenty Guineas given to Sailors for the Run to Europe."[37] Massachusetts seamen sailing on William Pepperrell's vessel *Charming Molly* received £16 (Mass., about 35 s. sterling) per month in 1747. This was four times higher than wages paid by Pepperrell during the 1730s.[38] The letterbook of Manhattan merchant Gerard Beekman reveals that New York tars also earned war-inflated wages. Two hands on Beekman's sloop *Dolphin* received 75 s. (N.Y., about 41 s. sterling) per month in 1748, while another "Mariner" was paid at the monthly rate of £5.15.0 (N.Y., about 61 s. sterling).[39]

The financial rewards of privateering are harder to determine. Unlike merchant seamen, mariners on private men-of-war earned no fixed wages, receiving instead shares of the prizes they intercepted. Obviously, if a privateer were unlucky in capturing enemy merchantmen, its crew members would receive little more than their provisions. On the other hand, successful privateering cruises offered the prospect of windfall gains. The crews of Captains Hall and Lamprier, two privateers sailing in consort in 1744, shared £200 each after capturing a rich Spanish ship which sold for £10,000.[40] Each tar serving on board a New Providence Island privateer, commanded by John Gardener, shared 1000 pieces of eight (about £163 sterling) from the proceeds of a 1745 cruise.[41] Shares of £70 per man were divided by the crew of the Philadelphia privateer *Cruizer* in 1745.[42] Although these examples are probably exceptional, the hands of a private man-of-war could expect to earn about 137 s. (sterling) per month if their vessel only took one prize of average value on a voyage.[43] This more than doubled the wages paid in the merchant service.

Mariners serving in the Royal Navy and on the colonial coast guard vessels earned much lower wages than their merchant marine counterparts. The rate of pay for seamen in the navy had not changed since the Interregnum. In 1653 Parliament set the wages for able seamen at 24 s. per month; this rate did not change until after the great mutinies at Spithead and the Nore in 1797.[44] Out of his monthly wages the British tar paid deductions to the sailors' hospital at Greenwich, to his ship's chaplain and surgeon, and, because the navy provided no uniforms, to his vessel's purser.[45] Thus, the lower deck sailor on a king's ship earned about 23 s. each month if he were lucky. Because pay in the Royal Navy was so low and the service so onerous, the navy was plagued by deserters. In an effort to curb desertion, the service continually withheld wages to deter their men from deserting. As a result, numerous tars in the Royal Navy were not paid for years.[46]

Wages in the colonial coast guard also held little attraction for provincial sailors. Table 1 presents the available data on wages in the Massachusetts and Rhode Island coast guard as well as the proposed wages for a Pennsylvania guard vessel. Only the Pennsylvania rate equaled the prevailing wages in the merchant service. The remuneration offered by the Bay Colony never approached these wages. The low pay, coupled with the inflation that afflicted New England currencies, combined to drive Massachusetts wages

TABLE 1

Monthly Wage Rates for Seamen in the Colonial Coast Guard
During King George's War

Year	Massachusetts		Rhode Island	Pennsylvania
1740	£6	(22s. 10d.)[a]		
1741	£8[b]	(22s. 2d.)		
1742	£8	(29s. 1d.)		
1743	£8	(29s.)		
1744	£8	(27s. 1d.)	£8 (27s. 1d.)	
1745	£8	(24s. 9d.)	£8 (24s. 9d.)	
1746	£8	(24s. 10d.)	£8[c] (24s. 10d.)	
1747	£8	(17s. 3d.)	£14 (30s. 3d.)	
1748	£12.10	(27s. 4d.)	£14 (30s. 8d.)	£5 (57s. 5d.)

Source: *Mass. House Journal*, XIX, 122-23; *Mass. House Journal* XX, 202; *Mass. House Journal*, XXI, 208-09; *Mass. House Journal*, XXII, 155-56, 216; *Mass. House Journal*, XXIII, 393-94; *Mass. House Journal*, XXIV, 12, 68, 96, 349; *Mass. Acts and Resolves*, XIII, 94, 106, 225, 367, 535; *Col. Rec. R.I.*, IV, 568, 575; *Col. Rec. R.I.*, V, 16, 90-92, 101, 167-68, 216, 246; *Pa. Arch.*, II, 67-68.

[a] The figures in parentheses are the sterling values of the colonial currencies. They are based on the exchange rates found in Table 5.2, "Colonial Exchange Rates: English Continental Colonies, 1649-1775" in John J. McCusker, *Money and Exchange in Europe and America, 1600-1775: A Handbook* (Chapel Hill, N.C., 1978), p. 316.

[b] The Massachusetts legislature enacted these wages as £2 new tenor. Table 1 expresses all Massachusetts wage rates in old tenor. £1 new tenor was approximately equal to £4 old tenor. See McCusker, *Money and Exchange*, p. 133.

[c] The Rhode Island legislature also paid a bounty of 40s. (R.I.) to each volunteer. In his discussion of New England exchange prior to 1750 when Massachusetts adopted the silver standard, Professor McCusker states "that with minor exceptions we are able to treat them [i.e., the currencies of Massachusetts, Connecticut, Rhode Island, and New Hampshire] as a unit." As a result, the Massachusetts rates of exchange were used to compute the sterling equivalents of Rhode Island paper money. See McCusker, *Money and Exchange*, pp. 131, 136.

down below even those of the Royal Navy in 1747! Rhode Island tars fared better than their northern neighbors, but they still lagged far behind the merchant service and the privateers.[47] Not surprisingly, the colonies often experienced difficulty in raising (and keeping) volunteers to serve on the patrol vessels. In January 1746 Captain Thomas Sanders, commander of the provincial sloop *Massachusetts,* petitioned the Bay Colony's government for higher wages for himself and his crew. Governor Shirley supported Sanders's request, and told the House that Sanders "was not able to support himself and Family nor to get able-bodied Seamen to navigate the Province Sloop, under the scanty Allowance you have made for them."[48] Sanders's plea was successful, and the House agreed to raise their wages.[49]

Prompted, perhaps, by the success of the colony's sloop crew, Captain Edward Tyng, commander of the province's ship *Massachusetts Frigate,* requested more money for himself and his crew. Tyng's application emphasized "the great Difficulty he meets with in manning the said Ship by Reason of the lowness of the Wages allowed by the Government." Shirley again strongly urged the representatives to increase the wages paid to the colony's tars "for it seems impracticable for Capt. Tyng to make up his Complement without it." After initially defeating two proposals to raise the mariners' wages, the legislators granted an increase to 40 s.[50]

The Bay Colony's legislators were not as sympathetic to the sailors in its employ the following spring. The lower House flatly refused another petition for higher wages presented by Captain Tyng, stipulating that wages for 1747 be continued at the level of the previous year. In case there should be a shortfall of recruits, the representatives decided to rely on coercion to fill the colony's manpower needs: "if a sufficient Number of Seamen do not appear to inlist, the Captain-General [Governor Shirley] be desired to cause an Impress for that Service."[51]

Throughout King George's War the low wages paid by the colonial governments and the Royal Navy were major obstacles hindering recruiting. The severity of naval discipline with is heavy reliance on corporal punishment was undoubtedly another.[52] To solve its manpower shortages the navy relied on impressment. Not surprisingly, the colonists were strongly opposed to this form of "recruiting," and press gangs were greeted with violence. In Boston and Charles Town lives were lost in confrontations between merchant seamen and the naval press gangs.[53] Despite this, it is interesting to note that many of the New Englanders who protested loudly against the Royal Navy's press gangs enacted legislation that set in motion press gangs of their own to recruit the colonial coast guard.

Since merchant shippers could not resort to impressment to obtain sailors, they too tried to attract men by offering high wages. Indeed ship owners were forced to offer wages that were sufficiently high to induce mariners to risk the press. In this way the mere presence of naval warships helped to push up the cost of merchant seamen's wages. The manpower requirements of the navy helped to create a vicious circle of an inadequate supply of seamen, higher wages, press gangs, and an exodus of merchant sailors to safer ports. The demand of privateers for seamen exacerbated the pressure on the number of men available for merchant vessels.

Even more than the merchant marine, privateers were seen as a drain on seamen from the navy and the coast guard vessels. But even the private men-of-war often faced shortages of men. They too were forced to advertise for crews in the newspapers or sail from port to port in quest of able-bodied seamen. It is incorrect to view the privateers as great magnets easily attracting a bountiful supply of mariners.

The shortage of seamen was one of the most serious problems affecting British naval administration in the eighteenth century.[54] There were not enough mariners in Britain to meet the needs of both the navy and the merchant fleet. This same problem clearly affected administrators in the colonies. American mariners avoided service in the navy and the coast guard as much as possible. The merchant vessels and privateers held forth more attractive possibilities. Yet, even these employers frequently suffered from a lack of sailors. In the colonies, as well as in the mother country, there was simply a shortage of seamen available for duty during wartime.

Carl E. Swanson
Brock University

Notes

[1] W.L. Grant and J. Munro, eds., *Acts of the Privy Council of England: Colonial Series, 1613-1783* (Nendeln, Liechtenstein, 1966), III, 636.

[2] *Boston Gazette*, 20 Aug. 1739; *New York Weekly Journal*, 27 Aug. 1739; *Pennsylvania Gazette* (Philadelphia), 23 Aug. 1739; *South Carolina Gazette* (Charles Town), 8 and 15 Sept. 1739.

[3] *Pa. Gaz.*, 30 Aug. 1744; *New York Post-Boy*, 17 Sept. 1744, quoted in Carl Bridenbaugh, *Cities in Revolt: Urban Life in America, 1743-1776* (New York, 1971), p. 61.

[4] Duke of Newcastle to the Governor and Company of Rholde Island, 18 Apr. 1740, Gertrude S. Kimball, ed., *The Correspondence of the Colonial Governors of Rhode Island, 1723-1775* (Freeport, N.Y., 1969), I, 149, hereafter cited as *R. I. Gov. Corr.* Newcastle sent the same letter to the other colonial governors.

[5] For the disastrous effects of the war on French colonial commerce, see Thomas M. Doerflinger, "The Antilles Trade of the Old Regime: A Statistical Overview," *Journal of Interdisciplinary History*, 6 (1976), 397-415; Dale Miquelon, *Dugard of Rouen: French Trade to Canada and the West Indies, 1729-1770* (Montreal, 1978), chapters 6 and 7. The number of British colonial privateers and the prizes they captured are presented in Carl E. Swanson, "Predators and Prizes: Privateering in the British Colonies during the War of 1739-1748," (Ph.D. Thesis, University of Western Ontario, 1979), chapters 3, 5, and 7.

[6] The rations of tons, guns, and men for merchantmen increased noticeably during wartime, thus indicating both larger crews and heavier armaments. See Swanson, "Predators and Prizes," 95, and James F. Shepherd and Gary M. Walton, *Shipping, Maritime Trade, and Economic Development of Colonial North America* (Cambridge, 1972), pp. 196-97.

[7] Daniel A. Baugh, *British Naval Administration in the Age of Walpole* (Princeton, N.J., 1965), 205, supports the larger figure; Ralph Davis, *The Rise of the English Shipping Industry in the Seventeenth and Eighteenth Centuries* (London, 1962), pp. 320-21, cites a peak strength of 52,000 in 1747.

[8] Swanson, "Predators and Prizes," p. 175.

[9] R. Pringle to Andrew Pringle, 31 Dec. 1742; Pringle to Richard Partridge, 5 Feb. 1743; Pringle to Francis Dalby, 23 May 1743; Pringle to Henry and John Brock, 12 Dec. 1744, Walter B. Edgar, ed., *The Letterbook of Robert Pringle* (Columbia, S.C., 1972), pp. 471, 496, 557, 777, hereafter cited as *Pringle Letterbook*.

[10] Worthington C. Ford, *et al.*, eds., *Journals of the House of Representatives of Massachusetts* (Boston, 1919-1971), XXII, 204-05, hereafter cited as *Mass. House Journal*; H.S. Vaughan, ed., *Voyages and Cruises of Commodore Walker* (London, 1928), pp. 93-94.

[11] See, for example, *Boston Gaz.*, 24 Nov. 1747, 3 May 1748; *Pa. Gaz.*, 25 Feb. 1746; *S.C. Gaz.*, 14 and 21 May 1744, 17 June 1745, 25 May 1747. Numerous examples from the *Maryland Gazette* are cited in Richard B. Morris, *Government and Labor in Early America* (New York, 1965), p. 247.

[12] *Boston Eve. Post*, 5 Nov. 1739.

[13] Journal of the privateer sloop *Revenge*, 5 June-14 May 1741, J. Franklin Jameson, ed., *Privateering and Piracy in the Colonial Period: Illustrative Documents* (New York, 1970), pp. 382-93.

128

[14] *Pa. Gaz.,* 10 Feb. 1747.
[15] *Ibid.,* 30 Aug., 6 Sept., 6, 14, 18, 25 Dec. 1744, 1, 8, 15, 29 Jan. 1745.
[16] See, for example, *Boston Gaz.,* 10 Feb. and 17 Nov. 1747; *Pa. Gaz.,* 4 Nov. 1742; *Virginia Gazette* (Williamsburg), 26 Oct. and 2 Nov. 1739; *S.C. Gaz.,* 4 Apr. 1740.
[17] *Mass. House Journal,* XX, 84.
[18] *Ibid.,* 98-99; Massachusetts Archives, 64, Maritime, 1740-53, 204-05, 209-11, State House, Boston.
[19] Warren to Thomas Corbett, 8 Sept. 1744, Julian Gwyn, ed., *The Royal Navy and North America: The Warren Papers, 1736-1752* (London, 1973), p. 36.
[20] Palmer to Masterson, 2 Aug. 1748, George E. Reed, ed., *Pennsylvania Archives, Fourth Series: Papers of the Governors* (Harrisburg, Pa., 1900), II, 80.
[21] See, for example, *S.C. Gaz.,* 4 Apr. 1740, 1 and 8 Nov. 1742, 3 Jan. 1743.
[22] Richard Pares, "The Manning of the Navy in the West Indies, 1702-63," *Transactions of the Royal Historical Society,* 4th Series, 20 (1937), 47.
[23] *Mass. House Journal,* XVIII, 90.
[24] Ellis Ames, Abner C. Goodell, *et al.,* eds., *The Acts and Resolves, Public and Private, of the Province of the Massachusetts Bay . . .* (Boston, 1869-1922), XIII, 427, hereafter cited as *Mass. Acts and Resolves.*
[25] *Mass. House Journal,* XXII, 203.
[26] *Mass. House Journal,* XXIII, 115, 121.
[27] See, for example, "An Act for equipping the colony sloop, and sending her out to cruise, &c.," enacted April 1741; "An Act for fitting out the colony Sloop Tartar, in company with the sloop kept by His Majesty's colony of Connecticut, for guarding the coast," enacted June 1744, John R. Bartlett, ed., *Records of the Colony of Rhode Island and Providence Plantations In New England* (New York, 1968), V, 17, 19, hereafter cited as *Col. Rec. R.I.*
[28] *Ibid.,* 253-54.
[29] Shirley to Wanton, 6 June 1745, Charles H. Lincoln, ed., *The Correspondence of William Shirley* (New York, 1912), I, 227-28, hereafter cited as *Shirley Correspondence.*
[30] Shirley to Newcastle, 31 Dec. 1747, *ibid.* 420-23.
[31] Wanton to Partridge, 26 July 1745, 1 *R.I. Gov. Corr.,* p. 367. This theme was reiterated many times in other letters; see 5 *Col. Rec. R. I.,* pp. 139-40, 148, 154, 183-84.
[32] Shirley and Warren to Rhode Island Governor William Greene, 4 July 1746, 1 *Shirley Correspondence,* pp. 329-32. Shirley and Warren actually complained that Rhode Island's bounty was too high.
[33] Sydney V. James, *Colonial Rhode Island: A History* (New York, 1975), pp. 274-75.
[34] Davis, *Rise of the English Shipping Industry, p. 137.*
[35] *Boston Eve. Post,* 5 Nov. 1739.
[36] Davis, *Rise of the English Shipping Industry,* p. 137.
[37] Pringle to Henry and John Brock, 12 Dec. 1744, *Pringle Letterbook,* p. 777.
[38] Byron Fairchild, *Messrs. William Pepperrell: Merchants at Piscataqua* (Ithaca, N.Y., 1954), p. 152. The exchange rates for sterling conversion employed here and throughout this paper are from John J. McCusker, *Money and Exchange in Europe and America, 1600-1775: A Handbook* (Chapel Hill, N.C., 1978), pp. 310, 316.
[39] Beekman to Captain William Collins, 3 Feb. 1748, Philip L. White, ed., *The Beekman Mercantile Papers, 1746-1799* (New York, 1956), I, 41. The wage rates cited in this discussion are for men who sailed before the mast. Captains and mates, of course, received much higher remuneration.
[40] *Pa. Gaz.,* 21 June 1744; *Boston News-Letter,* 16 Aug. 1744; *S.C. Gaz.,* 17 Sept. 1744.
[41] *Pa. Gaz.,* 23 May 1745.
[42] *Ibid.,* 20 June 1745.
[43] A detailed discussion of the procedures employed in arriving at this figure is presented in Swanson, "Predators and Prizes," pp. 312-20.
[44] Christopher Lloyd, *The British Seaman, 1200-1860: A Social Survey* (London, 1968), pp. 248-49; Baugh, *British Naval Administration,* p. 229.
[45] Lloyd, *The British Seaman,* pp. 235-36.
[46] J.R. Hutchinson, *The Press-Gang Afloat and Ashore* (London, 1913), 44; Jesse Lemisch, "Jack Tar in the Streets: Merchant Seamen in the Politics of Revolutionary America," *William and Mary Quarterly,* 3rd series, 25 (1968), 382-83; Pares, "Manning the Navy," *Trans. Royal Hist.*

Soc., 20 (1937), 38. In addition to monthly wages, naval personnel also received prize money from the enemy vessels intercepted by their ship. It is difficult to ascertain how much prize money augmented a mariner's income. Three-fourths of all prize money went to the officers. The remaining quarter was shared among all the lower deck sailors and marines. Moreover, the navy withheld prize shares, like wages, in an effort to prevent desertion. However much prize money supplemented the 24 s., it was insufficient to place naval wages on a par with the merchant marine or equal the potential offered by privateering.

[47] Like their naval counterparts, sailors in the coast guard were entitled to prize money. But since provincial guard vessels primarily patrolled their own coasts and rarely cruised in the enemy's shipping lanes, colony vessels made few captures. It is, therefore, doubtful if prize money significantly raised the level of wages in the coast guard.

[48] *Mass. House Journal,* XXII, 155-56.

[49] *Ibid.,* 170-71.

[50] *Ibid.,* 203-04, 224-25.

[51] *Mass. House Journal,* XXIII, 393-94.

[52] Lloyd, *The British Seaman,* pp. 239-45.

[53] *S.C. Gaz.,* 24 May 1740; *Pa. Gaz.,* 10 Dec. 1745. Impressment of Boston seamen caused a major riot in 1747, but there were no fatalities. See *Boston Gaz.,* 24 Nov. 1747 and Shirley to the Lords of Trade, 1 Dec. 1747, *Shirley Correspondence,* I, 412-19.

[54] Baugh, *British Naval Administration,* p. 147.

13. Bibliographical Control of Eighteenth-Century French Canadiana

An interdisciplinary volume like the present one is an ideal opportunity to attempt to jump the fences which the departmental structure of universities seems to have placed around the activities of scholars of a particular period of intellectual and cultural history. Even more important is the possibility of sharing insights between two or more disciplines when the barriers of subject and languge departmentalism are temporarily lowered. I want you first of all to look over your fence into the yard of library science. Some of the conceptualizations and theories being developed there owe a great deal to other disciplines but the practical application of some of the theory is to be found in many other people's yards. I have recently been applying an evolving theory of bibliographical control to the field of French Canadiana; I hope it will be of equal value in language departments other than French, and in subject departments other than Canadian history or literature. Indeed, it has significance well beyond even the cross-disciplinary field of the eighteenth century which brings us together. In order to make points about the eighteenth century I shall need to range into sixteenth and seventeenth-century areas as well and to make some remarks about the concepts of "bibliographical control" and "bibliographical universe."

The bibliographical universe consists of millions and millions of objects which we designate books, pamphlets, periodicals, maps, manuscripts, sheet music, etc.; for some people the universe would include postage stamps, theatre tickets, or any piece of paper or other material with human-produced signs on it, made with an enormous range of implements — from a sharp piece of stick to a printing press or a high-speed computer-driven machine. The very act of attempting an exhaustive list of either the categories of product or the categories of means of production would constitute a form of bibliographical control. Classification is a basic instrument of bibliographical control. Each individual object in the bibliographical universe can be assigned to a class, even though we would not find universal agreement on what are the most important or useful classes. Nevertheless, instinct tells us that the number of classes cannot be very great in number. S.R. Ranganathan stated in 1953[1] that any attempt to list all items in the bibliographical universe is impractical, but he proceeded to suggest that some usable substitutes for universal lists are certainly within the realm of possibility. In his book *Documentation and its Facets* (1963),[2] Ranganathan

132

spelled out five characteristics which might form the basis for restricting an "omnibus universal documentation list" to usable lists. I took the liberty in 1976 to expand these five characteristics to six and proceeded to divide them further into two classes. Reflection since then has led to the identification of three more and I am sure there are others. These generic characteristics still seem to fall into two main classes.

Those of you who want a more thorough investigation of the theoretical framework within which I will be proceeding, might like to struggle with the first chapter in *The Bibliographical Control of Early Books* (Bangalore, India, 1978).[3] There, in some close argumentation, I attempt to build upon, but modify, the fine philosophical endeavours of Patrick Wilson, in his *Two Kinds of Power: An Essay on Bibliographical Control* (Berkeley: University of California, 1968).[4] Wilson attempts to establish, with Carnap as his guide, a philosophical underpinning for the common use or uses of the term. But before using Wilson's ideas, let me state what the nine "characteristics" derived and expanded from Ranganathan are:

A Area of origin of the documents
B Language of the documents
C Period of production of the documents
D Physical process by means of which the documents were produced
E Author or group of authors of the documents
F Present location of the documents
G Subject of the documents
H Standard or quality of the documents
I Service aimed at by the documentation lists

When trying to classify objects in the bibliographical universe according to these limiting characteristics, we might note that the first six require a predominantly objective kind of judgment, while the other three imply a judgment of a more subjective kind in which knowledge of the *purposes* in the mind of the users of the list is all-important.

This distinction owes a great deal to Wilson's "two kinds of power" as it is based upon his maintenance of "our common-sense distinction between powers whose exercise requires appraisal and those whose exercise requires only bare description." Although I have asserted a more subtle interrelationship between what he calls "exploitative" and "descriptive" power than he is willing to accept, I thoroughly agree with Wilson that bibliographical control is a *power,* the power that can be exercised by individuals over a part or the whole of the bibliographical universe. And I agree that that power is both descriptive and evaluative. But I place much more emphasis than he on the primacy of descriptive power. Without thorough and accurate description, appraisal is arbitrary and partial.

Wilson, in pursuing his enquiry, asks a key question (beginning of Chapter II):

What might a person be able to do or have done to things in the bibliographical universe that would count as exercises of the power we call "bibliographical control"?

It seems to me the primary exercise of the power is to name and count those things. How powerful is your control? What eighteenth-century items of Canadiana are you able to name? How many are there? Let us use these questions to explore our chosen part of the universe.

The alternative phrase in Wilson's question, "to do or have done to," implies an *instrument* of power, so the concept of bibliographical instrument is fully discussed in Wilson. The most familiar bibliographical instrument is a list of books and articles arranged in a convenient, browsable and meaningful order — the familiar "bibliography" in its many printed and manuscript forms. But the development of machine-readable bibliographical data bases, with a theoretically infinite variety of possible forms of display is beginning to complicate (but in some ways also to simplify) the traditional forms of bibliographical instruments, or 'bibliographical tools' as the jargon of library and information science would have it. One needs a strong theoretical framework if one wishes to design a computer-based bibliographical tool that will optimize our bibliographical control over even a part of the bibliographical universe. That part of the universe which I want to exercise power over is limited by four of the nine characteristics mentioned above — to books printed in the French language, on a hand-operated letterpress machine, during the eighteenth century, on subjects relating to the geographical area we now call Canada. It should also be possible in the ideal bibliographical instrument to derive listings characterized by the other five as well. Moreover, the computer-based bibliographical tool that we ought to create must be capable of bibliographical control of other parts of the bibliographical universe in addition. The impracticality of attempting control of the whole of that universe has led me to design a system for control only of letterpress books printed before 1801, thus making a rational application of Ranganathan's classificatory underpinning. Attention to Wilson's very important distinction between descriptive and exploitative power has led me to incorporate access or indexing devices that will optimize the combination of those powers. The distinction should be kept in mind when assessing existing bibliographical tools as well as when imagining a more powerful one in machine-readable form. The computer should not be used as a mere mechanical substitute for human labour, but a "telescope of the mind" as one writer has put it. Just as the telescope enabled man to see things he could not see with the naked eye, the computer ought to be able to extend the use of the human mind, especially making use of the elusive elements of human memory that all forms of recorded knowledge exemplify.

With these thoughts in mind, I have been developing a computer-based bibliographical tool that should significantly improve our bibliographical control over French-language Canadiana before 1801, and, at a second stage, over French, Spanish, and Portuguese Americana, i.e. Western Hemispheriana in those three languages. Eventually, the system should be expandable to cover all letterpress production before 1801. Before imagining what the developing system should be able to do, and before describing what it can do now, a survey of what existing manually-based tools can do for us should be attempted.

The first requirement for minimal bibliographical control of French-language Canadiana of the eighteenth century would be an exhaustive list of all items in our limited part of the bibliographical universe enabling us both to identify and count those items. Although the definition of "Canadiana" is fraught with difficulties, the selection of items is a fairly simple exercise of appraisal: the choice of data for representing each item is an exercise of neutral "descriptive" power. The publication that comes nearest to an ideal tool is Tremaine's *Bibliography of Canadian Imprints 1751-1800*.[5] It is limited by (A) area of origin of the documents, (C) period of production, (D) physical process and to a certain extent (F) location. Even though the French-language and bilingual items are scattered among items in English or other languages, we may easily impose limitation (B) and isolate 546 items in roughly chronological order in the listing. (I should note in passing that no bibliography in our field is strictly chronological. Books of the same year of publication are nearly always listed in conventional author/title order, so the arrangement should probably be called more accurately "annalistical" rather than chronological.)

Although a small number of items has been and will eventually be found to augment Tremaine, it is safe to assume (an act of "appraisal") that this tool is very close to the ideal in exhaustive listing, for it includes items for which no surviving copy has been found. The index in the back of the book, however, leaves much to be desired when one wishes to apply our four other limitations and thus to exercise "exploitative" power as distinct from "descriptive" power.

Canadiana printed outside Canada have been listed in a large number of bibliographical tools, but none is comparable with Tremaine's listing of Canadian imprints. Tremaine's listing supersedes earlier partial attempts at chronological listings, such as Dionne's, which has at least one feature that makes it a better tool of bibliographical control. Dionne's Tome I (1905)[6] is limited to French-language items printed in Quebec. However, with 62 items between 1765 and 1800, his coverage is poor. (It is noteworthy, however, that the shortness of the individual entries makes scanning much more feasible than in Tremaine.) No annalistical bibliography supersedes Dionne's companion volume of imprints printed outside Quebec.[7] Although this Tome II includes 909 items before 1801, only 336 are, on rough count, in the French language. The words "rough count" are necessary because the language of some entries is not indicative of the language of the text, so precision is not feasible.

One of the major advantages of the annalistical or pseudo-chronological arrangement of Dionne and Tremaine is that we can select those items printed within a set period of time. For instance, Dionne lists roughly 131 French-language items of Canadiana that were printed between 1701-1750, and 101 between 1751 and 1800. If the user of a bibliographical tool were attempting to locate contemporary printed works covering, for instance, the Seven Years' War, this would greatly improve his bibliographical control. A subtle variation on the annalistical arrangement would improve it even more. One bibliography attempts to list all items according to the date of the *contents* of the book, even though first publication of the work may have been decades or even centuries later. This is Staton & Tremaine's *Bibliography of*

Canadiana,[8] a catalog of the Canadiana in the Toronto Public Library (now the Reference Library of the Metropolitan Toronto Library System). The 749 items before 1801 (in many languages) are in fact listed by the conventional author/title arrangement within each of the years, so the book *can* be read as the annals of Canadiana. Unfortunately, however, the actual coverage of French-language items is limited to the holdings of one library. A rough count made by quick scanning of the language of the title pages both in the bibliography and its 1959 Supplement,[9] indicates that about 287 of the 897 items before 1801 are probably in the French language. About 45 belong in the first half of the eighteenth century, but a considerable number of Canadian imprints are included in the 128 or so of the second half of the eighteenth century. If we discount nineteenth and twentieth-century imprints, this fine bibliography can compare favorably with Dionne for comprehensiveness only in the second half of the eighteenth century. However, the detailed general index to the text provides access points (other than annalistical) greatly superior to Dionne, but still well below the level needed for reasonable exploitative bibliographical control.

A bibliography based on a single library's collection is a severe limitation on the comprehensive element of bibliographical control that we are presently concentrating on. A union catalog (such as *The National Union Catalog: Pre-1956 Imprints)*[10] tends, on the other hand, to scatter items of our limited portion of the bibliographical universe among a preponderance of non-relevant items. Nevertheless, the limited tool, when used as an access device to the more comprehensive tool, frequently improves the quality of both tools as an instrument of bibliographical control. For this reason, *NUC: Pre-1956 Imprints* can be used as the most comprehensive listing of French Canadiana, but only in combination with more limited bibliographies organized on different principles. In general, then, a scholar wishing to exercise bibliographical control over a limited portion of the universe must use a number of even more limited bibliographical tools, despite the fact that they, too, frequently include non-relevant items.

Several lists of bibliographies of Canadiana are available, but all suffer from the same problem that union catalogs present to us. The Bibliothèque Nationale du Québec, for instance, has published a *Bibliographie de bibliographies québécoises* (1979).[11] The power of selecting bibliographies limited by the time and the language of the original items listed is not facilitated by the predominantly nineteenth and twentieth-century contents of most of the bibliographies listed, however, and the place limitation (Quebec) limits our access to items for the whole of Canada. Lochhead's *Bibliography of Canadian Bibliographies* (2nd ed., 1972)[12] transcends the space limitation, and provides readier access to major bibliographies of the kind most pertinent to our purposes partly because Peter Greig's index of subjects, localities, authors, and compilers helps to chart scope limitations.

Most of the largest bibliographies of Canadiana are in fact printed catalogs of individual collections, either of bookcollectors or of libraries. None of them is exactly alike in arrangement, scope, or bibliographical treatment of individual items. The very range of possibilities provides the designer of a computer-based bibliographical instrument with a host of ideas for imagining what devices might be incorporated in the system for maximal exploitative bibliographical control.

Laurentiana parus avant 1821[13] is probably the most useful bibliographical instrument for determining what Canadiana in French appeared before 1801, as it is a full-scale bibliographical catalog of 770 items in the largest single Canadian repository that has published such a catalog. But it is also useful because it has a larger number of different means of access to information contained in the catalog than is to be found in other printed catalogs.

The catalog proper of 416 pages, although arranged in conventional author/title/date order, can be used with reasonable convenience within four of our nine limiting characteristics, but the following indexes provided in the back of the book extend that convenience to encompass three others:

Index des titres	(15p)
noms	(26p)
matières	(21p)
illustrations	(6p)
cartes et plans	(8p)
lieux d'édition	(15p)
imprimeurs	(8p)
dates de l'édition	(16p)

The latter index provides information that can easily be scanned to identify and count (with the usual imprecision) items before 1801 in French. The total number is 263 (almost as rich as Dionne). No other printed library catalog can be so easily used to gain this simplest form of bibliographical control over the portion of the bibliographical universe that we are interested in. The Lawrence Lande Collection of Canadiana in the Redpath Library of McGill University has been catalogued in a sumptuous volume[14] in which the 2328 items are arranged in three categories, each of which is also arranged in conventional author/title/date order. The three categories are:

Basic Canadiana (915 items)
Canadiana in the West and North (608 items)
Cultural and Supplementary Canadiana (805 items)

The indexes at the end of the book are idiosyncratic:

Bibliographical Index (largely a nominal index of authors, both personal and corporate) (8p)
Index to Government Documents (largely an index to localities both as subject and source of the douments) (3p)
Title index (17p)
Subject index (7p)

One must search sequentially through the whole book to identify Canadiana in French printed before 1801, a very time-consuming process. A first rough count established that 32 French-language Canadian imprints and 124 other French-language Canadian items are listed. It would be very tedious to attempt to further subdivide the latter 124 into pre-1701 and eighteenth-century items. However, the rough count suggests that the McGill collection is only half as rich as the BNQ collection.

Rare and Unusual Canadiana,[15] the first supplement to the Lande bibliography, was published in 1971 in not quite so sumptuous a form, but again in conventional author/title/date order, thus making it comparable with *Laurentiana* and the three categories of the Lande bibliography. The first 667 pages contain 2335 items, and the next 67 pages an addendum of 206 items. An author index and a title index are provided, together with a "Special Subject Index" which intermingles broad subject headings with form (e.g. Broadsides, Circulars and Ephemera) and chronological headings (e.g. French Regime). Among the chronological headings is "Early Canadian Imprints dating up to 1800," but the addresses for the items are not themselves in chronological order. Once again, a sequential search through the thousands of items is required to discover what proportion might be Canadiana in French before 1801, or between 1700 and 1800 (or any other desired period). The figures are 53 French-language Canadian imprints and 110 other French-language items of Canadiana. McGill is beginning to rival BNQ!

Older catalogs and bibliographies are of varying quality and convenience for satisfying our modest desire for at least a simple quantitative answer to our original questions.

However, this is not meant to be a survey of *all* bibliographical tools, so we need not go on to analyse Gagnon, Faribault, and other tools of less comprehensive scope. But some brief comments on the amount of information provided in a range of the most useful tools is in order. In *Bibliographical Control of Early Books* I made the distinction between macroscopic and microscopic bibliographical control, with very detailed examples to illustrate the distinction. I shall give here only one or two examples from bibliographies of French Canadiana. Dionne is a fine example of *macroscopic* bibliographical control — he approaches more closely than any other bibliographer the criterion of comprehensiveness or exhaustivity, and he achieves this by reducing individual entries in his listing to minimal description. McCoy, in his *Jesuit Relations of Canada* (1937)[16] is a fine example of *microscopic* bibliographical control — he provides 132 entries for the 50 or so texts that constitute the 1632-1673 series of reports. Although his categorization of variations can be faulted by application of modern analytical techniques, McCoy has provided more detailed bibliographical analysis of individual copies of a group of French Canadian books than any other bibliographer, including his predecessors Harrisse or Cole, who provide more detail on the *content* of the books they describe. Dionne provides a rather skimpy "Table des Matières" which is derived completely from the information provided in his entries, not from the books themselves.

When considerable bibliographical detail in an entry is accompanied by valuable annotations (as in Staton & Tremaine) such derived indexes can be a valuable tool for bibliographical control. Indexes of information in the actual books for which the entries are a surrogate would improve our control even further, but, in practice most indexes to bibliographies provide information that is contained only in the surrogate or its accompanying annotations. Such limitations of a manually-produced bibliographical tool should not limit our approach to indexing devices in a machine-based system. Thus, a macroscopic tool like Dionne's could be complemented by indexing devices which *add* information to the minimal amount given in an entry designed for ease of scanning.

Observed weaknesses of existing bibliographical instruments make it highly desirable that the Western Hemisphere Short-Title Catalog system (WHSTC) will be essentially a *macroscopic* bibliographical control instrument with indexing features built into it so that the *microscopic* bibliographical control provided by other bibliographical tools can be made available by referral. A brief overview of the WHSTC system, with its retrieval and indexing program called "NOBLE" will suggest how this is being done.

First of all, a working definition of what constitutes an item or individual unit in the bibliographical universe has been devised. This is called a "bibliographically distinct volume." Second, rules for creating a record or surrogate for each 'bdv' have been devised. It is essentially an adaptation of a traditional short-title catalog record, and it is meant to *identify* not to *describe* a 'bdv'. It is also meant to be an index term for referring to other kinds of surrogates recorded in catalogs, bibliographies, and checklists. Third, the basic machine-readable files of the system are cumulated in a series of main files that are accessed through 26 "control" files by a user of the system. The user can employ a large number of "browsing files" which will maximize his or her power of selection, and a large number of "query files" which will maximize his or her power of aggregating records into a machine-produced bibliography. If you wish to have details of how the system works and is evolving, you might like to read *The HPB Project: Phase IV*.[17] The major end-products of the on-line system are bibliographies, annotated or unannotated, in various stages of development, which are generated from a "query file." These query files will proliferate as the system responds to the needs of users for exploitative bibliographical control. I have reproduced the bibliographies generated from two of these for illustration. They represent bibliographies in a transition stage from 'descriptive' to 'exploitative'. Both bibliographies require annotations representing appraisal of subject, quality, and potential use. More descriptive data may also be needed.

I have supplied the seventeeth-century bibliography for contrast with the less-well-developed eighteenth-century bibliography, but both have features in common that should be commented on first. The user of the system is first confronted with a "menu" and invited to choose among eight possibilities which are strongly related to the nine "characteristics" of limitation, derived from Ranganathan.

What point of access to the WHUC database do you want?
(type the letter corresponding to its description):

    A Anonymous titles
    P Personal authors
    C Corporate authors
    L Localities

S Subjects
F Forms
O Others
E Exiting from system

Although "FORM" then "RELATIONS" was chosen in this instance for the seventeenth-century listing, the so-called "tracings" under the heading of query file Q0011 indicate other possible access points.

Type first word of the form you seek
otherwise type 0 for none or type ? for index: relations

1) RELATIONS
    Q0011,Q0055
    2 specifications.   1 pages.

Which page do you wish to read? Type the number of the page you seek otherwise type 0 for none or press RETURN for all records:

Jesuit relations   Q0011
Recollet relations   Q0055

If you would like more information about one of these items, please type the numerical information as it appears against that item. If not, type NO: Q0011

JESUIT RELATIONS. Chronological listing of accounts of events in Canada, 1632-1673, sent by Jesuit missionaries to France

Jesuit relations (F)   Jesuits (S)(C)
Relations (F)   Jesuites (S)(C)
New France (S)   Nouvelle France (S)
Missions (S)

    56 addresses

Type in the letter corresponding to your wishes:

P the bibliography printed out
S the bibliography stored for COM
N none of the above

? n

Just to hint at the browsing possibilities, I have chosen "TITLE" and "LETTRES" as a first exploratory decision for finding the eighteenth-century listing, but used a more specific "FORM" approach as an alternative. Again, the tracings will suggest other alternatives, but more important still, will suggest access points to other query files that might be relevant to the user's purpose in retrieving this particular bibliography.

? a

Type first word of title you seek (avoid use of article) otherwise type 0 for none or type ? for index: lettres

1) LETTRES
    L0300342-995, A0148179-95, 201-10, C0752044*-6, D0440313-9*,

F0206450-0*, J0092998*-3021*, 200398, L0028668*, M0726808-13, 5-9, 22*, R0166593-4*, S0029845-50,2
17 specifications.   1 pages.

Which page do you wish to read? Type the number of the page you seek otherwise type 0 for none or press RETURN for all records:

Lettres a M. le marquis de L. C.   L0028668*
        monsieur N***   371*
        curieuses touchant la religion   J0200398
        d'amour d'une religieuse   A0148179*,82*
        d'Heloise a Abailard   486*
        d'un francois a un hollandais   521-2
        d'une demoiselle entretenue   C0752044*-5
            religieuse portugaise   A0148179*
            Turque a Paris   S0029847
        de la Fillon   C0752046
        ecrites d'Anvers par un officier   705*
        edifiantes et curieuses   J0092998*-3021*
        galantes et philosophiques   R0166593-4*
        historiques et galantes   D0440313-9*
        persanes   M0726808-13,5-9,22*
        sinceres d'un gentilhomme   F0206450-0*
        turques   S0029847*-50

If you would like more information about one of these items, please type the numerical information as it appears against that item. If not, type NO: no

What point of access to the WHUC database do you want?
(type the letter corresponding to its description):

    A Anonymous titles
    P Personal authors
    C Corporate authors
    L Localities
    S Subjects
    F Forms
    O Others
    E Exiting from system

?   f

Type first word of the form you seek
otherwise type 0 for none or type ? for index: ?

Type a letter to set all entries beginning with that letter: l
        5 records.   1 pages.

Which page do you wish to read? Type the number of the page you seek otherwise type 0 for none or press RETURN for all records:
LAWS
LEITOURGIKON

LETTERS
LETTRES
LITURGY

Type first word of the form you seek
otherwise type 0 for none or type ? for index: letters

1) LETTERS
Q0034
1 specifications.   1 pages.

Which page do you wish to read? Type the number of the page you seek
otherwise type 0 for none or press RETURN for all records:

From Jesuit missions   Q0034

If you would like more information about one of these items, please type
the numerical information as it appears against that item. If not, type
NO: Q0034

JESUIT LETTERS FROM MISSIONS. Chronological listing of 18th
century publications
Letters (F)   Lettres (F)
Jesuits (S)(C)   Jesuites (S)(C)
Missions (S)
48 addresses

Type in the letter corresponding to your wishes:

P the bibliography printed out
S the bibliography stored for COM
N none of the above

? p
1
J0092998* 50
[description not yet on file]
[Vol I, Le Clerc, 1702] [OClWHi]

2
J0092998* 55
[   ] Quelques missionnaires de la compagnie de Jesus
ed [Charles LE GOBIEN]
Lettres edifiantes et curieuses
[34 vols] Vol I
Paris,
Chez Jean Cusson.
1702
12mo 111p
DCU—IA

3
J0093002* 75
[   ] Quelques missionnaires de la compagnie de Jesus

ed [Charles LE GOBIEN]
Lettres edifiantes et curieuses
[34 vols] Vols I—III
Paris,
Chez Nicolas Le Clerc.
1703
12mo 136,194,225pp

4
J0093002* 85
Quelques missionnaires de la compagnie de Jesus
ed [Charles LE GOBIEN]
Lettres edifiantes et curieuses
[34 vols] Vol II
Paris,
Chez Jean Cusson.
1703
12mo 194p
DCU—IA

5
J0093993* 50
[   ] Quelques missionaires de la compagnie de Jesus
ed [Charles LE GOBIEN]
Lettres edifiantes et curieuses
[34 vols] Vol IV
Paris,
Chez Nicolas Le Clerc.
1704
443p

Each entry in both bibliographies consists of a short-title catalog entry selected by the machine from the "main" files. Each entry is preceded by two addresses and (optionally) an annotation; it may be followed by a list of library holdings and (optionally) another annotation. The list of library holdings comes from the 'control' file, which also instructed the machine what entry to select from the 'main' files. All the other information comes from the 'query' file.

A computer program has been used to give identifying addresses to each entry in the bibliographies (1-56 and 1-48), but a reference to the best available bibliographical description in another bibliography could be substituted if that would improve our bibliographical control. For instance, references to Harrisse[18] could be substituted in the seventeenth-century bibliography, or references to Conlon[19] could be substituted for the following 11 WHSTC addresses in the eighteenth-century bibliography:

WHSTC	Conlon
1 and 2	11035
3	11553
5	12046

6	12608
7	13082
8	13585
9	14113
11	15640
12	16636
17	17738

This would make it possible to consult Conlon's notes on each first edition. Although the cross-reference would also reveal that Conlon's description of each item does not identify the item as accurately as the short-title catalog entry (e.g. items 1 and 2 are not distinguishable), it would also reveal subtle differences that provide new information (e.g. Conlon 11553 lists only the first edition of Vols II-III, but WHSTC 3 suggests the possibility that they were issued simultaneously with a reprint of Vol I).

The second address is what we call the WHUC (i.e. the Western Hemisphere Union Catalog) address. It is derived from an address in *NUC: Pre-1956 Imprints,* to which the user is automatically referred if he or she wishes to find a regular library catalog description of the item, and a list of libraries in the U.S. (and occasionally Canada) where the item may be found. If the first 8 characters of the address are followed by an asterisk, the item is *not* described in NUC. Thus, in the seventeenth-century bibliography, WHSTC 28 and 39 are either subsumed in some other entry or are not recorded in NUC. In the eighteenth-century bibliography, the high proportion of entries with asterisks indicates that NUC has subsumed most bibliographically distinct volumes within sets of the 34-volume work, thus making identification of different editions virtually impossible. The last three characters in the WHUC address represent date of publication if the item *is* in NUC, and filing and individuation numbers for the machine if it is not.

We might concentrate on the differences between the two bibliographies rather than the similarities in order to put the eighteenth-century one into perspective.

Not everything in the two bibliographies is French-language Canadiana. In the seventeenth-century one, the language of 27, 29, 33, and 34 makes it obvious that they would be excluded. Everything in the eighteenth-century list is obviously in French, but the descriptive annotations inserted for illustrative purposes in the last three entries indicate that only No. 47 among the three contains Canadiana.

Memoires du Levant, vols 1-5:
    46
J0093018* 99
[   ]
ed [Yves Mathurin Marie TREAUDET DE QUERBEUF]
Lettres edifiantes et curieuses
New edn
[26 vols] Vols I-V
Paris,
Chez G. Merigot le jeune.

144

    1780
    12mo 453,483,480,496,534pp
    TxU CaOLU CaQMBN

Memoires d'Amerique, vols 6-9; des Indes, vols 10-15; de la Chine, etc.,
vols 16-24:
        47
    J0093021* 40
    [   ]
    ed [Yves Mathurin Marie TREAUDET DE QUERBEUF]
    Lettres edifiantes et curieuses, ecrites des missions
    New edn
    [26 vols] Vols VI-XXIV
    Paris,
    Chez J.G. Merigot le jeune.
    1781
    12mo 424, 456, 424, 416, 404, 423, 448, 463, 400, 430, 438, 452, 480,
    516, 462, 526, 532, 619, 552pp
    TxU CaOLU CaQMBN*

Memoires des Indes et de la Chine, vols 25-26:
        48
    J0093021* 60
    [   ]
    ed [Yves Mathurin Marie TREAUDET DE QUERBEUF]
    Lettres edifiantes et curieuses
    New edn
    [26 vols] Vols XXV-XXVI
    Paris,
    Chez J.G. Merigot le jeune.
    1783
    12mo 444, 518pp
    TxU CaQMBN* CaOLU

A similar annotation upon geographical coverage added to each entry in the query file would enable us to make a decision that WHSTC 12, 17, 18, 19, 20, 26, 32, 34, 36 contain Canadiana. Simple descriptive annotations of this kind can be augmented with evaluative ones, but might be better reserved for the nine items as they appear in the Canadiana query file. Simple appraisal of the descriptive elements in both bibliographies helps us to decide what should in fact be selected for inclusion in other query files. More evaluative annotations can serve other purposes.

The seventeenth-century bibliography illustrates how we can optimize our macroscopic bibliographical control by reducing the descriptive detail of McCoy to minimal identificatory data. No real loss in microscopic bibliographical control has taken place despite the fact that McCoy's 132 entries have been reduced to 56. Indeed, microscopic bibliographical control can in fact be increased by adding interpretative or evaluative annotations to the query file. To illustrate this, McCoy's first 27 entries have been appraised, and *bibliographical* annotations added to the first ten WHSTC entries. Evaluative *content* notes could also be added before or after each WHSTC entry in order to improve our exploitative power. Some might with profit be derived from Harrisse.

1
L0235511   632
LE JEUNE, Paul
Brieve relation dv voyage de la novvelle France
Paris,
Chez Sebastien Cramoisy.
1632
8vo 68p
McCoy distingujishes 2 variations: 1,2
McCoy gives details of 3 textually insignificant variant states of forme A(o)

2
L0235531   634
LE IEUNE, Paul
Relation de ce qvi s'est passe . . .1633
Paris,
Chez Sebastien Cramoisy.
1634
8vo   216p
McCoy distinguishes 2 edns: 1st, 3,4,5; 2nd 6-9. This is 1st edn
CaQMBN
McCoy gives details of a textually significant variant state of formes H(i&o) and O(o), and an insignificant one of A(o)

3
L0235534   634
LE IEUNE, Paul
Relation de ce qvi s'est passe. . .1633
Paris,
Chez Sebastien Cramoisy.
1634
8vo   216p
McCoy distinguishes 4 variations of 2nd edn: 6,7,8,9
McCoy gives details of a textually significant variant state of formes H(i) and O(o), and an insignificant one of A(o) and E(o)

4
L0235539   635
LE IEUNE, Paul
Relation de ce qvi s'est passe. . .1634
Paris,
Chez Sebastien Cramoisy.
1635
8vo   342p

McCoy distinguishes 2 edns: 1st edn, 10,11,12,13; 2nd edn: 14
CaOOP CaQMBN
1st edn: McCoy gives details of a textually significant variant state of
forme X(i) and an insignificant one of E(i) and I(i); 2nd edn: McCoy gives
details of a textually significant variant state of forme Y(o) and possibly
of a cancel A2

5
L0235543   636
LE IEUNE, Paul
Relation de ce qvi s'est passe. . .1635
Paris,
Chez Sebastien Cramoisy.
1636
8vo   246p
McCoy distinguishes 4 variations: 16-19
CaQMBN
McCoy gives details of 3 or 4 textually significant variant states of forme
E(o) and of a textually significant variant state of F(i)

6
L0235542   636
LE IEUNE, Paul
Relation de ce qvi s'est passe. . .1634. & 1635
Avignon,
De l'imprimerie de Iaqves Bramereav.
1636
8vo   416p
McCoy 15 distinguishes no variants, but gives second part a distinct
number: 20
McCoy claims Part II is a reprint of his 16-19

7
L0235547   637
LE IEUNE, Paul
Relation de ce qvi s'est passe. . .1636
Paris,
Chez Sebastien Cramoisy.
1637
8vo   272,223p
McCoy distinguishes 2 edns: 1st, 21,22; 2nd, 23. This is 1st edn
CaOTU
McCoy gives details of a textually significant variant state of formes
Ee(o), Ii(i), Kk(i)

8
L0235551   637
LE IEUNE, Paul
Relation de ce qvi s'est passe. . .1636
Paris,

Chez Sebastien Cramoisy.
1637
8vo 199,163pp
McCoy 23 distinguishes no variants

9
L0235555 638
LE IEUNE, Pavl
Relation de ce qvi s'est pass[e]. . .1637
Roven,
Chez lean Le Bovllenger.
1638
8vo 336,256pp
McCoy distinguishes 4 variations: 24,25,26,27. This is McCoy 24 and 25 (two distinct issues)
CaOOP CaQMBN
McCoy gives details of a textually significant variant state of formes E(o), H(o), P(o), T(o), Aa(o) and an insignificant one of L(i), O(o), and Aa(i). He also gives details of 4 textually significant variant states of Mm(i). A new gathering of four leaves, a(tilde), substituted for A1, distinguishes 1st and 2nd issue. He also provides evidence for two textually significant cancels, Bb8,Ff2

10
L0235556 636
LE IEUNE, Pavl
Relation de ce qvi s'est passe. . .1637
Roven,
Chez lean Le Bovlanger. El se vendent a Paris, Chez Pierre De Bresche.
1638
8vo 336,256pp
McCoy distingishes 4 variations: 24,25,26,27. This is McCoy 26 and 27 (2 distinct issues)
CaQMM CaOTU CaOOP
McCoy identifies a variant state of forme a(tilde) (o), which distinguishes two issues, but any or all other variant formes might be present in any of the 3 issues subsumed in McCoy's 24-27

11
L0235565 638
LE IEVNE, Pavle
Relation de ce qvi s'est passe. . .1638
Paris,
Chez Sebastien Cramoisy.
1638
8vo 78,67pp
McCoy distinguishes 2 edns: 1st, 28; 2nd, 29,30
CaOTU CaQMM CaOTP

The eighteenth-century bibliography is at a more primitive stage of development simply because no manually-produced bibliographical tool is available for us to make the computer, as yet, serve as a telescope of the mind. The highly-respected *Bibliothèque de la Compagnie de Jésus*, first published in 1853,[20] is the most comprehensive tool for bibliographical control of the writings of the Jesuits. Even the 1960 edition[21] of Sommervogel, who revised De Backer's monumental work, is limited by the fact that the entries in the bibliography are based on secondary sources and not on the books themselves. The 40 or so entries for the *Lettres édifiantes et curieuses* found under Gobien, Halde, Patouillet, and Querbeuf (nothing under Marechel or Marchal) are derived mainly from review notices such as those in the *Journal de Trevoux*,[22] and the books listed need to be matched with actual copies. Thus, WHSTC 7, 16, 24, 44, 45 still need checking. Obvious gaps in the De Backer/Sommervogel lists (e.g. Vols 21-26, 29-30, 32) have been supplied in our bibliography, and information derived from NUC or individual library catalogs has been added to the query files for confirmation as well.

For instance, WHSTC 1, 40, and 41 not only record from NUC some abbreviated bibliographical information within square brackets, but also record the location of the copy closest to London, Ontario, that could be used to create a short-title catalog record for the main files.

> 40
> J0093039   767
> [see description in NUC]
> [Memoires geographiques, Paris] [MiU]

> 41
> J0093040   767
> [this item not yet in control file]
> [Memoires geographiques, Yverdon] [NN]

WHSTC 44 and 45 indicate that a visit to the *Bibliothèque Nationale* in Paris might be necessary in order to improve our bibliographical control.

> 44
> J0093018*   90
> [description not yet on file]
> [Vol XXXI de Hansy le jeune 1774] [Bibliotheque nationale de la France]

> 45
> J0093018*   95
> [description not yet on file]
> [Vols XXXIII-XXXIV Pierre Berton 1776] [XXXIII in BN de la France]

Locations information is, of course, a very important element in improving our bibliographical control of a portion of the bibliographical universe. The locations information for Canadian libraries is as complete as use of the Canadian Union Catalog (CANUC) and serendipity can make it, but it must be obvious that early editions of early volumes are scarcer than later editions or later volumes in the series.

Early editions of particular volumes seldom appear in complete sets of the

Lettres, as they were long out of print when the sets were made up. It is ironic, therefore, that libraries that can boast of complete sets seldom have the earliest editions. One must look for broken or incomplete sets if one wants early editions. Item 3, for instance, was found in the William L. Clements Library in a mixed set of volumes 1-4, 10-15, 17, 23, 25, and 27. The first three volumes came from a seminary in Guelph, Ontario, where, presumably, later volumes were not to be found.

Locations information is also an important element in our bibliographical instruments because the powerlessness of scholars in the past to find actual copies of the earliest editions has led to heavy reliance on nineteenth- and twentieth-century reprints or editions of the earlier texts. Select bibliographies or primary sources (which scholarly practice demands should be included in an authoritative scholarly work) are very deficient in contemporaneous *printed* sources because of reliance on modern texts. Careful checking of the intermediary texts against the originals is not a common practice, and one suspects that this is because a copy of the originals is not easy to find. Locations information is too restricted in a library catalog, and tools such as Dionne do not have such information. As always, Tremaine is an honorable exception.

Indeed, the degree of bibliographical control provided by our bibliographical instruments is so poor that we cannot even estimate from them the total number of separate items that constitute French-language Canadiana in the eighteenth century nor what proportion of them are to be found in Canadian libraries. The definition of what constitutes an "item" differs considerably from one bibliographical tool to another, so the rough counts I have alluded to earlier are not very reliable. It seems almost certain, however, that manually-produced instruments give us more control over sixteenth and seventeenth-century French-language printed books than over eighteenth-century books (with the exception of Canadian imprints). The machine-based system which is now being developed as part of the WHSTC system is already more comprehensive than any one manually-produced tool and has indexing devices which provide more points of access or indexing capability than any one manually-produced tool. The data base does not yet incorporate material from Harrisse, Dionne, and other fairly comprehensive standard bibliographies, but it would, I think, be fitting to end this paper with the best estimate possible at this time of the size of that portion of the bibliographical universe that can be called French-language Canadiana of the eighteenth century. The WHSTC bibliographies you have seen demonstrate that the contents of the query file are automatically counted by the machine and printed out after the heading. The four query files containing lists of Canadiana show that, as of this moment, the number of items is as follows:

1545-1700	188
1701-1750	162
1751-1770	190
1771-1800	125
Total	665

Comparison of the pre-1701 printout with Harrisse demonstrates that 92 are identifiable in WHSTC, and that 65 items in the best manually-produced tool available may, eventually, after confirmation, be added to the file. Twenty items in Harrisse are not relevant, but the ease with which judgments can be made about items in Harrisse shows what a fine tool the 1872 bibliography really is. But our machine-readable file more than doubles our exploitative and descriptive power. The answer to "How many items of printed French Canadiana were published before 1701" can be answered "At least 253." "What are they" can be answered with a printout of a developing bibliography. "Where are they" can also be answered (at least partly) by the same printout.

Similarly, for the first half of the eighteenth century, although comparison of the 1701-1750 WHSTC bibliography with Dionne reveals considerable inaccuracy in the 1906 bibliography, 62 items are identifiable with reasonable certainty. The 65 possible additions to WHSTC may eventually be reduced to about 50 when all "ghosts" have been laid. So it would seem possible to state "At least 212 items of French-language Canadiana were published in the eighteenth century before printing was introduced into Canada." After printing was introduced, approximately 580 French-language items were published in Canada, and at least 250 were published outside Canada.

When the query files have been further developed, I hope to be able to locate copies of as many items as possible in Canadian libraries. A recent sampling of U.S. libraries suggested that holdings as high as 46% could be found in the richest collection in the U.S. — in the John Carter Brown Library, Brown University, Providence, Rhode Island. Present indications are that no one collection in Canada is likely to provide more than 30% of the possible range of books. We need to improve our bibliographical control in order to improve our bibliographical resources.

William J. Cameron
The University of Western Ontario

Notes

[1] Ranganathan, Shiyali Ramamrita, "Universal Bibliography and its Substitutes" *Libri* 1953: 2: 293.
[2] Ranganathan, Shiyali Ramamrita, ed, *Documentation and its Facets*; being *a symposium of seventy papers by thirty-two authors*, Bombay, New York, Asia Pub. House, [1963] 639p.
[3] Cameron, William J. *Bibliographical Control of Early Books*, Bangalore, India, Sarada Ranganathan Endowment for Library Science, 1978. ix, 78p.
[4] Wilson, Patrick, *Two Kinds of Power, An Essay on Bibliographical Control*, Berkeley and Los Angeles, Univ. of California Press, 1968.
[5] Tremaine, Marie, *A Bibliography of Canadian Imprints 1751-1800*, Toronto, University of Toronto Press, 1952. xxvii, 705p.
[6] Dionne, Narcisse-Eutrope, *Inventaire chronologique des livres . . . publiés en langue française dans la province de Québec. . . 1764-1905*, Québec, 1905 viii, 175p. (And *Premier Supplément* 1912).
[7] Dionne, Narcisse-Eutrope, *Inventaire chronologique des ouvrages publiés à l'étranger . . . sur Québec et la Nouvelle France . . . 1534-1906*, Québec, 1906. viii, 155p (And *Premier Supplément*, 1912.)

8 Staton, Frances M. and Marie Tremaine, *A bibliography of Canadiana, Being items in the Public Library of Toronto, Canada, relating to the early history and development of Canada,* Toronto, The Public Library, 1934. 828p.

9 Gertrude M. Boyle and Marjorie Colbeck, *A bibliography of Canadiana First Supplement, Being items in the Public Library of Toronto, Canada, relating to the early history and development of Canada,* Toronto, The Public Library, 1959, 333p.

10 *The National Union Catalog: Pre-1956 Imprints,* London, Mansell, 1968-, 674 vols + (still appearing).

11 Boivin, Henri-Bernard, compiler, *Bibliographie de bibliographies québécoises,* Montréal, Ministre des affaires culturelles, Bibliothèque nationale du Québec, 1979. 2 vols.

12 Lochhead, Douglas, *Bibliography of Canadian Bibliographies. Index compiled by Peter E. Greig* Second edition, [Toronto], University of Toronto, in association with the Bibliographical Society of Canada, [1972]. 312p.

13 Vlach, Milada, and Yolande Buono, compilers, *Laurentiana parus avant 1821.* Montréal, Bibliothèque nationale du Québec, 1976. xxvii, 413, 120p.

14 Lande, Lawrence. *The Lawrence Lande collection of Canadiana in the Redpath Library of McGill University* Montreal, Lawrence Lande Foundation for Canadian Historical Research, 1965. xxxv, 301p.

15 McGill University, *Rare and Unusual Canadiana; first supplement to the Lande bibliography,* Montreal, Lawrence Lande Foundation for Canadian Historical Research, 1971. xx, 779p.

16 McCoy, James Comly, *Jesuit Relations of Canada, 1632-1673; a bibliography,* Paris, Arthur Race, 1937. 310p.

17 Cameron, William J., *The HPB Project: Phase IV. The French Canadian Contribution to the Development of A Western Hemisphere Short-Title Catalog (WHSTC) of Spanish, French, and Portuguese books printed before 1801.* London, Ontario, University of Western Ontario, 1980, vi, 183, [128]p.

18 Harrisse, Henry, *Notes pour servir à l'histoire, à la bibliographie et à la cartographie de la Nouvelle France et des pays adjacents 1545-1700,* Paris, Librarie Tross, 1872, xxxiii, 367p.

19 Conlon, Pierre, *Prélude au siècle des lumières en France: Répertoire chronologique de 1680 à 1715,* Genève, Droz, 1970-75, 6 vols.

20 De Backer, Augustin, *Bibliothèque des écrivains de la Compagnie de Jésus,* Liège, Grandmont-Donders, 1853-1861. 7 vols.

21 De Backer, Augustin et Alois, *Bibliothèque des écrivains de la Compagnie de Jésus; nouvelle édition par Carlos Sommervogel,* Heverlé-Louvain, Editions de la Bibliothèque S.J., 1960. 12 vols.

22 *Mémoires pour l'histoire des sciences et des beaux-arts.* Trévoux, Impr. de S.A.S. Paris, Chez E. Ganeau, 1701-67. 265 vols.

14. La Visée historiographique de Charlevoix d'après ses "Liste et examen des auteurs consultés"

Je mettrai à la tête de chaque Histoire un Catalogue exact de tous les Auteurs, qui auront écrit sur le même sujet, ne l'eussent-ils fait qu'en passant, pourvû que ce qu'ils en ont dit, mérite qu'on y fasse quelque attention. Je marquerai en même tems les secours, que j'aurai tirés de chacun, et les raisons, que j'aurai euës de les suivre, ou de m'en écarter; en quoi je tâcherai de faire en sorte, qu'aucune prévention, ni aucun autre intérêt, que celui de la vérité, ne conduise ma plume.

. . . il étoit bien temps de rendre ce service au Public, tandis que nous avons encore des regles certaines de critique pour distinguer les Pieces légitimes et authentiques, de ce nombre prodigieux d'Ecrits hazardés, dont la plûpart altérent la vérité jusqu'au point de la rendre méconnoissable, et qui en feroient enfin perdre absolument la trace, si on laissoit aller le débordement plus loin.[1]

Le sort réservé à l'*Histoire et description générale de la Nouvelle-France* est paradoxal. Elle n'a été rééditée en français qu'en 1976 (Montréal; Elysée), et on la cite beaucoup moins que les *Relations* des Jésuites, Champlain ou même Sagard; et pourtant, elle constitue non seulement la première histoire d'envergure de la Nouvelle-France, mais encore elle a donné à notre histoire sa forme quasi définitive. On a souvent cité cette phrase de Fr.-X. Garneau:

Notre histoire qui n'était avant lui qu'une oeuvre imparfaite a pris sous sa plume les proportions, l'ordre et le développement d'une histoire en forme.[2]

Proportion, ordre, développement; ces mots, qui pourraient être de Charlevoix, renvoient à la double opération du travail historique: sélection des éléments diégétiques et mise en ordre dans une structure narrative et explicative. Dans cette optique, le jugement de Garneau me paraît très juste: de Garneau lui-même jusqu'à Groulx tout au moins, l'histoire du Canada semble avoir emprunté à Charlevoix un cadre global, une forme canonique, tant pour le choix des matériaux que pour le développement du commentaire et l'ordre du récit.

Mais chercher la visée historiographique de Charlevoix dans sa bibliographie critique peut ressembler davantage à une gageure qu'à une entreprise sérieuse. Je ne vous cacherai pas le caractère insolite de cette hypothèse de travail. A défaut de toucher l'essentiel peut-être, elle me permettra de questionner d'une manière différente un discours historiographique important du Siècle des Lumières. Un discours, qui, se situant en marge et à la suite d'autres *écrits,* vise un objectif à double volet — cumulatif et normatif — : *tout* dire de l'essentiel et *bien* dire la vérité.

L'Histoire comme anti-roman

Une lecture superficielle de la "Liste des auteurs" dégage une première ligne de force importante: l'insistance sur l'"Histoire suivie et complette," par opposition à l'"Histoire fort détaillée" de la colonie qu'avaient laissée les Jésuites avec leurs *Relations.* L'*Histoire suivie* hiérarchise les faits, leur donne liaison et vectorialité, dégage les causes et l'enchaînement, identifie les acteurs des événements; l'histoire détaillée, collée au quotidien, rend le discontinu, la poussière de mille gestes ponctuels, recueille les matériaux sur lesquels l'histoire suivie sera fondée. L'histoire suivie met de l'ordre dans une profusion regardée comme une espèce d'organisme vivant qui menace de s'amplifier au point de "noyer" l'histoire même et de rendre incompréhensible la logique des événements. Non maîtrisée, cette profusion devient fable proliférante occupant tout l'espace historique — comme le cadavre de l'Amédée d'Ionesco finit par occuper tout l'espace scénique. A trois reprises au moins, Charlevoix affirme préférer le vide ou l'exiguïté de la connaissance à la profusion fabuleuse. Les premiers auteurs, "par cela même qu'ils nous apprenoient très-peu de choses," "ne pouvoient pas nous jetter dans de grandes erreurs." On comprend au nom de quel principe un Lahontan est avec violence désavoué: il confond "tellement" "le vray avec le faux," qu'il plonge tout dans l'incertitude. Car en histoire, la fable ou le roman — cet adroit mélange de vérité et de mensonge, comme on disait fréquemment alors — est pire que l'ognorance. Dans son "Avertissement," Charlevoix reproche à Koempfer d'avoir "défiguré" les "trois ou quatre faits historiques" à quoi se réduit son *Histoire de Saint-Domingue*: "Koempfer en a fait un Roman, où la vraisemblance n'est pas même gardée."

Rappelons au passage qu'un autre Jésuite français, le P. Porée, publia en 1736 un violent réquisitoire contre le roman: *De libris qui vulgo dicuntur Romanses;* un an auparavant, le P. Bougeant, qui s'intéressa à l'âme des bêtes, publia son *Prince Fan-Féredin au royaume de Romancie* (XII-275pp.), parodie, qui relève sur le mode humoristique tous les clichés du roman.

La prolifération fabuleuse aura son exacte correspondance dans l'écriture: on pourrait regarder la "liberté de plume" reprochée à Hennepin et Lahontan surtout comme une manifestation stylistique de cette abondance trompeuse, mais c'est dans l'"enflure" verbale, le "style de déclamation" qu'on la retrouvera le mieux: assez curieusement, c'est à deux représentants de l'ordre mendiant, de l'ordre "pauvre", les Récollets Leclercq et Hennepin encore, que sont accolées ces qualifications comme si la pauvreté affirmée de l'extérieur était compensée par la boursouflure langagière. Faut-il encore rattacher à cette prolifération dangereuse les "indécences" et les "libertés" reprochées à Lahontan et Hennepin encore une fois? J'y serais porté, surtout si on les range sous la catégorie du désordre où entrerait encore le style

"barbare" et "embarrassé" (Lahontan), par opposition au style "simple et
naturel" d'un Champlain, par exemple. Car le bien écrire se confond avec la
simplicité (Mgr de Saint-Vallier): "Le style de ces relatons (celles des Jésuites)
est extrémement simple." On aurait tort de voir toutefois en Charlevoix un
adepte de l'ascétisme historique: il aime les amples portraits, les détails
nombreux, l'accumulation des questions hypothétiques. Dans le corps de son
récit, il ne veut rien sacrifier de la prodigieuse richesse de l'événement, il
accueille avec empressement le "curieux", l'"intéressant", l'énigmatique. Je
n'en fournirai ici que deux exemples, puisqu'ils ne touchent pas directement à
mon propos:
  1. Les "Hommes monstrueux" dont on parle dès les pages 15 à 20 du Livre
I. Charlevoix, qui écrit de Champlain: "On ne peut lui reprocher qu'un peu
trop de credulité pour des contes", s'attarde à parler de "choses
extraordinaires", non dénuées de "merveilleux" et "qui ne sont pas tout-à-fait
indignes de l'attention des personnes curieuses" (pp. 15-16). Par exemple, des
"Hommes d'une grandeur et d'une grosseur monstrueuses, qui rendoient leurs
excremens par la bouche, et urinoient par-dessous l'épaule," ou encore ce
"Peuple tout noir" aux "cheveux droits blancs" du Labrador ou bien ces
Pygmées qui "n'ont pas plus de trois pieds de haut, et sont d'une extrème
grosseur." Avant de "mettre fin à cette digression," Charlevoix s'interroge en
des termes peut-être un peu surprenants pour un Jésuite cultivé et orthodoxe:

> Qui peut s'assûrer de connoître tous les caprices et tous les mysteres de la
> Nature? On sçait combien l'imagination des Meres a de pouvoir sur le fruit
> qu'elles portent. L'experience, le témoignage même de l'Ecriture, en sont
> des preuves sans réplique: ajoûtons à cela les figures bizarres, où certaines
> Nations trouvent une beauté, dont elles sont si jalouses, qu'on y met les
> corps des Enfans à la torture pour achever ce que l'imagination des Meres
> n'a pû finir, et l'on comprendra sans peine qu'il peut y avoir des Hommes
> assez differens des autres pour donner lieu à certaines gens, qui saisissent
> vivement les objets, et ne se donnent pas le tems d'examiner les choses, de
> faire des contes absurdes, qui ne sont pourtant pas sans quelque réalité. Je
> reviens à mon Histoire.

"Je reviens à mon Histoire," conclut Charlevoix, conscient d'avoir cédé à la
"séduction de l'étrange" et à sa propension à formuler des hypothèses lorsque
celles-ci ne mettent pas en danger la belle ordonnance logique de
l'enchaînement événementiel.
  2. En étudiant de près certains passages de l'*Histoire et description,* j'avais
relevé un élément de stratégie narrative visant à dramatiser un événement
important. Par exemple, le récit de l'attaque de Phips devant Québec est
encadré par deux zones d'ombre laissées au début et à la fin. La première a
pour objet la culpabilité plus ou moins grande du Gouverneur de Plaisance
que les Anglais venaient de prendre; la seconde pèse les différents
témoignages touchant la mésentente de certaines tribus indiennes avec les
Anglais et qui empêcha de ces derniers d'attaquer en même temps les
Français sur le front de Montréal. Dans les deux cas, l'auteur ne décide pas, il
se contente de formuler des hypothèses comme s'il voulait créer un

156

contrepoint entre l'accessoire (certains éléments du contexte) et l'essentiel (le récit lui-même). Dans les deux cas, l'embrayeur autoritaire "quoiqu'il en soit" fait obliquer le texte vers un terrain plus sûr: on passe de l'énonciation à l'énoncé ou, si l'on me permet ce parallélisme aventureux, de l'hypothèse à la Vérité.

Je ne serais pas surpris que ce balisage de la diégèse entre deux signaux aussi voyants ne fasse partie d'une stratégie historienne visant à rejeter à la périphérie l'accessoire pour laisser bonne place à l'événement central sur l'interprétation duquel ne subsiste aucun doute. Comme par hasard, l'auteur affiche la carence de sa documentation ou de sa mémoire seulement pour l'accessoire. Le procédé a le double avantage de régler une fois pour toutes le sort de l'inclassable, de l'inexplicable en le refoulant aux confins du récit et, par la grâce d'un aveu d'humilité, de rendre l'essentiel d'autant plus crédible.

Contrairement à ce qu'on pourrait croire à première vue, la fable ou la "conjecture", peuvent être accueillies, du moment qu'elles ne mettent pas en danger la cohérence globale de l'éconcé historique et qu'elles donnent à celui-ci le tremblement du vécu, de la pensée en action.

Me voici un peu loin, me direz-vous, de ma liste d'auteurs. Comme Charlevoix, je reviens à mon histoire. La fiction, ai-je dit, est le danger suprême. Comment en sortir? Jugeant les premiers auteurs de dictionnaires géographiques et historiques, Charlevoix écrit:

> Ils n'avoient devant les yeux que peu de Memoires, dont les Auteurs se bornaient presque à rapporter ce qu'ils avoient vû, ou appris de témoins oculaires, et ne pouvoient quére être taxés que de quelque exaggeration.

On discerne bien ici le lieu commun de la source historique: la connaissance passe d'abord par le vu de témoins, mais doit devenir écrit (livre ou archive) pour servir à l'historien.

La primauté du vu

> Comme j'ay plus de connessance de ces choses que beaucoup d'autres, j'en parles hardiment. . . J'ay eu le bonheur d'estre témoin oculeire de presque tout,

écrit Marie Morin au début de son *Histoire simple et véritable,* communément appelée *Annales de l'Hôtel-Dieu de Montréal.* Le témoin fiable est celui-là seul qui *a vu.* Lafitau a vu de près les moeurs, les coutumes et la religion des Sauvages Amériquains; Sagard, présenté positivement, "raconte naïvement tout ce qu'il a vû," mais "il nous apprend peu de choses intéressantes" parce qu'"il n'a pas eu le tems de voir assez bien les choses, encore moins de verifier tout ce qu'on lui avoit dit." On peut compter sur ce que Bacqueville de la Potherie "dit comme témoin oculaire," mais "il n'a pas toujours été bien instruit sur le reste." Est-ce à dire que l'acuité de la vision est liée à l'agir? Je le crois. En tout cas, plus le vu est greffé sur un *faire* important, plus le témoignage sera précieux, comme le manifestent les Jésuites de la Nouvelle-France "répandus dans toutes les nations" et "entrés" "dans toutes les affaires de la Colonie." Mais encore faut-il que cet agir soit transparent, animé d'intentions droites.

Donc, primauté du vu, et méfiance du ouï-dire, comme chez Champlain. Le ouï-dire, c'est la voix anonyme collectivisée, la rumeur, la parole diffuse, fabulatrice, comme si la vue garantissait à elle seule la véracité. Charlevoix récuse davantage Hennepin et Lahontan en ne mentionnant pas leur qualité de témoin oculaire qu'en les attaquant violemment dans leurs thèses, leur comportement ou leur style. Voltaire, qui insistera tellement sur "l'incertitude de l'histoire," parlera de "cette certitude qui naît de la disposition unanime de mille témoins oculaires de différentes nations, sans que personne ait réclamé contre leur témoignage." (Article "Histoire" de l'*Encyclopédie*).

Si l'on se rappelle que la "Liste des Auteurs" se termine sur la mention "d'une aussi habile main," celle du cartographe Bellin, on se demandera si Charlevoix ne dépasse pas ici le cliché pour rejoindre une hantise de l'époque dont on verra des manifestations dix ans plus tard dans plusieurs articles et gravures de l'*Encyclopédie*: l'oeil et la main comme organes essentiels de saisie du réel. Je ne pense pas seulement ici à ces très belles planches représentant plusieurs dessins d'oeil ou de main, mais à d'autres mettant en scène un Monsieur bien habillé et très calme, montrant de sa main à une Dame le spectacle pas du tout effrayant d'un volcan dont la lave descend jusqu'à leurs pieds. Je pense à cette expression du médecin Tronchin que je choisis parce qu'elle n'est ni de d'Alembert, ni de Diderot, ni de Jaucourt: "l'inoculation confiée à des yeux éclairés et à des mains sages." Au départ, la fiabilité historique sera donc affaire d' acuité visuelle et de main-mise à la pâte de l'événement.

S'interroger sur le témoignage, c'est forcément s'interroger sur le témoin. On sait quelle importance y attachent les auteurs de l'*Encyclopédie* — Diderot plus particulièrement:

> Il faut considérer si les témoins sont oculaires ou non; ce qu'ils ont risqué pour se faire croire; quelle crainte ou quelles espérances ils avoient en annonçant aux autres des faits dont ils se disoient témoins oculaires: s'ils avoient exposé leur vie pour soûtenir leur déposition, il faut convenir qu'elle acquéreroit une grande force; que seroit-ce donc s'ils l'avoient sacrifiée et perdue?[3]

Détachée de son contexte, cette phrase semble un brin naïve; mais, faute de temps, je ne puis la replacer dans la discussion serrée à laquelle se livre Diderot sur la critique des sources historiques. Elle nous permet toutefois de mieux voir la position de Charlevoix. Celui-ci ne distingue pas comme Diderot, Voltaire, l'abbé de Prades, entre différents types de faits (simples/extraordinaires; transitoires/permanents; passés/présents; éloignés/rapprochés, etc.), entre différents types de témoins (oculaires, instruits, intéressés, nombreux, indépendants. . .); il ne pose le problème du témoin que par rapport à la contemporanéité de l'événement. Et encore, le témoin n'est accepté ou récusé que sur sa personne. Il s'agit moins de savoir si son témoignage est conditionné dans l'espace et le temps, limité par l'acuité de vision, la distance existentielle ou physique que d'établir d'abord la qualité de l'individu. Lahontan est récusé comme témoin en tant que "mauvais François" et "mauvais Chrétien," comme Hennepin qui aurait dû "se souvenir que c'étoit aux frais de la France, qu'il avoit voyagé dans l'Amérique, et que c'étoit au nom du Roy Très-Chrétien, que lui et le Sieur Dacan avoient pris possession des Pays, qu'ils avoient découverts." Il est symptomatique d'ailleurs que Charlevoix présente Lahontan comme un déclassé social, puis comme un chicanier qui subit la honte de la condamnation:

> L'Auteur, quoi qu'homme de condition, fut d'abord Soldat en Canada.
> . . . il se brouilla avec le Gouverneur, fut cassé, et se retira . . .

Pourquoi Charlevoix attribue-t-il l'initiative de la brouille à Lahontan alors qu'il connaissait le naturel chicanier et autoritaire du Gouverneur Brouillan et savait que celui-ci avait été condamné pour concussion? Charlevoix aurait fort bien pu écrire quelque chose comme: "le Gouverneur et Lahontan, tout aussi mauvais sujets l'un que l'autre, se brouillèrent. . . ."

Mais la valorisation/dévalorisation du témoin est habituellement beaucoup plus subtile. Champlain "étoit habile Navigateur, homme de tête et de resolution, désintéressé, plein de zéle pour la Religion et pour l'Etat"; Sagard "paroît homme fort judicieux, et très-zélé, non-seulement pour le salut des ames, mais encore pour le progrès d'une Colonie." Comme par hasard, l'*être* accompagne un témoignage semblable à celui des Jésuites — donc fiable — et le *paroître* est attribué à qui ne voit pas de la même manière. Autre subtile distinction, que je note sans généraliser: Lescarbot est présenté favorablement, mais comme un "Auteur" qui "a ramassé tout ce qui avoit été écrit avant lui": "il paroit sincere, bien instruit, censé et impartial" (On sait que les témoignages de Champlain et Lescarbot ne concordent pas toujours).

Une dernière distinction, beaucoup plus importante celle-là, s'attache à la mise en écriture du témoignage. Voyons-en un exemple: celui du Récollet Leclercq. Ne parlons pas de la *Nouvelle Relation de Gaspésie,* jugée péremptoirement inintéressante parce que la géographie humaine et physique en est pauvre, alors que pourtant la "description" de la même région par Nicolas Denys est fort vantée. Le *Premier Etablissement de la Foy* est dévalorisé dès le départ parce qu'"on a lieu de croire que le Comte de Frontenac a mis la main" à "Cet Ouvrage." Jugement surprenant à un double titre:

1) Justifiant à priori son entreprise historique, Charlevoix avait écrit dans son "Projet" qu'une histoire de la Nouvelle-France n'exigeait pas que "toutes les parties" "soient de la même main."

2) Charlevoix s'en prend souvent aux faiseurs de "conjectures" qui suivent la mode, la voix pubique ou simplement leurs préjugés, plutôt que d'adopter une attitude désintéressée. Or, l'insinuation par le biais de la parole diffuse, du ouï-dire dont je parlais plus tôt, est fréquente chez Charlevoix:

> Aussi passe-t-il pour constant que c'est Geudreville lui-même, qui a retouché la derniere Edition de ses *Voyages* [ceux de Lahontan].
>
> Il paroît même qu'il [Hennepin] avoit défense de retourner dans l'Amérique, et que ce fut le chagrin, qu'il en conçut, qui le porta à s'en aller en Hollande, où il fit imprimer un troisiéme Ouvrage . . . .
>
> On leur [les *Voyages* de Lahontan] a rendu plus de justice en Canada, où l'Auteur passe communément pour un Romancier.

Plus que mesquinerie ou concurrence dans le domaine du faire et de l'écrire, il faut retenir ici une conception de l'historien qui fait de celui-ci un analogue de Dieu, en ce qu'il sonde les reins et les coeurs, voit les ressorts cachés des actions les plus complexes, distingue sans possibilité d'erreur le vrai du faux, le sincère de l'apprêté; bref, il est le Créateur qui met ordre et lumière dans le Chaos.

L'intermédiaire de l'écrit

Un dernier point retiendra mon attention. Malgré la primauté du *vu* sur le *ouï-dire*, du *témoignage direct* sur l'*intermédiaire*, l'historien n'est pas celui qui table sur le témoignage direct du témoin, mais sur la transcription de ce témoignage. Dans le corps de son ouvrage, Charlevoix ne confirme ni n'infirme un fait par ce qu'il a vu lui-même, mais par *une autre pièce écrite*. Pour être valable ou même utilisé, le témoignage devra franchir l'oralité et se fixer dans l'écriture, plus particulièrement le livre. Autrement dit, le seul regard retenu en définitive, n'est pas le regard de l'observateur, mais celui du lecteur: les premiers historiens et géographes "n'avoient devant les yeux que peu de Memoires dont les Auteurs se bornoient presque à rapporter ce qu'ils avoient *vû*, ou appris de témoins oculaires." Malgré toutes ces phrases sur l'observation visuelle, le regard critique n'est donc en définitive qu'un regard de liseur; le réel historique qu'on prétend représenter n'est pas le vu concret mais une vue de l'esprit fixée dans un livre.

Je dis un livre et non pas l'archive comme j'avais d'abord écrit, puisque Charlevoix oppose justement le livre à l'archive, non pour privilégier cette dernière, mais pour lui accorder un rôle d'appoint: l'archive n'apporte en effet que des "éclaircissemens" aux "Livres imprimés"; "les pièces originales" citées à la fin ne servent qu'à "remplir" les "vuides."

"Eclaircissemens", "vuides": ces mots peuvent encore nous éclairer sur ce qui constitue l'histoire chez Charlevoix. Dans les dépêches des Gouverneurs et des Intendants, il a "puisé tout ce qui regarde le Gouvernement politique et militaire de la Nouvelle-France"; les mémoires de Perrot et Pénicault lui ont mieux fait comprendre les moeurs et coutumes des Indiens. C'est donc dire que ces deux sujets, moeurs et gouvernement, ne font pas fondamentalement partie de l'histoire. Se défendant d'avoir "voulu faire tomber" l'Histoire de Koempfer sur le Japon, Charlevoix affirme n'y avoir rien trouvé "pour l'historique" ("j'aurois bien eu de la peine à en tirer une feüille d'impression") même s'il contient "une Notice fort ample de cet Empire, qui renferme le Gouvernement, la Police, la Religion, la Géographie et le Commerce des Hollandois" (Avertissement). Ce resserrement du champ historique était présent dès le départ puisque dans son "Projet" de 1735, Charlevoix prévoyait disposer les données recueillies en deux groupes: celles qui, organiquement liées entre elles, hiérarchisées en système, constitueraient le corps de l'histoire et celles qui, simultanées dans la réalité, risqueraient d'interférer avec la séquence narrative. L'ordonnance même de l'Histoire publiée en 3 volumes va exactement dans le même sens.

T.I: — "Avertissement"
— *Histoire et description. . . .*, L.I-XIII, p. 1-571.

160

— "Particularités de la vie et de la mort de quelques sauvages chrétiens", pp. 572-600.
— "Table des matières"

T.II: — *Histoire et description*. . ., L.XIII-XXII, pp. 1-502.
— "Table des matières", pp. 503-582.
— "Description des plantes principales de l'Amérique septentrionale", paginé de 1 à 56.

T.III: — "Remarques de M. Bellin . . . sur des Cartes et des plans . . .", p. I-XIX.
— "Dissertation préliminaire sur l'origine des Amériquains", p. 1-43.
— *Journal historique*. . . p. 44-500.
— "Projet d'un corps d'histoires du Nouveau Monde", p. I-IV.
— "Fastes chronologiques du Nouveau Monde. . .", p. V-XL
— "Liste et examen des auteurs. . .", p. XLI-XLII.

Malgré que son auteur en ait contre le roman, l'*Histoire et description* est en réalité construite comme un roman sagement disposé en chapitres chronologiques. Tout ce qui ne touche pas à l'aventure collective du groupe colonisateur, tout ce que Charlevoix ne peut narrativiser (faune, commerce, culture matérielle) est habituellement refoulé en dehors des bornes strictes du récit. Pour le Diderot et le Voltaire de l'*Encyclopédie,* on s'en souvient, l'opération historique était une entreprise de totalisation du savoir sur tous les aspects du passé humain.

* * *

Je me résume. Les gloses de Charlevoix sur les auteurs utilisés ne relèvent pas d'un simple commentaire bibliographique. Elles mettent en cause une conception de l'histoire dont on peut maintenant tracer les grandes lignes, en s'inspirant de l'"Avertisssement" et du "Projet d'un corps d'Histoires . . . ." Tout d'abord, il faut distinguer l'*historique* de l'*énoncé historique:* ou, si l'on préfère, d'une part, la diégèse, c'est-à-dire l'ensemble des éléments événementiels retenus, et d'autre part, le récit, c'est-à-dire l'organisation linguistique, l'arrangement textuel qui permet de représenter le réseau diégétique.

Lettré cultivé, professeur et rédacteur au *Journal de Trévoux,* Charlevoix définit l'histoire par rapport aux grands genres littéraires comme l'épopée, la tragédie et la comédie avec lesquels elle entretient une parenté par le sujet traité, aussi bien que par les personnages mis en scène. Mais là même où elle prétend s'en éloigner, elle en demeure assez près malgré tout: les sources où elle puise sont essentiellement écrites (le livre, le papier d'archive, le "bon mémoire"). Ne devient source que ce qui a été bien "digéré" une première fois par un mémorialiste ou un scripteur quelconque et une seconde fois par l'historien. On est loin de l'entreprise encyclopédique où un Voltaire, un Boucher d'Argis, un Diderot interrogent, outre les sources utilisées pour l'*Histoire et description*, la tradition orale, les textes de lois, les "monuments" (médailles aussi bien que statues et édifices), les manifestations de la culture matérielle (artefacts, logement, outils, habillement) et spirituelle (Beaux-Arts et littérature, langue, religion, contes, légendes et chansons populaires. . .). Diderot était évidemment tout disposé à accueillir les sources les plus diverses, puisque dans sa propre ville de Langres (cf. article du même nom) des découvertes archéologiques et une sauvegarde systématique de "monuments" ont permis de déterminer qu'une colonie romaine avait existé, qu'on y avait présenté du théâtre, que les Gaulois vénéraient Pluton, etc.

Plus spécifiquement, l'Histoire de la Nouvelle-France ne sera pas celle d'un "grand Empire" avec ses "révolutions importantes" et ses personnages célèbres; elle s'apparente plutôt à la comédie qui, prenant "ses sujets" et "ses Acteurs dans la vie privée," n'offre rien d'éclatant mais "des graces naïves, beaucoup de varieté et de simplicité, une sage distribution." Bien à regret, semble-t-il, Charlevoix se voit presque condamné à relater l'évolution d'une colonie qui n'offre rien de palpitant: des personnages sans beaucoup de panache, des "détails peu interessans en soi," retenus seulement pour leur exotisme ("pays éloignés").

On peut même se demander si Charlevoix n'a pas eu l'impression de se livrer à un pensum:

"Pour venir au sujet de l'Ouvrage, que je présente aujourd'hui au Public, j'en connois tous les desavantages. Il s'agit d'un pays immense, et qui après plus de deux Siécles, qui se sont écoulés depuis que nous l'avons découvert, est encore moins peuplé qu'il ne l'étoit alors ,quoi qu'il y ait passé assez de François pour remplacer au triple les Sauvages qu'on y trouva, et qu'on ne puisse pas leur reprocher de les avoir détruits. Cela n'annonce point une Histoire remplie de faits interessans; mais on la demandoit cette Histoire, et on avoit raison de la demander. C'est celle de toutes les Colonies Françoises du nouveau Monde, qui ont été honorées du titre de la nouvelle France, ou qui en ont fait partie; et elle nous manquoit." (Avertissement)

Dans le même "Avertissement" Charlevoix écrit encore:

Il m'auroit sans doute été plus aisé et plus agréable de ne prendre, si j'ose ainsi m'exprimer, que la crême de l'Histoire du nouveau Monde. J'aurois été bien-tôt à la fin de ma carriere, et j'aurois eu apparemment plus de Lecteurs. . . .

En réalité, l'histoire de la Nouvelle-France, semblable à celle de Saint-Dominique publiée plus tôt est l'histoire d'un échec, comme l'expriment clairement les dernières lignes de l'"Avertissement."

Qui a donc arrêté le progrès de l'Evangile parmi ces Barbares, et d'où vient que la plus ancienne de nos Colonies, celle qui naturellement devoit se peupler davantage, est encore la moins puissante de toutes?

Mince consolation de savoir que cette histoire "ne présente, au moins dans l'origine du principal Etablissement, que des objets capables de faire estimer notre Nation, la seule, qui ait eu le secret de gagner l'affection des Amériquains."

Restent donc les "détails curieux," sur lesquels insiste tellement Charlevoix et qui, par leur pointillisme, forment une sorte d'"Histoire suivie" capable "d'interesser et d'instruire." Mais n'allons pas croire que la surabondance des détails fasse perdre l'ensemble de vue. L'entreprise historique est d'abord une opération sélective, classificatoire ensuite: "on pourra avoir une connaissance entiere de chaque region du Nouveau Monde . . . de ce qui s'y est passé de considerable . . .; de ce qu'elle renferme de plus curieux." Charlevoix veut rivaliser avec les Voyages et Mémoires pour l'abondance et la curiosité des détails, mais sauvegarder l'ordre, la précieuse unité d'ensemble. Une métaphore revient souvent chez lui: celle de la noyade:

> L'Histoire du Nouveau Monde ne sera plus en danger de périr par sa propre abondance; les choses, qui sont véritablement dignes de la curiosité des Lecteurs, n'y seront plus noyées dans les inutilités, pour ne rien dire de plus, ni embarassées dans les contradictions . . .
>
> ("Projet d'un corps d'histoire. . .")

Surabondance du détail, on le voit, mais surabondance maîtrisée, mise en ordre, passée à l'aune de la vérité. Car la mise en ordre, finalement, conduit à la vérité. Si elle peut accueillir les éléments les plus incongrus ou surprenants, la vérité exclut les contradictions. Une vérité dont on serait bien embarrassé de délimiter les contours et encore davantage les critères. Charlevoix écrit:

> nous avons encore des regles certaines de critique pour distinguer les Pieces legitimes et authentiques, de ce nombre prodigieux d'Ecrits hazardés, dont la plûpart altérent la vérité jusqu'au point de la rendre méconnaissable /. . ./ . . . il nous reste encore un rayon de lumiere, à la faveur duquel nous pouvons dégager la vérité de ce monstrueux amas de fables, qui l'ont presqu'entierement éclipsée . . .
>
> ("Projet d'un corps d'histoires. . .")

Mais on ne saura jamais en définitive d'où vient ce rayon de lumière, ni quelles sont ces règles certaines.

Le même mise en ordre, la même ordonnance générale devra prendre en charge l'énoncé historique. N'ayant pas le temps d'entrer dans le détail, je rappelle seulement quelques éléments. V. LeBlanc parle de la Nouvelle-France "d'une manière confuse, peu exacte, et sans ordre." Si l'on se rappelle que la grande faute de Lahontan, de Hennepin, de Leclercq était la boursouflure, la déclamation et l'embarras, on pensera aux règles de clarté, de simplicité, d'hiérarchisation des éléments de la phrase de l'idéal classique. Il faudrait encore ajouter une dernière remarque: si l'on franchit les limites de la phrase, si l'on déborde la stylistique, on trouve la vieille catégorie de la *disposition:* pas seulement celle des éléments verbaux en eux-mêmes mais celle touchant la distribution de la matière factuelle: dans l'Avertissement, Charlevoix parle de "l'ordre et la distribution des faits" comme d'un "vaste champ à la Critique."

Réal Ouellet
Université Laval

Notes

[1] "Projet d'un corps d'histoires du Nouveau-Monde", Publié d'abord dans le *Journal de Trévoux*, en janvier 1735, et repris à la fin du T. III de *L'Histoire et description de la Nouvelle-France* (Paris: Nyon Fils, 1744). Les "Liste et examen des auteurs que j'ai consultés pour composer cet ouvrage" sont aussi publiés aux T. III, tandis que l'"Avertissement," auquel je me référerai parfois est placé en tête du T. III. *L'Histoire et description* parut en 1744 chez cinq éditeurs différents et sous deux formats: in quarto en 3 volumes et duodecimo en 6 volumes. Je citerai ici l'édition Nyon Fils en 3 volumes. C'est celle que reproduisent anastatiquement les Editions Elysée (Montréal, 1976).

[2] Fr.-X. Garneau, "Préface," *Histoire du Canada* (Montréal: Beauchemin et Valois, T. I, 1889), pp. VI-VII.

[3] Article "Agnus Scythicus" de *l'Encyclopédie*. Cf. aussi, parmi beaucoup d'autres: "certitude", "critique", "fait", "histoire" . . . .

15. L'Érudition et la fonction du savoir au XVIIIe siècle: Pierre Potier chez les Hurons du Détroit

Qui était Pierre Potier?

Un jésuite belge,[1] missionnaire chez les Hurons du Détroit de 1744 à sa mort en 1781. A lire les notes personnelles qu'il a rédigées de son écriture fine et régulière,[2] témoignant d'une vaste érudition, de sa curiosité et de son savoir linguistique, littéraire et scientifique, on peut se demander quel miroir de la mentalité il reflétait au milieu du Siècle des Lumières.

Témoin étonnant? Il semble que non. Beaucoup d'esprits cultivés avaient, comme lui, répondu à l'appel des nouveaux mondes à évangéliser, sollicitant le privilège de partir pour les "Indes", comme on disait. Pourquoi partaient-ils ainsi? Que signifiait "convertir" les infidèles, "civiliser" les peuples nomades, soi-disant primitifs?

Bien que nous soyons ici en présence d'une longue tradition de conquête des espaces et des âmes depuis l'époque de la Contre-réforme, il convient de distinguer, dans le cas de Pierre Potier — tout comme dans bien d'autres — deux types de formation: d'abord la formation dite *classique,* que reçurent comme lui tous les écoliers des collèges et facultés de la Compagnie de Jésus en Europe d'Ancien Régime. Ensuite, la formation *personnelle,* acquise au gré de l'initiative de l'individu et qui, débordant le cadre conventionnel, organise progressivement les matériaux constituant l'outillage mental.

Une telle passion de connaître nous amène à poser la question suivante: quelle pouvait être chez Potier la fonction du savoir? Comment concevait-il l'oeuvre missionnaire et à quoi répondait la décision d'acquérir et, si possible, d'assimiler les langues indiennes, les sciences diverses? Malgré l'absence de plusieurs documents, il est possible d'en donner une idée assez précise.

Nous n'avons qu'à rappeler sommairement ici que les Jésuites français ou belges venus en Nouvelle-France — à l'instar de tous les missionnaires — accompagnaient marchands et explorateurs, en vue de travailler à la "conversion" des infidèles à la foi catholique et, dans une certaine mesure, au genre de vie des Européens. Ils se proposaient de "civiliser" les Indiens, pour les fixer, les établir, les soustraire au nomadisme à l'intérieur de "réserves", voire de "réductions".

La maîtrise de la langue indienne — en l'occurrence le huron — était perçue comme une nécessité, le "moteur" même de l'action apostolique et pastorale, permettant de catéchiser, d'instruire, de continuer la mission. Il importe de préciser que, dans la tradition dont il hérite, Pierre Potier fait servir à cette cause non seulement tout ce que l'étude des lettres classiques (le latin surtout) lui a transmis, mais également le vaste répertoire littéraire et scientifique acquis grâce à la diffusion de l'imprimé.

L'écolier Pierre Potier a environ 13 ans au moment de son entrée au collège de Tournai, situé à la frontière de la France et de la Belgique. L'établissement réglait son programme sur la tradition des autres collèges de la Compagnie de Jésus en Europe, adoptant une pédagogie conforme au *Ratio Studiorum* de 1598, charte traditionnelle imposant un ordre des études inspiré du *modus parisiensis*[3] dont la pratique avait été progressivement mise en vigueur dans les collèges.

Méthode d'étude essentiellement progressive, le *Ratio* fait avancer l'élève de classe en classe, en l'initiant aux lettres. Il a été adopté en France et dans les régions de langue française avec de légères variantes, en particulier grâce à la réforme du P. Jouvancy. En général, les collèges français suivaient la tradition du collège Louis-le-Grand, de Paris.[4]

L'émulation en est le grand ressort. L'effort principal portait sur la maîtrise de la langue latine, en vue d'aborder les auteurs classiques, surtout latins. On consacrait environ trois ans à l'étude de la grammaire latine. Celle de Despautère, traditionnelle à l'époque de la Renaissance, fut remplacée par d'autres manuels, comme celui du P. Emmanuel Alvarez, que le Père Potier a utilisé.[5] Les éditions en trois ou quatre volumes, correspondaient aux étapes de formation de l'écolier, qui s'initiait d'abord aux rudiments du latin (première Grammaire), ensuite à l'étymologie (seconde Grammaire), puis à la Syntaxe (troisième Grammaire), enfin à la prosodie et à la poésie. Ces étapes se concluaient par l'étude de l'éloquence (Rhétorique)[6] et de la philosophie.

En seconde classe, le grec s'ajoutait au latin. On employait ordinairement la grammaire grecque de Clénard. Toutefois, le latin était la langue courante des écoliers:

"C'est en latin que se font les classes de lettres et les cours de dialectique, de philosophie, de théologie, d'Ecriture Sainte; en latin que l'on apprend, récite, disserte, discute, harangue les grands personnages en vers et en prose; en latin que l'on joue la comédie, la tragédie, ou la pastorale . . ., que sont rédigés bien des actes officiels."[7]

Les cours étant dictés, l'écolier, privé de livres ou de manuels, rédige des cahiers de notes, où se retrouve la leçon dictée.[8]

La liste des ouvrages de la bibliothèque du Père Potier montrerait chez cet esprit curieux de s'informer de tout, le souci constant, non seulement d'enrichir son vocabulaire latin, français et huron, mais aussi, comme il convient à un missionnaire que le zèle inspire, d'utiliser ce savoir, de l'ordonner, comme le dit G. Bollème,[9] à ce "qui possède une valeur morale et religieuse."

Notons que si les documents prouvent à quel point le Père Potier a toujours cherché à enrichir sa culture littéraire et scientifique, jamais la passion de l'érudition ne lui a fait franchir les limites de la plus stricte orthodoxie catholique. Loin, dans les espaces à peine connus, il demeure fidèle à la tradition qu'il véhicule. Nous en examinerons ici quelques secteurs.

a. Langue et littérature

Dès son entrée au collège, Pierre Potier s'initie, en suivant l'*ordo studendi*,[10] aux rudiments du latin et il suivra, en progressant de classe en classe, le livre des *Institutiones* du P. Alvarez. En première classe: déclinaisons, conjugaisons, parties du discours; en seconde classe: grammaire; en troisième classe: syntaxe; ensuite: prosodie, poésie. Son ouvrage préféré, toutefois, noté avec soin, demeure le traité du Père Ducygne sur l'art métrique, l'art poétique et l'art de l'éloquence, traité qu'il note sous le titre de *Excerpta ex Patre Ducygne*.[11]

Après six ans au collège de Tournai (1721-1727) et deux ans à celui de Douai (1727-1729), Potier fait deux ans de noviciat chez les Jésuites de Tournai, et une année d'étude de lettres à Lille, avant d'être nommé régent au collège de Béthune (1732-1738), ce qui lui donne l'occasion de reprendre plus à fond tout le cycle des humanités — latines, grecques, françaises — en suivant le progrès de ses écoliers depuis les classes de grammaire jusqu'aux classes de poésie et de rhétorique.

Le maître par excellence de l'éloquence latine, Cicéron, demeure l'idéal dont s'inspire le professeur d'humanités et de rhétorique, qui enseigne l'art de bien dire et de persuader. On ne saurait trop souligner à quel point on cultivait cet art dans la formation de l'homme moderne: qu'il fût destiné à la carrière d'homme d'église ou à celle d'homme du monde.

En principe, le cycle des études grecques commençait en seconde année. Les manuscrits soulignent l'intérêt de Potier pour l'antiquité et la langue grecques. On y trouve des notes sur les fables d'Esope,[12] sur les poètes, sur les dieux et déesses de la mythologie, sur la langue grecque,[13] y compris un lexique latin-grec.[14] En fait, la plupart des écrits de Potier porteront sur les trois langues qui lui sont les plus familières: le latin, le français, le huron.

L'étude du latin est demeurée une préoccupation constante du missionnaire, même après le cycle des études théologiques et philosophiques (dont il a conservé plus de 20 cahiers de notes, en latin). Quantité d'extraits d'auteurs figurent dans les cahiers: Quinte-Curce, Térence, Cicéron, Virgile, Horace, Ovide.[15] On y trouve aussi des fables de Phèdre et des chants héroïques,[16] des notes sur le vocabulaire français-latin,[17] des titres de tragédies et de comédies,[18] des extraits d'opuscules latins sur l'histoire poétique, une lettre latine de Sadolet,[19] des vers latins contre les jansénistes,[20] des notes sur l'étude de la langue latine,[21] sur la rhétorique des Pères Ducygne et Jouvancy,[22] sur les caractéristiques du dialogue et de l'épître, sur l'*ordo studendi*,[23] des extraits du *Dictionnaire poétique* du Père Vanière,[24] dont il a tiré un vocabulaire latin-français, des textes de caractère insolite, tel que le *De Vino*.[25]

Du côté de la langue française, le Père Potier a recueilli des morceaux disparates:

épîtres, fables, stances, vers, logogryphes, énigmes,[26] des pièces de poésie tirées des gazettes du temps, telle qui la *Suite de la Clef* (1747),[27] des extraits de Boileau,[28] des notes de vocabulaire tirées de pièces de théâtre,[29] des fables de Lafontaine,[30] des proverbes, 142 sentences, 30 maximes, 147 pensées diverses,[31] un recueil de 147 bons mots et de pensées choisies des auteurs anciens et modernes.[32]

Il est particulièrement intéressant de découvrir que le Père Potier a rédigé un glossaire[33] sur le vocabulaire, les manières de parler et le langage au XVIIIe siècle. Ce répertoire comprend environ 3500 termes, répartis sous les titres qui suivent:

Façons de parler proverbiales, triviales, figurées, tirées du P. Joubert. Effets de quelques plante. Termes français, tirés du Dictionnaire de Trévoux. Extraits des Entretiens entre la Prieure et la Comtesse, par le P. Lallement. Termes français recueillis çà et là (356 termes). Termes français recueillis durant la traversée (134 termes). Termes français recueillis à Québec (27 termes), à Lorette (566 termes), de Québec au Détroit (142 termes), au Détroit (1327 termes). D'autres termes ont été tirés des gazettes et journaux du temps et de l'Histoire de France, de Larrey. Enfin, Potier a rédigé son propre Dictionnaire français.[34]

Dès son arrivée en Nouvelle-France, le Père Potier se rend à la mission huronne du P. Richer, à Lorette, près de Québec et y transcrit les notes du P. Etienne de Carheil sur les conjugaisons de la langue huronne.[35] Durant les années suivantes, il rédige un recueil original sur les éléments de la grammaire huronne, suivies d'études sur les racines.[36] Même après trois ans d'efforts, il ne fait que "bégayer" le huron, comme il l'avoue au P. de Saint-Pé, en mars 1746.[37] Des rédactions diverses nous apprennent, par exemple, qu'il a compilé un vocabulaire huron-français[38] de 1588 mots d'usage plus courant, extraits, semble-t-il, d'un dictionnaire non retrouvé. Plusieurs manuscrits, rédigés en huron, ne sont pas encore traduits et il faudra un spécialiste de cette langue très difficile pour estimer ce qu'un si patient travail représente de soins constants et d'érudition.

b. **Philosophie, théologie, Ecriture Sainte, spiritualité, pastorale**
Convaincus de l'importance des humanités, les jésuites avaient fait de grands efforts "pour rétablir l'étude de la philosophie, rejetée par les humanistes et les réformés.[39] Cette discipline était souvent considérée comme superflue. Sur cette matière, Potier a rédigé un cahier de notes, résumant la métaphysique d'Aristote (appelée philosophie transcendentale) et un autre sur la philosophie morale (appelée éthique).[40] Encore là, rien d'original dans ces notes. Potier se contente, à la manière du Journal de Trévoux, d'exposer, sans critique, le contenu d'une oeuvre nouvelle, à titre d'information, sinon de "curiosité", au sens que lui prêtent les littérateurs de l'époque.[41]
Le cycle des études théologiques — quasi ne varietur — représente un ensemble de traités, dont Pierre Potier a rédigé plus de 20 cahiers durant les années passées au théologat de Douai (1738-1742). Les traités sur le dogme et les sacrements sont les plus abondants et révèlent la préoccupation de réfuter les thèses protestantes. Il y est fréquemment question de controverses, soit contre les protestants, soit contre les athées et les déistes.
Deux cahiers résument les ouvrages de Tirinus sur les controverses.[42] Un autre s'intitule Instructions sur les matières controversées.[43] Trois cahiers analysent les Entretiens sur la religion contre les athées et déistes, du Père du Tertre et touchent à la problématique posée par la campagne des philosophes des Lumières contre toute religion révélée. Les multiples questions disputées

évoquent précisément ces inquiétudes de la scolastique aux aguets, gardienne des vérités "reçues".[44] D'emblée, toute matière théologique contenait une partie importante, réservée à l'arsenal des arguments des "adversaires", qu'il fallait passer au crible de la dialectique thomiste et réfuter. Ici encore: transposition en joute théologique, du tournoi, où entre en lice le guerrier féodal, le chevalier qui se mesure à l'ennemi. Pour l'honneur! Certes! Mais davantage par conviction: le soldat du Christ, de l'Eglise militante, s'engage à la conquête des âmes, à l'avant-garde du combat. Il faut tenir compte, sur le plan de la motivation, de ces attitudes fondamentales, inscrites dans la mentalité des générations que, toutefois, deux siècles de Contre-réforme ont commencé à essouffler.

Même s'il nous manque l'une des sources les plus importantes, — i.e. les notes spirituelles et des lettres nous révélant l'âme et la vie intérieure du missionnaire — les notes en spiritualité et en pastorale n'en sont pas moins le cadre d'un univers religieux assez nettement défini.

Que ce soit au noviciat ou durant les années de formation qui l'ont suivi — philosophie, régence, théologie, 3e an de probation — la division et l'utilisation maximum du temps[45] facilitent l'activité intellectuelle en vue d'un meilleur service des âmes. Tout s'ordonne selon des activités pastorales multiformes. Le Père Potier a donc pris soin de noter de nombreux ouvrages de spiritualité et de pastorale:[46] extraits du Père Bordier, de la retraite du Père Bourdaloue, des méditations du Père Segneri et du Père Le Maître, de la retraite du Père Maillard, extraits du Père Lallemant et du Père Saint-Jure, de *L'Introduction à la vie dévote* de Saint François de Sales, de *L'Imitation de Jésus-Christ*, de Thomas à Kempis; extraits de Saint Paul, de la retraite du Père Crasset, de *La Perfection chrétienne et religieuse* du Père Rodriguez, des *Méditations* du Père Busée; les *Sermons* du Père Bretonneau, les *Méditations* et les *Réflections chrétiennes* du Père Croiset, le *Pédogogue chrétien*, les catéchismes de Montpellier, de Sens, du Concile de Trente, *La Maison de l'éternité* du Père Coret, des extraits de la vie de saint Ignace, de saint François-Xavier, de saint François Régis. Ajoutons enfin: des extraits du rituel de Québec, les cas réservés en confession, deux mandements de l'évêque de Québec, un traité des dîmes et trois sermons, donnés à Béthune (1734) à Douai (1732) et à Tournai (1743).[47]

c. Les connaissances scientifiques

On ne saurait sous-estimer le soin avec lequel le Père Potier s'est appliqué à enrichir ses connaissances scientifiques, dès le moment où elles ont été abordées, au cours des années de philosophie. On y enseignait la cosmologie héritée d'Aristote et de Ptolémée. A cette conception traditionnelle, enrichie toutefois de quelques éléments plus modernes discrètement intercalés, se rattachaient les divers traités dont il a rédigé des notes,[48] sous la dictée des Pères Jean Thomas et Joseph Le Mire: *Mathematica, Traité de Méchanique, Traité des projections astronomiques ou de la construction des planisphères.* Parmi les achats de livres faits à Paris et à La Rochelle[49] figurent sans doute un certain nombre d'ouvrages de science, puisqu'ils font l'objet du travail de rédaction des années en huronnie. Même s'il est assez difficile de préciser dans quelle mesure ces connaissances scientifiques ont été parfaitement assimilées, il reste que le fait d'en avoir fait des notes précises ne peut manquer d'attirer notre attention. Il y a lieu d'en donner ici un sommaire.

1) L'ouvrage de Noël Regnault *Les Entretiens physiques d'Ariste et d'Eudoxe ou Nouvelle physique en dialogues*[50] traite des questions suivantes:

corps, matière, vide, mouvement, sphère, terre, minéraux, aimant, pesanteur, air, feu, froid, chaud, fermentations chimiques, mer, corps humain, anatomie, organes, sons, lumière, optique, miroirs, couleurs (selon Newton), plantes (corail, champignons, genseng), botanie, animaux, météores, planètes, système du monde (selon Copernic et Tycho Brahé), comètes, système de Newton, l'existence de Dieu.

2) Dans l'*Origine ancienne de la physique nouvelle,*[51] le même auteur passe en revue ce que les physiciens anciens ont dit des sujets analysés dans les *Entretiens physiques d'Artiste et d'Eudoxe.* En comparant la nouvelle physique à l'ancienne, Regnault y analyse l'hypothèse de Descartes et sa méthode, montrant que Descartes a eu le mérite d'approfondir les causes secrètes de nos connaissances, allant plus loin qu'Aristote, dégageant ce que la physique nouvelle doit aux observations et à l'expérience, aux instruments nouveaux, à l'établissement des Académies, à l'institution des journaux et mémoires littéraires.

3) C'est dans *Le Spectacle de la nature*[52] de Noël Antoine Pluche que s'élargit particulièrement le panorama des connaissances scientifiques. Cet ouvrage de vulgarisation a souvent été réédité et le Père Potier en a résumé des parties considérables.[53] C'est une petite encyclopédie des connaissances scientifiques, assorties d'autres connaissances d'usage, resumées avec minutie.

4) L'auteur du *Spectacle de la nature* a aussi publié une *Histoire du ciel,*[54] où l'on recherche l'origine de l'idolâtrie et les méprises de la philosophie sur la formation des corps célestes et de toute la nature. Cet ouvrage résume ce que l'on connait du ciel poétique (zodiaque, écriture symbolique, théogonie, mythologie grecque, les mystères égyptiens, la divination), la cosmogonie des philosophes (Aristote, Epicure, Gassendi, Descartes, Newton), la physique de Moyse, les conséquences de l'histoire du ciel.

5) Dans son *Abrégé complet de chirurgie,* Guy de Chauliac traite de la physiologie, des humeurs (selon les anciens et les modernes), des facultés, des sensations, de l'hygiène, des passions de l'âme, de pathologie (tumeurs, plaies, ulcères), d'ostéologie, de la saignée, des médicaments.

6) *La Médecine, chirurgie et pharmacie des pauvres*[55] de Hecquet traite des maladies diverses, de la pharmacie des pauvres, en particulier des remèdes domestiques pris dans les aliments, graines, herbes, plantes.

7) Un autre traité non moins pratique que les deux précédents, surtout en huronnie, est celui de Louis Liger, *La Nouvelle Maison rustique ou l'économie générale de tous les biens de campagne . . . mise en meilleur ordre, avec la vertu des simples, l'apothicairerie.*[56] On y renseigne le lecteur sur la basse-cour, les chevaux et bêtes de somme, les terres labourables, les eaux, les plantes, le jardinage, la vigne, les boissons, les fleurs, le jardin des simples ou la botanie et une pharmacie ou apothicairerie familière, les boissons telles que l'eau de vie, l'esprit de vin, la pêche, la chasse et autres amusements de campagne, la cuisine et l'office.

Que retenir de cet imposant ensemble de sujets à la fois scientifiques et pratiques, notés avec patience, précision constante et curiosité envahissante? Potier y ajoute parfois les formules mathématiques, les figures géométriques et, en suivant l'effort des hommes de science, il s'est demandé comment harmoniser la science nouvelle avec l'ancienne, comme l'indique le titre de l'ouvrage de Regnault: *l'Origine ancienne de la physique nouvelle*. C'est presque toute la création qui figure dans ces notes, chaque être étant situé dans le cosmos selon son espèce et sa fonction, en sorte que le *Spectacle de la nature* forme un tableau complet, comme le fait voir Potier. S'il a pris soin de noter les ouvrages de médecine, de pharmacie et de chirurgie, il faut supposer qu'il a dû remarquer les traditions médicales des Hurons, qui connaissaient la vertu curative des herbes. Toutefois on ne retrouve que quelques bribes de cette tradition dans les cahiers de notes du missionnaire. Ainsi, par exemple, "les feuilles de hêtre trempées dans l'eau sont bonnes contre la brûlure,"[57] "la farine qui sort de dessous la meule est un bon remède contre la brûlure." Quelques mots du vocabulaire huron sont à signaler: *otraouita* (racine de la grappe de vinaigrier, qui procure l'avortement), *enra* (autre racine, contre la brûlure) et *ochraouata* (onguent divin).[58]

d. **Les connaissances en histoire et en géographie**
Naturellement le spectacle de la nature qui se déploie dans les écrits du Père Potier s'élargit constamment, non seulement à partir des ouvrages scientifiques dont il tire ses notes, mais également lorsqu'il se passionne pour les nouvelles récentes et prend la peine de noter tous les lieux qu'il traverse. C'est à la mission huronne de l'Ile-aux-Bois-Blancs qu'il reçoit les gazettes et journaux du temps. Il en extrait une quantité considérable de nouvelles de France ou d'Europe (Vienne, Londres, Turin, etc.).[59] Au milieu de nombreuses chroniques, mêlés aux multiples faits divers notés au jour le jour, figurent des curiosités sur les inventions, sur les institutions, un compte rendu fort circonstancié de la bataille de Carillon, tiré d'une relation.[60] Divers ouvrages d'histoire ont fait l'objet de résumés.[61]

Il semble qu'une érudition aussi envahissante que celle du Père Potier l'aurait amené à poser le problème de la qualité des sources et à dépasser par l'attitude critique, une érudition plutôt quantitative. Sur ce point, les cahiers de notes non retrouvés auraient peut-être révélé quelque chose de plus qu'une infatigable curiosité et auraient répondu à la question entrevue au départ: quels rapports y a-t-il entre les acquisitions de l'esprit et le service de l'Eglise en pays de mission?

À côté d'une vision fort stéréotypée du temps historique s'ordonne celle de l'espace géographique, éparpillée dans les ouvrages d'histoire, dans les journaux du temps. Les cahiers du Père Potier contiennent une grande quantité de notations géographiques, d'itinéraires ou guides de voyage. Outre le journal de voyage depuis la Belgique jusqu'au Détroit, dont il a dressé un double itinéraire, d'abord sur le vaisseau le *Rubis* et ensuite en canot, il y a 14 itinéraires détaillés des chemins ou routes des voyageurs dans la région de Détroit, avec mention de tous les points, des distances parcourues (parfois avec les dates précises et les escales), avec noms de lieux (rivières, montagnes, baies, détours).[62] Potier a aussi compilé les itinéraires détaillés dressés par d'autres voyageurs, tels que ceux de Charleau, Chevalier, Derouen. L'étude des noms de lieux, leur comparaison avec les noms actuels et la vérification des distances restent à faire.

Du côté de la sociologie et de l'anthropologie culturelle, les spécialistes pourront avec fruit utiliser les listes des Hurons occupant chacune des 33 cabanes de la mission en 1747.[63] Ces listes donnent le nom d'un grand nombre de Hurons, leurs liens de parenté, leur nombre dans chacune des cabanes. Outre quelques fragments sur les mariages, les décès, les comptes de la mission, Potier a dressé la liste de tous les baptisés de la mission depuis 1728 jusqu'en 1781.[64] Le prénom chrétien, latinisé, nous renseigne aussi sur leur sexe.

Malgré l'aspect fragmentaire de ce compte rendu des connaissances du Père Potier, leur analyse sommaire nous oriente considérablement, surtout si l'on cherche à déterminer comment il concevait et organisait, au XVIIIe siècle, non seulement l'univers intellectuel, mais aussi le rapport qu'il entretient avec les conditions de l'existence. Sur ce plan, on ne saurait trop souligner l'importance de l'étude des humanités, du latin en particulier, qui le prépare directement à l'étude de la langue huronne. En effet, c'est principalement en latin que Potier explique la grammaire huronne. Si le besoin d'écrire et de s'instruire demeurent en lui une passion, c'est qu'il nourrit, en même temps que les exercices spirituels et les travaux de la mission, une vie intellectuelle qui cherche sa mesure dans des espaces plus vastes, situés bien au-delà de la huronnie. Ainsi le nouveau monde aiguise-t-il l'appétit de redécouvrir l'ancien, où il s'enracine.

Robert Toupin
Université Laurentienne

Notes

[1] Né à Blandain le 21 avril 1708, entré au noviciat de Tournai le 30 septembre 1729, régent au collège de Béthune de 1732 à 1738; en théologie à Douai de 1738 à 1742; il prononce les derniers voeux le 2 février 1743, quitte La Rochelle pour le Canada le 29 avril 1743, arrive à Québec le Ier octobre 1743, étudie la langue huronne à Lorette, quitte Québec le 26 juin 1744, arrive à l'Ile-aux-Bois-Blancs, mission huronne du Détroit le 25 septembre, s'établit à Sandwich où il fonde, en 1767, la paroisse de l'Assomption de Windsor; décédé le 16 juillet 1781.

[2] Outre la bibliothèque de Potier, dont un grand nombre de titres nous sont connus, il existe au moins 35 cahiers manuscrits (ou fragments de cahiers), dispersés dans divers fonds d'archives (ASQ — archives du Séminaire de Québec; ASJCF — archives des Jésuites de Saint-Jérôme; MBM — archives de la bibliothèque municipale de Montréal. Autres dépots: Détroit, Windsor, London). Au moins 35 autres cahiers n'ont pas été retrouvés. N.B. Aucun écrit personnel n'évoque la vie spirituelle ou morale de Potier.

[3] G. Codina Mir, S.J., *Aux sources de la pédagogie des Jésuites, le modus parisiensis* (Rome, 1968).

[4] G. Dupont-Ferrier, *Du collège de Clermont au lycée Louis-le-Grand: la vie quotidienne d'un collège parisien (1563-1920)* (Paris, 1922-25).

[5] P. Delattre, S.J., *Les Etablisements des Jésuites en France depuis quatre siècles* (Enghien-Wetteren, 1947-1957), II, col. 203.

[6] ASJCF, Ms. Potier, *Gazettes*, 34, 36, 42, 45, 46.

[7] P. Delattre, II, col. 244.

[8] F. de Dainville, *L'Education des Jésuites* (Paris: Minuit, 1978), p. 286. Dans ses cahiers de notes, Potier indiquait souvent le nom du professeur et la date de la fin de la rédaction.

9 "Littérature populaire et littérature de colportage au XVIIIe siècle," dans *Livre et société dans la France du XVIIIe siècle* (Paris: Mouton, 1965), p. 75.

10 ASQ, ms. Potier 97, tables, liste (p. 10).

11 *Ibid.*, p. 1.

12 ASQ, ms. Potier 97, pp. 37-39.

13 *Ibid.*, pp. 49-52.

14 *Ibid.* ms. Potier /&/, pp. 1-33.

15 *Ibid.* ms. Potier 97, pp. 26, 30, 47-48; aussi ms. 102, pp. 187-204. La liste des ouvrages de la bibliothèque Potier signale les oeuvres de Virgile et d'Horace, les *Satires* de Juvénal, cf. ASJCF, copie D-7, p. 3-4.

16 ASQ, ms. Potier 97, pp. 39-42.

17 *Ibid.*, pp. 57-66, 67-104, 106-119.

18 *Ibid.*, p. 49.

19 *Ibid.*, pp. 24, 44.

20 *Ibid.*, p. 43.

21 *Ibid.*, pp. 1-4: *rudimenta, excerpta, carminum species.*

22 *Ibid.*, p. 5-6.

23 *Ibid.*, p. 10.

24 *Ibid.*, pp. 67-68.

25 *Ibid.*, ms. Potier 99, pp. 141-144.

26 ASJCF, ms. Potier, *Gazettes*, pp. 146-153.

27 *Ibid.*, p. 63.

28 ASQ, ms. Potier 97, p. 22.

29 *Ibid.*, pp. 30-33.

30 *Ibid.*, p. 41.

31 *Ibid.*, ms. Potier 102, pp. 205-214.

32 *Ibid.*, pp. 215-222.

33 MBM, coll. Gagnon, ms. Potier, 447.9714 P863fa, pp. 103-161. Edition partielle dans le *Bulletin du parler français au Canada*. Québec/Paris, t. III, 1904-5, pp. 213-220, 252-255, 291-293; t. IV, 1905-6, pp. 63-65, 103-104, 146-149, 224-226, 264-267.

34 ASQ, ms. Potier 95, pp. 1-192.

35 ASJCF, ms. Potier, ms. *huron* 1, pp. 1-260, ms. *huron* 2, pp. 1-302.

36 *Ibid.*, ms. *huron* 3: *Elementa grammaticae huronicae. Radices huronicae.* (pp. 1-105, 111-148); ms. *huron* 4 *Radices huronicae* (pp. 1-295).

37 *Ibid.*, ms. Potier, *Registres hurons*, copie Potier sur feuillet attaché à la couverture.

38 MBM, coll. Gagnon, ms. Potier 497.922 P863vo, pp. 175-194.

39 De Dainville, pp. 207, 273.

40 ASQ, ms. Potier 92, 93. Un ms. non retrouvé, *ibid.*, no. 97, contenait des notes extraites de la *Logique en forme d'entretiens*, de Regnault. Même après l'installation à l'Ile-aux-Bois-Blancs, Potier rédige un sommaire d'un nouvel ouvrage de Condillac, intitulé *Essai sur l'origine des connaissances humaines*, d'après le périodique *Suite de la clef*, mars, 1747. Potier semble s'être abonné à quelques gazettes du temps.

41 Cf. J. Ehrard et J. Roger, "Deux périodiques français du XVIIIe siècle: le *Journal des Savants* et les *Mémoires de Trévoux*," dans *Livre et société dans la France du XVIIIe siècle* (Paris: Mouton, 1965), p. 33.

42 ASQ, ms. Potier 82, 83. Ces cahiers, intitulés *Controversiae*, résument un ouvrage intitulé: *R.P. Jacobi Tirini Antverpiani e Societate Iesu commentarius in Sacram Scripturam*.

43 *Ibid.*, manuscrit non retrouvé, signalé dans ASQ, ms. Potier 97.

44 *Ibid.*, ms. Potier, 94.

45 Cf. ASQ, ms. Potier 99, pp. 1-28: *Distributio temporis in novitiatu.* Sur un plan plus global, lire: Jean Delumeau, "Le développement de l'esprit d'organisation et de la pensée méthodique dans la mentalité occidentale à l'époque de la Renaissance," dans *XIIIe Congrès International des Sciences Historiques*, Moscou, 1970.

46 ASQ, ms. Potier 99, pp. 61-213. Un ouvrage projeté sur l'oeuvre du Père Potier inclura la liste des volumes de sa bibliothèque.

47 *Ibid.*, ms. Potier 101, pp. 84-245.

48 Cf. ASQ, ms. Potier 96, 160 p. Aussi: De Dainville, *op. cit.* pp. 355-391: "L'enseignement scientifique dans les collèges de jésuites au XVIIIe siècle."

[49] ASJCF, ms. Potier *Gazettes,* p. 55 (il visite à Paris la librairie Guérin et y fait des achats) et p. 56 (il achète des livres à La Rochelle et un certain Ranjard, de cette ville, lui écrit: "Je prie le R.P. Potier, s'il trouve quelque curiosité en coquillages, pierres figurées, pétrifications, insectes, et autres curiosités de m'en faire part.").

[50] Edité en 4 volumes, 3e édition, Paris, 1737. D'autres éditions remontent à 1729 et 1733.

[51] (Paris, 1734).

[52] *Le Spectacle de la nature, ou Entretiens sur les particularités qui ont paru les plus propres à rendre les jeunes gens curieux et à leur former l'esprit* (Paris, 1732-1750). Pour les tomes I-IV, Potier a utilisé la 8e édition, de 1741-42.

[53] Le ms. Potier *Le Spectacle de la nature 3* (ASJCF) résume les t. V (161 p.), VI (174 p.) et VII (152 p.), notes complétées le 3 janvier 1751 (t. V), le 21 février 1752 (t. VI) et le 20 mars (t. VII). On trouvera, aux pages 90-91 (résumant le t. V), des dessins de cadrans, de l'instrument horaire, de la gnomonique. Aux pages 93-94 (résumant le t. VII), des dessins de planches, de figures, et l'année de l'édition 1747.

[54] (Paris, 1742).

[55] Philippe Hecquet, *La Médecine, la chirurgie et pharmacie des pauvres* (Paris, 1740).

[56] (Paris, 1736).

[57] Cf. MBM, coll. Gagnon, 497.922 P863vo, p. 117.

[58] *Ibid.,* pp. 120, 183, 184, 192.

[59] ASJCF, ms. Potier, *Gazettes,* pp. 10-51, 66-84, 98-130, 134-139, 141-144. Périodiques mentionnés: *Etrennes mignonnes, Suite de la Clef.*

[60] *Ibid.,* pp. 132-133. Relations incluses dans la lettre de M. Godefroi.

[61] Cf. ASQ, ms. Potier 98, pp. 1-148 (*l'Histoire de tous les peuples du monde,* de Jovet); pp. 160-232 (histoire des conciles généraux et particuliers); pp. 243-292 (*Histoire de France sous le règne de Louis XIV,* de Larray); ms. Potier 102, pp. 138-186 (*Instruction sur l'histoire de France et Romaine* de Le Ragois); pp. 223-238 (*Histoire de l'Amérique septentrionale* de Bacqueville de la Potherie), pp. 239-262 (*Histoire de l'Amérique méridionale,* ms. Potier 103, pp. 122-138, *Histoire de la Nouvelle-France,* de Charlevoix; pp. 146-165 (*Les Eléments de l'histoire.)*

[62] ASJCF, ms. Potier, *Gazettes,* pp. 52-59, 166a-172, 177, 181, 185.

[63] ASJCF, ms. Potier, ms. *huron 3,* pp. 149-153. MBM, ms. Potier 497.922P863vo: *Village huron de l'île aux bois blans en 1747. 33 cabanes ou loges,* pp. 195-214.

[64] ASJCF, ms. Potier, *Registres* de la mission, pp. 3-5, 29-48.

16. Le Retable de Saint-Augustin-de-Desmaures: une oeuvre d'architecture intérieure du XVIIIe siècle (1746) transplantée dans un ensemble plus tardif¹

Une recherche menée dans les archives de la paroisse de Saint-Augustin-de-Desmaures, située dans le comté de Portneuf à quelques kilomètres de la ville de Québec et une confrontation des résultats de cette recherche avec les éléments du décor existant dans l'église actuelle de Saint-Augustin (fig. 1) nous ont permis de mettre au jour l'existence d'un retable du XVIIIe siècle, transplanté dans un ensemble plus tardif, une église du XIXe siècle.

L'intérieur des églises du Régime français nous est peu connu et peu d'exemples des oeuvres de cette époque nous sont parvenus. Des gravures nous transmettent l'image de l'intérieur de l'église des Jésuites (CA 1666) (fig. 2) et celui de l'église des Récollets (CA 1693) (fig. 3) deux édifices prestigieux du XVIIe siècle érigés à Québec. Le seul exemple d'un décor intérieur du XVIIIe siècle encore en place aujourd'hui est celui de la chapelle des Ursulines de Québec construit après 1730 (fig. 4). Quelques pièces du premier retable de l'Ange-Gardien (CA 1706) sont conservées au Musée du Québec; nous disposons cependant d'un document photographique qui montre une partie de ce retable, avant qu'il ne soit complètement désassemblé (fig. 5). On comprend dès lors l'intérêt que suscitent l'existence et la connaissance d'une autre oeuvre de l'architecture intérieure du XVIIIe siècle, soit le retable de l'église de Saint-Augustin-de-Desmaures, exécuté à partir de 1746 (fig. 6).

Qu'entendons-nous par le décor intérieur d'une église? Il se compose de divers éléments dont les principaux sont la chaire, le tabernacle, la voûte, le retable principal et les retables latéraux. Nous retenons parmi ceux-ci et pour fins d'étude ici le retable principal qui est la pièce de mobilier liturgique la plus importante et une oeuvre d'architecture et de sculpture imposante nécessitant plusieurs mois, sinon quelques années de travail, et des sommes d'argent élevées pour couvrir les frais de production.

Nous abordons l'analyse du retable de l'église de Saint-Augustin par le biais de l'histoire de l'architecture. Cette oeuvre, comme nous le verrons, est intimement liée sur le plan formel à l'espace dans lequel elle prend place. Aussi traitons-nous à la fois du retable et de son environnement physique.

Par ailleurs, les mentions au sujet de son ornementation sculptée n'interviennent dans notre propos, que lorsque nous le jugeons opportun.

C'est un devis et un marché datés de 1822 qui nous révèlent la présence d'un retable ancien dans l'église de Saint-Augustin (construite en 1816).

> . . . savoir, Que le dit Sieur Joseph Frigon tant pour lui que pour le dit François Xavier Leprohon et le dit Joseph Houde leur caution s'est obligé solidairement avec eux envers la dite Fabrique de Saint-Augustin, à continuer à leurs frais et dépens L'ancien Retable dans l'Eglise nouvelle de la dite paroisse. . . .[2]

Les documents d'archives du XVIIIe siècle sont clairs au sujet de "l'ancien Retable" qui est mentionné dans le devis et le marché. Son auteur, Charles Vésina maître sculpteur, signe en 1746 le contrat d'exécution des travaux de ce retable et s'engage envers la paroisse de Saint-Augustin pour une période de trois ans.[3] Conçu pour le choeur de l'église de l'Anse-à-Maheu (fig. 7), le troisième édifice religieux construit dans la paroisse de Saint-Augustin en 1720, le retable de Charles Vésina adopte la forme de l'arc de triomphe, c'est-à-dire un retable droit qui occupe la largeur du choeur et qui comprend une partie centrale destinée à recevoir le maître-autel et le saint patron de l'église, ainsi que des volets latéraux plus petits.[4] La plupart des édifices religieux de la première motié du XVIIIe siècle sont dotés de retables en arc de triomphe adossés soit à un chevet plat, soit à la cloison qui sépare le choeur de la sacristie. Le choeur de l'église de l'Anse-à-Maheu s'inspire du modèle de l'église des Récollets et (fig. 3), comme celui-ci, il remplit une double fonction, car il abrite à la fois le choeur et la sacristie. Cette disposition est obtenue par la cloison qui délimite ces deux parties et qui sert d'appui au retable. Il faut attendre la fin du siècle, lorsque la disparition de la sacristie intérieure permet le dégagement du rond-point, pour voir apparaître un autre décor, comme celui de l'église des Jésuites du XVIIe siècle, le retable à trois volets ou à pans coupés (fig. 2).

En 1822, le retable sculpté par Charles Vésina soixante-seize ans auparavant est intégré au décor intérieur de l'église de Saint-Augstin-de-Desmaures et s'y retrouve aujourd'hui dans sa presque totalité, non sans avoir subi quelques modifications lors de son insertion (fig. 6). Il n'a été l'objet d'aucun changement important depuis cette date. Les maîtres d'oeuvre chargés de l'adapter à son nouvel environnement font face à un défi de taille, à cause de la forme et des dimensions, d'une part, du retable lui-même, et d'autre part, du nouveau sanctuaire, deux entités complètement différentes. En effet, l'église de Saint-Augustin est érigée sur un plan en croix latine avec un choeur de 28 pieds de large, en forme d'hémicycle, et une sacristie extérieure (fig. 8). Le retable droit de Charles Vésina, pour sa part, mesure environ 20 pieds.

Afin de présenter une image de l'état original de l'oeuvre de Vésina, nous éliminerons du retable actuel les changements apportés au début du XIXe siècle et qui sont décrits dans le marché et le devis de 1822. De plus, nous procéderons à une vérification des fragments et nous compléterons l'analyse par des comparaisons avec d'autres modèles de retable.

177

Figure 1. La façade l'église actuelle de Saint-Augustin-de-Desmaures (Photo Archives de l'Université Laval).

Figure 2. Québec. Vue de l'intérieur de l'église des Jésuites. Gravure de Short, 1759 (photo Musée du Québec).

178

Figure 3.   Québec. Vue de la nef et du retable de l'église des Récollets. Gravure de Short, 1759 (photo Musée du Québec).

Figure 4.   Québec. Vue de l'intérieur de la chapelle du monastère des Ursulines (photo Éditeur officiel du Québec).

Figure 5. L'Ange-Gardien. La partie centrale du retable avant qu'il ne soit complètement désassemblé (photo Q.Q.A.N.).

Figure 6. Vue du choeur et du retable de l'église actuelle de Saint-Augustin-de-Desmaures (photo I.B.C.).

180

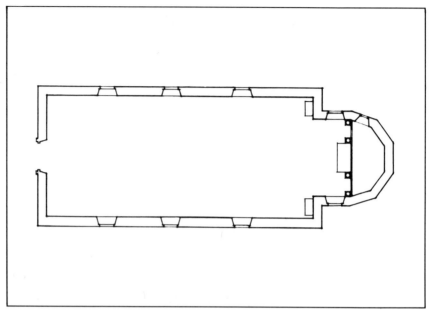

Figure 7. Reconstitution du plan au sol de l'église de l'Anse-à-Maheu (dessin d'André Cloutier).

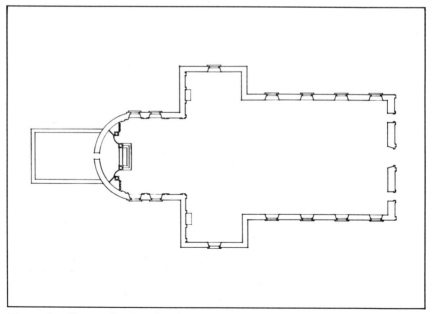

Figure 8. Reconstitution du plan original de l'église de Saint-Augustin-de-Desmaures (dessin d'André Cloutier).

Figure 9.   L'arrière du retable de l'église actuelle de Saint-Augustin-de-Desmaures (photo Archives de l'Université Laval).

Figure 10. Reconstitution hypothétique du retable de l'église de l'Anse-à-Maheu (dessin d'André Cloutier).

Le marché spécifie qu'on a installé le retable "suivant les dimensions proportions, règles et mesures de L'ordre corinthien déjà observé. . .",[5] Selon l'ordre retenu, la colonne de 11 '-10 " et la base de 3 '-5 " respectent le rapport de proportions entre ces membres, soit le 1/3 de la hauteur. Aucun changement n'a été apporté à ce niveau. Par ailleurs, une légère modification a pu se glisser au niveau des socles surélevant la base et au niveau de l'entablement qui, par un excès de quelques pouces, échappent aux proportions de l'ordre corinthien. Exception faite de ces détails mineurs, la hauteur du retable actuel semble conforme à celle du modèle original.

Devant l'impossibilité de placer le retable tel quel dans l'église de Saint-Augustin, les maîtres d'oeuvre le modifient au moyen des opérations suivantes:

> Premièrement changer les Placages attachés à l'ancien Retable en panneaux d'assemblage de deux parties, tant dans les Panneaux que dans leurs montants, en changer la position de manière à ne laisser que la Place des fenêtres, et de leurs ornements. . . .[6]

La partie centrale reste intacte et conserve la même largeur, 12 pieds. La première opération consiste à "changer la position" des volets latéraux, c'est-à-dire de les reculer par rapport à la partie centrale, ce qui a pour effet de projeter cette dernière vers l'avant et de créer un effet baroque. Cette action s'explique ainsi: le couronnement élaboré du retable nécessite un recul suffisant par rapport à l'inclinaison de la voûte au cul-de-four; force est, pour dégager la partie centrale du retable, d'avancer ce dernier dans le choeur. On l'installe donc au début du rond-point, non loin des fenêtres latérales. Or le marché indique de "laisser la Place des fenêtres, et de leurs ornements", ce qui sous-entend que l'emplacement du retable obstrue celles-ci à la vue. Afin de dégager les fenêtres et leurs boiseries, on détache les panneaux latéraux, qui ont un couronnement plus bas que celui du panneau principal, et on les place dernière les boiseries.

Ensuite, on procède à l'élargissement des volets latéraux, "changer les Placages attachés à l'ancien Retable en panneaux d'assemblage de deux parties", une opération qui implique l'adjonction de pans incurvés de part et d'autre de la partie centrale et le déplacement des volets anciens vers les extrémités. D'ailleurs, on peut aisément discerner l'âge de chaque partie en se rendant sur le terrain. Le panneau central ainsi que les panneaux des extrémités sont de la même époque, car on y reconnaît les mêmes matériaux, le même assemblage. Les pans courbés, composés de planchers embouvetées placées verticalement ont été ajoutés en 1822 (fig. 9). L'élargissement du retable est imposé par les dimensions du sanctuaire de l'église de Saint-Augustin. Cependant, on peut se demander ce qui justifie le choix de panneaux incurvés pour combler le vide. Selon les termes du marché, il s'agit de continuer le décor intérieur du choeur à partir du retable. Au XIXe siècle, la conception du décor intérieur d'une église englobe tout l'édifice et non plus différentes pièces de mobilier liturgique comme c'est le cas au XVIIIe siècle. Pour atteindre cette continuité, le morcellement est à toutes fins pratiques exclu. Dès lors, le lien par une forme circulaire va de soi.

Pour redonner sa forme au retable de l'Anse-à-Maheu, il suffit essentiellement d'enlever les pans courbés, de les remplacer par les volets anciens qui ont chacun 4 pieds de large et de placer ceux-ci en ligne avec la partie centrale. On obtient un retable droit, adoptant la forme de l'arc de triomphe. Cependant, pour l'harmonie de l'ensemble, l'ornementation sculptée nécessite des rajustements, particulièrement en ce qui a trait à l'emplacement des pilastres et de la frise de la corniche. C'est ainsi que se poursuivent les modifications décrites dans le marché.

> . . . changer également la position de la corniche des pilastres de leurs chapitaux Piedestaux et socs en y substituant l'assemblage qui leur manque, changer aussi en un autre plus proportionné à l'Espace le descendant de l'autre pilastre qui servira à l'autre pilastre du premier trumeau s'il peut être conservé en entier Lorsqu'il sera Détaché.[7]

Les pilastres ainsi que leur chapiteau, leur piédestal et leur socle, placés à l'origine derrière les colonnes ont été détachés de leur assemblage et jumelés aux volets anciens. La frise de ces parties est également détachée et incorporée aux pans courbés. Chacun de ces éléments sculptés remis en place, l'image du retable de Vésina se précise davantage.

Nous connaissons différents modèles de retable en arc de triomphe. Le premier exemple, dont nous possédons une illustration, est celui de l'église des Récollets (fig. 3). Le seul retable encore en place du même type est celui de la chapelle du monastère des Ursulines (fig. 4). Le retable de l'Ange-Gardien reprent également la forme de l'arc de triomphe (fig. 5). Tous ces documents sont essentiels pour la compréhension du retable de l'église de Saint-Augustin, car ce sont les seuls exemples que nous possédions.

Le retable de l'église des Récollets de Québec a pu inspirer Charles Vésina, du moins par ses proportions. En élévation, on y retrouve l'ordre corinthien et le développement en largeur comme à Saint-Augustin; la partie centrale est trois fois plus large que les volets latéraux. Des pots de feu couronnent l'entablement au-dessus des colonnes et des niches (ou tableaux) ornent les volets latéraux surmontés de reliquaires. La différence principale entre ce retable et celui de Saint-Augustin, se situe au niveau de l'entablement, qui, dans le premier cas, est ininterrompu et coiffé d'un fronton en segment de cercle alors que le second comporte un entablement ouvert et incurvé en forme de segment de cercle.

Le retable des Ursulines, par la richesse de son ornementation, est sans contredit un des plus grandioses qui ait été réalisé sous le Régime français. On y retrouve des niches dans les volets latéraux, un entablement rectiligne et un amortissement massif. Parmi ces exemples, le retable de l'Ange-Gardien se rapproche le plus, à notre avis, de celui de Saint-Augustin. Mais là aussi il s'agit d'un ensemble transformé au début du XIXe siècle, à l'occasion de travaux dans le choeur de l'église. Ceux-ci affecteront les volets latéraux; la partie centrale demeure intacte.[8] La ressemblance entre les deux oeuvres est frappante: un entablement de même forme et un couronnement presque identique.

Abstraction faite des pans incurvés qui sont un apport du XIXe siècle, la comparaison du retable de l'église de Saint-Augustin avec des retables du Régime français nous a permis de reconstituer théoriquement le retable de

184

Charles Vésina que nous proposons ici (fig. 10). Les couronnements sont replacés selon les modèles vus ailleurs, les statues intègrent les niches que devaient abriter les volets latéraux et les pilastres retournent derrière les colonnes.

La rareté des vestiges du Régime français en architecture religieuse n'est plus à démontrer et il existe un vide certain dans ce domaine. La présence du retable de Charles Vésina dans l'église de Saint-Augustin, en plus d'apporter une contribution importante à l'Art ancien du Québec, soulève une question: la réutilisation des retables serait-elle une pratique courante dans d'autres églises du Québec? Le cas de Saint-Augustin n'est sans doute pas unique.

Madeleine Gobeil-Trudeau
Université Laval

Liste des Abbréviations

(Références et notes et légendes des figures)

Q.Q.A.N.   Archives nationales du Québec

S.M.E.   Archives du Séminaire de Québec

I.B.C.   Inventaire des Biens culturels

Notes

[1] Ce texte est tiré d'un ouvrage du même auteur intitulé "Bâtir une église au Québec," Montréal, Libre Expression, 1981, 125 p., ill.
[2] Q.Q.A.N. Minutier de Mtre F.-X. Larue, 28 mai 1822, devis et marché.
[3] Archives de la fabrique. 2.1, F.104 et 9.1.
[4] Archives de la paroisse. 21.1, F. 81.
[5] Q.Q.A.N. *loc. cit.*
[6] *Ibid.*
[7] *Ibid.*
[8] "Explications Principales des ouvrages à faire à l'Église de l'Ange Gardien", S.M.E., Polygraphie 8, no 29.

17. William Blake and Westminster Abbey

The profound impression made on Blake's mind by "those neglected works of art, called Gothic monuments"[1] has been emphasized by all his biographers since Benjamin Heath Malkin who, in 1806, the same year that Blake began work on his *Canterbury Pilgrims,*[2] wrote the first memoir of the artist's life. Blake's early assignment to sketch old monuments — primarily in Westminster Abbey — was a "circumstance he always mention[ed] with gratitude."[3] Undoubtedly the five years he spent there making drawings laid the foundation of his life-long belief that Gothic form 'is Living Form' and exemplifies true art.[4] Attribution to Blake the apprentice of drawings made from effigies in the Abbey to illustrate Richard Gough's *Sepulchral Monuments in Great Britain*[5] and other Abbey subjects executed for the Society of Antiquaries[6] have broadened our knowledge of Blake's experience in the Abbey church and his awareness of its treasures. Yet beyond allusions to gothic motifs decorating Blake's illuminated verse[7] or lending symmetry to some of his designs[8] there has been little interest in what he may have learned there. We are told in a general way that Blake used the sculpturesque forms in the Abbey to frame his idea of "the aspect of an angel,'"[9] the calm recumbance of death[10] and "the pure & spiritual character of the female expression & form"[11] but the monuments in Westminster Abbey have never been examined with a view to their specific impact on Blake's art and thought.[12]

Gilchrist pictures Blake in the Abbey as quite alone — limited in his movements only "during service and in the intervals of visits from strangers."[13] Malkin's description of him frequently standing on monuments "and viewing the figures from the top"[14] hardly suggests the supervision of anyone concerned about either damage or decorum. Blake probably saw few people; the three weekday services[15] were open only to the Chapter, members of the foundation and Westminster School.[16] Congregations were lamentably small.[17] The choir and organ accompanying every service[18] would, however, have lent atmosphere to his task and punctuated his working day. Other ceremonies were infrequent. The House of Lords attended twice a year.[19] Funerals, numbering about twenty *per annum* in the eighteenth century, usually took place at night or were performed perfunctorily, the body never being carried into the Abbey at all.[20] As to visitors, until 1826 it was impossible to enter any part of the Abbey outside the hours of service without paying a fee.[21] From the beginning of George III's reign, as Jocelyn Perkins

185

writes, "the neglect suffered by the fabric was unbelievable . . . the condition of the monuments was filthy in the extreme . . . No one troubled to emphasize its sacred character."[22] Had Blake not been sent there, it is likely that his idea (especially during these formative years) of the Abbey's interior and monuments would have come from Sir Roger de Coverley's[23] and Lien Chi Altangi's[24] accounts of them rather than from the freedom to touch and climb on, to visit and re-visit, daily, for a period of years, some of the most beautiful relics of mediaeval craftsmanship in all England.

It was probably in the Abbey that Blake's fierce sense of the unity of art and craft took root[25] for it was no doubt here that he first gained access to original works of art executed in precious materials. His previous studies had been with plaster casts and copies.[26] Here were effigies carved in alabaster or cast in bronze, comatesque mosaics,[27] magnificent brasses like huge engraved plates,[28] the *opus Alexandrinum* pavement in the presbytery, "unequalled outside of Rome itself,"[29] and the fourteenth-century Sedilia which, in W. Burges's view, is "quite equal, if not superior, to contemporary Italian art."[30] Although not instructed to sketch them, he must have seen John of St. Albans' thirteenth-century angel spandrels in the south transept[31] and Lawrence Imber's sculptured saints, "in good preservation and . . . full of character"[32] ranged in Henry VII's Chapel, itself a magnificently exuberant Gothic structure.[33] The Chapel choir stalls were carved from motifs after Blake's favourite Albrecht Dürer and other German artists.[34] The bronze effigies of its founder, Henry Tudor, his queen, Elizabeth of York, and Lady Margaret Beaufort, his mother, all justly regarded as "among the very noblest [monumental effigies] in Europe"[35] were executed by Torrigiani, who worked in the same studio with another of Blake's idols, Michelangelo.[36] It must have been with such works in mind that Blake later deplored the contemporary approach to beautifying public buildings, "[which] lament and desire," Laurence Binyon writes, "show how [Blake] conceived of the function and need of art in national life. Isolated in his own age, he was ever conscious of the lost medieval tradition and striving to take up again its broken threads."[37] The Abbey's beautiful originals represented the tradition that wedded art to craft, sculpture to stonemasonry,[38] goldsmithing to foundry work,[39] conception to execution, before the fragmentation that relegated craft to drudgery and disrepute.

In 1779, just before he was free of his indentures, Blake applied for admission to the Royal Academy of Arts.[40] At this time, history painting, albeit with little pretence to historical accuracy as yet, was the dominant genre.[41] Fresh from contact with mementos of the heroic past as exemplified by Abbey monuments, Blake no doubt had some basic knowledge of the dress appropriate to various periods; yet his early history paintings, as Anthony Blunt points out, employ the mixed costume favoured by Angelica Kauffmann and John Hamilton Mortimer.[42] With the '80s and '90s, and the artist-antiquarian approach to history painting introduced by Benjamin West and John Singleton Copley, however, research and historical accuracy began to take on new importance.[43] Illustrations of authentic historical costume and armour, published by Joseph Strutt,[44] Francis Grose[45] and others,[46] became routine sources for the history painter. In this context, it is not surprising that

PLANCHE I   PLATE I

I a. The Pardoner from Blake's
Canterbury Pilgrims

I b. The Sedilia, Westminster
Abbey

I c. Coat of arms, Westminster
Abbey

I a, II a, IV a from *Chaucer's Canterbury Pilgrims* by William Blake,
reproduced by permission of the Department of Rare Books and Special
Collections, McGill University Libraries, Montreal.
I b, II b, c, d, IV b reproduced by permission of the Dean and Chapter,
Westminster.

188

PLATE II

II a. The Prioress and the Nun

II b. Tomb effigy, Elizabeth of York, Westminster Abbey

II c. Tomb effigy, Elizabeth of York, Westminster Abbey

II d. Partial view of bronze grille showing greyhound and dragon badges. From Scott's *Gleanings* . . . (see note 28)

III a. Partial view of bronze grille showing rose and portcullis. From Scott's *Gleanings* . . .

III b. Partial view of Henry VII's Chapel gate. From Scott's *Gleanings* . . .

III c. Tomb effigy, Lady Margaret Beaufort, Westminster Abbey

190

IV a. The Wife of Bath

IV b. St. Dunstan's in the East.
From Bohn's *Pictorial Handbook*
. . . (see note 86)

IV c. Tomb effigy, Elizabeth I,
Westminster Abbey

Blake, in 1810, should emphasize his fidelity to the architectural style of the Tabard Inn, in his *Canterbury Pilgrims,* and that he should describe the costume of his characters as "correct according to authentic monuments."[47] Blake made these claims, no doubt with an eye to Thomas Stothard's *Pilgrimage to Canterbury,* the costumes for which were taken from Strutt's *Dress and Habits of the People of England.*[48] What better counter-thrust at this thief of his subject, as Blake believed Stothard to be, than impugning the accuracy of his reading of Chaucer and claiming rival researches — not in antiquarian volumes but directly from authentic monuments? At first glance, one might suppose that Blake's assertions were mere bravado, for the *Canterbury Pilgrims* obviously employs the mixed costume of an earlier style of history painting. Yet since, as we shall see, many of his pilgrims do exhibit striking similarities in costume, and indeed in other features, to specific Abbey monuments, Blake's claim was well-founded and intended to be taken literally. Here, it would seem, is a fruitful means of gauging the Abbey's impact on a particular composition long recognized as central to Blake's philosophy of criticism, history and the nature of poetic vision.

Details of the Pardoner's costume — his gloves, for example — illustrate Blake's fidelity to monumental originals in the Abbey. They closely resemble those on Robert Waldeby's brass in St. Edmund's Chapel where Blake sketched the effigies of John of Eltham and Edward III's infant children. The fourteenth-century likeness shows him in archiepiscopal robes, the right hand raised in benediction, the left holding a cross.[49] Similar jewelled gauntlets figure in Henry III's portrait on the Sedilia, faithfully rendered in Blake's copy of it,[50] and are clearly suggested by the metal quatrefoils on the backs of Edward I's hands, the exhumation and unwrapping of whose corpse Blake is believed to have both witnessed and progressively recorded in sketches.[51] The *croix patonce* on the Pardoner's back appears as part of the inscription on Henry III's tomb.[52] More importantly, it forms the basis of Edward the Confessor's Cross, seen sculptured in the south aisle[53] and featured most prominently in the Abbey's coat of arms. The usurpation of symbols and garments appropriate to leaders of the Church and State underscores the Pardoner's will to power. Blake describes him as "the Age's Knave, who always commands and domineers over the high and low vulgar. This man is sent in every age for a rod and scourge, . . . he is in the most holy sanctuary, and he is suffered by Providence for wise ends. . . ."[54] The costume to which he has no just claim serves to emphasize his presence among the upper classes near the front of the cavalcade, where he has no right to be.[55] The cross on his back recalls the Confessor's shrine in the heart of the Abbey and parodies its use on crusaders' tunics — a habit alluded to in Edmund Crouchback's name[56] whose sanctuary tomb Blake sketched. Chaucer's Pardoner, on concluding his Tale, attempts to wrest the leadership of the pilgrims from Harry Bailly.[57] Blake's rendition of the Pardoner's costume reinforces this element of Chaucer's characterization.

Of all Blake's pilgrims, it is the Prioress and the Wife of Bath whose costumes and characters have received the greatest critical attention. That he intended them to be regarded as complements of each other seems clear from Blake's comment, that "the characters of Women Chaucer has divided into two classes, the Lady Prioress and the Wife of Bath. Are not these leaders of the ages of men? The Lady Prioress, in some ages, predominates; and in some the Wife of Bath, in whose character Chaucer has been equally minute and exact. . . ."[58] Karl Kiralis, elaborating on Foster Damon's initial insight, analyzes the Prioress and the Wife of Bath, their jewelry, costume and paraphernalia to demonstrate the identification of the two women as Tirzah the Prude and Rahab the Whore, respectively.[59] The Wife's 'morning draught of comfort' emphasized in all three of Blake's descriptions of his design[60] is interpreted as Rahab's, that is the Whore of Babylon's, cup of fornications.[61] Although Kiralis does not cite it, Blake's contemporary illustration of Revelation 17:1-4, featuring the Great Whore posed on the seven-headed Beast, holding her cup and wearing a large heart-shaped pendant gives good evidence for the identification in Blake's mind of the Wife of Bath with the Whore of Babylon.[62] The Wife's sensual, manipulative nature, as well as her frankly expressed desire to have "al the soveraynetee,"[63] are indeed appropriate to Blake's characterization of Rahab as the Female Will. To demonstrate the Prioress's identification with Tirzah, Kiralis points to her posed position, uncovered forehead and teasingly-revealed upper arms, breasts and shoulders.[64] He further interprets the reticulated trappings of her horse as the Veil of Vala,[65] and the small white dogs beside her as her inner impulses. They "are the picture of prim dignity," he writes, "the image the Lady Prioress tries to reflect, though the jumping one suggests some kind of anxiety, which the female Prioress must have under her calm exterior."[66] Although he did not, Kiralis might have pointed out a persuasive link between the Prioress and the idea of prudery, for Blake's tenth and eleventh illustrations to Thomas Gray's "A Long Story" feature women wearing various old-fashioned head-dresses, among them the pedimental form worn by the Prioress, and accompanying the lines "The ghostly prudes with haggard face/ Already had condemn'd the sinner."[67] This peaked head covering is Blake's own detail, but many other features of clothing come directly from Chaucer's text. One is always aware, as Warren Stevenson points out, of "the subtlety of Blake's technique, and . . . his skillful efforts to reconcile reasonable fidelity to Chaucer's text with fidelity to his own vision. . . ."[68] Where fidelity is achieved, however, his suspected divergence from the spirit of the original must be explored with caution.

For his own part, Blake discusses the Prioress at some length, giving particular emphasis to her youth and her attendant greyhounds.[69] "This Lady," he states further, "is described also as of the first rank, rich and honoured. She has certain peculiarities and little delicate affectations, not unbecoming in her, being accompanied with what is truly grand and really polite; her person and face Chaucer has described with minuteness; it is very elegant, and was the beauty of our ancestors, till after Elizabeth's time, when voluptuousness and folly began to be accounted beautiful."[70] Blake's comments and his visual representation of the Prioress take on new significance when viewed in terms of the monumental effigy of Elizabeth of York, whose granddaughter, Elizabeth I, Blake associates with the turning-point in tastes concerning feminine beauty. Torrigiani's bronze effigy portrays the former as young and beautiful, her forehead and neck uncovered and her long hair hanging over her shoulders under her pedimental head-dress. Her arms are cased in tight sleeves to the wrist, and a horizontal line under her breast suggests a difference of cut or material in the upper part of her robe. All these features are reflected in Blake's portrait of the Prioress. The metal grille through which the tomb must be viewed adds further details. It is, in W.R. Lethaby's words, "an extraordinarily beautiful work, . . . conceived with great frankness as a little building of brass, all of open-work lattices, traceries, and brattishings . . . the details sharp and vivid; and the inscriptions, badges of greyhounds and red dragons, and images, are triumphs of skill."[71] Blake in his comments on the *Canterbury Pilgrims* is at great pains to ascribe the "greyhounds" in the design — which in Chaucer's text are merely "smale houndes" — to the Prioress. The Monk, who rides close by, Chaucer describes as given to hunting with "Grehoundes"[72] and Blake, it would appear, took no chances that the "fair prelaat" might be mistaken for their owner. The animals on the screen confronting the dragons are very like the Prioress's dogs, and represent the Beaufort greyhound, badge of the King's mother's family.[73] Anyone looking at these creatures might conclude, though incorrectly, that since the dragon obviously represents the House of Tudor, the greyhound must logically stand for the House of York, and thus be the badge of the Queen. But understood this way or not, Elizabeth of York's effigy cannot be viewed without numerous and conspicuous decorative greyhounds lying directly in one's line of vision. The additional presence of roses, on the tomb, on the grille and carved throughout the Chapel — appropriate to Tudor, Lancaster and York — is a happy coincidence, for the Prioress's name, Eglantine, is also that of the sweet briar rose. A further motif, the Beaufort portcullis, prominent on the grille, the tomb, the Chapel gates and indeed throughout the decorative carving, bears striking resemblance, despite its different orientation, to the trappings on the Prioress's horse. That Blake had this badge of the Beauforts in mind while working on the *Canterbury Pilgrims* is clear from his contemporary illustration to *Paradise Lost, Satan Comes to the Gates of Hell*,[74] which features both the arrow-footed portcullis and the accompanying chain motif so conspicuous on the perforated panels of Henry VII's Chapel gates. Even the crown in this version of the portcullis badge suggests the Prioress's "crowned A" in Chaucer's text. The Nun by her side has a wimple, in contrast to the Prioress's bare neck, like that shown on Lady Margaret Beaufort's effigy which, similar in style and materials, and sharing the decorative motifs of the portcullis and the rose, lies in the south aisle of Henry VII's Chapel. The Nun's head-dress is less peaked than Lady Margaret's but is still roughly pedimental in form; a head covering beneath it, while present, does not hide her hair as Lady Margaret's does. Elizabeth's youthfulness and Lady Margaret's elderly appearance are also reflected in Blake's characterization. These two tombs, in fact, exemplify a turning-point in the Abbey's history. Although expressive of the purest Renaissance tradition,[75] they represent the last of the mediaeval royal monuments and the last, indeed, before the great upheaval in the English Church. Writing of Lady Margaret who outlived both her son and daughter-in-law, Dean Stanley observes: "Strikingly are the old and the new combined as, round the monument of that last mediaeval

Princess, we trace the letters of the inscription written by [Erasmus] the first and most universal of the Reformers. We feel, as we stand by her tomb, that we are approaching the great catastrophe.''[76]

By the time Elizabeth Tudor came to the throne, a drastic change had taken place. Blake's reference to "the beauty of our ancestors till after Elizabeth's time when voluptuousness and folly began to be accounted beautiful" could well apply to tastes in monuments for, in this reign, the Abbey took on the new function of 'Temple of Fame',[77] with memorials to great ladies of the court predominating. These monuments in Lawrence Tanner's words were "monumental in every sense of the word, and . . . were so designed that they had perforce to be fixed for support against the walls of the Church. As their height would have obscured the windows many of them occupy the site of the former altars, which were usually placed against windowless walls in the side Chapels."[78] The first tomb to displace an altar was that of Frances Grey, Duchess of Suffolk, who died in the year of Elizabeth's accession.[79] Elizabethan effigies display the form-distorting dress that was the fashion: farthingales, ruffs and showy sculptured jewelry. On the evidence of Abbey monuments, "voluptuousness and folly" were accounted beautiful from the beginning of Elizabeth's reign, and not merely after her death.

That the Wife of Bath's costume has an Elizabethan air can be seen at a glance, but comparing the Wife's overall appearance with that of Elizabeth Tudor's effigy produces surprising similarities. Physically they are both of advanced years, with aquiline noses, thick necks and faces wide at the cheekbones. Although Chaucer describes her as well-wimpled,[80] Blake's Wife reveals her neck and bosom as does Elizabeth, and both wear heavy beads and pendants matched with dangling ear-rings. Each wears a point lace frill to her chemise turned back, although the Wife lacks Elizabeth's broad plaited ruff beneath it. The Queen, like the Wife, wears a close coif but lacks the Wife's head-dress, specified by Chaucer, which Kiralis describes as "resembling the Pope's tiara with an ironic suggestion of a halo."[81] These papal associations would of course be appropriate to Elizabeth as head of the English Church. As Queen she calls to mind the Elf Queen in the Wife's Tale. Ever courted, ever virgin, she epitomizes both Rahab's role of Virgin Whore and her characterization as the Female Will. In illustration 11 to Gray's "The Bard" Blake depicted a youthful Elizabeth wearing a frill very like the Wife of Bath's, which Geoffrey Keynes describes as "conspicuously spiked, shewing again Blake's hatred of the Monarchy."[82] It is worth noting that in his *Vision of The Last Judgment,* roughly contemporaneous with the *Canterbury Pilgrims,* Blake wrote: "In Eternity Woman is the Emanation of Man; she has No Will of her own. There is no such thing in Eternity as a Female Will, & Queens [of England *del.*]"[83] Northrop Frye has pointed out the poet's affinity to the Elizabethans, but there is no reason to suppose Blake admired the Elizabethan Establishment.[84] Among his annotations to Bacon, his comment that "It was a Common opinion in the Court of Queen Elizabeth that Knavery Is Wisdom,"[85] suggests far otherwise. Significantly, the Merchant, positioned confidentially at the Wife's left ear, bears a suggestive resemblance to portraits of the Lord Chancellor. A further hint of the connection between these two and its destructive nature is the apparently gothic steeple above their heads. It is, in fact, a faithful rendition of the belfry of St. Dunstan's in the East, a gothic imitation by Sir Christopher Wren.[86] Blake accused Bacon of being a Contemplative Atheist, making "Pretence to Religion to destroy Religion."[87] Wren's imitation, obvious from "the flatness, shallowness and littleness of its mouldings",[88] he would no doubt have considered, as he did Reynolds' *Discourses,* "A Pretence of Art, To destroy Art."[89] Church Establishment — State Religion — traceable to Elizabeth Blake refers to as "The Abomination that maketh desolate,"[90] an epithet he also uses of Rahab:

> . . . thus Rahab is reveal'd,
> Mystery, Babylon the Great, the Abomination of Desolation,
> Religion hid in War, a Dragon red & hidden Harlot.[91]

To return to the *Canterbury Pilgrims:* if the greyhound is appropriate to the Prioress, the dragon facing it on Henry VII's grille is equally appropriate to the Wife in her association with Rahab as well as to Elizabeth Tudor, whose dynasty it represents. In fact Blake's reference, elsewhere in *Jerusalem,* to "Babylon the Great" as "The Druid Dragon"[92] makes such an association difficult to refute. Elizabeth of York and Elizabeth Tudor can be seen to confront each other much as the greyhound and the dragon do: the one whose marriage ended the Wars of the Roses and whose children established the Tudor dynasty; the other whose refusal to marry, and thus relinquish power over Church and State, brought the dynasty to an end. The one belonging to the Old Dispensation of "true enthusiastic superstition,"[93] as Blake calls mediaeval Catholicism; the other initiating a state religion and appropriating the churches for the glorification of courtiers and politicians rather than the glory of God. A reversal of civil status, associating the mother of the Tudors with the celibate Prioress and the much-married Wife with the Virgin Queen, is fully consistent with Blake's theory of history as he expounds it in *A Descriptive Catalogue,* his apologia for the *Canterbury Pilgrims:*

> The characters of Chaucer's Pilgrims are the characters which compose all ages and nations: as one age falls, another rises, different to mortal sight, but to immortals only the same; for we see the same characters repeated again and again. . .
> . . . some of the names or titles are altered by time, but the characters themselves for ever remain unaltered, and consequently they are the physiognomies or lineaments of universal human life. . . .[94]

In his apprentice years Blake's studies, as Malkin writes, took him "over all the old monuments in Westminster Abbey . . . ,"[95] and must have early impressed upon him the co-occurrence of varying styles of dress and beauty there, embodying simultaneously the linear and the cumulative view of history and taste. Given his interpretation, thirty years later, of Chaucer's pilgrimage as that of every age involving universal human types, Blake's use of costumes drawn from various times is more suited to the spirit of this view than dress uniformly representative of Chaucer's day could be. One wonders if the germ of this visionary concept of history may first have been implanted in the Abbey where, as Malkin affirms, "he drew [its monuments] in every

196

point he could catch, . . . The heads he considered as portraits; and all the ornaments . . . as miracles of art."⁹⁶ What better source than these could Blake have chosen when illustrating Chaucer in his later years to exemplify the "lineaments of universal human life"?

M.E. Reisner
Laval University

Notes

¹ *A Father's Memoirs of His Child,* reprinted in G.E. Bentley, Jr., *Blake Records* (Oxford: Clarendon Press, 1969), p. 422.
² Mona Wilson, *The Life of William Blake,* new ed., Geoffrey Keynes (London: Oxford Univ. Press, 1971), p. 233.
³ Malkin, *op, cit.,* p. 422.
⁴ All Blake quotations are from *The Complete Writings of William Blake,* ed., Geoffrey Keynes (London: Oxford Univ. Press, 1966) and are identified as K. K 461, 604, 610 and 778; also designs to *Jerusalem* plates 46, 57 and 84.
⁵ Paul Miner, "The Apprentice of Great Queen Street," *BNYPL,* 67, (Jan.-Dec. 1963), 639-40. Geoffrey Keynes, *Blake Studies,* (Oxford: Clarendon Press, 1971), pp. 16-18.
⁶ Anthony Blunt, *The Art of William Blake* (London: Oxford Univ. Press, 1959), pp. 3-4 and p. 3 n. 4; Miner, pp. 641-42; Keynes, *Blake Studies,* pp. 20-24.
⁷ Especially in Jean H. Hagstrum, *William Blake: Poet and Painter* (Chicago: The Univ. of Chicago Press, 1964), p. 77 *et passim.*
⁸ Blunt, plates 42a-d.
⁹ William Gaunt, *Arrows of Desire* (London: The Museum Press Limited, 1956), p. 32.
¹⁰ Kathleen Raine, *William Blake* (New York, Washington: Praeger Publishers, 1970), p. 19.
¹¹ Part of the information about Blake sent by John Linnell to Alexander Gilchrist, cited by Bentley, p. 318 n. 2.
¹² The two most recent studies of the impact of Gothic art on Blake pay only the slightest attention to his contact with it in the Abbey: cf., Roger R. Easson, "Blake and the Gothic," *Blake in His Time,* ed. Robert N. Essick and Donald Pearce (Bloomington and London: Indiana Univ. Press, 1978), pp. 145-54; and Edward J. Rose, "The 'Gothicized Imagination' of 'Michelangelo Blake'," *ibid.,* pp. 155-69.
¹³ *Life of William Blake, A New and Enlarged Edition* (New York: Phaeton Press, 1969), p. 18.
¹⁴ Bentley, p. 422.
¹⁵ Jocelyn Perkins, *Westminster Abbey: Its Worship and Ornaments* (London: Humphrey Milford, Oxford Univ. Press, 1938), III, p. 131. Services in the summer were held at 6, 10 and 3.
¹⁶ Perkins, III, p. 149. See also Lawrence E. Tanner, *Westminster School* (London: Country Life Ltd, 1934), p. 68.
¹⁷ Perkins, III, p. 143.
¹⁸ Perkins, III, p. 154.
¹⁹ January 30th and May 29th: Perkins, III, p. 131. A third official service was held on November 5th: Perkins, III, p. 144.
²⁰ Perkins, III, pp. 145-46.
²¹ Adam Fox, *The Pictorial History of Westminster Abbey* (London: Pitkin Ltd, 1962), p. 18.
²² Perkins, III, pp. 141-42.
²³ *Spectator,* No. 329: "Sir Roger Visits Westminster Abbey".
²⁴ *The Citizen of the World,* Letters XII and XIII.
²⁵ Cf. K 592-93; 596.
²⁶ Blunt, pp. 2-3; Hagstrum, p. 24; Raine, p. 12; and Morton D. Paley, "'Wonderful Originals' — Blake and Ancient Sculpture," *Blake in His Time,* p. 171.
²⁷ W.R. Lethaby, *Westminster Abbey Re-examined* (London: Duckworth & Co., 1925), p. 217.
²⁸ Especially Eleanor de Bohun's fourteenth-century brass: cf. George Gilbert Scott, *Gleanings from Westminster Abbey* (London: John Henry and James Parker, 1863), pp. 189-90, and

Francis Bond, *Westminster Abbey* (London: Henry Froude, Oxford Univ. Press, 1909), p. 180.

29 Lethaby, p. 217. Cf. also p. 220.

30 "The Sedilia", in Scott, *Gleanings*, p. 119.

31 Lawrence E. Tanner, *Unknown Westminster Abbey* (Harmondsworth, Middlesex: Penguin Books, 1948), p. 15.

32 W.R. Lethaby, *Westminster Abbey and the Kings' Craftsmen* (London: Duckworth & Co., 1906), p. 230.

33 Bond, pp. 132-34, and *Westminster Abbey*, Vol. I of *Royal Commission on Historical Monuments (England)* (London: His Majesty's Stationers' Office, 1924), p. 20.

34 *Westminster Abbey and the Kings' Craftsmen*, p. 239 n.

35 Bond, p. 205.

36 *Westminster Abbey Re-examined*, p. 203.

37 *The Drawings and Engravings of William Blake*, ed. Geoffrey Holme (London: The Studio Limited, 1922), p. 28.

38 *Westminster Abbey and the Kings' Craftsmen*, p. 240.

39 Elspeth M. Veale, *Studies in London History*, ed. A.E.J. Hollaender and William Kellaway (London: Hodder & Stoughton, 1969), p. 147.

40 Bentley, p. 15.

41 Roy Strong, *And when did you last see your father?* (London: Thames and Hudson, 1978), p. 13.

42 Blunt, p. 7.

43 Strong, p. 24.

44 *The Regal and Ecclesiastical Antiquities of England* (1773), *Complete View of the Dress and Habits of the People of England* (1796-99), and *The Sports and Pastimes of the People of England* (1801).

45 *Treatise on Ancient Armour and Weapons* (1786).

46 Richard Gough's *Sepulchral Monuments of Great Britain* (1786-99) and Charles Alfred Stothard's *The Monumental Effigies of Great Britain* (1811-33).

47 K 567.

48 Strong, p. 58.

49 W. Burges's "The Brasses", in Scott, *Gleanings*, p. 189.

50 Blunt, plate 2a.

51 Keynes, *Blake Studies*, p. 23.

52 W. Burges's "The Tombs", in Scott, *Gleanings*, p. 150.

53 "Ancient Arms in Westminster Abbey", in Scott, *Gleanings*, p. 298.

54 K 570.

55 S. Foster Damon, *A Blake Dictionary* (Providence, R.I.: Brown Univ. Press, 1963), p. 79, comments on rank; Walter Clyde Curry, *Chaucer and the Mediaeval Sciences*, rev. ed. (London: Allen and Unwin, 1960), p. 65, states that there is no evidence that the pilgrims of high rank have had "any close association whatever with the Pardoner."

56 Arthur Penrhyn Stanley, *Historical Memorials of Westminster Abbey* (London: John Murray, 1868), p. 134.

57 James Winny, *The General Prologue to the Canterbury Tales* (Cambridge: Cambridge Univ. Press, 1965), p. 22.

58 K 572.

59 Damon, p. 79. Karl Kiralis, "William Blake as an Intellectual and Spiritual Guide to Chaucer's *Canterbury Pilgrims*," *Blake Studies*, 1 (Spring 1969), 148-62 *et passim*. Warren Stevenson, "Interpreting Blake's *Canterbury Pilgrims*," *Colby Library Quarterly*, 13, (June 1977), 120-25 and Orphia Jane Allen, "Blake's Archetypal Criticism: *The Canterbury Pilgrims*," *Genre*, 11, (1978), 181-83 adhere to this interpretation.

60 K 567, 588, 590.

61 Revelation 17:4.

62 Stevenson, pp. 119, 124 cites it.

63 *The Works of Geoffrey Chaucer*, ed. F.N. Robinson, 2nd ed. (Boston: Houghton Mifflin Company, 1957), *WBP*, 1. 818.

64 Kiralis, p. 148.

65 Kiralis, pp. 154-55.

[66] Kiralis, p. 161.

[67] *William Blake's Water-Colour Designs for the Poems of Thomas Gray,* intro. Geoffrey Keynes (London: Trianon Press for the William Blake Trust, 1971), designs 32 and 33.

[68] Stevenson, p. 119.

[69] K 566, 588, 589.

[70] K 568.

[71] *Westminster Abbey and the King's Craftsmen,* p. 232.

[72] *Gen Prol,* 1. 190.

[73] John Woodward and George Burnett, *Woodward's A Treatise on Heraldry British and Foreign* (Rutland, Vt.: Charles E. Tuttle Co., 1969), p. 595; use as supporters, p. 662.

[74] *Catalogue of William Blake's Drawings and Paintings in the Huntington Library,* enlarged and rev. R.R. Wark (San Marino, Ca.: The Huntington Library, 1969), plate II, dated (1807).

[75] *Westminster Abbey Re-examined,* p. 203: "The tomb portraits of Henry VII and his Queen, with a third figure of the King's mother near by . . . are really great works of the Italian Renaissance. . . . They follow the tradition of Donatello and, if they were in Italy, they would be noted among the most wonderful things that could be seen on tour."

[76] Stanley, p. 166.

[77] Stanley, p. 200.

[78] Lawrence E. Tanner, *The History and Treasures of Westminster Abbey* (London: Pitkin Pictorials Ltd, 1953), p. 66.

[79] Stanley, p. 198.

[80] *Gen Prol,* 1. 470.

[81] Kiralis, p. 148.

[82] *Water-Colour Designs for the Poems of Thomas Gray,* p. 59.

[83] K 613.

[84] Northrop Frye, *Fearful Symmetry* (Boston: Beacon Press, 1962), p. 9. S. Foster Damon, *William Blake: His Philosophy and Symbols* (Gloucester, Mass.: Peter Smith, 1958), p. 172, suggests that Blake did, in fact, admire it.

[85] K 397.

[86] See engravings of "Wren's Steeples", in *The Pictorial Handbook of London* . . . (London: Henry G. Bohn, [1861]), and pp. 196-197 on St. Dunstan's in particular.

[87] K 403, 398.

[88] *The Pictorial Handbook of London,* p. 196.

[89] K 452.

[90] K 393.

[91] K 716: plate 75, 11. 18-20.

[92] K 741: plate 93, 1. 25.

[93] K 575.

[94] K 567.

[95] Bentley, p. 423.

[96] Bentley, pp. 422-23.

18. Women Artists in Eighteenth-Century France

The Eighteenth Century in Perspective

The decade of the 1970s will undoubtedly go down in history as a period that witnessed a dramatic renaissance (some might say revolution) in the history of women artists. The birth of the Women's Caucus for Art, the *Feminist Art Journal,* and the Center for Feminist Art Historical Studies, all established in the early seventies, are but a few milestones in the movement.[1] The celebration of International Women's Year in 1975 stimulated the publication of bibliographical sources, notably Vicki Lynn Hill's *Female Artists, Past and Present.* Capping the decade, Germaine Greer published her comprehensive but controversial *Obstacle Race* which will undoubtedly spark a new wave of reactions in the 1980s.[2]

In spite of the dramatic increase in interest in women's art, no one has made a quantitative analysis of women artists of a particular period. No one, for example, has attempted to analyze and evaluate the phenomenal increase in the number of French women artists during the Enlightenment. It was for this reason that the present investigation of women artists was initiated several years ago. The study is more concerned with women artists as a professional group than as individuals. The approach is both analytical and biographical, examining such questions as why escalating numbers of French women turned to art as a vocation in the eighteenth century; from what economic classes they emerged; from whom they learned their crafts; the nature of their marital relationships; and the extent of their success, financially and professionally, in competing with male artists.

Within Europe, France clearly excelled in the number and quality of active women artists during the Enlightenment. This is not surprising because France contained the three essential ingredients necessary for the emergence of women as professionals: an abundant supply of male artists, a society sufficiently mobile to encourage women to enter the professions, and a substantial middle class. The first ingredient was necessary because almost all of the women learned their crafts in the workshops of male artists. Only toward the end of the century did an increasing number of women learn to paint in the studios of other women, but this practice was the exception rather than the rule. Consequently, the number of female artists in a particular locality or country tended to be proportional to the number of male artists, provided that the other prerequisites existed.[3] In a century which produced

Watteau, Boucher, Greuze, Chardin, Fragonard, and David, France could be expected to give birth to a proportionally large number of female painters as well. And this was true; indeed, as France displaced Italy as the cultural center of Europe in the eighteenth century, Paris and its environs also became the artistic showcase for women artists.[4]

The second ingredient, social mobility, was equally important in motivating women to turn to the brush and palette for a livelihood. In such socially rigid countries as Russia and Spain the number of women who became professionals was small even though there was an adequate supply of male artists.[5] In France the social conditions were favorable in the eighteenth century because French society gave women increasing independence. The literary salons in the seventeenth and eighteenth centuries had already given a small but influential number of women unprecedented opportunities to exhibit their wit and literary talents. Through the salons French women had gained higher stature and influence in society. It is not surprising, therefore, that women artists were welcomed into the art salons of the Enlightenment. Women artists with great talent, e.g., Rosalba Carriera, Vigée-Lebrun and Angelica Kauffmann, were universally respected and celebrated. It is in this sense that Vigée-Lebrun's comment that women "reigned" in French society before the revolution "dethroned" them must be understood.[6]

Without the third ingredient — a sizeable middle class to buy art and artifacts — few women artists could have survived in the competitive marketplace. It was largely the mercantile, financial, and professional bourgeoisie that bought their works. Without this increasingly significant group of art patrons, the number of women who could have supported themselves solely through the sale of their works would have been appreciably smaller. A few women, notably Vigée-Lebrun, Labille-Guiard, and Marie Benoist, who found royal and noble patrons to buy their large canvasses, were not as dependent upon the middle classes, but even they found a ready market in the affluent bourgeoisie. Most of the other women artists in France (and elsewhere in Europe) found buyers almost solely in the upper bourgeoisie and country gentry.

This correlation of economic activity and cultural creativity was clearly manifested throughout Europe in the Enlightenment, and it explains the meteoric increase in women professionals in what might be called the Golden Age of women's artistry. In such countries as the Netherlands and in the city states of Renaissance Italy, this new class of bourgeois patrons had emerged earlier, explaining in part the earlier emergence of women professionals in these states. It was not until the eighteenth century with the five-fold expansion of trade in France that the stage was set for a "cultural explosion," to use Professor J.H. Plumb's expression. And as commercial wealth increased almost geometrically from generation to generation in the course of the eighteenth century, the number of women artists increased correspondingly. In the judgment of Elinor Barber, a leading authority on the bourgeoisie in 18th-century France, the new class of wealthy financiers and merchants became "the new patron of arts and letters." As a result, there were more French women artists active in the second half of that century than in all of the preceding centuries in French history.[7]

These three conditions — an abundance of male tutors, a relatively open society, and an expanding middle class — account for the phenomenal increase in women artists in France in the Enlightenment. The contrast between that period and the preceding centuries is striking. If one were to plot the number of known women artists for each century on a bar graph, the curve would rise slowly for the centuries before the seventeenth, rise more rapidly in the seventeenth, and then escalate sharply in the eighteenth. In terms of numbers, there were only three active women artists in France in the sixteenth century, about thirty in the seventeenth, and over two hundred in the eighteenth. The Académie du Saint-Luc alone registered 130 women as master painters in that century.[8] Admittedly the number of women artists who worked prior to the eighteenth century may be greater than these figures indicate because of fewer extant records and greater anonymity in the earlier periods, but even if allowances are made for these considerations, the figures speak tellingly for the important rise of women artists. By the end of the century French women could boast that in the Salon of 1800 twenty-five of the 180 exhibitors were women.

French Women Artists of the Enlightenment

The identification of female artists in the eighteenth century is not difficult. By examining the registers of the art academies in the most important cities one can list the names of several hundred. The more difficult task is to separate the professionals from the amateurs and the successful from the dilettantes. The list below is compiled from research in the Bibliothèque d'Art et d'Archéologie in Paris, from visits to most of France's important art museums, and from a study of the literature and art exhibitions of the eighteenth century.[9] The women are listed alphabetically in the second and third groups, but in the first group they are listed in the order in which they were generally ranked by their contemporaries. The sixth person in this category, Collot-Falconet, is listed last because she is the only sculptor. No two critics will agree upon any listing of artists, male or female, but for the purpose of making a study of the social, economic, and aesthetic aspects of women's art in the eighteenth century, the twenty-three women analyzed in this study should suffice. Even if one were to replace the names of five or six artists with others, none of the generalizations in this study would change appreciably.

A. *Most Successful:*	Married (M) Single (S)	First Art Teachers	Academies
1. Marie Louise Elisabeth Vigée-Lebrun (1755-1842)	M	Father, Davesne, Briard	Saint-Luc Académie Royale Eight Others
2. Adélaïde Labille-Guiard (1749-1803)	M (Twice)	F. Vincent, La Tour, F.A. Vincent	Saint-Luc Académie Royale
3. Anne Vallayer-Coster (1744-1818)	M	Father	Académie Royale
4. Marguerite Gérard (1761-1837)	S	Brother-in-Law (Fragonard)	None

5.	Marie-Guillemine Benoist, née Leroulx-Delaville (1768-1826)	M	Vigée-Lebrun David	Société des Arts de Grand
6.	Marie-Anne Collot-Falconet (1748-1821)	M	Falconet	Imperial Academy in St. Petersburg

B. *Moderately Successful:*

1.	Madeleine-Françoise Basseporte (1701-1780)	S	P.A. Robert, Aubriet	None
2.	Anne Rosalie Bocquet-Filleul (1753-1794)	M	Father, Briard	Saint-Luc
3.	Marie Geneviève Bouliar (1762-1825)	S	Greuze	None
4.	Gabrielle Capet (1761-1818)	S	Labille-Guiard	None
5.	Françoise Marie-Thérèse Duparc (1726-1778)	S	Father, Van Loo, Chardin ?	Académie de Marseille
6.	Marie-Suzanne Giroust-Roslin (1734-1772)	M	Vien, La Tour, Roslin	Académie Royale
7.	Jeanne Philiberte Ledoux (1767-1840)	S	Greuze	None
8.	Marie-Victoire Lemoine (1754-1820)	S	Ménageot, Vigée-Lebrun ?	None
9.	Marianne Loir (ca. 1715- after 1769)	S	Father, Brother, J. de Troy	Académie de Marseille
10.	Adèle de Romance-Romany (1769-1846)	M	Regnault	None

C. *Honorable Mentions:*

1.	Gabrielle Bertrand Beyer (1730-1790)	M	Husband	Imperial Academy of Vienna
2.	Marie-Renée-Geneviève Brossard de Beaulieu (1755-after 1835)	M	Father, Greuze	San Luca (Rome), Académie de Lyon
3.	Aimée Duvivier (active 1786-1824)	S	Father, Greuze ?	None
4.	Marquise de Grollier, née de Fuligny-Damas (1742-1828)	M	Spaendonck	None
5.	Catherine Lusurier (1753-1781)	S	Cousin (Drouais)	None
6.	Marie-Thérèse Reboul-Vien (1735-1806)	M	Vien	Académie Royale, San Luca (Rome)
7.	Nanine Vallain-Piètre (active 1787-1810)	M	David, Suvée	None

Analysis and Evaluation

All but four of the twenty-three women emerged from the broad spectrum of the middle class. If their fathers were not artists, they were goldsmiths, merchants, shopkeepers, tailors, jewelers, distillers, or government officials. Of the remaining four, two rose from the lower class — Capet and Collot-Falconet — and two from the aristocracy — the Marquises of Grollier and of Romance-Romany. Another, the Comtesse Benoist, married into the nobility of the robe, but came from solid bourgeois stock.

These statistics should not be surprising because most of the intelligentsia — writers, musicians, *philosophes* — also emerged from the bourgeoisie, but what is different in their origins is that artists came from a lower stratum in that nebulous class. None of the female artists in the eighteenth century, for example, came from families engaged in the practice of law or jurisprudence, which was so often true for writers not only in France but throughout Europe.

Perhaps the most important change in the origins of the female artist is the tendency for an increasing number to come from non-painting families. Insofar as we have been able to study their lives, only eight of the twenty-three women received instruction from their fathers or brothers. Two others — Gérard and Lusurier — learned from a brother-in-law and a cousin, respectively. Six married artists, but to say that the wife learned to paint from the husband is to conjecture erroneously because all six had learned to paint before their marriages.[10] In sum, 50 percent of the women emerged from families in which painting was neither the vocation of the father nor of a close relative. Compared with earlier centuries this is a high percentage, and it negates the widespread myth that virtually all of the female artists prior to the nineteenth century were trained by their fathers or close relatives. More cases need to be studied, but it would appear that the familial, social, and economic ties of the medieval and Renaissance eras were breaking down along with the guild system in the century of the Enlightenment. By the middle of the century it was common for a bourgeois father to have a promising daughter tutored in the fine arts. The quality of the training depended upon the availability of tutors, female as well as male, and the pocketbook of the father.

Except for the two representatives of the aristocracy, the common motivation of women artists was economic gain, the driving force behind most entrepreneurs and professionals. It had long been fashionable for women, especially noble ladies, to dabble in art, but what was different in the eighteenth century was that it became increasingly profitable for them to become professionals. Most of the artists found painting to be a lucrative field of self-employment. The most successful — Vigée-Lebrun, Labille-Guiard, Benoist, and Collot-Falconet — received commissions as large as most of the male artists. In fact British male artists complained that Vigée-Lebrun was getting three times as much for a painting as Reynolds. Women also competed increasingly with males for royal patronage. The Bourbons patronized Vigée-Lebrun, Labille-Guiard, Vallayer-Coster, Basseporte, Bocquet-Filleul, and Marie Brossard; the Habsburgs employed Bertrand-Beyer at Schönbrunn; the Orange family commissioned Collot-Falconet at the Hague; Catherine the Great supported Collot-Falconet for twelve years and Vigée-Lebrun for six; the French revolutionary governments subsidized Labille-Guiard, Benoist, Capet, and Vallain-Piètre; Napoleon rewarded Benoist, Labille-Guiard, Capet and Gérard; and the aristocracy supported others, including Loir, Romance-Romany, and Duvivier.

Women's changing role in the arts was also reflected in their memberships in the art academies. Even though the Académie Royale of Paris set the quota of women artists at four during the beginning of the century, five of the twenty-three women analyzed in this study were admitted: Reboul-Vien in 1754, Giroust-Roslin and Vallayer-Coster in 1770, Vigée-Lebrun and Labille-Guiard in 1783. Vigée-Lebrun, Labille-Guiard, and Bocquet-Filleul were also members of the Académie de Saint-Luc. Within France Vigée-Lebrun held memberships in four academies and outside she had memberships in six of the most prestigious academies of Europe.[11] Duparc and Loir were members of the Academy of Marseilles; Brossard was a member of the Academy of Lyons; and Benoist was an honorary member of the Société des Arts de Grand. Outside of France Collot-Falconet was given the status of *agrégée* in the Academy of Fine Arts of St. Petersburg; Reboul-Vien and Brossard were members of the Accademia di San Luca in Rome. In total, more than half of the women held memberships in one or more academies — an important achievement; and though they were not given the same privileges as men, this influx indicates again the great distance that they had advanced in the course of the eighteenth century.

Moving from the social to the psychological realm of the female artist, we walk with greater trepidation. What kind of woman became a professional painter? Most of the successful female artists either remained single (approximately 50 percent), left their husbands shortly after an unhappy marriage (a 17 percent divorce or separation rate), or married after their careers were well established. In short, 80 percent of the women were either single or were for all practical reasons unencumbered by marriage during the first twenty-five or thirty years of their lives. Few of the women combined an early, happy marriage with a successful career, and of these only three managed to raise a family: Benoist and Reboul-Vien each with three children and Giroust-Roslin with six.[12] Even these exceptions fall far below the national average of children per French family for the century. For the most part, most women artists either did not marry or married late because they wanted to be free to pursue an independent career or because many men, aside from male artists, found them to be a strange breed of women: intellectually too independent, socially less acceptable, or politically too libertine. Relatively few of them played the dual role of wife and artist successfully. A high percentage escaped from unhappy marriages because a successful career made them economically independent of their husbands, and, in a few cases, Vallayer-Coster and Bocquet-Filleul in particular, their productivity dropped significantly after a late but happy marriage.

Why did most of the women artists avoid making historical, mythological, and allegorical pictures? In our judgment, the answer lies in the basic economic motivation behind the emergence of women in the fine arts in the eighteenth century. As we have seen, most of the women came from bourgeois families and depended upon the sale of portraits for their livelihood. They followed the example of the Italian artist, Rosalba Carriera, whose entrepreneurial techniques proved that a woman could ignore the academy's preference for history paintings and make a fortune in the less prestigious field of portraiture. Taking Paris by storm in 1720-21, she had more orders for portraits from the aristocracy and bourgeoisie than her studio could produce. Similarly, most of the female professionals in that century found instant markets for pictures of heads, busts, or half-lengths from the portrait-hungry clientele. The proud country gentry and the nouveau-riche bourgeoisie wanted portraits which female artists could turn out in great numbers. They were not interested in historical or mythological scenes to cover their drawing rooms. They shared Dr. Johnson's disdain for symbolic art: "I would rather see the portrait of a dog that I know than all the allegorical paintings they can shew me in the world."[13]

It was this changing taste of the new *Kulturtraeger* — the affluent bourgeoisie and the country gentry — that dictated the style and genre of art for women in the marketplace in the eighteenth century. Why should Vigée-Lebrun produce history paintings when she could make over a million dollars selling portraits? Why should Labille-Guiard spend two years making a history painting for eight thousand francs, when she could earn many times that amount by painting portraits? With few exceptions most women had little desire to compete with male academicians in the production of the more prestigious but less profitable genre of history painting. Putting it differently, the typical female artist, a middle-class professional, was persuaded more by the profits of portraiture than by the prospects of academic praise through history paintings, whereas the male artist, longer associated with the hierarchical values of the academy and still looking in terms of royal and church patronage, was influenced more by the hope of artistic immortality through history painting than by the pursuit of lucrative portraiture.

The most controversial issue regarding women artists concerns the quality of their achievements. Was their collective effort significant? Were the most gifted women equal to or better than some of the male artists? When viewed in its entirety, the artistic production of women in eighteenth-century France is staggering, measuring into the thousands of separate pieces and covering the entire gamut of the fine arts.

Even if it is true that never before in history had so many female artists risen as professional competitors to males, were they as good? Could any of them compare in importance with the best male painters of the period: Boucher, Chardin, David, Fragonard, Greuze, La Tour, Robert, Vernet, Vincent, or Watteau? Most of the traditional art historians apparently do not think so for rarely is a French woman artist mentioned in the standard histories of the century.[14] Why not?

In the judgment of most traditional art historians none of these women artists was an important innovator or painter of history. Most of the art critics from the eighteenth century to the present insist that artists must meet one of these requirements before being taken seriously. Few French women of the period met either. For the most part they were portraitists or painters of still lifes, and they often emulated the styles of their male tutors, sometimes so slavishly that their paintings are inseparable. Only a few were innovative: Vigée-Lebrun and Labille-Guiard were creative in positioning and adorning their subjects, and others, especially Vallayer-Coster, were creative in their floral and still-life arrangements, but, for the most part, they accepted and worked within the confines of the rococo or neoclassical styles of their time. In this sense the bold innovators of the century were men — Watteau, Chardin, Greuze, and David — and the women were creative disciples. The argument of the traditionalists follows, therefore, that even though Vigée-Lebrun,

206

Labille-Guiard, and Benoist were superb portraitists, they have been
excluded from art textbooks because they failed to measure up to the
orthodox concepts of "great" art.

If art histories, however, are to go beyond the presentation of individual
works of art within periods of stylistic development and to include the life of
artists within the historical context, no significant art history can ignore the
role of women artists within the art community of certain historical periods.
Not all of the women artists merit inclusion, but certainly no art history of
eighteenth-century France is complete without some discussion of the
portraits of Vigée-Lebrun, Labille-Guiard, and Benoist, the still lifes of
Vallayer-Coster, the genre paintings of Gérard, and the sculptures of Collot-
Falconet. In their time they were as celebrated as most of the male artists,
earned as much money, received as favorable reviews, and fulfilled the artistic
needs of their society. Undoubtedly a few were overpraised in their day, but
the time has come for historians to restore some of them to the respected
positions they enjoyed in the age of the Enlightenment.

Howard V. and Charlotte B. Evans
Central Michigan University

Notes

[1] The literature of the early seventies is replete with feminist topics: Jacqueline Skiles and Manet McDevitt, *A Documentary Herstory of Women Artists in Revolution* (New York: Know Press 1971); Lucy Lippard, "Sexual Politics: Art Style," *Art in America* (September-October 1971); Ann Sutherland Harris, "College Art Association's Women's Caucus," *Feminist Art Journal* (April, 1972); Cindy Nemser, "The Women Artists' Movement," *Feminist Art Journal* (Winter 1973-74). The *Feminist Art Journal* ceased publication in 1977.

[2] Vicki Lynn Hill, *Female Artists, Past and Present* (Berkeley: Women's History Research Center Inc., 1974); Germaine Greer, *The Obstacle Race* (New York: Farrar Straus Giroux, 1979).

[3] Great Britain, for example, which produced a number of important male artists for the first time in the eighteenth century, also produced a number of women artists for the first time.

[4] Only a few Italian women artists — Rosalba Carriera, Giovanna Fratellini, and Giulia Lama — stand out in the eighteenth century, whereas France produced a score or more.

[5] The Westernization of Russia in the eighteenth century included the Westernization of its art, but most of Western art, in contrast to the production of icons, was either imported or created by Western artists in Russia until the end of that century. Consequently, it was not until the nineteenth century that Russian women became artists in the Western tradition. In Spain, where Western art reached its peak in the seventeenth century, Spanish women also learned to paint and sculpt in the same century, but few of them except Luise Roldán enjoyed the international reputation of the early Italian and Dutch women artists.

[6] Marie Louise Elisabeth Vigée-Lebrun, *Souvenirs de Madame Vigée Le Brun*, (Paris: Charpentier et Cie, 1869), I, p. 107, states: "Les femmes régnaient alors, la révolution les a détrônées." For support of the statement that life had become difficult for women painters during the revolution see Antoine Schapper, "Painting During the Revolution 1789-1799," *French Painting 1774-1830, The Age of Revolution*, pp. 108-9, hereafter cited as *The Age of Revolution*; also, *Women Artists: 1550-1950*, p. 45.

[7] Elinor G. Barber, *Bourgeoisie in 18th-Century France* (Princeton: Princeton Univ. Press, 1955), p. 97. For names and numbers of women artists one can turn to the collective findings of such writers as Ernst Guhl, *Die Frauen in der Kunstgeschichte* (Berlin: J. Guttenberg, 1858); Elizabeth F.L. Ellet, *Women Artists in all Ages and Countries* (New York: Harper, 1859); Hans Hildebrandt, *Die Frau als bildende Künstlerin* (Berlin: Mosse Buchhandlung,

1928); Clara Erskine Clement, *Women in the Fine Arts* (Boston and New York: Houghton, Mifflin, and Co., 1904); Carmen G. Perez-Neu, *Galeria universal de pintoras* (Madrid: Editora Nacional, 1964); and Greer, *Obstacle Race*.

[8] For a list of members in the academy see Jules Guiffre, "Histoire de l'Académie de Saint-Luc," *Archives de l'art français,* nouvelle periode, 9 (1925), p. 161ff.

[9] As a rule of thumb, we have used the years 1665 and 1765 as the limits of the birthdates of the artists, reasoning that anyone born before 1665 belongs to the seventeenth century and anyone born after 1765 belongs to the nineteenth. In a few instances an individual born after the year 1765 is included if she exhibited enough paintings before 1800. A number of women straddle the century, such as Benoist, Bouliar, Capet, Duvivier, Gérard, Ledoux, Lemoine, Romance-Romany, Vallain-Piètre, and Vigée-Lebrun, but no discussion of the eighteenth century would be complete without them. On the other hand, as much as we would have liked to include Pauline Auzou, Constance Marie Charpentier, Eulalie Cornillaud-Morin, Jeanne-Elisabeth Gabiou-Chaudet, Marie Eléonore Godefroy, Antoinette Cecile Hortense Haudebourt-Lescot, Elise Lebarbier-Bruyère, Césarine-Henriette-Flore Mirvault-Davin, and Mme Villers, they clearly lie outside the eighteenth century. Of these, Charpentier comes closest to the cutoff date, but almost all of her surviving works belong to the nineteenth century.

[10] These include Bertrand-Beyer, Collot-Falconet, Giroust-Roslin, Labille-Guiard (second marriage to Vincent), Reboul-Vien, Romance-Romany.

[11] On the title page of her *Souvenirs* Vigée-Lebrun lists the nine academies of which she was a member. A complete title of her memoirs thus reads: *Souvenirs de Madame Vigée Le Brun de l'Académie Royale de Paris, de Rouen, de Saint-Luc de Rome et d'Arcadie de Parme et de Bologne, de Saint-Pétersbourg, de Berlin, de Genève et Avignon.* As we have seen, she also was a member of the Academie de Saint-Luc in Paris before it was abolished.

[12] The women who remained single were identified in the lists of women artists. Vigée-Lebrun, Collot-Falconet, Labille-Guiard (her first husband), Romance-Romany were unhappily married. Vallayer-Coster married at age 36, Giroust-Roslin at 25, and Bertrand-Beyer at 25 or older. Vigée-Lebrun, Collot-Falconet, and Bocquet-Filleul had one child each, but they do not fall into the category of women who combined an early marriage with a successful career. The number of children, if any, of Bertrand-Beyer, Grollier, and Vallain-Piètre, who all seemed to have been successfully married, is not known.

[13] Dorothy M. Mayer, *Angelica Kauffmann, R.A.* (Gerrards Cross, Buckinghamshire: Colin Smythe Ltd., 1972), p. 28.

[14] This statement is true for most art histories, but it is particularly true for Julius S. Held and Donald Posner's *17th and 18th-Century Art* (Englewood Cliffs, N.J.: Prentice-Hall, Inc., and New York: Harry N. Abrams, Inc., n.d.). Not a single name of a woman artist appears in the index, and when Posner discusses Falconet's *Equestrian Monument of Peter the Great,* he does not mention Collot-Falconet who sculpted the head of Peter.

19. Physiological Mechanism from Boerhaave to Haller

Albrecht von Haller (1708-1777) was trained under Herman Boerhaave (1668-1738) who can be regarded as a dedicated iatromechanist. The influence of Boerhaave on Haller was well marked, as is indicated in the *Praelectiones academicae* (1739-1744), the very impressive collection of Haller's notes and commentaries to his teacher's *Institutiones medicae* (first published in 1708). However, in his *Primae lineae physiologiae* (first published in 1747) and *Elementa physiologiae corporis humani* (1757-1766), Haller took issue with central points of Boerhaavian doctrine, e.g. the general vascular model for tissues and membranes, the theory of generation, etc. Not only did the contents of physiological theory radically evolve (especially with the "De partibus corporis humani sensilibus et irritabilibus," 1752), but methodologies also tended to differ on some relevant points. In addition the subject matter of physiological analysis seems to have shifted in the transition.[1]

I will try and develop three theses relevant to that change in research programme:

(1) Boerhaave's methodology seems significantly incoherent when confronted with the principles of his physiological theory. Boerhaave tried to find a way of reconciling these two differing tendencies of his thought.

(2) Some iatromechanist doctrines were already beginning to incorporate theoretical elements that did not seem compatible with a mechanistic analysis. I refer specifically to Baglivi's fibre theory. The way Baglivi was proceeding must have seemed both progressive and regressive to someone like Haller, who was well aware of Boerhaave's problematic attempts to reconcile mechanistic theory with empirical methodology.

(3) Haller made a decisive step to resolve those conceptual problems at the time he renounced Boerhaave's doctrinal model in physiology. This step coincided with the advent of the irritability theory. However we can best account for it through an investigation of the initial tenets of the *Elementa*.

(1)

C. Daremberg describes Boerhaave's doctrine this way: "His theory echoes an iatromechanism [inherited from Pitcairne], blended with Hippocratism and with chemical medicine, according to a formula similar to Baglivi's."[2]

210

This needs clarification and adjustment. True: Boerhaave's doctrine is a blend, but not a kind of glueing together of different types of systems. He had a significant model of the organism, but he had to frame the right type of methodology to build the theory. There is tension between his theoretical and methodological presuppositions.[3] The geometric and mechanical analysis of motion should be used in the explanation of operations of solid parts articulated together, as well as in the explanation of the determined effects of fluids in the economy of organic parts. Boerhaave points out that "these actions are produced according to the hydrostatic, hydraulic, and mechanical laws." The mechanical model seems to suggest extending the laws of mechanics to the explanation of vital motions, since for a Cartesian physicist, such laws made for the intelligibility of all natural phenomena. But applying the rule of intelligibility of functions to organic operations depends on a theory which assumes that the ultimate structure of the live anatomic whole determines all those functions.

To solve this problem, the suggested key is an analysis of anatomic structures into their compounding parts: the system of functions, Boerhaave believes, is deducible from the nature of the elements. But since the mechanical model fails to connect the nature of each organic fluid with the operations depending thereon, it is necessary to call upon experience to provide data (e.g. from recording significant humoral phenomena and from observing chemical reactions between humoral parts and the various solid materials). This is not contradictory to Boerhaave's general methodological stand. He is critical of purely speculative hypotheses of the Cartesian type, and he finds himself in agreement with Newton's rejection of superfluous causes. Direct observation bears on the organic phenomena, and their variations according to either internal or external conditions. Rational investigation purports to reveal the concealed dispositions producing observable phenomena and determining the sequential operations in observable structures. Clear and determinate principles should articulate any inference from known to unknown. In his rectoral address of 1715, *De comparando certo in physicis,* Boerhaave summarizes such a view.[4] As a matter of fact, the principles to guide inferences can only be provided by mechanics and physics, because only their concepts and experimental data enable us to ascertain the general and special powers of bodies. But, with Newtonian physics, some unknown material dispositions are invoked to justify a method of geometrical deduction from the observed order and quantitative features of phenomena. The *"Hypotheses non fingo"* tends to suggest a purely operational scope for scientific demonstration. Computation of the effects and mathematical inference from that computation are sufficient to set a system of laws without ontological support in the nature of causal agents, unknown and methodologically presumed unknowable. Suspending the ontological causal reference makes it possible to derive from an interplay of structures and forces a principle of explanation for the regularly observed phenomena. I do not mean that this is the ultimate interpretation of Newtonian methodology. It is rather an expression of what Boerhaave took it to mean.

Newton wanted to restrict the role of unknowns to serve as postulates in the general mathematical expression of mechanical phenomena and determinations to motion in the universe. Boerhaave will postulate species of functional attractions specified in accordance with the observed and experienced properties: *"gravitas, magnetismus, electrica vis, salium efficacitas, seminum actio, singularium denique corporum vires."*[5] Indeed, he uses the Newtonian model to stress the difficulty of understanding the more special kinds of motions and to suggest that an unknown real element should be supposed in the internal disposition of submicroscopic parts to account for particular effects manifested in the phenomena. So, let us postulate internal dispositions in the material parts linked with the resulting effects by some significant connection, provided those phenomena are taken to conform to the general laws of mechanism.

Two axioms permit the use of such a postulate in physiological explanation. The first axiom is clearly stated in the explanation of reproduction, but it prevails elsewhere as well: there is an unexceptionable law of nature maintaining the identity of specific organic types, the consensus of compounding parts, and the modality of organization. There is teleological causality at the source of composition and activity for each type of organism. Newtonian methodology lets one leave behind the scene the determining conditions for enacting of the organic "project". The second axiom states the circularity of organic determinations. In the *Institutiones,* this axiom is presented as a mere empirical statement about the interconnection of anatomical parts.[6] In the *De comparando certo in physicis,* the axiom evolves to mean that the action of individual parts is somehow determined by the whole structure, or rather, by a correlation of the unperceivable parts echoed at the level of the whole structure. This second axiom limits the possibility of deduction from the general principles of Mechanics.[7] One must rely on the empirical features to show the type of order that corresponds to the integrative operation of organism. And so, general principles of geometrical kind cannot apply strictly to explain the causal disposition of minute parts resulting in the integrative activity. The presumed causal property, which had been defined in analogy with gravitational force, strays from the model to become a postulate of internal organicity based on an unknown principle.

Accordingly, one would tend to limit mechanistic explanation to the operational description of certain effects, that are accounted for, at a more basic level, by the general axioms of organic order. But, as a matter of fact, Boerhaave's system of physiology is more dogmatically mechanistic, partly because it had preceded the recasting of his methodology in Newtonian mould and partly because it employs a general vascular model to account for all elements of the organic structure and for all functions. Boerhaavian methodology would recommend analyzing and classifying the complex empirical data (1) with the help of mechanical concepts proper (stage of *De usu ratiocinii mechanici in medicina,* 1702), (2) with the help of physiological concepts framed in the analogy of Newtonian dynamical concepts (stage of *De comparando certo in physicis,* 1715). In building his system, Boerhaave tends to apply some *a priori* reductionist schemes (such as the vascular model), which show closer affinity with the theoretical practice of the Cartesian iatromechanists.

212

(2)

My second point is that some late iatromechanist theories incorporated conceptual elements which were not reducible to the mechanist model. I will take the example of Baglivi's fibre theory, which opens, in a problematic fashion, the road to a new doctrine of the physiological element.

Giorgio Baglivi (1668-1707) starts from the "structural micrology" of the Malpighi school. He takes the functioning of organs to depend on juxtaposed *machinulae* of microscopic or submicroscopic size. His ambition is to relate a model of *machinulae* with the empirical data of pathology, collected according to Sydenham's method.[8] The *De fibra motrice et morbosa* (1700) is the first of the collection of essays in which Baglivi works out his fibre theory as the model applying to all physiological *machinulae*.[9] From there, the doctrine develops along four lines: (1) an anatomical study of fibre structure in the different parts of the body; (2) an analysis of the general functioning conditions for the organism; (3) a determination of the dynamic properties in fibres; (4) an hypothesis on fibrillar motion. The structural analysis indicates two levels; plain fibres, which can be described *more geometrico,* and complex *aequilibria* of fibres, which cannot be accounted for geometrically: wherefore it is necessary to subordinate geometry to observation. References to mechanical analogues, such as the *horologium oscillatorium,* act as conjectural approximations of what the fibrillar *machinulae* are. The conjecture has then to be checked against the empirical functional features of the various organic systems. But Baglivi is convinced that the explanatory model for fibrillar activity should be built in conformity with a system of general functions for the whole organism. So, he contrives his dual system of integrated parts, combining either nervous fibres or membranous fibres *jure originis, officii, consensus et societatis.*[10] The model refers to a twofold geometrical apparatus for mechanical activity, which strays from the professed empiricist methodology: the organic twin *horologia oscillatoria* are interpreted *au pied de la lettre,* and, as a matter of fact, the presumed discovery of contractile motions in the *dura mater* ("*cor cerebri*")[11] ties in with this same system. However, Baglivi is convinced that the essential motive force for the physiological clock is afforded by the fibrillar structure. The main role should be allotted to the systaltic and diastaltic motions in fibres, even if they remain unperceivable. The *proportio impetus et resistentiae* which the whole structures seem to display, suggests such an hypothetical point of theory.

This way, Baglivi initiates research into properties of the fibre "*tanquam radicem, et principium partium.*"[12] He will show phenomena in the muscular fibres equivalent to what will later be identified with Hallerian irritability (experiments on excised heart, on fragments of the cardiac muscle). To explain such contractions, he does not appeal to the nervous fluid, but to a kind of spring inside the heart fibres. The facts are clearly evidenced. Whether we are faced with Hallerian irritability or not, is a matter of theoretical interpretation. The step in Haller's direction consists in severing the phenomenon from the activity of animal spirits, and linking it with a specific "mechanism" within fibres. But live fibrillar contraction is made to depend on the diffusion of an impulse through the whole *horologium oscillatorium,* which initiates from the *dura mater* as the organism's main spring. The property is also generalized to glands. And the other membranes, instead of being restricted to a mere wrapping function, are taken to exert oscillatory, dynamical, and equilibrating action. Indeed, fibres are presented as minute *automata,* which act as so many small levers, when stimulated by the contact of fluids, but those levers are activated by a first impulse coming from the centre, and they are kept in sufficient tension by the centre's oscillatory action.

When Baglivi tries to identify the property that resides in the fibre, he seems to resume Borelli's theory of muscular motion: organic parts are endowed with given quantities of moving force *"a varia gravitate ac minimorum componentium structura."*[13] This way, phenomena of organic motricity are seen to depend on a *nisus solidorum ad contractionem.* Such a kind of representation serves to keep animistic or iatrochemical principles at bay. This iatromechanistic conviction, however, is mainly programmatic. To apply axioms of Mechanics to physiological phenomena, one must account for the functional features evidenced by macroscopic or microscopic observation and frame acceptable hypotheses on the structure of submicroscopic physiological elements: *Necesse est in hoc practices negotio Geometra famuletur observationi.* Baglivi tries some mechanical models to account for contraction in the muscle fibre. The inadequacy of such models is so evident that Baglivi calls them *opiniones.* In spite of the mechanical ideal, concepts creep in to describe the functional aspect of phenomena. (They will reappear in Haller's physiology to identify the fibrillar elements as irreducible organic structures). For instance, Baglivi states that the *fibrarum crispatura,* which he also calls *solidorum irritatio,* is produced by a limited variety of stimuli (within thresholds of variation), whether these stimuli be internal or external, natural or pathological. But, besides this *prima facie* functional characterization, the structural conditions for fibrillar properties exceeded Baglivi's possibilities for observation and demonstration. Vital contractility, as specific property, is interpreted within a very general framework of methodologically abstract mechanism. It may be noted that in the pathology part of the doctrine, vital contractility is assigned back to ancient Methodism and its couple *strictum-laxum.* As basic pathological states, spasm and atony express the proper dynamism of fibrillar structures. Curiously enough, this trend brings the anatomo-physiological analysis of fibrillar structure closer to the consensus of organic parts in the Hippocratic tradition.

This shows as well that a unitary model of organic function rules over Baglivi's explanations. Accordingly, was it really possible to grant distinct orders of fibres specific and autonomous properties? In contraposition to Baglivi's combined skepticism and mechanical dogmatism, Haller develops his theory of the elementary organic structures. He gives fibre theory a different meaning from Baglivi's by avoiding a priori reference to a global and unifying mechanical model. For Baglivi, fibre was a *machinula* functioning within an integrated machine, which was somehow considered to be the meaningful prototype. This global machinery would determine by interplay of antagonistic forces the functional activity of the *machinulae* in the mechanical harmony of the whole. With Haller, fibre becomes a physiological element endowed in certain cases with specific functional properties.

(3)

When the ultimate anatomic element, the fibre, becomes the *substratum* for a system of vital operations, physiology gets involved in studying vital motions and in taking account of the manifold arising therefrom. The definition which opens the *Elementa physiologiae corporis humani* bears witness to this trend.[14] Physiological research must be based on the study of the anatomical structure on which vital motions depend. This structure may be compared with the ordering of wheels and cogs of a mechanism; in this respect the physiologist faces the material organization of his subject matter the way a mathematician aims at expressing in a calculus the interplay of forces and the mechanical functions: the operation can be achieved only insofar as the structure of parts may be analytically disassembled. However, the connection of motions with the so-called geometrical structure of organism raises problems which break precise analogy with the model to be inferred from mechanical investigations. Though physiology is the theory of motions taking place in the animated machine, and though principles of mechanics, hydrostatics, and hydraulics can apply, attempts at reduction hardly succeed because of specificity in the organic motive phenomena.[15] The apparent mechanical anomaly in phenomena requires one to resort to an empiricist methodology. Haller does not reject the principle that the laws of Mechanics apply to forces and effects which experience identifies as specific to the living. But the transfer of principles and models must be subordinated to a systematic experience of vital phenomena that may indicate legitimacy conditions for applying the explanatory scheme. There seems to be incommensurable complexity between the circulatory function of blood in functionally diversified vessels endowed with tonicity, differential resistance, and special dynamics on the one hand, and the circulation of fluids in lifeless canalizations with standing properties on the other. Haller keeps a certain number of the iatromechanist hypotheses, which, by the way, experience confirms, but those corroborated hypotheses remain within bounds of a macroscopic analysis pertaining to elementary mechanics and geometry. This was the theoretical level of explanatory schemes in Borelli and Hales: there is no guaranty that one can proceed with this model of mechanical intelligibility beyond such a level. Haller adopts the same agnosticism in regard to calculus and probability measurement in application to the theory of vital motions: he relativizes the hoped-for results of a minute quantitative decomposition.

As a counterpart, Haller sets up a composite experimental methodology: use of comparative and pathological anatomy, microscopic investigation of elementary structures, organic devices made conspicuous through diverse preparation techniques, and above all, experiments on living animals. The aim is to establish, by means of correlated experiences at various levels, a determined connection between structure and function, in the numerous cases where first-hand description does not enable us to perceive clearly nor set precisely the functional correlations of vital motions. On the other hand, the principle of repetitive experimentation is to guaranty that through structure-function description, one can reach to an equivalent of organic laws. This is done by eliminating adventitious or casual phenomena which form sorts of parasitic qualitative variables.[16] Indeed, Haller falls back on Bacon's methodology, but he cannot operate within the bounds of too strict an empiricism. He rejects hypotheses framed as *a priori* presuppositions to explain phenomena, but he maintains at the same time a role for hypotheses that have been suggested by experience, insofar as they determine explanatory schemes and analogy transfers from one field of observation to another: they may give meaning to facts that have been revealed by observation but seem to fall short of any direct empirical correlation. Experimentally controlling and classifying facts is not enough to render useless any attempt at theoretical systematization. Thus, a framework for analysis is afforded by a theory, or an hypothesis which anticipates the theory to be formulated. Converging and concurring facts warrant legitimate, though ever probabilistic, use of theoretical concepts. This is the case with Haller's views on the organic structure.

In the *Primae lineae physiologiae* (1747), Haller had stated his aphorism: physiology is *anatome animata*. This methodological paradox gets analyzed at the beginning of the *Elementa*. Since the Italian iatromechanists of the mid-seventeenth century, anatomy had been conceived as a descriptive science of structures which could make the deduction *de usu partium* possible. Haller will affirm that the order cannot be geometrical in the subject matter of physiology.[17] From the geometer's method, Haller draws a distinction between degrees of truth, stretching from certainty to mere conjecture. And so, the definition of fibres as similar to elements in geometrical combinations is paradoxical. Haller's definition runs this way: "Fibre is for the physiologist what the line is for the geometer, *scrire* that which all figures derive from."[18] Canguilhem's interpretation is that this doctrine of physiological element is jointly based on an analytic investigation of observable structures and on a rational jump to a unit of organisation according to the pattern of elements in Geometry.[19] Fibre is a pluralistic and manifold genus of elements which could be indefinitely distinguished, a material homologous with the complex special features of organic wholes. Three quarters of a century before Haller, Malpighi, developing the methodological presuppositions of his micrology, had acknowledged the need for principles of integration to explain the structural anatomy of living beings. His principle of integration was a principle of mechanical explanation of phenomena expressed by the organism as a whole. It resulted in the notion of complex anatomical structures that might be reduced to a juxtaposition of *machinulae*. If the structure of *machinulae* and their mode of juxtaposition were known, could the function of the integrated systems be deduced *ex hypothesi*? Haller's definition of fibre ruins the possibility of such a deduction *more geometrico*, because the determination of what counts as a structural element depends on the special order of properties in physiological systems, and this order is to be told empirically. Analysis shows that the physical and chemical properties of fibre components could be given, but one must transcend the mechanico-chemical effects to account for the observed and concealed features of physiological phenomena. At this exact point, theoretical anticipation intervenes. Haller presumes that the element in the animal body is not the fibril shown by microscopic analysis, because such a fibril seems to be itself decomposable in yet smaller fibrils, but the element is an unperceivable fibril reached by the sole force of mind (*sola acie mentis*) which would not be itself divisible into further organic constituents.

I will be content at this stage to stress two features of the Hallerian analysis. First, the organic element is taken to be simple only insofar as it can account functionally for observable systems at a higher level: as "simple", it affords explanatory ground for the organic properties of structurally complex wholes. Haller enumerates all anatomical structures where fibrillar elements are observed, then he postulates a common nature for all those elements in the elementary or primordial fibre: "The fibre is elastic; flexible, it contracts and recovers its reduced size. This nature has been observed even in the bones, it would be made manifest generally, if one produced the separation of the most minute filaments."[20] This kind of elasticity represents a basic physiological property corresponding to the fibrillar structure; it will determine, through integration of the organic systems, the enactment of complex functions. Indeed Haller, following indications of anatomical observation, will distinguish elasticity, as universal property of fibres, from irritability, which belongs to fibres of muscular tissues, and sensibility which is conditioned by the activity of the nervous network. Nevertheless, it remains significant that only the elasticity of primordial fibre appears as *raison d'être* of functions performed by integrated systems: this chemically complex fibre is a simple structure, if one analyzes the structural ground for organic functions.

The Hallerian model possesses a second noteworthy feature: the rational requirement that justification for the organic functions be sought for in a submicroscopic elementary structure. The theoretical extrapolation beyond observable data is not a mere inference justified by limited technical means; it is a logical requirement of the model of order referred to.[21] On the one hand, microscopical observation gives evidence of fibrillar structures "emboîtées" one inside the next down to an infinitesimal order compared with global organic structures at the macroscopic level. If one relied on a methodology of strict *anatome animata,* it would mean a constantly widening gap between the physiological functions to be accounted for (at the global level) and the structural conditions to count in the mechanical explanation. In Hallerian physiology, objective explanation of the structure-function tie implies that the anatomic elements be homogeneous in their dispositional properties with organic wholes, provided one follows the thread of analogy with observed phenomena: otherwise, this science would reinstate substantial forms and occult qualities, or at least, Van Helmont's *archeus* and Stahl's *logos*.

Haller is a follower of Boerhaave, and Boerhaave himself felt that empiricist requirements of Newtonian methodology had to be extended to physiology. Haller must maintain this analogy with observed phenomena under his conception of natural order and his knowledge of data, even though the gap may seem to widen between global activities and elementary structures. And so, we have his postulate of a primordial fibre, itself unanalyzable in terms of *structures emboîtées,* and, as such, inaccessible to microscopical investigation. But it affords the theoretical condition and paradigmatic element for integrating of complex structures, since it contains the dynamical *raison d'être* of organic properties, and since it keeps within compass of analogy with the observed features of fibrillar components at an intermediate structural level.

This way, with Haller as well as with Maupertuis, but in a more experimental and structuralist perspective, tying in with a methodology of *anatomia subtilis*, a new concept is developed to represent the integrative order of organic structure.

The shift in theory and in method cleared the ground insofar as late iatromechanical models are concerned. It probably launched a new research programme which has supported physiological theorizing up to the advent of cellular physiology. It may help our understanding of that theoretical shift to have recalled Boerhaave's and Baglivi's ambiguous problematics, whence Haller deviated, not without further integrating in a complex fashion methodological and theoretical models, which had been initially cast in the mould of iatromechanism.

François Duchesneau
Université de Montréal

Notes

[1] Arguments and textual evidence in support of my interpretation are presented here in a condensed form; they are more fully spelled out in my forthcoming book, *La Physiologie des lumières* (The Hague: Martinus Nijhoff, 1981).

[2] C. Daremberg, *Histoire des sciences médicales* (Paris: J.B. Baillière, 1870), II, p. 889.

[3] Herman Boerhaave, *Institutiones,* §§40-41, quoted by Daremberg, p. 892: "Les solides sont ou des vaisseaux qui contiennent les humeurs ou des instruments tellement construits, figurés et liés entre eux, qu'il se peut faire, par leur fabrique particulière, certains mouvements déterminés, s'il survient une cause mouvante. On trouve en effet dans le corps des appuis, des colonnes, des poutres, des bastions, des téguments, des cordes, des leviers, des aides de levier, des poulies, des pressoirs, des soufflets, des cribles, des filtres, des canaux, des auges, des réservoirs. La faculté d'exécuter des mouvements par le moyen de ces instruments s'appelle fonction; ce n'est que par des lois mécaniques que ces fonctions se font, et ce n'est que par ces lois qu'on peut les expliquer. Les parties fluides sont contenues dans les solides, mues, déterminées dans leur mouvement, mêlées, séparées, changées. Elle meuvent les vaisseaux avec les instruments qui sont liés avec eux; usent, changent leurs parois, et réparent les pertes qu'elles y ont causées. Ces actions se font selon les lois hydro-statiques, hydrauliques et mécaniques. On doit donc les expliquer conformément à ces lois, quand on est venu à bout de connaître auparavant la nature de chaque humeur en particulier, et les actions qui en dépendent uniquement, autant qu'on peut les découvrir par toutes sortes d'expériences."

[4] *Sermo academicus De Comparando Certo in Physicis* . . . (Lugduni-Batavorum: Apud Petrum Vander Aa, Bibliopolam, 1715), pp. 2-3: "Paucis enim conabor evincere, *rerum principia omnino nos latere, solis noscuntur, aut quae ex his,* una tantum hac via prius exploratis *geometrici ratiocinii firmitate elici possunt.*"

[5] *Ibid.,* p. 19.

[6] *Institutiones,* §47, (1727), p. 15: "Verum omnia illa ita cohaerent inter se ut, quasi in orbem eundo, mutuas causae et effectuum vices agant."

[7] *De comparando certo in physicis,* p. 38: "Omnia, nisi fallor, haec docent, humani corporis particulam simplicissimam a tot aliis pendere singulatim definitis, ut principiorum universalium usu nihil huic intelligendae prodesse queat, sola autem exempli praemonstratione fabricam patescere."

[8] This is evident in Baglivi's major treatise *De praxi medica* (1696). For the story of Baglivi's research on fibres, see M.D. Grmek, "La notion de fibre vivante chez les médecins de l'école iatrophysique," *Clio Medica,* 5 (1970), 297-318.

9 My analysis will be mainly based on *Specimen de fibra motrice et morbosa, in quibus de solidorum structura, vi, elatere, aequilibrio, usu, potestate, et morbis disseretur* (1702).

10 *Opera omnia,* 6e éd. (Parisiis: Apud Claudium Rigaud, 1704), p. 270.

11 *Ibid.,* p. 273, cf. p. 282: "dura mater, alterum quasi cor solidum validumque."

12 *Ibid.,* p. 268.

13 *Ibid.,* p. 321.

14 Albrecht von Haller, *Elementa physiologiae corporis humani,* 8 vol., (Lausanne: M.M. Bousquet — F. Grasset; Berne, Societas typographica, 1757-1766), I, Praef. autoris, p. i: "Qui physiologiam scribit, corporis animalis internos motus, viscerumque munera, et humorum mutationes, et vires exponendas sumit, quibus vita sustentatur; quibus vicissim lacerti valent, qui mentis reguntur imperio; quibus alimenta in succos nostros, adeo varios, convertuntur; quibus demum ex iis succis, et nostra corpora conservantur, et humani generis jactura novis partubus reparatur."

15 *Ibid.,* pp. V-VI: "Multa enim sunt in animali machina, quae a communibus legibus mechanicis valde aliena sunt: motus magni a parvis causis excitati; celeritas humorum per eas causas parum diminutae, a quibus per receptas leges frangi opportuerat: motus a causis penitus incognitis irrepentes: motus vehementes a debilibus fibris producti: decurtationes fibrarum omni calculo majores, et quae alia."

16 *Ibid.,* p. V: "Nullum unquam experimentum, administratio nulla, semel debet institui; neque verum innotescit, nisi ex constante repetitorum periculorum eventu. Plurima sunt aliena, quae se in experimenta inmiscent: discedunt ea repetendo, ideo quia aliena sunt, et pura supersunt, quae ideo perpetuo similiter eveniunt, quod ex ipsa rei natura fluant. Sed et natura variabilis est, et sola repetitione ejus quasi sensus et voluntas, dispalescit. Haec lex, prioribus temporibus parum perspecta, Morgagno inprimis auctore in anatomen illata est."

17 *Ibid.,* I, p. 1: "[Physiologiae] auctorem plurima ex physicis, chemicis, anatomicis, aliisque artibus repetere necesse est: neque ipsi circa simplicia corpora, quae facillimae definitionis sint, unice versari licet, ut utroque modo a Geometra differat, qui suae artis principia ab ipsa arte sumat, et lineas punctaque, aliaque mirae simplicitatis elementa tractanda nactus sit."

18 *Ibid.,* I, p. 2.

19 Cf. G. Canguilhem, *La Connaissance de la vie,* 2e éd., (Paris: Vrin, 1967), p. 51.

20 *Elementa,* I, p. 8.

21 *Ibid.,* I, p. 7: "Ex his nunc elementis, terra, aqua, oleo, ferro et aere conjunctis *fibra* nascitur, elementum corporis animalis, invisibile ubi simplex, multo minus, quam quod microscopiorum vi augente adhibita oculis nostris subjici queat, cum minima animalia, quae ipsa vehementissima lentium et sphaerarum vitrearum vi aucta demum oculis nostris conspicua fiunt, tamen ipsa perinde fibris fiant, multo certe mole totius animalis minoribus."

Index of names/Index des noms

222